1995

Until now, little attention has been paid to the political and ideological significance of the exemplum, a brief narrative form used to illustrate a moral. Through a study of four major works in the Chaucerian tradition (the *Canterbury Tales*, John Gower's *Confessio Amantis*, Thomas Hoccleve's *Regement of Princes*, and Lydgate's *Fall of Princes*), Scanlon redefines the exemplum as a "narrative enactment of cultural authority." He traces its development through the two strands of the medieval Latin tradition which the Chaucerians appropriate: the sermon exemplum, and the public exemplum of the Mirrors of Princes. In so doing, he reveals how Chaucer and his successors used these two forms of the exemplum to explore the differences between clerical authority and lay power, and to establish the moral and cultural authority of their emergent vernacular tradition.

CAMBRIDGE STUDIES IN MEDIEVAL LITERATURE 20

NARRATIVE,
AUTHORITY, AND POWER

This series of critical books seeks to cover the whole area of literature written in the major medieval languages – the main European vernaculars, and medieval Latin and Greek – during the period *c.* 1100–*c.* 1500. Its chief aim is to publish and stimulate fresh scholarship and criticism on medieval literature, special emphasis being placed on understanding major works of poetry, prose and drama in relation to the contemporary culture and learning which fostered them.

Recent titles in this series include
10 *The Book of Memory: A study of memory in medieval culture*, by Mary J. Carruthers
11 *Rhetoric, Hermeneutics and Translation in the Middle Ages: Academic traditions and vernacular texts*, by Rita Copeland
12 *The Arthurian Romances of Chrétien de Troyes: Once and future fictions*, by Donald Maddox
13 *Richard Rolle and the Invention of Authority*, by Nicholas Watson
14 *Dreaming in the Middle Ages*, by Steven F. Kruger
15 *Chaucer and the Tradition of the 'Roman Antique'*, by Barbara Nolan
16 *The 'Romance of the Rose' and its Medieval Readers: Interpretation, reception, manuscript transmission*, by Sylvia Huot
17 *Women and Literature in Britain, 1150–1500*, edited by Carol M. Meale
18 *Ideas and Forms of Tragedy from Aristotle to the Middle Ages*, by Henry Ansgar Kelly
19 *The Making of Textual Culture:* Grammatica *and literary theory, 350–1100*, by Martin Irvine

NARRATIVE, AUTHORITY, AND POWER

The medieval exemplum and the Chaucerian tradition

LARRY SCANLON

Associate Professor of English, Rutgers University

CAMBRIDGE
UNIVERSITY PRESS

Published by the Press Syndicate of the University of Cambridge
The Pitt Building, Trumpington Street, Cambridge, CB2 1RP
40 West 20th Street, New York, NY 10011-4211, USA
10 Stamford Road, Oakleigh, Melbourne 3166, Australia

First published 1994

Printed in Great Britain at the University Press, Cambridge

A catalogue record for this book is available from the British Library

Library of Congress cataloguing in publication data
Scanlon, Larry.
Narrative, authority, and power: the medieval exemplum and the
Chaucerian tradition / by Larry Scanlon.
p.   cm.–(Cambridge studies in medieval literature; 20)
Includes bibliographical references and index.
ISBN 0-521-43210-3 (hc)
1. English poetry–Middle English, 1100–1500–History and
criticism. 2. Didactic literature, Latin (Medieval and modern)–
England–History and criticism. 3. Chaucer, Geoffrey, d. 1400–
Knowledge–Literature. 4. Power (Social sciences) in literature.
5. Influence (Literary, artistic, etc.) 6. Exempla–History and
criticism. 7. Authority in literature. 8. Narration (Rhetoric)
9. Rhetoric, Medieval. 1. Title. 11. Series.
PR311.S33 1994
821'.109–dc20   93-25371 CIP

ISBN 0 521 43210 3 hardback

for Aline

Contents

Acknowledgments   *page* xi

INTRODUCTION: EXEMPLARITY AND AUTHORITY IN
THE MIDDLE AGES   I

1   Chaucer's Parson   3

2   Redefining the exemplum: narrative, ideology, and
    subjectivity   27

3   *Auctoritas* and *potestas*: a model of analysis for medieval
    culture   37

PART I: THE LATIN TRADITION   55

4   The sermon exemplum   57

5   The public exemplum   81
    John of Salisbury: *Policraticus*   88
    Aegidius Romanus and the Parisian tradition   105
    Giovanni Boccaccio: *De casibus virorum illustrium*   119

PART 2: THE CHAUCERIAN TRADITION   135

6   Exemplarity and the Chaucerian tradition   137

7   *Canterbury Tales* (I): from preacher to prince   146
    The *Friar's Tale*: Chaucer's critique of the proprietary Church 147
    The *Summoner's Tale*: Chaucer's anti-fraternal critique   160
    Power and pathos: the *Clerk's Tale*   175

ix

8   *Canterbury Tales* (II): from preaching to poetry   192
    The *Pardoner's Prologue and Tale*: the affirmations of
    anti-clericalism   193
    Chaucer's *Fürstenspiegel*: the *Tale of Melibee* and the *Monk's Tale*   206
    The *Nun's Priest's Tale*: the authority of fable   229

9   Bad examples: Gower's *Confessio Amantis*   245
    Simulating the voice of God (I): the anti-clerical critique 248
    Simulating the voice of God (II): the critique of romance   267
    Simulation as authority: Book VII, Gower's *Fürstenspiegel* 282

10 The Chaucerian tradition in the fifteenth century   298
    The king's two voices: Hoccleve's *Regement of Princes*   299
    Translation without presumption, or, the birth of tragedy out
    of the spirit of the exemplum: Lydgate's *Fall of Princes*   322

Bibliography   351
Index   367

Acknowledgments

One of the few unalloyed pleasures of finishing a first book as long in the making as this one is to acknowledge all the people who have helped along the way. I had the good fortune to begin graduate study at the moment when interest in literary history was reviving. The seminars I took with Jerome McGann, Stanley Fish, and Lee Patterson opened up a world of possibilities I scarcely knew existed. The dissertation I went on to write under Lee Patterson's direction formed the basis of this book; his consummate skill at that most delicate of pedagogical tasks made it a solid basis indeed. I also benefited from the guidance of John Baldwin, who introduced me to the endless intellectual intricacies of medieval kingship. Winthrop Wetherbee was an early and enthusiastic supporter; he read the complete manuscript in one form or another, and offered many invaluable suggestions, as did the anonymous reviewers for Cambridge University Press. Equally good advice on smaller portions came from Carolyn Dinshaw, Seth Lerer, Charles Blyth, David Aers, and Nicholas Watson. Derek Pearsall gave me the benefit of his awe-inspiring erudition in the course of a number of extended conversations. The editors I worked with at Cambridge, Katharina Brett, Andrea Smith, Kevin Taylor, and Joanna West were sage and unflappable throughout.

This book was finished at the University of Wisconsin-Madison, where I was blessed with four extremely supportive senior colleagues: A. N. Doane, Sherry Reames, Richard Ringler and Donald Rowe, who have all helped in large ways and small. I owe a special debt to Donald Rowe, whose scrupulous reading of the entire manuscript in its penultimate stage helped keep the twin demons of obscurity and prolixity at bay. The already legendary English department Draft Group helped me reshape chapters one and seven. Gail Berkeley, Linda Lomperis, Richard Kroll, Victoria Silver, Rafael Pérez-

xii   *Acknowledgments*

Torres, Elizabeth Marchant, Ellen Rooney, Jane Tylus, William Klein, Colleen Dunlavy and Ronald Radano have all contributed encouragement, advice, and good fellowship – intellectual and otherwise – along the way. Moral support, and on numerous occasions, food and shelter, has been lent by my family and in-laws.

Part of Chapter 8 appeared as "The Authority of Fable: Allegory and Irony in the *Nun's Priest's Tale*," in *Exemplaria* I (1989), 43–51; and part of Chapter 10 appeared as "The King's Two Voices: Narrative and Power in Hoccleve's *Regement of Princes*," in the anthology *Literary Practice and Social Change in Britain* 1380–1530, edited by Lee Patterson (Berkeley, Los Angeles and Oxford: University of California Press, 1990), 216–47. I received research support from Temple University and the University of Wisconsin. Much of the new research for this book took place during an idyllic year spent at the Center for the Humanities at Wesleyan University on a post-doctoral fellowship from the Andrew W. Mellon Foundation. The book benefited from my exchanges with all the fellows at the center that year, and in particular with its director Richard Vann. The formal or informal presence of Nancy Armstrong, Hazel Carby, Noel Carroll, Michael Denning, Richard Ohmann, Fred Pfeil, Leonard Tennenhouse, and Khachig Tölölyan gave me an intensive, hands-on introduction to Cultural Studies. I am particularly grateful to Fred Pfeil, whose good-humored but insistent skepticism about metaphors of the social body expressed at several Center colloquia sent me back to medieval political theory with a new orientation.

My largest debt has already been acknowledged on the dedication page. I have benefited from Aline Fairweather's help and encouragement at every stage in this project, frequently from her specific suggestions, and always from her inspiring intellectual energy – an energy that can only be described as exemplary.

Exemplarity and authority in the Middle Ages

CHAPTER I

Chaucer's Parson

I begin this study of narrative and authority where Chaucer ends: with the Parson. The *Parson's Tale*, and the *Retraction* which follows it, constitute the last and most definitive of a series of moments in the *Canterbury Tales* where Chaucer's self-conscious and apparently insatiable appetite for narrative complexity gives way to an affirmation of a dominant form of medieval authority. Previous scholarship has tended to deal with this dilemma by privileging one side of the opposition or the other – arguing either that Chaucer's narrative complexity subverts, or at least holds at a distance the simple verities of medieval authority, or, conversely, that his complexity can be reduced to these verities after all. The dilemma took its purest and most contended form in the formalist/patristic debates of the fifties and sixties.[1] While Chaucer Studies have moved beyond these debates, this opposition they assumed – that is, between the complexity of the textual and the simplicity of authority – continues to structure the field. The goal of this study is to move the field beyond this opposition as well, by means of a reexamination of the medieval exemplum and its role in four major works of the Chaucerian tradition: the *Canterbury Tales*, Gower's *Confessio Amantis*, Hoccleve's *Regement of Princes*, and Lydgate's *Fall of Princes*.

As many other scholars have argued, this narrative form dominated later medieval culture, particularly in England.[2] Its dominance

---

[1] For a critical history of these debates, see Lee Patterson, *Negotiating the Past: The Historical Understanding of Medieval Literature* (Madison: University of Wisconsin Press, 1987), 3–74.

[2] This claim has been made by, among others, D. W. Robertson, *Preface to Chaucer* (Princeton: Princeton University Press, 1962), 171–285 – though he tends to prefer the term exemplification, and tends to restrict *exemplum* to the sermon exemplum; Dieter Mehl, *Middle English Romances of the Thirteenth and Fourteenth Centuries* (London: 1969), 253; John Burrow, *Ricardian Poetry* (London: Routledge & Kegan Paul, 1971), 78–92; Judson Boyce Allen, *The Ethical Poetic of the Later Middle Ages: A Decorum of Convenient Distinction* (Toronto: University of Toronto Press, 1982), 95. Cf. Jacques Le Goff, "The Time of the *Exemplum*

raises a number of interrelated questions. The most obvious of these are questions about the exemplum's rhetorical status, as a narrative form which explicitly combines narrative with cultural authority. What is the relation between an exemplum's narrative and the cultural authority embodied in its *sententia*, or moral? Is this really a matter of the moral, as a simple, unchanging essence, subordinating the potential complexities of narrative? Or is what we have instead two differing orders of complexity, the one (authority) primarily social, but with an irreducibly rhetorical component, and the other (narrative) primarily rhetorical, with an irreducibly social component? For the most part, twentieth-century scholarship has failed to recognize the exemplum's specificity as narrative. The following definition, first offered in 1911, expresses a view of the exemplum that is still widespread, despite (or perhaps because of) its imprecision: "a short narrative used to illustrate or confirm a general principle."[3] In this definition, the exemplum's function is entirely determined by an external "general principle," whose own discursive status is assumed to be immediately obvious and unproblematic. The exemplum's specificity as a discursive form cannot be narrative, because its narrative does no more than illustrate or confirm this principle which is completely sufficient without such illustration or confirmation. Denying the exemplum's specificity as narrative raises larger problems. If the form is entirely superogatory, why was it so important to

(Thirteenth Century)," in *The Medieval Imagination*, tr. Arthur Goldhammer (Chicago and London: University of Chicago Press, 1988), 78–80.
[3] J. A. Mosher, *The Exemplum in England* (New York: Columbia University Press, 1911), 1. For a comprehensive survey of previous definitions, see Claude Bremond, Jacques Le Goff, and Jean-Claude Schmitt, *L' "exemplum"* (Turnholt: Brepols, 1982), 27–36. Le Goff concludes with a definition of his own, which is less useful than the incisive discussion which leads up to it: "un récit bref donné comme veridique et destiné à être inseré dans un discours (en général un sermon) pour convaincre un auditoire par une leçon salutaire." *Un récit bref donné comme véridique* is hardly more precise than the vagueness Le Goff finds endemic to his predecessors. The one precision of this definition concerns the exemplum's function, which is well in keeping with the Middle Age's own view (see 27 below). But even here the precision is achieved at the cost of considerable oversimplification. One can say only of the exempla appearing in post-twelfth-century collections that they were designed to be inserted in another discourse, and even then one cannot say it of all exempla or all collections. There is no evidence, for instance, that the exempla in Cesarius of Heisterbach's *Dialogus miraculorum* (see Chapter 4 below, 63–66) were intended to be used elsewhere, though subsequently they certainly were. And many of the exempla in later collections were adapted from older, self-contained texts like Gregory's *Dialogues*, or from a wide variety of non-exemplary sources. The narrowness of his definition forces Le Goff to restrict the exemplum to the period between the thirteenth and fifteenth centuries, and to the sermon, ignoring the substantial tradition I have labeled the public exemplum (see Chapter 2 below, 81–134).

later medieval culture? Why, in particular, was it so important to developments like the Chaucerian tradition, a lay, vernacular tradition that emerged in a culture previously dominated by the Latin traditions of the Church? What has been missing, both in accounts of the exemplum, and of the larger developments it facilitated, is an adequate notion of power. The history of medieval political thought makes it abundantly clear medieval culture could not understand *auctoritas* apart from the *potestas* to which it was typically opposed. But modern students of that culture, too often committed to a monolithic ideal of medieval authority, have been slow to grasp the implications of this dichotomy when exploring problems of transmission and change. In the pages that follow I will argue that the exemplum was not static, but active and dynamic, that it did not merely "confirm" moral authority, but reproduced it, and that that process of ideological reproduction opens up complex questions of power that have been largely ignored. More specifically, I will argue that the exemplum served as the principal means by which the Chaucerian tradition established its cultural authority. The congruence between narrative discourse and moral authority the exemplum asserts is precisely what enabled it to transmit previous forms of authority to this new vernacular tradition. This transmission was social as well as rhetorical: it must be viewed as a process of empowerment and appropriation.

As the most authoritative tale in the Canterbury collection, the *Parson's Tale* provides the ideal place to begin exploring the political contours of these questions. It is precisely the place where authority seems least discursive, and most closed and static. Exposing the hidden marks of its discursive construction will suggest an alternative view of Chaucer's relation to it, both in terms of the cultural materials he inherits, and in terms of what he passes on to his fifteenth-century posterity.

We need to recognize from the outset that Chaucer works very hard to keep these marks hidden, to produce the effect of closure and stasis, not only in the tale's internal avoidance of narrative, but in the prologue and *Retraction* as well. Harry Bailly begins the prologue by announcing that his "ordinaunce," the command establishing the tale-telling game, is nearly fulfilled, lacking only one tale. For this he turns to the Parson, requesting a "fable," which the Parson adamantly refuses to provide. Declaring fables to be a turning aside from "soothfastnesse," the Parson offers instead "Moralitee and vertuous mateere," a "myrie tale in prose" that turns out to be a penitential manual. As the collection's close, the tale thus seems to involve a generic shift away from the narrative *game* that has constituted the collection to the non-narrative genre, perhaps even non-generic discourse of "moralitee and vertuous mateere." The shift takes on even grander proportions in the *Retraction* which follows the tale. Ostensibly disavowing "what generations of readers have experienced as the best of Chaucer's poetry,"[4] the *Retraction* confirms the generic opposition between authority and *game* when it disclaims the tales of Canterbury which "sownen into synne" (X, 1085) in favor of his books of "moralitee and devocioun" (X, 1087). A more definite ending is hard to imagine. The *Parson's Tale* closes the collection, announces the end of Chaucer's authorial career, and conclusively subordinates the *game* of narrative to the authority of Christianity, in the form of the clerical treatise.

And yet, for all its definiteness and all its conclusiveness, this closure is still irreducibly narrative. The tale's isolation of Christian authority from the tale-telling game that precedes it is itself part of the collection's frame tale. It is a gesture produced out of narrative, and it draws its meaning from its relation to the narrative that produced it. Many scholars have legitimately suggested the tale functions in relation to the rest of the collection like the *sententia* in an exemplum. But the full power of this analogy has been missed because they have underestimated the interdependence between the authority the *sententia* embodies and the narrative it authorizes. In some versions of this view, the analogy is literal and explicit. The tale becomes a systematic compilation of *sententiae* applicable to specific tales. In less literal versions it becomes *sententia* to the world of the pilgrims generally, or indeed to "experience as a whole."[5] All of these

---

[4] Siegfried Wenzel, "Explanatory Notes" to Fragment X, in *The Riverside Chaucer*, ed. Larry Benson (Boston: Houghton-Mifflin Co., 1987), 955.

[5] Lee Patterson, "The 'Parson's Tale' and the Quitting of the 'Canterbury Tales,'" *Traditio* 34 (1978), 347. The suggestion that the *Parson's Tale* be used to gloss individual tales begins with Frederick Tupper, "Chaucer and the Seven Deadly Sins," *Publication of Modern Language Association* 29 (1914), 93–128. The most recent version is Bernard F. Huppé, *A Reading of the* Canterbury Tales (Albany: State University of New York, 1964), 231–41. See also Ralph Baldwin, *The Unity of the* Canterbury Tales (Copenhagen: Rosenkilde and Bassen, 1955), 95–105; and Robert Jordan, *Chaucer and the Shape of Creation: The Aesthetic Possibilities of Inorganic Structure* (Cambridge, MA: Harvard University Press, 1967). Most critics take the tale as Patterson does, as a more generalized accession to Church authority. For a more detailed critical history, see Patterson, 333–34. It is worth noting that even recent political readings view the tale as a capitulation. See Carolyn Dinshaw, *Chaucer's*

readings, while considerably different from one another, are alike in taking the tale's closure to represent a total capitulation to Church authority.[6]

Nevertheless, it is possible to move beyond this sense of closure, without denying the opposition between authority and narrative on which it is based. If one understands the opposition in more pragmatic terms, as precisely a rhetorical strategy with a particular ideological goal, it becomes possible to read the tale as an appropriation of clerical authority rather than a capitulation to it. If we ask how its closure might have been produced out of the narrative collection which precedes it, rather than simply assuming it was imposed from without, we will begin to understand the authority of that closure in ways that will make it at once more rhetorically complex and more historically specific. Indeed, its rhetorical complexity and its historical specificity are so intertwined it is impossible to separate them. As a matter of rhetoric, even the most elemental attention to the tale's form must recognize that the tale is not simply imposed on the collection from without, but is spoken from within, in the Parson's voice – in the voice, that is of one of the characters of the frame tale. And yet, even at this elemental level, rhetorical complexity depends on historical specificity; the Parson's voice can be distinguished from the collection's other voices only on the basis of his social differentiation from them. Though it is obviously meant to embody clerical authority, his voice cannot be specified even so generally as the voice of the Church. He is not a monk or a friar. Still less is he a bishop or a pope. He is a parson, occupying the lowest position within the hierarchy of the secular clergy. If one examines

---

Sexual Poetics (Madison: University of Wisconsin Press, 1989), 183–84; Peggy Knapp, *Chaucer and the Social Contest* (New York and London: Routledge, 1990), 92–94; Stephen Knight, *Geoffrey Chaucer* (Oxford: Basil Blackwell, 1986), 153–57; and Paul Strohm, *Social Chaucer* (Cambridge, Ma.: Harvard University Press, 1989), 174–82.

[6] Even the sporadic attempts to read the tale ironically have assumed the tale as a text represents a capitulation. They locate its irony in its relation to the narratives which come before it. In recent scholarship, this view seems to have been restricted to four articles: Judson Boyce Allen, "The Old Way and the Parson's Way: An Ironic Reading of the *Parson's Tale*," *Journal of Medieval and Renaissance Studies* 3 (1973), 255–71; John Finlayson, "The Satiric Mode of the *Parson's Tale*," *Chaucer Review* 6 (1971), 94–116; Laurie A. Finke, "'To Knytte Up al this Feste': The Parson's Rhetoric and the Ending of the *Canterbury Tales*," *Leeds Studies in English* n.s. 15 (1984), 95–105; and Carol V. Kaske, "Getting Around the *Parson's Tale*: An Alternative to Allegory and Irony," in *Chaucer at Albany*, ed. Russell Hope Robbins (New York: Burt Franklin, 1975), 147–77. David Aers, *Chaucer, Langland and the Creative Imagination* (London: Routledge & Kegan Paul, 1980), 106–16, modifies this ironic reading to make it the vehicle of an ecclesiological critique.

this narrative voice more closely one finds that the exchange between the rhetorical and the social continues.

For Chaucer defines the Parson's social location in rhetorical terms. He describes the Parson as an "ensample" three times in the portrait in the General Prologue. The Parson's moral effect on the social world he inhabits is a narrative one, and this characterization circumscribes even the ostensibly non-narrative textual authority he exerts in his tale:

This noble ensample to his sheep he yaf,
That first he wroghte, and afterward he taughte. (I, 496–97)

The Parson's teachings are authorized by his doings – indeed the simultaneity in the Middle English "wroghte" of both the notion of doing and the notion of creating by doing gives these lines a much stronger sense of the symbolic power of social action than is possible in modern paraphrase. They clearly establish that his access to the doctrinal and didactic authority he exerts within his tale comes primarily from his individual integrity and only secondarily – if at all – from his institutional position.

The lines draw on Christianity's own profound anti-institutional bias. They recall Christ's critique of the Pharisees from the Sermon on the Mount:

Whoever then relaxes one of the least of these commandments and teaches men so, shall be called the least in the kingdom of heaven; but he who does them and teaches them shall be called great in the kingdom of Heaven. For I tell you, unless your righteousness exceeds that of the scribes and Pharisees, you will never enter the kingdom of heaven. (Matthew, 5: 19–20)

At the same time, Chaucer's emphasis on the Parson's personal sanctity approaches a central tenet of Lollardy: the belief that sacerdotal authority "depended on the state of grace of the man wielding it."[7] Chaucer even seems to acknowledge this proximity when he has Harry Bailly refer to the Parson as a Lollard (II, 1173). Rather than viewing Chaucer as a crypto-Lollard, however, it is more plausible to see both his anti-clericalism and Lollardy as specific instances of the general anti-clericalism that was widespread

[7] Anne Hudson, *The Premature Reformation: Wycliffite Texts and Lollard History* (Oxford: Clarendon Press, 1988), 315. A good deal of ambiguity surrounds the exact nature and extent of this claim. Most Lollards, for instance, apparently did not push it to the Donatist extreme of holding that a priest's immorality invalidated the sacraments he administered. See Hudson, 314–89.

in English society in the last decades of the fourteenth century. That anti-clericalism had its specific cause in resentment against the vastness of Church property, but it is also related to the accelerated laicization of governmental structures at both the local and national levels.[8]

It is not surprising that Chaucer should draw on this anti-clericalism in attempting to establish his own authority. What is more striking is that the strategy he follows in doing so is exactly the same as his contemporary, Gower, from whom he is so often distinguished. Gower attacks ecclesiastical corruption in the *Confessio Amantis* by appealing to the same notion of exemplarity as Chaucer, connecting it even more explicitly to Christ:

> Crist wroghte ferst and after tawhte,
> So that the dede his word arawhte; [explained]
> He yaf ensample in his persone,
> And we the wordes have al one...[9]

He also uses the same rhetorical strategy, defining the ideal role of the cleric as an exemplary one. In the *Prologus* Gower invokes the purity of the Church's early days, when, unlike the present, clerics "weren tho / Ensample and reule of alle ... (Pr., 195–96)," and when "Thei were ek chaste in word and dede, / Wherof the poeple ensample tok" (Pr., 228–29), and he closes with the injunction that the Church should be "The Mirour of Ensamplerie" (Pr., 496). If ecclesiastical authority is equal to the sum of the exemplary achievements of individual clerics, it is an authority which in no sense resides in the institution. To define the Church as a "Mirour of Ensamplerie" is in fact to reduce it to an assemblage of individuals, without corporate authority.

There is nothing heterodox in this redefinition. Indeed, clerical writers themselves frequently described Christ as an exemplum.[10] Yet the emphasis both Chaucer and Gower place on exemplarity as

---

[8] Margaret Aston, "'Caim's Castles': Poverty, Politics and Disendowment," in *The Church, Politics and Patronage in the Fifteenth Century*, ed. R. B. Dobson (Gloucester: Alan Sutton Publishing, 1984), 49–54; Peter Heath, *Church and Realm 1272–1461* (London: Fontana Press, 1988), 189–222. On laicization see Janet Coleman, "English Culture in the Fourteenth Century," in *Chaucer and the Italian Trecento*, ed. Piero Boitani (Cambridge: Cambridge University Press, 1983), 33–63.

[9] *The Complete Works of John Gower*; vols. 2–3, *The English Works*, ed. G. C. Macaulay (Oxford: The Clarendon Press, 1901), v. 2, p. 452, V, 1825–28. Subsequent citations from this poem will be from this edition. Book and line numbers will be given in the text.

[10] For instance, Augustine, *De Civitate Dei*, IX, xxii.

doing, as *factum*, rather than *dictum*, distances clerical authority from the textual. If even Christ's *dicta* depend on his *facta*, then the textual authority of the clergy must always be secondary to their actual piety as a group of historical individuals. The emphasis on exemplarity carries the burden of the anti-clerical polemic, and if anything Chaucer's greater reliance on narrative makes his text the more polemical on this point. Gower's prologue, like Chaucer's, is in the form of an estates-satire. But Gower's follows a more traditional topical format, treating each estate in turn. To this extent he allows the Church to retain some residual corporate status. Chaucer's prologue is entirely narrative, enabling him at once to celebrate the Parson's exemplarity and to deny it institutional status. He is able to be more polemical precisely because he is more narrative. The point is worth stressing, because Gower's preference for abstract hierarchies is often contrasted to Chaucer's preference for narrative in order to demonstrate Chaucer's anti-didacticism.[11] In this case, Chaucer's use of narrative is anti-clerical rather than anti-didactic; his motives are polemical and not exclusively aesthetic or formal.

The Parson's exemplarity consists almost entirely of his disavowal of institutional prerogatives. Ostensibly echoing his voice, Chaucer the Pilgrim tells us, "Wel oghte a preest ensample for to yive," then lists all the things the Parson does not do: he does not sell his benefice for hire, or seek chantry, or retreat into a brotherhood (I, 505–14). Nor does he stand on ceremony, refusing the "pompe or reverence," of his position, and pursuing correction of his flock discreetly and benignly (I, 515–26). Earlier in the portrait we are told he is loath "to cursen for his tithes," and more often gives out of his own funds to poor parishioners (I, 486–90).

His self-abnegation is summed up best in the striking image that occurs toward the beginning of the portrait.

> Wyd was his parisshe, and houses fer asonder,
> But he ne lefte nat, for reyn ne thonder,
> In siknesse nor in meschief to visite
> The ferreste in his parisshe, muche and lite,
> Upon his feet, and in his hand a staf.   (I, 491–95)

The Parson entirely constrains his body to the geographical extent of his parish, incessantly retracing its limits with his feet. This image is

---

[11] For a representative view, see Paul Strohm, "Form and Social Statement in *Confessio Amantis* and the *Canterbury Tales*," *Studies in the Age of Chaucer* 1 (1979), 17–40.

a stark contrast to the outriding Monk, with his stable full of horses, overseeing the far-flung properties of a prosperous abbey. The Parson's exertions are restricted to the smallest ecclesiastical unit – a unit moreover with its roots not in ecclesiastical organization, but in the feudal estate. The parish was originally coextensive with the feudal manor, and although nominal control of the parish was transferred to the Church in the thirteenth century, many parishes were still patronized by local landowners.[12] The Parson's institutional functions are entirely localized, and unlike the Monk, who embodies the Church's capacity to rival secular landowners, he presents no threat to lay power.

This is perhaps the most significant feature of the Parson's exemplarity: it is almost entirely negative. His activity is directed entirely toward restraining his effect on the world around him. Not only does he refuse all institutional prerogatives, but he also restrains himself even in his pastoral correction of his parishioners. His every act has as its goal the maintenance of an absolute *status quo*, and the model he presents to his parishioners is self-abnegation in the face of existing social forces. The model is self-abnegating not only in its content but in the very exemplary form of its presentation. That is, the Parson does not teach his parishioners to be self-abnegating by directly instructing them. Rather, he acts in a self-abnegating way and hopes they will imitate him.

As an ideal, the Parson bespeaks a point of view at once profoundly conservative and profoundly laicist. The commitment of this view to an absolute *status quo* makes it conservative. Its commitment to restraint of ecclesiastical prerogative in the name of this *status quo* make it laicist. Chaucer implicitly maintains this point of view throughout the General Prologue. The ecclesiastical and quasi-ecclesiastical figures he presents unfavorably, the Prioress, the Monk, the Friar, the Summoner, and the Pardoner, are almost all evil primarily by virtue of their unfettered exercise of prerogatives that come to them through their institutional positions. The one other favorable ecclesiastical figure, the Clerk, is, like the Parson, a self-abnegating character more interested in his scholarly pursuits than in institutional preferment. As the discourse of a character the sacerdotal value of whose words is dependent on the sanctity of his

---

[12] G. H. Cook, *The English Mediaeval Parish Church* (London: Phoenix, 1954), 18–20. Heath, *Church and Realm*, 18.

actions, the *Parson's Tale* ceases to be institutionally specific, and becomes a form as accessible to the lay as the clerical. The shift is reinforced by the tale's genre, which characterizes Church authority as specifically as Chaucer's social location of its teller.

As a penitential manual, the tale presents a very distinctive and specific form of clerical authority, the authority of the confessor – whose precise concern is to elicit the voice of the laity. This is an authority that is ecclesiological rather than philosophical, historically specific, and institutionally localized. At this time, it was also relatively new.[13] This tradition of the penitential manual begins after the Fourth Lateran Council of 1215, which mandated yearly confession to all believers.[14] The tradition of such manuals written in English is of even more recent vintage. P. S. Jolliffe reports that no extant English work of spiritual guidance dates from before 1340.[15] Thus, the *Parson's Tale* is appropriating quite a new genre. Moreover, as a new genre it represents nothing less than the production of a new form of subjectivity. The confessant, or confessional subject, if we may call him that, confronts Christian authority in an individuated, secularized, and most importantly, eminently secularizable form. Christian authority as an ideal is simple, total, and unchanging; it resides in the ultimate *auctor*, God. But by its very nature it is also an ideal which demands to be put into practice. Its practical expression depends on a series of mediations which expose it at every point to the fallen secular world it aspires to transform – the human language of the biblical text, the institutional structures of the Church, and the ritual forms through which individual devotion is enacted. By their fallen status, none of these mediations can ever fully capture the Divine authority they express, and its presence in the world depends on their continual reiteration.

The penitential manual takes this necessity to its limit. It aspires to reorganize every moment of the penitent's conscious life. As the

---

[13] There was an older tradition that died out around 1000, but it was more concerned with defining the nature of sin than it was with establishing confession as a ritual. See J. T. McNeill and H. M. Gamer, *Medieval Handbooks of Penance* (New York: Columbia University Press, 1938).

[14] Patterson, "The 'Parson's Tale,'" 335–39; Leonard E. Boyle, "The Fourth Lateran Council and Manuals of Popular Theology," in *The Popular Literature of Medieval England*, ed. Thomas J. Heffernan (Knoxville: University of Tennessee Press, 1985), 30–43; and Fritz Kemmler, "*Exempla*" in *Context: A Historical and Critical Study of Robert Mannyng of Brunne's* "*Handlynge Synne*" (Tubingen: Gunter Narr Verlag, 1984), 24–59.

[15] P. S. Jolliffe, *A Checklist of Prose Writings of Spiritual Guidance* (Toronto: Pontifical Institute of Mediaeval Studies, 1974), 23.

Parson warns, "contricioun most be continueel" (X, 304). It is not enough simply to internalize the categories of the Church so as to recognize sin when it occurs: one must also demonstrate the success of the internalization through the quasi-public act of confession, the "verray shewyng of synnes to the preest" (X, 319). The demonstration cannot be partial: "Al moot be seyd, and no thyng excused ne hyd ne forwrapped." Nor is even a complete demonstration sufficient: a confession must be followed by satisfaction, the new disposition of the mind must be registered in the actions of the body. Nor is the process complete even there. Once absolved the penitent is immediately subject to the temptation of sin once again, and once he or she succumbs the process must begin again as quickly as possible.

The penitential manual envisions Christian faith as an endless internalization accomplished against continual resistance. Indeed this resistance is anticipated even by that aspect of the genre that seems most closed and self-assured: its intricate system of taxonomy. For this very intricacy demonstrates the multiplicity, the endless variety of forms the resistance of sin can take. The penitential manual is thus a closed, stable text, whose very stability is nevertheless predicated on disorder and flux. Its authority, total and unassailable within the text, must nevertheless be continually reasserted in the resistant world outside of it. That resistant world begins in the consciousness of the penitent, and this dependence makes the practice of penance enabling as well as constraining. It provides a framework through which the believer can understand not simply the nature of God or the world at large, but every one of his or her own acts. In exchange for a more intimate submission to Church authority, it offers the believer a more complete comprehension of his or her own subjectivity.

Chaucer does not merely draw on this form of empowerment; he takes control of it. The *Parson's Tale* represents an authorization of his own voice, an authorization so implicit it has gone unnoticed. Yet it is an obvious fact which cannot be ignored: despite the apparent deference to the Church in the guise of the Parson, in the last analysis it is not the Parson but Chaucer who speaks. Having made doctrinal authority accessible to the lay by restricting the Parson's authority to the exemplary value of his actions, Chaucer can close his collection with a systematic exposition of doctrine which at once rounds out the Parson as a moral ideal and asserts Chaucer's own right as a lay poet to establish such ideals. In all probability, the *Parson's Tale* is the first extant penitential manual in English to be compiled by a non-cleric; certainly it was the first to which a non-cleric affixed his name.[16] This fact alone would make the tale a central instance of the cultural shift whereby "the literate laity were taking the clergy's words out of their mouths."[17] The tale's placement in a lay poetic collection makes its ecclesiological status that much more attenuated. A penitential manual is, in fact, a radically open text: its purpose is not achieved until its prescriptions are enacted within the life of the penitent who reads it. To the extent the *Parson's Tale* actually serves as *sententia* to the tales that precede it, it ceases to be a real penitential manual, and to the extent it actually serves as a penitential manual it ceases to be a purely textual *sententia*. The tale becomes an image of Church authority rather than the thing itself, and the image serves Chaucer rather than the Church.

It serves Chaucer in the first instance precisely by virtue of the strict rhetorical opposition the tale maintains between lay discourse as entirely narrative, and clerical discourse as entirely non-narrative. Despite its generally hortatory stance, the tale differs from its models in its exclusion of specific hortatory rhetorical effects, most notably in its exclusion of the exemplum.[18] Because of its power to move its audience, the exemplum was employed widely in the penitential tradition, and some penitential manuals were outright exemplum collections, including the influential early fourteenth-century work, *Handlyng Synne*. Chaucer's general fascination with the exemplum makes its exclusion here all the more striking. As it developed within the Church, the exemplum's narrative component came more and more to be identified with the lay audience and its *sententia* comes

---

[16] The present state of knowledge regarding this corpus of material is still too preliminary to enable us to make statements about the social position of its compilers with complete certainty. Moreover, many of these works are anonymous. Nevertheless, most of the major works in the tradition have been edited, or at least examined. To date, no lay author before Chaucer has been discovered. For a brief sketch of the tradition, see Patterson, "The 'Parson's Tale'," 338–39. For a more extensive overview, see Jolliffe, *A Checklist*, and A. I. Doyle, "A Survey of the Origins and Circulation of Theological Writings in English in the Fourteenth, Fifteenth, and Early Sixteenth Centuries, with Special Consideration of the Part of the Clergy Therein" (unpub. Ph.D. diss., Cambridge University, 2301–2302, 1951). See also Vincent Gillespie, "Vernacular Books of Religion," in *Book Production and Publishing in Britain 1375–1475*, ed. Jeremy Griffiths and Derek Pearsall (Cambridge: Cambridge University Press, 1989), 317–44.

[17] K. B. McFarlane, *Lancastrian Kings and Lollard Knights* (Oxford: Oxford University Press, 1972), 204; cited in Gillespie, "Vernacular Books," 317.

[18] Patterson, "The 'Parson's Tale'," 345–46.

more and more to be identified with the doctrinal discourse of the Church. However, for Church commentators, the Christian exemplarist ultimately controlled both discourses. Chaucer accepts the distinction between narrative and doctrine, but widens it, so that the opposition is no longer simply an opposition between two discourses. Instead narrative becomes the discourse of the world *tout court* and doctrine becomes a body of truth beyond all human discourse, including the specific institutional discourses of the Church. Exemplary narrative leads to doctrinal authority, but not as the smooth translation of one discourse to another. Rather it leads to it as something beyond, which it can never quite reach. The Parson's rejection of narrative cuts clerical discourse off from the form which, in the penitential tradition and elsewhere had been its most powerful means of persuasion.

In this "tale to end all tales,"[19] Christian authority becomes the end of discourse, a set of stable, abstract categories equally available to all believers. By making the *Parson's Tale* non-narrative and setting it apart from the rest of the collection, Chaucer completes his de-privileging of the ecclesiastical. Where narrative becomes the language of the lay, the ecclesiastical is signified only by the end of discourse. It hovers beyond the discursive as the definitive form of closure, but without any discursive features of its own. In this way, Chaucer appropriates ecclesiastical authority not by repudiating it but by exaggerating its claims to closure. He places it beyond the discursive and makes its enactment dependent on him.

Moreover, this placement is itself metaphorical. The Tale *seems* to be at the end of discourse, but it only seems so, for this seeming is itself rhetorically produced. The Tale's ostensibly complete closure is in fact an effect that results primarily from the dominance of its relentless taxonomizing. But it has other rhetorical strategies as well, which tend to return it to the lay world it claims to leave behind. The most striking of these is the metaphorization of the opposition between *lord* and *thral*. This metaphor recurs throughout. It illustrates a central fact about authority modern thought has been slow to recognize. Authority is as dependent on power as power is on authority. Chaucer's appropriation of clerical authority in this tale is not a simple act of resistance; it is simultaneously an affirmation of his own, gendered, class-specific lay privilege. The affirmation begins

---

[19] Patterson, "The 'Parson's Tale'," 380.

with the biblical citation "whoso that dooth synne is thral of synne"
(X, 141).

Chaucer insists on the metaphor's literal force.

Ne a fouler thral may no man ne womman maken of his body than for to
yeven his body to synne. / Al were it the fouleste cherl or the foulest
womman that lyveth, and leest of value, yet is he thanne moore foul and
moore in servitude. (X, 145–46)

This passage clearly collapses the spiritual back into the social
categories of *cherl* and woman. It stops short of actually making social
inferiority itself a sin, but, it makes the pursuit of Christian virtue a
natural extension of the social exertion of ruling class privilege. It
clearly assumes male, ruling class readers. Drawing on their fear and
loathing of those beneath them it transfers the foulness of the
"fouleste cherl" and "fouleste womman" to the thraldom of sin, and
thus collapses their desire to avoid sin with their desire to maintain
their distance from those beneath them.

This gendered, class-specific understanding of sin is supported by
the frequent recourse to social commentary that occurs throughout
the discussion of the Seven Deadly Sins. *Superbia* contains a long
attack on "outrageous array of clothyng," and the "holdynge of
greet meynee" (412–79). *Invidia*, defined as "sory of alle the bountees
of his neighebor" (488), ends with a discussion of the "Murmure"
that is "ofte amonges servauntz that grucchen whan hir sovereyns
bidden hem doon leveful thynges" (506–14). *Ira* is presented as the
source of "werre and every manner of wronge that man dooth to his
neighbor in body or in catel" (563). The major subcategory of *Ira* is
cursing; this is contrasted to juridical oath-taking (591–96). *Ira* is also
taken to include such politically significant speech as flattery and
false counsel (567–69, 612–18). In the course of a justification of
social hierarchy, *Avaricia* discusses at length the contrast between
social servitude and thralldom to sin (752–75). In the last section, one
of the arguments offered against *luxuria* is its disruption of primogeniture: "of which brekynge comen false heires ofte tyme, that
wrongfully ocupien folkes heritages" (883–85).

The catalog of sins is by no means dominated by this social
commentary. But the conflation of socially oriented sins with the
more theologically oriented (such as anger against God) and the
more private (such as *wanhope*) collapses the social into the theological, and literally puts the existing social hierarchy beyond

question. That hierarchy becomes part of an absolute status quo which the sinner faces in his or her struggle against sin. The sinner's first duty is self-restraint, and that self-restraint applies with equal force to the social hierarchy as it does to the divine hierarchy. The transcendence of social relations which the sinner's self-restraint demands has the effect of leaving the social relations entirely intact. Even as Chaucer acknowledges their inequity, he uses that acknowledgement as an argument for their preservation.

He begins the long discussion in *Avaricia* with the Augustinian argument that source of social hierarchy is original sin: "the first cause of thraldom is for synne" (X, 755). This leads him immediately to the observation that lordship is contingent and arbitrary:

Wherfore thise lordes ne sholde nat muche glorifien hem in hir lordshipes, sith that by natural condicion they been nat lordes over thralles, but that thraldom comth first by the desert of synne. (X, 757)

Lords spring of "swich seed as cherles spryngen"; they die "the same death." Therefore, Chaucer advises, "do right so with thy cherl, as thou woldest that thy lord did with thee, if thou were in his plit" (X, 761–62).

Chaucer's acknowledgment of the historical contingency of lordship is in no way an argument for radical social change; it is rather an incitement to empathy.[20] This empathy is antithetical to social reform, for it assumes the very power relation it might seem to ameliorate: it is conditioned on the opposition between lord and cherl. The lord is to treat the cherl as he would like to be treated *if he were a cherl*. There is no question of treating the cherl as an equal. The empathy extends only to preventing "extorcions and despit of... underlynges" (X, 764), it assumes the lord's dominance, and by placing the responsibility for lord/cherl relations solely in his hands, it also perpetuates that dominance.

---

[20] We can confirm this in a rough way by comparing this view of social hierarchy with that expressed by radical contemporaries of Chaucer's like John Ball. As quoted by Froissart, Ball asks,

In what way are those whom we call lords greater masters than ourselves? How have they deserved it? Why do they hold us in bondage? If we all spring from a single father and mother, Adam and Eve, how can they claim or prove that they are more lords than us, except by making us produce and grow the wealth which they spend?

(Jean Froissart, *Chronicles*, selected, tr. and ed. Geoffrey Brereton (London: Penguin Books, 1968), 212.) Where Chaucer, in accordance with the dominant medieval view, will justify bondage despite its historical contingency by making its contingent status an inevitable result of the Fall, John Ball will draw on the same argument but make bondage's connection with the Fall that much more compelling a reason to reject it as contingent.

The profound conservatism that motivates this Chaucerian empathy is a point worth stressing. Chaucer's empathy has long been one of the defining characteristics of his continuing authority; it has its roots in Dryden's description of the Canterbury collection as "God's plenty."[21] This empathy has often been connected to Chaucer's rhetorical complexity and offered as evidence of his resistance to Christian moralizing, and as evidence even of some innately democratic spirit. This passage suggests that it was neither. Here, the explicit motive for such empathy is the Christian recognition of the equality of all humanity before God. Moreover, Chaucer defines this spiritual equality in a rigorously conservative manner. He not only places it beyond the inequality of material social relations; he makes social inequality necessary to produce spiritual equality. It is the lord's very social superiority to the cherl which obliges the lord to treat him as a spiritual equal.

This dependence of the spiritual on the material becomes even more marked as the passage continues. I cite at length.

Now as I have seyd, sith so is that synne was first cause of thraldom, thanne is it thus: that thilke tyme that al this world was in synne, thanne was al this world in thraldom and subjeccioun. / But certes, sith the time of grace cam, God ordeyned that som folk sholde be moore heigh in estaat and in degree, and som folk moore lough, and everich sholde be served in his estaat and in his degree. / And therfore in somme contrees, ther they byen thralles whan they han turned hem to the feith, they make hire thralles free out of thraldom. And therfore, certes, the lord oweth to his man that the man oweth to this lord. / The Pope calleth hymself servant of the servantz of God; but for as much as the estaat of hooly chirche ne myghte nat han be, ne the commune profit myghte nat han be kept, ne pees and rest in erthe, but if God hadde ordeyned that some men hadde hyer degree and som men lower, / therfore was sovereyntee ordeyned, to kepe and mayntene and deffenden hire underlynges or hire subgetz in resoun, as ferforth as it lith in hire power, and nat to destroyen hem ne confounde. / Wherefore I seye that thilke lordes that been lyk wolves, that devouren the possessiouns or the catel of povre folk wrongfully, withouten mercy or mesure, / they shul receyven by the same mesure that they han mesured to povre folk the mercy of Jhesu Crist, but if it be amended. (X, 769–75)

This is a remarkable passage. In a culture whose extant political writings are notoriously oblique on the question of power relations, it is as explicit as any I have seen in asserting: (1) that class hierarchy

21 John Dryden, "Preface to Fables Ancient and Modern," in *Of Dramatic Poesy and Other Critical Essays*, ed. George Watson (London: J. M. Dent, 1962), 284–85. See Lee Patterson, *Chaucer and the Subject of History* (University of Wisconsin Press, 1991), 14–22.

is a product of Christian grace, and (2) that the Church, even in its spiritual functions, was dependent on the forms of lay sovereignty growing out of such hierarchy. There is nothing democratic about this text. It provides a strong counterexample to recent considerations of Chaucer's politics which emphasize his commitment to "counter-hegemony."[22] It is true that the tone here is still admonitory and that Chaucer is clearly concerned that his audience understand the exact limits of ruling class power, and the spiritual obligation to which they give rise. Nevertheless, his very articulation of those limits entails a strict affirmation of the *status quo*. Human equality is restricted to a single privileged site, the purely spiritual "hooly chirche." The equality within that site is so radical that even the pope, nominally its supreme officer, is a servant of the other members, themselves "servants of God." But the very existence of that site depends on a material inequality Chaucer flatly declares divinely ordained. God's decree "that som folk sholde be moore heigh in estaat and in degree, and som folk moore lough," is coincident with Christianity's New Dispensation, "the time of grace." This New Dispensation is contrasted to the moment of universal thralldom that preceded it. Its form of hierarchy is orderly, not purely repressive. It brings with it the obligation that "everich sholde be served in his estaat and in his degree," and had the result that thralls were freed from their thralldom. But this obligation strengthens the importance of hierarchy rather than weakening it. The previous moment of universal thralldom which this view posits serves to legitimate the divinely inspired benevolence of present class relations, and make them the source of community: if God had not ordained "that some men hadde hyer degree and som men lower," then "the commune profit myghte nat han be kept." Community not only depends on hierarchy, it is hierarchy.

When Chaucer goes on to declare "therfore was sovereyntee ordeyned," he clearly means the term in a fairly technical sense. The weak passive construction is revealing. Unlike the more general inequality between degree mentioned in the previous clause, "sovereyntee" is not so clearly a divine invention. Chaucer may have in mind the specific power structures of his own time, which were undergoing increasing consolidation, often under the auspices of the sovereign figure of the king. During the course of the fourteenth

---

[22] Strohm, *Social Chaucer*, xiii.

century the judicial system became centralized under royal control; Parliament, originally conceived as an extension of the king's counsel, provided the landowning classes for the first time with the possibility of a nationally unified voice; and the royal bureaucracy, in which Chaucer spent most of his adult life, continued to grow despite baronial resistance. While these newly emergent national forms of sovereignty could not be presented as divinely ordained in the same way as the general principle of social inequality, they could nevertheless be seen as following in the same spirit, particularly since they all involved the routinization of power through standardized administrative procedures and written records.

The implication that the "estaat of holy Church" depends on such lay forms of sovereignty connects this text to such royalists as Dante, who argued in *De monarchia* that men would "fling aside" spiritual guidance if they "were not held to the right path by the bit and the rein." This was the office of the Roman Prince: "to provide freedom and peace for men as they pass through the testing time of this world."[23] The Church's dependence on lay political power was a mainstay of medieval political theory, acknowledged by even as anti-secular a figure as Augustine.[24] Nevertheless, it was only in royal responses to the papal publicists that this dependence began to take on the status of a sacral duty, and the office of king was seen as deriving as directly from God as that of the pope. Chaucer's suggestion that the estate of the Church depends on lay sovereignty clearly grows out of that position, but also generalizes it, connecting sovereignty to the hierarchy of class relations. This synthesis gives the spirituality elaborated throughout the tale a specific political location. This passage figures the tale's general appropriation and internalization of Church authority as enacted from the position of one who holds political sovereignty over others. In the image of sovereignty as empathy exercised with proper Christian restraint – at once upholding the holy Church, and keeping, maintaining, and defending its underlings and subjects – Chaucer affirms both Christianity's authorization of political hierarchy, and that hierarchy's sacral importance.

This affirmation is by no means restricted to this tale. We can find

---

[23] Dante, *Monarchy and Three Political Letters*, tr. Donald Nicholl and Colin Hardie (London: Weidenfield and Nicolson, 1954), 93.

[24] R. A. Markus, "The Latin Fathers," in *The Cambridge History of Medieval Political Thought c. 350-c. 1450*, ed. J. H. Burns (Cambridge: Cambridge University Press, 1988), 108–10.

a similar affirmation in another passage that is much better known. This is Chaucer's announcement of his aesthetic program at the end of the *General Prologue*. It defines his commitment to empathy and narrative capaciousness in more explicitly rhetorical terms, but it just as explicitly marks that commitment in terms of class:

> ... I pray yow, of youre curteisye,
> That ye n'arrette it nat my vileynye,
> Thogh that I pleynly speke in this mateere,
> To telle yow hir wordes and hir cheere,
> Ne thogh I speke hir wordes proprely.
> For this ye knowen al so wel as I:
> Whoso shal telle a tale after a man,
> He moot reherce as ny as evere he kan
> Everich a word, if it be in his charge,
> Al speke he never so rudeliche and large,
> Or ellis he moot telle his tale untrewe,
> Or feyne thyng, or fynde wordes newe.   (I, 725–36)

In begging his audience's indulgence to allow him to speak in the words of others no matter how "rudeliche and large," he presents his audience's prospective acceptance as a function of their "curteisye." They will affirm their own "curteisye," their own cultural claim to ruling class status, by assigning the *vileynye* Chaucer may speak not to him but to the lower class world to which Chaucer implies such speech belongs. This passage frames the collection's entire exploration of its socially diverse narrative voices as conducted from a position of class superiority. The aristocratic *curteisye* from which the collection begins moves easily into the more specifically spiritual empathy with which I have been arguing it ends. In between Chaucer demonstrates the textual integrity of the lay experience, its capacity to tell its own story, in its own terms, even where those terms are morally and socially degraded.

If this demonstration presents a challenge to the textual authority of the Church, and at various points it clearly does, it also affirms the capaciousness of the class perspective from which it begins. As the narrative expression of a politically conservative Christian empathy, Chaucer's textual complexity, his capacious ability to speak in voices other than his own, affirms rather than contests the hierarchical social formation from which those voices issue. For this reason, Chaucer moves more easily than is usually acknowledged from the subversion of one form of social authority to the affirmation of

another. His final justification of lay political sovereignty in the
Parson's Tale is anticipated at earlier points throughout the collection,
as I shall argue below.[25] He usually resists ecclesiastical authority just
as far as he needs to in order to appropriate it, and that appropriation
is usually motivated by his commitment to the ruling class to which
both he and his audience belong. The authority to which he lays
claim in the *Parson's Tale* provides this audience with a form of
textuality of their own. This textuality, produced in the vernacular
outside the institutional confines of the Church, occupies a specifically
lay social space, which its audience more clearly controls. As a
rhetorical matter, it is less distinct from the clerical traditions which
enable it. But even here it is weighted more heavily toward the lay
language of narrative, and even where, as in the *Parson's Tale*, it
emphasizes the separation between that language and the language
of doctrine, this separation tends, albeit ironically and indirectly, to
affirm narrative. For it exalts doctrine so completely as to place it
entirely beyond history, and therefore beyond the institutional grasp
of the Church. Even when it is not exemplary, Chaucerian narrative
resembles the exemplum in its striving after a moral authority which
it implies, but which lies beyond it. It finds its own authority in
precisely this striving; in what we can call its self-conscious
acknowledgment of its own incompletion. That acknowledgment is
always ironic, often corrosively so. But its self-confessed dependence
on the very clerical authority it ironizes means it should be
understood as appropriative rather than subversive.

Reading Chaucer's narrative as appropriative not only offers a
more plausible account of his relation to the culture which produced
him, it also offers a more plausible account of his relation to his
immediate posterity. As a hard material fact, Chaucer's abiding
canonical status depended in the first instance on the fifteenth
century's designation of him as England's first vernacular *auctor*.
While the twentieth century has cheerfully accepted the fifteenth's
assessment of Chaucer as the chief poet of his age, we have also
viewed their celebration of him as pre-eminently a moral authority
as entirely wrong-headed, and part of their "regression into the worst
vices of medieval literature."[26] Yet if we see Chaucer's narrative

[25] See 146–244.
[26] E. Talbot Donaldson, "The Middle Ages," in *The Norton Anthology of English Literature*, fifth
ed., ed. M. H. Abrams (New York and London: W. W. Norton and Co., 1986), 12. The best
recent discussion of this issue is A. C. Spearing's magisterial *Medieval to Renaissance in English*

complexity (which is where *we* locate his authority) as designed less to subvert clerical authority than to laicize it, his canonizers' subsequent affirmation of his authority becomes more intelligible. I can illustrate this point more clearly by a brief consideration of the *Retraction*.

The *Retraction* follows the same double logic as the tale, and like the tale it has usually been read as an act of submission. The direct appeal to the autobiographical fulfills the penitential manual's performative demands. Having systematically laid out the requirements of Christian penitence, Chaucer proceeds to enact them with respect to his own life. "Wherefore I biseke yow mekely," he asks his readers,

... for the mercy of God, that ye preye for me that Crist have mercy on me and foryeve me my giltes; / and namely of my translacions and enditynges of worldly vanitees, the whiche I revoke in my retracciouns. (X, 1084–85)

He then lists the *Troilus*, the *House of Fame*, the *Legend of Good Women*, the *Book of the Duchess*, the *Parliament of Fowls*, and those *Canterbury Tales* "that sownen into synne," along with others (X, 1086–87). Then, he thanks "oure Lord Jhesu Crist and his blisful Mooder, and alle the seintes of hevene," for his translation of Boethius and "othere bookes of legendes of seintes, and omelies, and moralitee, and devocioun" (X, 1088–89).

The submissive aspect of this retraction is obvious. Its appropriative aspect is less obvious, but no less crucial. The autobiography Chaucer presents here is entirely textual. It consists not of his actions generally, but only of his writings. What is at stake, then, is not his sins, but his claim to *auctoritas*. Those works which lack moral authority he disclaims in favor of those which possess it. The rejection of the other works is obviously a rejection of sin. It cannot, however, be viewed as a rejection of the lay. On the contrary, it is spoken from a position which never ceases to be lay. Its authority is dependent not on his ecclesiological status, or lack thereof, but rather on his own individual penitential integrity – an integrity he has defined in

Poetry (Cambridge: Cambridge University Press, 1985). Spearing is clearly bothered by the standard view, yet he never seems to be able to break entirely free of it. Early on in his discussion of the Chaucerian tradition he warns, "It would be quite wrong to suppose that the transition from medieval to Renaissance in English poetry could be seen simply in evolutionary terms..." (89). Nevertheless, he concludes the discussion by declaring, "The persistent distortion of Chaucer's achievement that is represented by the poetry of most of his disciples meant that the work of the literary Renaissance, which Chaucer had begun singlehanded, had to be done all over again in the sixteenth century" (120).

purely textual terms. Because he retextualizes Christian authority at
the very moment that he is ostensibly submitting to it, his submission
is an appropriation. For this reason the retraction should be
considered a consolidation and not a rejection. Though it de-
authorizes the "sinful" tales, it does not necessarily deprive them of
all value. They were an integral part of the narrative logic that leads
up to this point; Chaucer never repudiates this logic, and in fact rests
his claims of authority upon it. The gap he has erected between them
and his authoritative works is crucial, but if the *Retraction* banished
them entirely, the opposition on which its own authority depends
would also collapse. The tale he began in the voice of the Church he
now closes by investing his own voice with a quasi-sacral status.
Having distanced himself from the works that "sownen into synne,"
he is now poised to be remembered as the author of saints' lives,
homilies, and works of morality and devotion.

Thus, the fifteenth century's notorious "narrowing" of the
Chaucerian tradition in fact begins with Chaucer himself.[27] The
didactic Chaucer which they make the first *auctor* in English and the
father of their tradition is a Chaucer first produced by Chaucer
himself. It is true that the work of Chaucer's successors is more
explicitly didactic, and more explicitly royalist, and less explicitly
playful than his. But if we read this explicitness as a necessary part of
the consolidation of the vernacular authority he initiated, it becomes
intelligible. Though the fifteenth century valued his didactic works
over the others, there is no evidence that it ceased reading them.
Nearly two-thirds of the extant manuscripts of the *Canterbury Tales*
are complete or were clearly intended to be so. The preference for
such tales as the *Clerk's Tale*, the *Monk's Tale*, the *Prioress's Tale*,
Melibee, and the *Parson's Tale* represents a privileging of particular
elements within what was taken to be a larger *oeuvre*; it certainly does
not represent a suppression of the other elements. Indeed, on the face
of it, the fifteenth century's reading of Chaucer is no narrower than
the twentieth's. Where the fifteenth century concentrated on the tales
I have mentioned above to the neglect of others, the twentieth
century, in its ostensibly more capacious reading, has concentrated
with similar narrowness, on a different set of tales: the *Knight's Tale*,
the *Miller's Tale*, the *Wife of Bath's Tale*, the *Pardoner's Tale*, and the
Nun's Priest's Tale. To term the fifteenth century's reading narrow

---

[27] Cf. Paul Strohm, "Chaucer's Fifteenth-Century Audience and the Narrowing of the
'Chaucer Tradition,'" *Studies in the Age of Chaucer* 4 (1982), 3–32.

from that perspective is rather more self-congratulatory than historically accurate.

I would like to suggest instead that we should understand the development of Chaucer's posterity as a consolidation rather than a narrowing. This consolidation was marked thematically by an increasingly explicit and increasingly specific affirmation of kingship, a source of secular authority in both material and ideological terms. The consolidation was marked rhetorically by a nearly exclusive use of the exemplum. The *Confessio Amantis*, the *Regement of Princes*, and the *Fall of Princes* are all exemplum collections addressed to the issue of kingship. But both the theme and the form are already evident in Chaucer, where they play a crucial, if somewhat less obvious role in establishing his own authority. Without their appearance in Chaucer, their more explicit role later would not have been possible.

Redefining Chaucer's authority as exemplary enables us to move beyond his mythic status as the father of English poetry to specify his historical relation to the culture he inhabited. Moreover, an exemplary model of authority, with its complex interdependence between past and present, comes much closer to the role which Chaucer declares for himself in the prologue to *Melibee*, and which Lydgate reiterates in the *Fall of Princes* a half-century later, the role of translator. Chaucer's frequent recourse to the exemplum enabled him to translate cultural authority from the Latin discourse of the Church to the vernacular; it enabled his successors to complete the process by producing him as an *auctor*. This process obviously began not with Chaucer himself, but with the models of authority carried to him either through the Church, or through lay writers like Petrarch and Boccaccio engaged in their own appropriations of Church authority. It also began with the exemplum itself, as one of the Church's chief vehicles for the reproduction of authority. In the chapters which follow, I will trace the exemplum's transmission from the Latin traditions of the Church to the vernacular tradition initiated by Chaucer and Gower, and continued by Hoccleve and Lydgate. Before I do that, however, we need to look more closely at exactly what it was that was being transmitted. What I am calling an exemplary model of authority depends on an understanding of exemplarity and authority which differs markedly from the way these notions are usually understood.

Chaucer scholarship has failed to appreciate the full importance of the exemplum in large part because the exemplary, as a narrative instantiation of cultural authority, runs athwart one of modern literary studies' most fundamental assumptions. Recognizing formal analysis, "close reading," as a distinctive feature of its own historical moment, it tends to regard such consciousness of formal complexity as the barrier which separates it from the past. While it certainly recognizes formal complexity in the past, it tends to treat its presence there as anomalous or illicit. Modern literary criticism tends to isolate form as precisely that which resists the cultural materials out of which it is constructed. Post-structuralist scholarship has made this approach more theoretically rigorous by replacing "form" with "textuality," but retains the same politics on this point. The dispersions of the textual are generally taken to be a force which, by its very nature, inevitably resists all established forms of cultural authority. This predisposition against authority either makes didactic forms like the exemplum unreadable, or in special cases (like some of Chaucer's tales) reads the narrative element as a dispersive force necessarily subverting the authority it ostensibly supports. Authority is treated as simple, closed, and unchanging. It is a pure given, an inherited ideal which exercises absolute constraint over an unquestioning present. Narrative, by contrast, is treated as complex, dynamic, and liberating.

The exemplum will not be adequately understood until we refuse this crude opposition between simplicity and complexity. On the one hand, we need to recognize that narrative complexity is a structural feature whose ideological value is variable. On the other, we need to see that authority's ostensible simplicity is no less variable: that authority is not some pure given, but an ideological structure that must be produced and maintained. I turn now to a more general reconsideration of the exemplum as a narrative form, and authority as a cultural and ideological structure. The instance of the *Parson's Tale* has already shown the two are inextricably related.

CHAPTER 2

Redefining the exemplum: narrative, ideology, and subjectivity

In his excellent study of *Handlyng Synne*, Fritz Kemmler astutely diagnoses a problem that has hampered all modern attempts to define the exemplum. Medieval discussions of the exemplum were much more interested in its function than its form.[1] This often neglected fact demonstrates two things: medieval culture was keenly interested in using narrative, but it was less interested in discussing it. While it recognized narrative form had ideological functions, such recognitions remained largely implicit. It clearly valued the ideological utility of the exemplum, but it gives us little explicit guidance as to what it considered that utility to be.

Kemmler's solution to this problem is to set the formal aside, and to concentrate on the empirical totality of an exemplum's functions from its immediate rhetorical function in the particular text in which it appears, to the text's immediate social uses, to its broader *Sitz im Leben*, "the communicative situation in a social and cultural context."[2] That solution will not work for this study, which is concerned with the exemplum's transmission from Latin to the vernacular, and indeed, with its power to produce the very *Sitz im Leben* in which it functions. Without some notion of its formal specificity, there will be no basis on which to assess the obvious changes in its social and cultural functions. Nevertheless, Kemmler's diagnosis remains useful, for it reminds us how historically specific the opposition between the formal and the functional actually is. In this chapter and the next I will appeal to three current theoretical notions to help bridge the gap between the formalist emphasis of modern literary studies and the understanding of narrative and authority implicit in medieval functional explanations. These notions are

---

[1] Fritz Kemmler, "*Exempla*" in Context, 60–67, 155–92.
[2] Kemmler, "*Exempla*" in Context, 172–92.

ideology, hegemony, and subjectivity, and I will use them to show that both authority and narrative share a performative, empowering aspect, which provides the grounds on which the exemplum connects them.

My understanding of these terms derives from the eclectic tradition, both Marxist and feminist, which follows Louis Althusser's pioneering reconsideration of ideology in the late sixties, a tradition which has increasingly come to be described by the umbrella term "Cultural Studies."[3] In appealing to Cultural Studies I am fully aware of, and indeed, sympathetic to the unease many medievalists feel regarding the importation of twentieth-century theoretical constructs into discussions of medieval cultural forms. Janet Coleman speaks for many when she pleads, "Can we not be satisfied with an ordinary language which speaks of historical events and literary style and content, without demanding a third, higher critical diction, a professional jargon?"[4] The problem is that in the case of the exemplum ordinary language has simply not done the job. It is not hard to see why. Without some attempt to redefine its own assumptions, the ordinary language of criticism will inevitably reinforce them. In treating medieval authority as at some basic level entirely given, static, and unquestioned, many medievalists simply reinforce the modernist view of the past, even those who are explicitly anti-modernist in their celebration of such authority. Such idealizations are every bit as anachronistic as the crassest post-structuralist appropriation. My recourse to theory is not an evasion of history, but a return to it. We cannot define the exemplum formally until we free ourselves at least somewhat from the modern predisposition to separate narrative form entirely from ideological function. This predisposition is a theoretical one, even if it expresses itself in

---

[3] See especially Louis Althusser, "Ideology and Ideological State Apparatuses: Notes Toward an Investigation," in *Lenin and Philosophy*, tr. Ben Brewster (New York: Monthly Review Press, 1971), 127–86. Despite its brevity, the best history of the term *ideology* is Stuart Hall's "The Hinterlands of Science: Ideology and The 'Sociology of Knowledge,'" in *On Ideology* (Birmingham: Centre for Contemporary Cultural Studies, 1977; London: Hutchinson, 1978), 9–33. See also Jorge Larrain, *The Concept of Ideology* (London: Hutchinson, 1979), and *Marxism and Ideology* (London: Macmillan, 1983); and David McLellan, *Ideology* (Minneapolis: University of Minnesota Press, 1986). For subjectivity, see Kaja Silverman, *The Subject of Semiotics* (Oxford and New York: Oxford University Press, 1983). The best introduction to Cultural Studies is Patrick Brantlinger, *Crusoe's Footprints: Cultural Studies in Britain and America* (New York and London: Routledge, 1990). See also Anthony Easthope, *Literary into Cultural Studies* (New York and London: Routledge, 1991).

[4] Janet Coleman, *Medieval Readers and Writers 1350–1400* (New York: Columbia University Press, 1981), 273.

ordinary language and shifting it requires explicit reconsideration of its theoretical basis.

John Burrow observes that:

The exemplary mode is not very attractive to modern readers. We have been taught by so many good critics to respond sympathetically and intelligently to allegorical stories that the allegorical mode has once more become acceptable; but stories which represent themselves as "examples," whether in medieval or in Renaissance literature, are something of an embarrassment. In a fiction which merely exemplifies an ethical concept ("patience," "gluttony") or an accepted truth ("Woman are fickle," "*Radix malorum est cupiditas*"), literature condemns itself to an ancillary role as the servant of the moral or political or religious beliefs of its age. The process of metaphorical transfer, or *translatio*, necessary to allegory ensures, we may feel, some degree of imaginative independence in that mode, but in the literal mode of "exemplification," the story may do no more than illustrate slavishly *idées reçues*. Such is indeed the case with most of the illustrative stories, or *exempla*, to be found in medieval sermons and books of religious instruction.[5]

Burrow's "we" is more than formulaic. He has identified the response that the modern reader brings almost instinctively to a didactic form like the exemplum. To the exent that we – despite the critiques of postmodernism – remain modern readers, we inevitably respond to such didacticism as pure mystification, a tired reiteration of some bankrupt morality, which denies narrative any rhetorical specificity and effectively pre-empts critical analysis. This response is central to a modernist consciousness, which is precisely why it seems so instinctive.

It is not surprising that Burrow names the religious exemplum as the most slavish of a slavish form. Because modern scholars have considered the exemplum entirely dependent on established authority, they have also considered it at its most characteristic when the authority it transmits is most purely religious. Accordingly, treatment of the exemplum in Middle English literary studies tends to be restricted to the sermon exemplum. The more clearly political public or classical exemplum has been largely ignored, although it was no less characteristic of the Latin tradition than the sermon exemplum – as the next chapters should make clear. In offering a new definition, however, it will be useful to attack the problem at precisely the place where scholars like Burrow have found the exemplum at its most unpromising. The following can be found in a late thirteenth-

---

[5] Burrow, *Ricardian Poetry*, 82.

century English collection, the *Speculum laicorum*, under the rubric *De nomine Jhesu*:

One time Christians were fighting against the pagans. When they saw their enemies prevailing in the fight and feared being vanquished, they all began, in one voice, to cry out "Jesus" and suddenly, almost unexpectedly, the pagans turned their backs and they were vanquished by the Christians.

Christiani quodam tempore pugnantes contra paganos, cum vidissent inimicos suos in pugna prevalere et metuissent vinci, ceperunt omnes, una voce, Jhesum acclamare et subito quasi insperate pagani terga vertentes Christianis victi sunt.[6]

I choose this exemplum because it seems at first glance to confirm completely the modern stereotype. A doctrinal truth, the omnipotence of Christ's name, is imposed on a barely formed narrative, completely determining its outcome. However, if one attempts to trace this apparent translation of moral to plot, one quickly discovers that the two are inseparable, that the moral can only be apprehended narratively. Indeed, it can only be apprehended narratively because it is produced narratively, and the manner of its production is as much a theme of this story as it is a feature of its structure.

This exemplum is quite literally about the maintenance of Christian authority in the social space of historical reality. It takes that authority not as a given but as something which must always be reproduced out of continuous struggle. To describe such authority as an *idée reçue* would surely be to deny completely this exemplum's narrative logic. While Christ's omnipotence may be inevitable, there is nothing inevitable in the structure of this narrative about the acclamation of his name; it occurs unexpectedly and has an unforeseen result. The acclamation itself is the generation of a new voice, a quintessentially narrative act. Yet this narrative act is simultaneously socially transformative: the single voice which the Christians produce in coming together to call Jesus's name makes his omnipotence communally manifest in a way that it was not before. And even at this point the transformation is still not instantaneous. It is delayed by a duration which is narrative and almost entirely formal. Between the acclamation and the miraculous pagan retreat stands the phrase *subito quasi insperate*. In its delay right at the point of dénoument, the phrase reads like a general formula for Peter Brooks's narrative "middle as detour," the "struggle toward the end under

---

[6] J.Th. Welter, ed., *Le Speculum laicorum* (Paris: Auguste Picard, 1914), 81.

the compulsion of imposed delay."[7] At the same time, the almost purely formal status of this phrase retains a thematic connection to the exemplum's moral. *Insperate* in its etymological sense ("unhoped for") ironically heightens the effect of the transformation, for Christ's omnipotence is precisely what is always to be hoped for. This thematic connection does not inhibit the phrase's narrative function. On the contrary, it simply assigns this narrativity the name of Christ. As a generic moment of delay, this phrase enables the exemplum to assert that Christian authority is at once always triumphant and always to be struggled for.

The Church valued the exemplum not because it passively submitted to Christian doctrine, but, on the contrary, because the exemplum's status as narrative gave it an ideological power doctrine often lacked. That ideological power is constituted by its rhetorical specificity as narrative. The recurrent theme in ecclesiastical commentary on the exemplum from the fifth century onward was its persuasive power in contrast to reason or doctine. Opposing examples to doctrine (*verba*), Ambrosiaster suggested preachers append examples "in order to persuade more easily."[8] Gregory I, who compiled the first Christian exemplum collection, repeatedly observed in a variety of contexts that the exemplum aroused the heart to the love of God, in contrast to biblical commentary, which engaged the intellect. A later authority on preaching, Humbertus Romanus, described the form as capturing the intellect and imprinting the mind.[9]

Humbertus recapitulates this point narratively in an exemplum from his *De dono timoris*, which also occurs in the fourteenth-century *Alphabetum narrationum* of Arnold of Liège, one of the most widely circulated of all medieval exemplum collections.[10] In this exemplum, incorrectly but strikingly attributed to Bede, the story of the conversion of England is told in this way: after a learned and subtle

---

[7] Peter Brooks, *Reading for the Plot: Design and Intention in Narrative* (New York: Vintage Books, 1985), 107–08.

[8] He make this point twice in *Commentarium in epistolam ad Corinthius primam*: "Exemplum subjicit, ut facilius suadeat; quia cui verba satis non faciunt, solent exempla suadere;" and "Quoniam exempla facilius suadent quam verba, exemplis commendat per quae facile assequantur non debere illos in Ecclesia loqui linguis, qui interpretari non possunt" (J.-P. Migne, *Patrologiae Latinae Cursus Completus* (Paris: 1879), columns 249 and 268). Cited in both J.-Th. Welter, *L'exemplum dans la litterature religieuse et didactique du Moyen Age* (Geneva: Slatkine Reprints, 1973; reprint of Paris-Toulouse edition of 1927), 13; and Bremond, Le Goff, and Schmitt, *L'"exemplum"*, 48, but in both cases the column numbers given are inaccurate. [9] Welter, *L'exemplum*, 14–15, 72.

[10] Bremond, Le Goff, and Schmitt, *L'"exemplum"*, 77.

(*litteratus et subtilis*) bishop came to England and preached sermons of great subtlety but converted no one, a friar (*minoris litterature*) using stories and exempla converted *pene totam Angliam* (almost all of England).[11] The misappropriation of Bede gives this exemplum the quality of a foundation myth: here we have an exemplum locating its own discursive power at one of Christianity's most important points of historical origin, the conversion of Anglo-Saxon England. Moreover, what we find at this point of origin is not a complacent faith in the inevitable power of Christian doctrine, but an active insistence on the recourse to ideological expediency in the form of narrative. Indeed, this exemplum not only asserts the ideological power of narrative, but also uses that assertion to bolster one form of institutional spirituality (the friars) over another (the diocesan hierarchy).

Like that of *De nomine Jhesu*, the narrativity of this exemplum is thoroughly ideological, and its ideology is thoroughly narrative. The lay exemplum will exploit this interdependence even more fully. For instance, as I shall argue below, in the *Friar's Tale*, Chaucer retells a sermon exemplum of some currency. Naming its protagonist a summoner, rather than a *miles*, or bailiff or *avocatus*, he transforms what was an ecclesiastical critique of the worldly rapacity of judicial officials generally into a specifically lay critique aimed at the ecclesiastical courts alone. Even more strikingly, like a number of royalists before him, Gower uses the story of Constantine's Donation, invented by Church publicists, to repudiate the very institutional prerogatives they intended it to legitimate. This transformative rhetorical power, which lay poets will appropriate from the Church, the Church itself had appropriated from the classical Roman exemplum.

The Roman exemplum was modeled on the Greek *paradeigma*, a narrative inserted into a public discourse (either deliberative or judicial). From the beginning it was a narrative used to persuade. Indeed, Aristotle elevates it to a distinct form of thinking, opposing *paradeigma* to enthymeme as one of the two forms of persuasion common to all oratory.[12] While Latin rhetoricians are less clear about the exemplum's logical status,[13] they are even more direct than

---

[11] Cited in Thomas F. Crane, ed., *The Exempla or Illustrative Stories from Sermones Vulgares of Jacques de Vitry* (London: 1890), note on xviii.   [12] *Rhetoric*, II, 20.

[13] Bennet J. Price, "*Paradeigma* and *Exemplum* in Ancient Rhetorical Theory," (unpub. Ph.D. diss., University of California, Berkeley, 1975), 84–147, esp. 130–47.

Aristotle regarding its ideological function. In Quintillian's formulation, the exemplum "is the relation (*commemoratio*) of a thing done (*rei gestae*) or that might have been done, which is useful in the persuasion of that which you have claimed."[14] In this definition the exemplum is at once discursive and material. It is a *commemoratio* used to persuade, but a *commemoratio* which rests on a *res gesta* – a *res gesta* which, accordingly, produces not only an immediate historical effect, but an enduring moral value. Augustus Caesar dramatically anticipated this point in the dedication of the statues of Roman leaders he had installed in his new forum. He caused the statues to be built in order that he "and future rulers would be required by the people to live according to the example of [such] lives."[15]

By the first century BC the exemplum had become such a staple of oratorical discourse that exemplum collections began to appear for the first time.[16] The Roman sense of history was itself characteristically exemplary. Livy's *Ab urbe condita* is frequently compared to an exemplum collection, and indeed, later exemplum collections were sometimes epitomes of Livy.[17] The classical exemplum persuaded by appealing to heroic figures and *auctores* the audience already venerated. This appeal was never static because it was precisely the capacity to produce moral authority which the figures being appealed to embodied. And it was precisely this productive capacity that Christianity appropriated when it adopted the exemplum as a form particularly suited to indoctrination and conversion.

This capacity, functional though it is, is also a formal property. That is to say, the exemplum's specificity as narrative is defined precisely by its constant movement between the historical and the textual. And yet it is precisely this formal specificity that is ignored by formal definitions like the one I cited at the beginning of this chapter: "a short narrative used to illustrate or confirm a general principle." The exemplum illustrates a moral because what it recounts is the enactment of that moral. The moral does not simply gloss the narrative. It establishes a form of authority, enjoining its audience to heed its lesson, and to govern their actions accordingly. It is more than an abstract principle. It would be better described as a moral

---

14 Quintillian, *Institutio oratoria*, V 11.6; cited in Price, "*Paradeigma* and *Exemplum*," 150.
15 Suetonius, *De vita Caesarum*, II, 31: "commentum id se, ut ad illorum vitam velut ad exemplar et ipse, dum viveret, et insequetiam aetatium principes exigerentur a civibus." Cited in Arvast Nordh, "*Exemplum* in Martial," *Eranos* 52 (1954), 228–29.
16 Price, "*Paradeigma* and *Exemplum*," 85–87; Nordh, "Historical *Exempla* in Martial," 227.
17 Price, "*Paradeigma* and *Exemplum*," 86.

law: a value which the exemplarist assumes already binds the community together, or which he or she is strenuously arguing should bind it together. In short, the exemplum is not a purely textual exchange between two discursive genres, the narrative and the interpretive, in which the narrative supports some proverb-like interpretation. In its narrative the exemplum reenacts the actual, historical embodiment of communal value in a protagonist or an event, and then, in its moral, effects the value's reemergence with the obligatory force of moral law. For the purposes of this study, I offer a new definition: an exemplum is a narrative enactment of cultural authority.

Though as a formal term, "enactment" may seem ambiguous, its ambiguity fits precisely the cultural propensity my definition is meant to highlight. An enactment can either be ideological or more directly historical. That is, to enact social authority can mean either to represent it ideologically before the community or actually to exert it within the community. But the point of the exemplum is precisely to connect these two possibilities – to give the ideological representation of authority a specific historical source. The pseudo-Ciceronian *Rhetorica ad Herennium* defines the exemplum as either *dictum* or *factum*, a saying or a doing, a definition echoed in the title of one the most widely disseminated of the classical exemplum collections, the *Facta et dicta memorabilia* of Valerius Maximus. The exemplum could be either a saying or a doing because it is always both. An exemplary action is already a saying because it transmits its authority to the community. An exemplary saying is already a doing because it produces a moral obligation which must be enacted. For this reason, the distinction that is sometimes drawn between the use of the term *exemplum* to describe a narrative form, and its use to describe a person who serves as an example is misleading. A person who serves as an example becomes exemplary precisely by transforming his or her actions into a moral narrative.

This fluidity in the distinction between narratives and people may strike modern sensibilites as even more incoherent than the exemplum's didacticism. After all, one of the most basic and enduring postulate of formalist analysis is that characters are not people; that they have no existence outside of the narrative in which they appear. Such passing back and forth between the formal and actual is precisely what formalism cannot allow. Nevertheless recent theorists of subjectivity, be they feminist, Marxist, or post-structuralist, have all shown that the distinction between selfhood and language is by no means as hard and fast as formalism assumes it to be. Following the insights of Emile Benveniste, Jacques Lacan, and especially Louis Althusser, these theorists posit a dialectial relationship between the formation of identity and the structures of language and ideology. Selves become selves by filling subject positions, the slots which ideological or linguistic systems create for them. At the same time, all such systems are predicated on the external existence of subjects to propel them, not as already formed, independent selves, but as agents motivated by interests to some extent external to the systems they enter. The power of this view of identity is acknowledged even by narratology, the most prominent of formalism's heirs.[18]

While a detailed account of current theories of the subject is beyond the scope of this study, it is well worth noting the striking similarity at this basic level between them and the formal logic of the exemplum. For the exemplum's enactment of authority in fact assumes a process of identification on the part of its audience. That is to say, the exemplum expects the members of its audience to be convinced by its *sententia* precisely because it expects them to put themselves in the position of its protagonists, to emulate the protagonist's moral success, or avoid his or her moral failure. It persuades by conveying a sense of communal identity with its moral lesson.

In this way, a performative model of exemplarity assumes a model of cultural authority that is equally performative. The authority an exemplum enacts cannot be a static, self-contained entity, defined purely by some abstract, propositional core. It too must be defined, at least in part, by the production of subject positions. Exemplary authority resembles ideology as defined by Althusser: "all ideology has the function (which defines it) of 'constituting' concrete individuals as subjects."[19] In order to increase the flexibility and specificity of this notion, Stuart Hall has recently suggested a return to Antonio Gramsci's notion of "hegemony," the complex of interdependent political, social, and intellectual forces that produce an ideological consensus at a particular moment within a social

---

[18] So that for example, Gerard Genette's *Narrative Discourse: An Essay in Method* (tr. Jane E. Lewin (Ithaca: Cornell University Press, 1980; orig. "Discours du récit," a portion of *Figures III* (Paris: Editions du Seuil, 1972))) ends with a consideration of voice derived from Benveniste's account of subjectivity (212–62).

[19] Althusser, "Ideology and Ideological State Apparatuses," 171.

formation.[20] In contrast to older models of ideology, which make the cultural to one extent or another a secondary effect of material relations, hegemony is irreducible as a component of ruling-class dominance. If the term emphasizes ideology's connection to material relations, it also emphasizes ideology's constitutive role in producing those relations. Because it crosses class boundaries it can never become complete. As Hall puts it, "Hegemony, once achieved, must be constantly and ceaselessly renewed, re-enacted."[21] The notion thus bears an even closer relation to medieval *auctoritas* than ideology, both in its constitution of material relations (in medieval terms, *potestas*), and in its constant need for renewal and reenactment.

[20]   Stuart Hall, "The Toad in the Garden: Thatcherism among the Theorists," in *Marxism and the Interpretation of Culture*, ed. Cary Nelson and Lawrence Grossberg (Urbana: University of Illinois Press, 1988), 35–73. Gramsci himself never produced a comprehensive defintion of the term. I have adapted this definition from Raymond Williams, *Marxism and Literature* (Oxford: Oxford University Press, 1977), 108.

[21]   Hall, "Toad in the Garden," 54.

CHAPTER 3

"*Auctoritas*" and "*potestas*": a model of analysis for medieval culture

Authority is an important term in at least four disciplines besides literary studies: history, philosophy, political science, and sociology. Nevertheless, general discussions of the term are relatively rare.[1] In normal usage, it generally describes a constraint handed down by a repressive past accepted compliantly by an unquestioning present. It is treated as a binary structure, which involves the simple deference

---

[1] An important exception for literary studies in the Middle Ages is A. J. Minnis, *Medieval Theory of Authorship: Scholastic Literary Attitudes in the Later Middle Ages* (London: Scolar Press, 1984). For some thoughtful reservations about the extension of scholastic models to lay poets like Chaucer, see Bella Millett, "Chaucer, Lollius, and the Medieval Theory of Authorship," *Studies in the Age of Chaucer, Proceedings, No. 1, 1984: Reconstructing Chaucer*, ed. Paul Strohm and Thomas J. Heffernan, 93–115. The term *authority* is frequently used in critical discussions, but is rarely treated as posing any particular problem of definition. More than a dozen recent volumes which use the term in their titles treat it rather vaguely as a constraining, repressive past, which the works with which they are concerned struggle against, but they take this view of authority to be sufficiently obvious as to need no particular defense. The treatment of the problem I have found the most useful conceptually is Jacqueline T. Miller's *Poetic License: Authority and Authorship in Medieval and Renaissance Contexts* (New York and Oxford: Oxford University Press, 1986). Though Miller restricts her attention to literary authority, her emphasis on authority's enabling power applies to social authority as well, and provides the basis for understanding the link between the two which medieval culture maintained. Ralph Flores, *The Rhetoric of Doubtful Authority: Deconstructive Reading of Self-Questioning Narratives, St. Augustine to Faulkner* (Ithaca and London: Cornell University Press, 1989) convincingly demonstrates authority is a rhetorical construction through a series of elegant readings of major canonical texts. Nevertheless, his acknowledged exclusion of authority's social dimension leads him to underestimate its ideological efficacy – to assume that because authority is always rhetorically constructed, it is therefore "doubtful" and disempowered. I have also benefited from John Guillory's *Poetic Authority: Spenser, Milton, and Literary History* (New York, Columbia University Press, 1983) – though ultimately I find his notion of authority too idealized – and from briefer discussions in Michel Foucault, "What is an Author?," in *Textual Strategies: Perspectives in Post-Structuralist Criticism*, ed. Josue V. Harari (London: Methuen, 1980), 141–60; Sandra M. Gilbert and Susan Gubar, *The Madwoman in the Attic: the Woman Writer and the Nineteenth-Century Literary Imagination* (New Haven and London: Yale University Press, 1979), esp., 3–104, and Edward Said, *Beginnings: Intention and Method* (New York: Columbia University Press, 1985), 13–17, 81–93. The problem of authority has received somewhat more sustained reflection in the fields of sociology and legal theory. I discuss the tradition in these fields in note 7 below.

37

of present to past. From my perspective, the problem with this view is that it ignores the problem of agency, the production and assumption of subject positions, which, as I have just argued, necessarily characterizes all systems of belief. I propose instead that we think of authority as triangulated. For it involves not just deference to the past but a claim of identification with it and a representation of that identity made by one part of the present to another. In this way the constraint of authority can also be empowering. The power to define the past is also the power to control the constraint the past exerts in the present. Authority, then, is an enabling past reproduced in the present.

There is much in classical and medieval notions of *auctoritas* to support this view. Jacqueline Miller, in a brief but richly suggestive discussion of medieval poetic authority, cites Abelard's famous observation that medieval writers were dwarves standing on the shoulders of the giants of classical antiquity. She points out that standing on the shoulders of giants makes the dwarves dependent on them, but it also means the dwarves could see further than the giants.[2] This insight can be extended from medieval notions of poetic and textual authority to public and political ones as well. Indeed, medieval *auctoritas* in the textual sense is not easily detached from *auctoritas* in the public sense. The term certainly designated the cultural prestige and ideological value of the works of *auctors* like Augustine or Virgil. But this sense was supplemented and framed by the opposition between *auctoritas* and *potestas*, which defined the institutional relation between the Church and lay power. First proposed at the end of the fifth century by Gelasius, the dichotomy received its fullest exposition between the ninth and twelfth centuries, during the great period of papal expansion, though it continued to have force to the end of the Middle Ages. In the papalist view which the Church historian Walter Ullmann calls "hierocratic," *auctoritas* designated the overriding sovereignty the Church wielded through the pope over all *societas Christiana*, while *potestas* designated only the power of execution, and the day-to-day overseeing of administrative matters to which lay princes were restricted.[3] Not suprisingly, many

---

[2] Miller, *Poetic License*, 9–20. The record of Abelard's observation comes not from Abelard himself, but from John of Salisbury (*Metalogicon*, III, 4). As we shall see in Chapter 5, John of Salisbury's *Policraticus* contains an even more emphatic assertion of the power of the present over the past in the invocation of authority (90–93).

[3] Walter Ullmann, *The Growth of Papal Government in the Middle Ages*, 3rd ed. (London: Methuen, 1970).

secular princes responded with a markedly weaker interpretation of *auctoritas*, which understood it as strictly spiritual. The prince followed the Church's counsel in spiritual matters, but his own in all things temporal. Even in the stronger version, however, no matter how far-reaching it gets, the social dimension of *auctoritas* is irreducibly textual. For the Church's institutional *auctoritas* was dependent on its ideological privilege; indeed, that was its *raison d'être*. The Church existed to interpret and disseminate the sacred text of the Bible, which it alone could interpret, by virtue of its privileged access to the ultimate *auctor*, God.

Conversely, it should also be clear that the textual dimension of *auctoritas* was politically enabling. The Church had power in the present because it had the power to redefine the past. I mean the past here both in an absolute sense, that is, human society's divine origin, but also in a more immediately historical sense as well. The Church's privileged relation to the sacred text was the source of its virtual monopoly on textual production of all sorts, administrative records as well as less practical texts. It exercised this monopoly both in actual production of texts and in the training of producers well into the later Middle Ages, and it retained much of its influence even thereafter.

The dichotomy of *auctoritas* and *potestas* came originally from Roman constitutional usage. In classical and late antique Rome, *auctoritas* designated the social as well as cultural power of an *auctor*, but both terms had a much wider semantic range. *Auctoritas* could describe a judgment, advice, persuasion, a command, political influence, and institutional power. *Auctor* could mean author in the modern sense, but it could also mean a founder, originator, inventor, or instituter of any sort. Most relevant to our concerns, however, are two early uses which both foreground the issue of power. The earliest attestation for either term is for *auctoritas*, and comes from the Twelve Tablets, where it is used to designate the right of ownership. If this was the earliest sense of *auctoritas*, it seems likely the earliest sense of *auctor* meant seller or vendor, one with the right to alienate property.[4]

I am less interested, however, in setting some absolute and stable point of origin than I am in suggesting the interchange between ideology and power that these terms signified from early on. This is a dimension which modern theoretical and philosophical discussions of authority have completely neglected, and which is well worth

---

[4] *Oxford Latin Dictionary*, (Oxford: Clarendon Press, 1968), vol. 1, 204–07.

pondering. For it not only gives the cultural senses of the term a material horizon; it also zeroes in on that material horizon at the point where it is, paradoxically, at both its most dynamic and its most constrained: the point of economic exchange. This is the point where the confrontation between present and past takes on its most material form, and where the categorical imperative to get the most for your money insures that here at least the present will try to keep intact the very past it is transforming. That is to say, economic exchange presents a model of the continuity between past and present which is conservative and transformative at once, because the property exchanged stays the same while its ownership changes. The early economic sense of *auctor* and *auctoritas* suggest that the conservatism the term comes to describe in its extension to the realm of culture is never conservatism for conservatism's sake alone, but is always admixed with self-interest.

The other early sense involves an even more complicated exchange between ideology and power. This is the sense of *auctor*, which means "father" or "progenitor" in such phrases as *auctor gentis*.[5] The *gens* was a sacral entity, the formation of which was originally restricted to the aristocracy.[6] In this sense of *auctor*, religion and power are inextricably intermixed. To claim an *auctor* was to announce oneself the possessor of aristocratic power even as one piously venerated the founder of one's clan. Moreover, even the power such piety claimed was itself not a single form of dominance, but inhered in the relation between two such forms, the dominance of gender and the dominance of class. This is a point worth stressing: both Marxists and feminists have too often tried to reduce the power of patriarchal figures like the *paterfamilias* to a single substance, either making gender dominance a secondary effect of class, or class dominance a secondary effect of gender. The figure of the *paterfamilias* should remind us that patriarchal power is both at once. And his veneration of the *auctor gentis*, suggests the early Roman *paterfamilias* fully recognized his power's relational essence. For in identifying himself with his

---

[5] Lewis and Short (*A Latin Dictionary* (Oxford: Clarendon Press, 1879), 198) list this sense first. The editors of the recent *Oxford Latin Dictionary* inexplicably list it last, although their first citation for it comes from Cicero, which would make it roughly contemporary with the economic sense which they list first, also attested from Cicero. (Their establishment of the economic sense as earliest seems based on their first citation for *auctoritas*, from the Twelve Tablets.)

[6] Geza Alfoldy, *The Social History of Rome*, tr. David Branaud and Frank Pollock (Totowa, New Jersey: Barnes and Noble, 1985), 8.

founding father, what he celebrates is not so much some simple paternal substance as patriarchy's discursive power to declare itself foundational, a discursive power extending out of its relational network of distinct forms of dominance. What I am suggesting is that the *auctor gentis* was a principle of hegemony that recognized itself as such – a self-conscious acknowledgment of material power's dependence on the systematic articulations of ideology.

It is clear that *auctoritas* and patriarchy are continually related from early Rome to the end of the Middle Ages. I do not mean to argue that patriarchy underwrote *auctoritas* during all that time as some stable set of material relations; rather that the two were always related in principle, that *auctoritas* was always associated with the continuing possibility of maintaining an ideological relation between gender and class dominance. For this reason, I have felt justified in using the term *patriarchy* throughout this study despite the well-founded objections of many recent feminist theorists that it lacks specificity. What I mean by the term is an ideological predisposition rather than a specific set of social relations.

Understanding Roman *auctoritas* as a self-conscious principle of hegemony may help explain the large gap between modern idealizations of the term and the political realities of the Roman state. Perhaps the most famous of these idealizations is Hannah Arendt's "What is Authority?" Citing Cicero's claim that *cum potestas in populo auctoritas in senatu sit* ("while power resides in the people, authority rests with the Senate"), she rather wishfully concludes that in Republican Rome "the most conspicuous characteristic of those in authority is that they do not have power."[7] Even a cursory glance at

---

[7] Hannah Arendt, "What is Authority," in *Between Past and Future: Eight Exercises in Political Thought* (Harmondsworth: Penguin Books, 1977), 122. This line of argument comes to Arendt from Theodor Mommsen, *Romisches Staatsrecht*, 3 vols. (Leipzig: Verlag von S. Hirzel, 1888), vol. 3, part 2, 1034, 1038–39; via Carl J. Friedrich. Friedrich's own version occurs in *Tradition and Authority* (New York, Washington, and London: Praeger, 1972), esp. 13–56. The argument has been reiterated as recently as 1979, by April Carter in *Authority and Democracy* (London, Henley, and Boston: Routledge and Kegan Paul), 41–59. A different tradition descends from Max Weber, who saw the history of the Western state as characterized by the transformation of what he called charismatic (as exemplified by figures like Christ) and traditional authority into the "rationalized" authority of modern bureaucracy. (See Max Weber, *The Theory of Social and Economic Organization*; tr. A. N. Henderson and Talcott Parsons (New York: The Free Press; London: Collier-Macmillan, Ltd., 1964; copyright, Oxford University Press, 1947), 152–53, 324–86.) This Weberian tradition differs from the one I have just mentioned in that it does not idealize authority as a lost consensus. But both are similar to the extent that they view authority as pure constraint. The most notable later works in the Weberian tradition are T. W. Adorno, Else-

the actual institutional structure of the Roman senate exposes the anachronism of such a direct translation. As P. A. Brunt has demonstrated, the *potestas* granted the people was largely putative. The people could only assemble on the summons of a magistrate; once assembled they could only speak by his invitation and could only vote yes or no to the laws he proposed, without power of amendment. The magistrates were themselves senators, elected to annual terms. The shortness of these terms and the magistrates' lifetime membership in the Senate meant they were very unlikely to act in any but the Senate's interest.[8]

In this context, it seems likely the emphasis in Cicero's formulation is not so much on the purely advisory role of *auctoritas*, as modern idealizations would have it, as it is on the putative nature of *potestas*. That is, while granting that power ultimately rests with the people in some abstract sense, he is insisting that the authority for making concrete decisions rests with the Senate alone. To the extent that the *potestas* of the people remains abstract, without concrete means of exercise, its status is better described as ideological than constitutional. Considered in context, Cicero's formulation suggests that the concentration of actual power in the hands of the aristocratic families assembled in the Senate was secured only by their reaching out to the plebeians, and persuading them the patrician exercise of power in the name of the plebeians actually served plebeian interests as well. The magistratically initiated and controlled popular assemblies were obviously designed with that goal in mind.[9]

In the *Res gestae*, the summary of his achievements intended to be engraved on his tomb, Augustus one-upped the Ciceronian version of this dichotomy. He assigned *potestas* to the Senate and the people, and reserved *auctoritas* to himself: at his accession to emperor, he "surpassed all in authority," but "had no more power than" his

---

Frenkel-Brunswick, Daniel J. Levinson, R. Nevitt Sanford, in collaboration with Betty Aron, Maria Hertz Levinson, and William Morrow, *The Authoritarian Personality* (New York: Harper and Row, 1950) and Richard Sennett, *Authority* (New York: Alfred Knopf, 1980). A minor, more properly Marxist tradition stressing the enabling aspect of authority begins with Friedrich Engels's letter "On Authority," in *The Marx-Engels Reader*, ed. Robert C. Tucker, 2nd ed. (New York and London, W. W. Norton, 1978), 730–33, and includes Herbert Marcuse, "A Study of Authority," in *Studies in Critical Philosophy*, tr. Joris de Bres (London: New Left Books, 1972), 49–135.

[8] P. A. Brunt, *Social Conflicts in the Roman Republic* (London: Chatto & Windus, 1971), 8–9, 45–47.

[9] This dynamic seems to illustrate perfectly the Gramscian notion of hegemony. See 35–36 above.

fellow magistrates.[10] It is entirely possible to idealize this development as well, and, indeed, Augustus's formulation encourages it. Nevertheless, both the immediate occasion and the wider context suggest that Augustus's reformulation has an ideological function similar to that of the senatorial original. After more than a century of civil war, Augustus's institution of the principate reconstituted a unified ruling class by drawing on the disaffections of both the lower classes and the provincial landowners, while still protecting the basic privileges of the senatorial orders.[11]

The absolute power the office of Emperor was to acquire depended in part on its ideological claim to speak for the Empire as whole. In Gibbon's memorable remark, the Empire was "an absolute monarchy disguised by the forms of a commonwealth."[12] Defined as the successor of the elected Republican magistrates, and subject to law, the Emperor derived his sovereignty from its voluntary surrender by the people, which was ratified by the Senate at his assumption of power. As G. E. M. de Ste. Croix has argued, these constitutional limitations were primarily fictions. Popular sovereignty had already been absorbed by the Senate. Early on in the Principate, the Senate itself became much more a consultative than a legislative body, with the result that the laws to which the Emperor was subject were primarily laws of his own making.[13] In practical terms, "the *princeps* enjoyed power which was … unlimited: there was no power in the Roman state which could be employed as an alternative to that of the emperor."[14]

Nevertheless, the actual exercise of this unlimited power depended precisely on the maintenance of its constitutional "disguise," fictional though this disguise might have been. Throughout the Principate, emperors avoided explicit claims of absolute, or even monarchical power.[15] At the same time, they also devoted much energy to enhancing the specifically imperial character of their *auctoritas*, from the gradual development of an imperial titulature to the adoption of

---

[10] *Res gestae divi Augusti*, in *Documents Illustrating the Reigns of Augustus and Tiberius*, collected by Victor Ehrenberg and A. H. M. Jones, 2nd ed. (Oxford: Clarendon Press, 1955, repr. 1976), 34.3, 28: "post id tempus auctoritate omnibus praestiti, potestatis autem nihilo amplius habui quam ceteri qui mihi quoque in magistratu conlegae fuerunt."

[11] G. E. M. de Ste. Croix, *The Class Struggle in the Ancient Greek World: From the Archaic Age to the Arab Conquests* (London: Duckworth, 1981), 350–78. See also Brunt, *Social Conflicts*, 112–56; and Alfoldy, *Social History of Rome*, 65–105.

[12] Gibbon, Edward, *The Decline and Fall of the Roman Empire*, 7 vols. (London: Methuen, 1896–1900), vol. 1, 68.   [13] de Ste. Croix, *Class Struggle*, 384–92.

[14] Alfoldy, *Social History of Rome*, 99.   [15] de Ste. Croix, *Class Struggle*, 367–77.

special dress, insignia, and ceremonies, to the cultivation of their divine or quasi-divine status.[16] These ideological forms alone are enough to give the lie to modern idealizations of *auctoritas* as an unchanging essence of Roman polity. *Auctoritas* was a complex ideological structure which was constantly being rearticulated and reformulated. Indeed, in the brief sketch I have just presented, we can see that the term passed through at least three historically distinct phases: the patriarchal authority of the archaic *auctor gentis*, the Senatorial authority of the Republic, and the imperial authority of the Empire.

Both of the later stages have obvious links to the patriarchal sense of authority expressed in the notion of the *auctor gentis*. The Senate, the assembly of the *senes*, or *patrifamilias*, literally exercised the *auctoritas patrum*. With the advent of the Empire, this patriarchally defined authority passed on to the emperor, the *pater patriae*, the title Augustus took in 2 BC.[17] This development from *paterfamilias* to *pater patriae* is marked by two contrary but complementary aspects: an increasing material consolidation and an increasing ideological dependence on collectivity. The collective significance of the *auctor gentis* is fairly slight. The figure unites the *familias*, but makes little ideological claim on those outside it. The assembly of separate *patrifamilias* in the Senate constitutes the claim of specific patriarchs to speak for Roman society as a whole. The consolidation of *auctoritas* in the single figure of the Emperor meant a much more collective appeal, as evidenced by both the indirectness of imperial claims of supremacy, and the growing profusion of ideological forms in which those claims were made. The singularity of imperial *auctoritas* enabled it to transcend material relations of class much more successfully than the previous two versions. The emperor's patriarchal status was essentially symbolic. Though as an ideological figure he affirmed the patriarchal privilege of the ruling class, his material power did not in fact proceed directly from his status as patriarch. His definition as *pater patriae* refracted a set of power relations which were considerably more complex. While he spearheaded the material interests of the ruling class, his ideological singularity presented him to Roman society as a whole as distinct from that class and above its interests. This, of course, only made him that much more effective as an agent

[16] Alfoldy, *Social History of Rome*, 100.		[17] Alfoldy, *Social History of Rome*, 101.

of such interests.[18] The figure of the emperor offered to the rest of the society ideological participation in the power from which they were materially excluded.

One need look no further than Virgil's *Aeneid* to suggest that Roman notions of the poetic *auctor* were intertwined with *auctoritas* in its political sense. Nevertheless, it was Christianity's appropriation of these terms which drew textual and political *auctoritas* definitively together. The relation between Christian and Roman notions of *auctoritas* is a vexed issue, so vexed it has led some commentators to the dubious conclusion that Gelasius's adaptation of the *auctoritas* and *potestas* dichotomy has no relation at all to earlier Roman usage.[19] In fact, this issue is part of the larger problem of how to make comprehensible the Christianization of the Roman empire. This process has been difficult to understand largely because the essence of Christian authority is so often taken to be its status as pure constraint, its self-denying givenness. To believe in Christianity is to embrace eternity and renounce all interest in history. However, if we grant the ideological, as opposed to strictly constitutional, value of Roman, and especially imperial, *auctoritas*, Gelasius's appropriation of the term becomes both more plausible and more interesting.[20] It helps explain not only why the Church might want to appropriate the term but also why Roman rulers might let them do it. In claiming the *auctoritas* which the emperors had formerly claimed as their own, Gelasius is claiming the specifically ideological power that imperial *auctoritas* represented. He is replacing the figure of the emperor with the Church as the source of Roman society's collective sense of itself. Redefined as ecclesiastical, this collectivity becomes even more independent of class relations than imperial *auctoritas* had been. Imperial *auctoritas* was independent of class but it still rested on a historically specifiable and localizable political entity. Ecclesiastical

---

[18] My argument at this point assumes the conclusions of de Ste. Croix, who views the emergence of the Principate as assuaging some lower class resistance without disturbing the basic privileges of the Senatorial orders and characterizes the subsequent development of the Empire as an increasing concentration of power in a smaller and smaller ruling elite. See *Class Struggle*, 332–408, 453–503.

[19] Robert L. Benson, "The Gelasian Doctrine: Uses and Transformations," in *La notion d'autorité au Moyen Age: Islam, Byzance, Occident; Colloques Internationaux de La Napoule, Session des 23–26 Octobre 1978*, organized by George Makdisi, Dominique Sourdel, and Janine Sourdel-Thomine (Paris: Presses Universitaires de France, 1982), 15.

[20] In any case, the strictly constitutional value of imperial *auctoritas* remains unclear. See Francesco de Martino, *Storia della Costituzione Romana*, 6 vols.(Naples: Casa editrice Jovene, 1974), vol. 4, part 1, 278–85.

auctoritas, though filtered through the institutional structures, is ultimately dependent on the sacred text alone. Obviously, this involves a denial of the historically immediate, but it is precisely that self-denial which is politically enabling, which gives Christianity its collective power. Christianity's renunciation of direct political attachment in favor of a sacred text theoretically available to all who can read gives it a socially unifying character. For the rulers, it establishes an ideological space where the contingency of material power can be renounced without material cost. For their subjects, this renunciation offers an ideological empowerment to counter their material deprivation.

Even this explanation, however, is too ahistorical. It appeals to a functionalism that denies Christianity's positive specificity. Even if its transcendental status is rigorously denied and it is considered strictly as an ideology, Christianity is always more than a simple alibi, an illusion that functions simply to disguise real relations of material power. The very labyrinthine complexity of its doctrine, and the massive, seemingly endless institutional forms to which it has given rise testify to its material, as well as ideological, autonomy. If this autonomy continues to defy the many attempts of twentieth-century thought to demystify and move beyond it once and for all – to be able to declare "God is dead," and have done with it – that is because Christianity's autonomy inheres finally in its textuality.

From the beginning Christianity has been marked by a double insistence: that it bespeaks a Spirit which transcends all material circumstance, but that its believers have to make that Spirit manifest in the very materiality it transcends. The agency which unites these two antithetical tendencies is precisely Christianity's sacral textuality. The New Testament's earliest extant documents are the Pauline letters, the longest of which, Romans, has been justly described as an "instrument of Church policy."[21] Yet the core of that ecclesiological policy is an exegetical strategy: the one whereby Paul displaces the Old Law with the New. Figural reading is what unlocks the spiritual superiority of the New Law over the Old. Paul's exegetical program enables him to find the Living Spirit of the New Law behind the dead letter of the Old. As a form of collectivity, then, the New Law is

---

[21] Helmut Koester, *History and Literature of Early Christianity*, v. 2 of *Introduction to the New Testament*, 2 vols. (Philadelphia: Fortress Press, 1982), 5. For a different view, see Norman Perrin, *The New Testament, An Introduction: Proclamation and Paranesis, Myth and History* (New York: Harcourt Brace Jovanovich, 1974), 106–14.

grounded on the figural, that is, on the continual possibility of displacing the literal constraint of any particular historical limit. As living Spirit hovering continually beyond the dead Letter, the New Law constitutes a text which continually transcends its own textuality, a signifier grounded on the endless possibilities of signification. A later text, the Gospel According to John, will declare these possibilities in the nature of the Christian deity himself: " In the beginning was the Word and the Word was with God and the Word was God. "

Such a deconstructive reading of these biblical cornerstones may seem anachronistic. I offer two justifications. The first is one of the fundamental postulates of modern biblical scholarship: namely, that historical consideration of Christianity must remain strictly neutral in relation to its transcendental claims. The surest evidence we have on which to base our assessment of Christianity's development are its texts. This is not only because like any historical phenomenon, most of its documentation is textual, but also because, as we have just seen, that documentation proclaims the centrality of its own textuality. If we are to apply the postulate of neutrality with the rigor it demands, we must avoid any positing of Christian belief as some pre-textual core entirely distinct and prior to the actual texts we use to evaluate it. For if we posit such a pretextual belief, the development and spread of Christianity becomes as inevitable a given as if we accepted it as the direct expression of the one, true God.

On the other hand, locating Christianity's ideological power in its textuality is precisely what produces the impression of anachronism, for we take a self-conscious interest in textuality as the distinctive mark of our own postmodern moment. This leads me to my second justification. The modern scholarly taboo on anachronism is actually the flip-side of the modernist conviction that modernism represents a complete break with the culture of the past. The taboo on anachronism erects this notion of the break into a methodological principle: the past is defined in the first instance by its radical difference from the present. Modernism's veneration of the break has proved to be one of postmodernism's most important sites of contest. Theorists such as Jacques Derrida and Jean-François Lyotard take their exposure of modernity's hidden debts to the past to mean the postmodern should strive for an ever purer break, while others have identified the notion of the break itself as that part of the modernist legacy that most needs interrogating. As Umberto Eco observes, "The postmodern reply to the modern consists of recognizing that the past, since it cannot really be destroyed, because its destruction leads to silence, must be revisited, but with irony, not innocently."[22] My reexamination of Christian authority is just such a return, and extending it to Christian notions of textuality enables the return to be made with the self-consciousness Eco calls ironic. For textuality is the ground on which postmodern theory characteristically locates its own self-conscious distance from the past.

Deconstruction treats Christianity's God as a "transcendental signified," a stable, non-linguistic ground.[23] This ground represents a point of absolute stasis not only so far as its believers are concerned, but so far as any possible critique is concerned as well. Paradoxically, the transcendental signified can never signify anything more than the point where all signification stops, where a system of thought gives way to the purely mystified desire for absolute presence. This is the point where the deconstructive critique must itself stop, and accept at face value what it finds. For Derrida, this moment of pure mystification is most characteristically expressed as a desire for the *phone*, the moment when text coincides with voice:

In every case, the voice is closest to the signified, whether it is determined strictly as sense (thought or lived) or more loosely as thing. All signifiers, and first and foremost the written signifier, are derivative with regard to what would wed the voice indissolubly to the mind or to the thought of the signified sense, indeed to the thing itself (whether it is done in the Aristotelian manner ... or in the manner of medieval theology, determining the *res* as a thing created from its *eidos*, from its sense thought in the logos or in the infinite understanding of God).[24]

The attribution of phonocentrism to all of previous Western tradition is essential to the Derridean metanarrative. It puts self-conscious textuality entirely on the side of deconstruction, and insures the privilege of the deconstructive critique as the definitive means of breaking with the mystifications of the past. If we actually test this metanarrative against Christianity, however, a more complicated picture emerges.

---

[22] Umberto Eco, *Postscript to the Name of the Rose*, tr. William Weaver (San Diego: Harcourt, Brace, Jovanovich, 1984), 67; cited in Lee Patterson, "On the Margin: Postmodernism, Ironic History, and Medieval Studies," *Speculum* 65 (1990), 87.
[23] Cf. Jacques Derrida, *Of Grammatology*, tr. Gayatri Chakravorty Spivak (Baltimore and London: The Johns Hopkins University Press, 1974), 30.
[24] Derrida, *Of Grammatology*, 11.

As Mary Carruthers observes, Derrida's "'logocentricism' bears most resemblance to the rationalist enterprise of modern scientific positivism": early and medieval Christianity present a radically different profile.[25] In fact, what is most distinct about the notion of God as Word is that in it, the term God never ceases to be a signfier. A transcendental signified is precisely what it isn't. The notion is certainly logocentric in that it literally centers Christian divinity in the Logos, but at the same time it is decidedly not phonocentric. God as Word is much more text than voice.[26] Its very free-standingness, its endless signifying of itself suggests language as text – that is, as already formed, as standing between speakers – rather than language as spoken, as the property of a particular speaker. Here the particular speaker is the Word itself, devoid of any further positive content. For the term "word" (in Derrida's terms the "signifier of the signifier") contains no inherent characteristic of its own, past the general capacity for articulation upon which all language, and therefore, all redefinition and specification, depend.

It is here, at the essential textuality of Christian belief, that we arrive at its most neutral, least reducible historicity. Focusing on the biblical text allows us to confront Christianity in general as a historical movement without committing us either to accepting the veracity of its belief or dismissing it as a superstitious alibi. But focusing on that text specifically as text in all its complexity, and not as the derivative register of already fully formed system of belief, also commits us to recognizing its essential self-reflexiveness. The God it names as its origin it also characterizes as a textual principle, God as Word. Given the massive positive doctrinal and institutional identity Christianity has acquired, it is difficult from this distance to

[25] Mary Carruthers, "Review of *Medieval Texts and Contemporary Readers*, ed. Laurie A. Finke and Martin B. Schichtman," *Studies in the Age of Chaucer* 11(1989), 223.

[26] In his recent discussion of early Christianity, Brian Stock (*Listening for the Text: On the Uses of the Past* [Baltimore and London: The Johns Hopkins University Press, 1990]), asserts that the scriptural word is phonocentric: "[Christianity and Judaism] are both scriptural, and yet they both envisage themselves as obeying the word of God.

"What kind of 'word' is this? In large part, it is a metaphor that uses orality to describe interchanges between God and Man. In monotheism it is necessary to establish a direct link between the authority behind Scripture and the obligations of man." Stock does not defend this claim, and in fact metaphors of orality are fairly rare in the New Testament. When New Testament writers wish to demonstrate the directness of their authority they much more characteristically adopt metaphors of vision, a vision which is not immediate but much more characteristically deferred: "For now we see in a mirror dimly, but then face to face." (I Cor., 13:12) The Book of Revelations might be cited as the most obvious place where the text is authorized as the direct transcription of Divine speech. But even here Christ's speech quickly gives way to John's vision, a vision not of immediate reality, but of one to come.

conceptualize the negativity that characterized its originary textuality. It is instructive to remind ourselves that Christianity, which we
normally take as the archetype of theological plenitude, was
considered by many of its earliest contemporaries to be a form of
atheism.[27] This is in no way to deny that the biblical text characterizes
its divine source in many other ways: as God the Father, as the
author of the Ten Commandments, and so on. From the very
beginning Christianity's textual indeterminacy is framed by the
patriarchal character of its deity, the ethical imperatives of the Judaic
tradition it appropriated, and its political quietism ("Render unto
Caesar what is Caesar's"). Nevertheless, all of these commitments
depended on the very textual indeterminacy they constrained. Like
the God it represents, the biblical text never ceases to be a signifier.
This may well be the secret of its historical success. Its essential
textuality ensures that it always knows itself not simply as a set of
collective beliefs, but also as a textual practice, that is, as a way of
producing and maintaining such beliefs. It may also explain why, for
all of Christianity's support of the status quo, it has never been
without its dissident and subversive traditions, from the Gnostics to
liberation theology. Christianity's politically conservative, socially
limiting tendencies have never been able to escape its subversive
tendencies. The latter are a function of the textual indeterminacy
which the conservative tendencies need in order to present themselves
as collective.

This originary textuality anticipates Gelasian *auctoritas*, though it
does not contain it, just as, in more specific terms, Gelasius himself
anticipates without containing the Gregorian institutional program
which was to take up his *auctoritas/potestas* dichotomy some five
centuries later.[28] He offers the Church to secular political power as an
independent agent of the societal-wide ideological solidarity upon
which political stability depends. What Gelasius takes away from the
emperor in terms of immediate control over *auctoritas*, he returns to
him in the form of greater autonomy for the collective sense of
identity *auctoritas* is designed to signify. In this dynamic lies the
political motivation for secular rulers as a group to support the
Church's political autonomy. The inherent textuality of the Church's
auctoritas enables it to affirm the collective status quo on entirely

---

[27] Ramsay Macmullen, *Christianizing the Roman Empire* (*A.D. 100–400*) (New Haven and
London: Yale University Press, 1984), 15, 110–111.
[28] Cf. Benson, "Gelasian Doctrine," 21.

autonomous terms. On the whole this *auctoritas*, if politically constraining, was also ideologically empowering. The empowerment proceeded directly from its textual autonomy in relation to all historical forms of *potestas*.

Such textuality prevents us from construing *auctoritas* as either given or unself-conscious. It also prevents us from restricting it entirely to the past. Whatever claims postmodern theory can make to have left the conundrums of modernism behind, it still has yet to escape the much larger riddle of Christianity. For what the postmodern present faces in its Christian past, a living, breathing past that still walks among us, is a form of ideological self-consciousness every bit as textual as its own. That is, despite the characterizations to the contrary, Christianity does not represent a metaphysics of pure presence unaware of its own textuality. Instead, it represents a different form of textual self-reflexiveness, one every bit as global as deconstruction's own. What Derrida calls *différance*, Christianity calls God. Derrida's deconstruction of modern positivism may not be a pure leap into the future so much as a return in a different guise to a form of knowledge Christianity already had and positivism repressed.

I can push this point even further. Is it too outrageous to suggest that the ultimate precursor of Derrida's "transcendental signified" is Paul's dead letter? That deconstruction is indebted to Christianity not only for its notion of textuality but also for the very mode of appropriation that represses, or at least disguises that debt. Paul's dead letter is a moment of pure mystification. Ascribing this deadness to Judaic tradition enables him not only to treat that tradition with impunity, but, more importantly, to deny its authority, to announce he is breaking with it even where he is not. Could this not be the ultimate source of modernism's ideal of a pure break with the past, an ideal it (paradoxically) inherited from Romanticism (which may itself have inherited the ideal from the Enlightenment), and which much postmodernism retains in its notion of history as radically disjunct. If this is the case, then Eco's call to revisit the past falls with particular urgency on the problem of Christian authority. If the notion of a self-authorizing break with a mystified past is Christian, even if only in part, and if this mode of self-authorization continues to operate in covert fashion in subsequent systems of thought, even where the break they posit is a break with Christianity itself, then when postmodernism declares that claims of a pure break with the past are illusory, it necessarily commits itself to a reexamination of precisely that past that even it has considered the most regressive, the deadest of the dead letters, Christianity.

Two final points will return us to the exemplum. First: the terms *ideology* and *hegemony* are crucial to redefining the problem of authority, because they correct the idealizations of traditionalists like Hannah Arendt. At the same time, we cannot use them as simple replacements for the older term. As terms developed primarily within Marxist tradition, they participate in the same general mythology of the modernist break as most other post-Christian systems of thought. They tend to be primarily synchronic in emphasis, while authority is more diachronic. Moreover, its diachronies are largely textual. Accordingly the term can deal more easily with precisely the problem on which recent theories of ideology have concentrated: subjectivity. The greater prominence *authority* gives to textuality brings it much closer to the dynamics of subject formation, inasmuch as subjects produce themselves in and through language. Its emphasis on the diachronic spotlights the role historical sedimentation plays in the process of subject formation, a question on which discussions of ideology and hegemony have been largely silent. Indeed, it may well be the very modernity of these terms that has prevented them from addressing this question. This leads me to my second point.

The modernist myth of the break has been particularly powerful within literary thought. Modern literature focuses on the figure of the author, whom it defines largely by his or her resistance to authority, especially religious authority. Yet modern literature also offers itself as a replacement for this authority it wants so fiercely to resist. In response to this contradiction, postmodern theory has declared the author to be either dead or at best an ideological construct.[29] The first response obviously demystifies one mythic figure of resistance by dreaming of a resistance that would be even purer (and therefore even more mythic). I offer my study of the exemplum more in the spirit of the second. Yet the *Parson's Tale* alone shows that an adequate understanding of how the notion of authorship has come to be produced will require more than the deductive isolation of a few defining characteristics. It will involve a bracketing of precisely that ideal of autonomy and resistance which has defined for modern

---

[29] The classic statements of these two positions are Roland Barthes, "The Death of the Author," in *Image, Music, Text*, essays selected and tr. Stephen Heath (New York: Hill and Wang, 1977), 142–48; Michel Foucault, "What is an Author?"

thought not only the author but the very movement of literary history. The modern conception of medieval culture is massively post-figured by the modern notion of the Renaissance; after modernity itself, the quintessential model of the cultural break. The very term *Renaissance* signifies a break, a break with nothing less than death.

Paired against it, the Middle Ages inevitably signifies fallow quiescense waiting for culture to begin again. The implications of this pairing are not so much complicated as reinforced by a second opposition, that of humanism to Christianity, with which the first is often overlaid. The Christocentric Middle Ages are seen as a long period of cultural stasis, or ideal balance, a monolith of "quiet hierarchies" and common assumptions which every cultural form shared by virtue of simply being *medieval*.[30] At some moment never finally to be determined, this culture with its eyes permanently fixed on the ideal unities of the divine gives way to the noisy, contradictory, and capacious realities of the human. The medieval is consigned to a past forever lost and the Renaissance begins. What is described here, of course, are two realities so completely distinct that it is never clear how we get from one to the other.

Few scholars, if any, would admit to this view in the bald manner I have just stated it. Nevertheless, both David Aers and Lee Patterson have recently demonstrated the widespread persistence of its assumptions.[31] To their eloquent accounts I have only one thing to add. The recent drive to rename the Renaissance the Early Modern, while eliminating the idealization implicit in the term itself, merely exacerbates the specific problem of transition with which I have here been concerned. For the new term makes even more total the break between the Middle Ages and everything that comes afterward. As this study of the exemplum offers a new view of the emergence of the Chaucerian tradition, it will of necessity also offer, albeit intermittently and incompletely, a new view of the cultural changes designated by the terms *humanism* and the *Renaissance*. Without in any way denying the specificity or importance of these changes, it will

---

[30] The phrase is D. W. Roberston's (*Preface to Chaucer*, 51). Cited and discussed in Aers, *Community, Gender and Individual Identity: English Writing 1360–1430* (London and New York: Routledge), 6–19.

[31] David Aers, "A Whisper in the Ear of Early Modernists, or, Reflections on Literary Critics Writing the 'History of the Subject,'" in *Culture and History 1350–1600: Essays on English Communities, Identities, and Writing* (Detroit: Wayne State University Press, 1992), 177–202; Patterson, "On the Margin," 92–101.

nevertheless suggest that they took longer, and owe more to the religious forms they came partially to displace than is usually acknowledged. More specifically, I want to suggest, as I have already begun to in my reading of the *Parson's Tale*, that what is usually seen as the transition from the medieval to the humanist might be more fruitfully understood as one from clerical to lay. The authority the Chaucerian tradition derived from the exemplum was an authority many of whose contours had already been produced from the largely clerical Latin traditions which preceded it. It is to these traditions we now turn.

PART I

The Latin tradition

CHAPTER 4

The sermon exemplum

The exemplum appears in nearly every form of serious medieval discourse, and is parodied in comic forms such as the fabliau and the beast fable. Within this broad cultural propensity, it is possible to discern two central strands. The first is the sermon exemplum, which evolved out of the earlier monastic tradition initiated by Gregory's *Dialogues*. The second is usually described as the classical exemplum, but I will call it the public exemplum.[1] The public exemplum was most prominent in the *Fürstenspiegel*, the Mirrors of Princes, but also occurred in other political, ecclesiological and historiographical contexts.[2] In modern scholarship, these two strands have been treated as entirely distinct. The sermon exemplum is usually the province of folklorists and social historians; the public exemplum, of intellectual historians. There is a good deal of justification to this separation. The sermon exemplum draws most of its material from folkloric and hagiographic traditions; the public exemplum from classical antiquity.

Nevertheless, this separation also completely obscures the exemplum's considerable political significance. Viewed as folklore, the sermon exemplum becomes spontaneous and unself-conscious, the product of an undifferentiated popular imagination, without any specifiable political interest. The public exemplum, by contrast, is viewed as self-consciously learned, but for that very reason, equally apolitical. It becomes the vehicle for the timeless moral teachings of classical tradition. This folklore/learned dichotomy reproduces the high modernist distinction between high and low culture, and should be suspect for that reason alone. One of postmodernism's many

---

[1] See 81–87 below.

[2] For a concise discussion of exemplarity in medieval historiography, see Gabrielle M. Spiegel, "Political Utility in Medieval Historiography: A Sketch," *History and Theory* 14 (1975), 314–25.

beneficial effects has been to expose the speciousness of such a distinction defined as a rigid boundary.[3] In this case, however, the objection can be made considerably more specific. The high/low separation between public and sermon exemplum completely ignores the social location they share. Both are narratives employed by clerics to persuade lay audiences. Both, therefore, have an inescapably polemical and ecclesiological dimension. The exemplum, a prominent feature of later medieval culture in its own right, was also part of the even larger process whereby the Church established itself as an international institution, and as a force in every aspect of social existence.

This dimension is not incidental, but definitive. For the exemplum is defined as much by function as by form, and its ecclesiological motivations define its function. That is, the ecclesiological motivation oriented the use to which the exemplum put the material it draws from previous traditions. Through the sermon exemplum, the Church attempted to establish its ideological authority among subordinate classes it had previously largely ignored. Through the public exemplum, it attempted to extend its authority at court. Its putative transcendence of class boundaries, its capacity to speak for all of society, was an important part of the ideological power it brought to court. As primarily a court tradition, the Chaucerian tradition attempted to reappropriate the textual authority of the Church largely on the terrain of the public exemplum. But it also, especially in the case of Chaucer himself, needed to contest clerical authority on the terrain of the sermon exemplum as well.

Some measure of the self-conscious complexity of which the sermon exemplum was capable can be gained by a closer examination of the following narrative, which occurs in the *Liber exemplorum ad usum praedicantium*, a thirteenth-century Franciscan collection, under the rubric "How Christ appeared to his disciples after the resurrection" (*Qualiter Christus, apparuit discipulis suis post resurrectionem*). After a list of the appearances, one finds this exemplum:

There was a certain bishop in Campania, a man endowed with great sanctity, to whom it befell, as pleased God, to become blind. Once, on the day of the resurrection of the lord, while this holy man sat alone in church, it happened that a boy crossed by him. Hearing but not seeing him the

---

[3] Frederic Jameson, "Periodizing the Sixties," in *The 60's Without Apology*, ed. Sohnya Sayres, Anders Stephanson, Stanley Aronowitz, and Frederic Jameson (Minneapolis: University of Minnesota Press, 1985), 194–201.

bishop said, "Who is there?" He answered, "I, my lord," and the bishop said, "What's new? Have you any gossip?" To which the boy: "Rumor has it, my lord – and it's a good one – that the Lord is risen." With that word, the bishop conceived an extremely great joy in his heart, and these words burst out: "May the lord bless you, my son, for this, truly, is a wonderful rumor. No one ever heard a better one." It happened not long afterward that a good benefice was open in the bishopric. When the bishop became aware of this, he remembered the boy and had him called in. The bishop said to him, "Dearest one, you brought me that best of rumors, namely, that the Lord is risen, and I, for love of Him about whom you brought news, give this benefice to you." The boy, hearing this and not expecting it, returned thanks as he ought. After some time passed, as the bishop slept one night, the Queen of the World, the Mother of Mercy, came to him in a dream and said, "Lord bishop, you have given this benefice to the boy who announced to you the good news of my son's resurrection. Now, indeed, let me give this to you." And placing her hand on one of her blessed breasts, she poured milk in his eyes, drops from a full breast. Awakened by these drops, the bishop opened his eyes and immediately discovered he could see so clearly it was as if he never saw more clearly.

Episcopus quidam in Campania, vir catholicus vite sanctitate preditus, tandem sicut Deo placuit cecitatem incurrit. Vir iste sanctus quodam die resurrectionis dominice, cum sederet solus in ecclesia, contigit ut transiret per eum puer unus. Quem non videns sed audiens episcopus dixit: "Quis es ibi?" Qui respondit: "Ego, domine." Et ait episcopus: "Qui sunt rumores tui?" Cui puer: "Hic est rumor, domine, bonus valde, videlicet, quia resurrexit Dominus." Ad quod verbum episcopus magnam iocunditatem valde concepit in corde suo, et in huiusmodi verbum prorupit: "Benedictus sis, fili, a Domino, quia verrissime bonus rumor est. Nunquam rumor melior auditus est." Contigit autem non multo post ut quoddam vacaret beneficium bonum in episcopatu. Quod cum episcopus accepisset, fecit ad se vocari puerum memoratum: cui et dixit episcopus: "Karrissime, cum mihi rumorem illum optimum detulisti, quod videlicet resurrexit Dominus, et ego, pro amore illius de quo rumorem detulisti, illud beneficium do tibi." Puer autem hoc audiens ex inopinato gratias sicut debuit retulit episcopo. Postea vero aliquanto tempore interiecto, episcopo nocte quadam dormienti adest in sompnis regina mundi mater misericordie dicens ei: "Domine episcope, tu dedisti beneficium illud puero qui rumorem illum bonum nunciavit tibi de resurrectione filii mei. Nunc autem hoc faciam tibi." Et apposita manu ad unam mamillarum beatarum plena mamilla lac utrique oculo episcopi instillavit. Ad quam quidem instillacionem episcopus evigilans oculos aperuit et statim videre se ita clare reperit sicut numquam clarius vidit.[4]

---

[4] *Liber exemplorum ad usum praedicantium*, ed. A. G. Little (Aberdeen: British Society of Franciscan Studies, 1908), 9, p. 5. The translation is mine. The compiler claims to have

Despite its spareness, and its lack of interest in character and setting, this is a spectacular narrative. Its very compression gives it an austere intensity which more detail might dissipate, and its abrupt plot shifts are all the more dislocating for the singularity of focus. This sermon exemplum takes up, self-consciously and with some thoroughness, the very problem which has defined the form for modern scholars: the absorption of folklore into ecclesiastical discourse. The exemplum records the displacement of the chaotic, oral realm of *rumor* by the master narrative of Christian salvation. But, unlike much modern scholarship, it in no way treats that absorption as a simple, straightforward affair. Instead, it traces a complex process of appropriation, whose very complexity insures its durability: in its displacement of *rumor*, Christian discourse comes, like Christ, to a place where it already was.

The boy in this story is a folk-tale archetype, the clever young hero tested for cleverness, but his cleverness is played out in an arena already defined by Christian discourse.[5] As a spokesman from the world of folklore, the boy enters the church as an outsider. The bishop, his Easter meditation interrupted by the entrance of an outsider, addresses the outsider in secular terms ("Quod rumores?") only to find the outsider is already on the inside. Confronting the irony of a sacral observance so universally acknowledged as to have become entirely banal, the bishop finds in its very banality a demonstration of its enduring significance. It is precisely because Christ's resurrection has become banal that the boy could mistake it for a rumor, by hearing it at the same times and in the same places as ordinary conversation. If his spontaneous recognition of the Resurrection's power demonstrates that it retains its sacral privilege even as a banal social fact, that very demonstration depends on the narrativity of that sacral privilege. The Resurrection is memorable because it is a good rumor: it distinguishes itself from the other banalities which surround it by its superiority as a story. The bishop's response, "This truly is a wonderful rumor," ironically accepts the boy's generic classification, and the exemplum will continue to refer to the Resurrection as a rumor until the end.

This recuperation of the oral is entirely narrative, operating

---

found the exemplum in the *Gemma Ecclesiae* of Gerald of Wales, although it does not occur there.

[5] Cf. Antti Aarne, *The Motif Index of Folk Literature*, rev. and enlarged by Stith Thompson (Bloomington: University of Indiana Press, 1956), vol. 3, H500.

through a formal mechanism which at least one contemporary theorist has made narrative's defining feature. This is Tzvetan Todorov's "narrative transformation."[6] He defines it as the combining of two narrative propositions in a single predicate (a narrative "function or motif"). In the hypothetical predicate "X plans to commit a crime," for example, two separate propositions, the planning of a crime, and the committing of a crime are transformed into a single narrative moment. In this schematic illustration, the transformation takes the literal form ABBC: the "planning to commit" and the "committing of a crime" are two distinct propositions brought together in the single predicate "commit," which they share. But he gives the term a much broader application as well. As the capacity of narrative to organize the facts it draws together,

transformation represents precisely a synthesis of differences and resemblances, it links two facts without their being able to be identified. Rather than a two-sided unit, it is an operation in two directions: it asserts both resemblance and difference; it engages and suspends time in a single movement...

"In a word," he concludes, "it makes narrative possible and yields us its very definition."[7]

This exemplum provides a clear instance of narrative transformation in the Todorovian sense. In the single predicate, "*rumor*," two motifs, the secular world of everyday existence and the sacred world of the Resurrection, are brought together, and the transformation is recapitulated and reenacted from the opening exchange between the boy and the bishop to the closing exchange between the bishop and the Virgin. Moreover, it is the nature of this particular transformation to proclaim itself as transformative. That is to say, the Christian transformation of *rumor* is a transformation of the power of narrative transformation. As a predicate which "asserts both resemblance and difference," *rumor* demonstrates the capacity of Christian discourse to become fully narrative without ever losing its specificity, without, that is, losing its superiority to the world of folkloric narrative it has transformed.

Demonstrating the narrativity of Church discourse enables this exemplum to draw its lay audience into an affirmation of the privilege of such discourse. The exemplum extends the boy's

[6] Tzvetan Todorov, *The Poetics of Prose*, tr. Richard Howard (Ithaca: Cornell University Press, 1977), 218–33.　　　[7] Todorov, *Poetics*, 233.

narratorial spontaneity by quite literally institutionalizing it: the bishop offers the benefice as a straight exchange for the rumor of the Resurrection. The bishop answers the boy's spontaneity with a spontaneous act of his own, but one which is far more definitive than the boy's in scope. Once the boy and the spontaneity he represents are absorbed into the Church, the audience is led to seek the ultimate reward for his sanctity in the reward to the Bishop, a member of the Church hierarchy. This reward, though it comes through divine intervention, is temporal, indeed bodily, in nature.

It would be wrong to overplay the eroticism latent in the narrative's execution of its reward, but it would be equally wrong to ignore it. The nearly pornographic emphasis on the literal tactility of Mary's gesture – her manipulation of her own "full" breast – makes her as much female body revealed to the gaze of male desire as the sacred Virgin mother ministering to one of her earthly children. Indeed, to return to Todorov's terminology, the rhetorical power of this image is precisely its "suspense" between the sacred and the profane. As the closure of a narrative of Christianity's appropriation of the secular, this suspension demonstrates Christianity's capacity to recuperate the secular at even its most resistant, namely, the erotic. This final image's latent eroticism insists on the materiality of divine intervention. Miracles happen within the world, on the world's terms, without ever losing their own, other-worldly privilege. In the manner of its production Mary's breast milk is erotically charged and tactile. In effecting its miraculous result, it is invisible and without substance. It simply dissolves into the clarity of the bishop's new-found vision. Despite its clarity, this vision is not a vision of anything in particular. The Church's power retains the character of an empty form – an empty form with nonetheless greater material effect than any material reality.

If any doubts linger about the capacity of didactic narrative to operate as fully as any other form of narrative, I hope my examination of this exemplum has dispelled them. This exemplum's didactic claims are not tacked onto the narrative; they are driven by it. And they are driven specifically by the narrative capacity for rhetorical complexity, a complexity which extends to the easy accomodation of the non-narrative. This elasticity enables the discourse of church doctrine to be at once fully outside the exemplum, as the immutable truth toward which it tends, and completely within the exemplum as the motor of its plot. Narrative becomes the discourse of the secular world, but a discourse continually amenable to incursions from the doctrinal. In this way, the Church is able to assert fully its institutional prerogatives without weakening its claims to transcend social concerns. The broad ideological power of this doubleness can be seen in the very way this exemplum constructs its subject-positions.

If the audience identifies first with the young boy, it is led through that identification to identify with the bishop, who, as a member of the ecclesiastical hierarchy, becomes the focus of communal desire. Yet that focus never leaves his institutional position. To the end he remains nameless, his individuality knowable only throught his institutional identity. When the audience focuses on him what they focus on is precisely the Church's capacity to produce subjectivity. As we shall see, this is a dominant pattern in the sermon exemplum: the form continually diverts the ideological sense of identity it solicits to specific institutional mechanisms whereby that sense is produced.

The sermon exemplum of the later Middle Ages evolved out of the monastic tradition of the earlier Middle Ages. Although our current state of knowledge regarding the middle of this earlier tradition remains inconclusive,[8] both its point of departure and its terminus are clearer. It begins with Gregory the Great, known in the later Middle Ages as the father of the exemplum, and his collection, *Dialogues*, and it ends with works like the early thirteenth-century collection *Dialogus miraculorum* by the Cistercian Cesarius of Heisterbach.[9] Though apparently intended for a monastic audience, Cesarius's work soon became a source for sermon exempla, as the appearance of its material in later Franciscan and Dominican collections indicates. Gregory was the first monk to become pope, and many of his considerable energies were devoted to promoting monasticism, the primary institutional vehicle through which the Church's westward expansion occurred in the earlier Middle Ages.[10] The *Dialogues* represent his attempt to provide the new Benedictine monasticism with its own hagiography.[11]

[8] For a brief discussion, see LeGoff, Bremond, and Schmitt, *L'"exemplum,"* 50–55.
[9] *Caesarii Heisterbacensis monachi ordinis Cisterciensis dialogus miraculorum*, ed. Joseph Strange, 2 vols. (Cologne, Bonn and Brussels: H. Lempertz and Co., 1851).
[10] Jean Decarreaux, *Monks and Civilization*, tr. Charlotte Haldane (London: Allen and Unwin, 1967), 246–52; R. W. Southern, *The Making of the Middle Ages* (New Haven and London: Yale University Press, 1953), 154–69.
[11] Cf. J. A. Mosher, *The Exemplum in England* (New York: Columbia University Press, 1910), 10. My reading of the institutional politics of the *Dialogues* draws on that strand of recent scholarship on Gregory which holds that, in the words of Carole Straw, "Gregory's

The work is presented as a conversation between Gregory and a novice named Peter. It is in four books: the first contains exempla drawn from the *vitae* of notable monks; the second is a *vita* of Benedict; and the third and fourth are devoted to a mixture of episcopal and monastic figures. Although it is frequently dismissed as a popular work, of less interest than Gregory's more contemplative writings, Gregory himself did not view it this way. Speaking through Peter, he declares its exempla no less edifying than scriptural commentary, and adds that "there are those who come to love the celestial homeland more through example than through pronouncement."[12] Gregory addresses Peter as *dilectissimus filius meus* (I, Prol., 2); Gregory's exempla makes the authority of the fathers available to him, but only if he first learns to become a good son, subordinating himself fully to his superiors.

For the most part, the listener to stories of the fathers gains a double advantage in spirit. He is inflamed with love for the life to come by comparing it to that of predecessors, and if he has any self-esteem, he learns to be humble before the superior goodness of others.

Fit vero plerumque in audientis animo duplex adiutorium in exemplis patrum, quia et ad amorem venturae vitae ex praecedentium comparatione accenditur, et iam si se esse aliquid aestimat, dum de aliis meliora cognoverit, humiliatur. (I, Prol., 9)

Submission to monastic authority brings with it a share of its sacral power. In the *exempla patrum*, a son may find his *vita ventura*, so long as he learns to be constrained only by the humility such examples will inevitably bring. His self-esteem and his humility become the same: he derives his sense of identity from his submission to the authority of the fathers. In distinction to previous monasticism, the Benedictine Rule stressed obedience and life-long commitment to the order, which gave it much greater viability than the earlier moments.[13] Gregory's exempla gave this ecclesiological impulse narrative expression, and the deference to institutional authority they establish carried over into the sermon tradition.

achievement in the *Dialogues* lies in placing these servants of God with their real power of divine inspiration firmly within the Church's hierarchy." For a fuller discussion and further bibliography, see Straw, *Gregory the Great: Perfection in Imperfection* (Berkeley, Los Angeles, London: University of California Press, 1988), 66–89.

[12] *Gregoire le Grand: Dialogues*, ed. Adalbert de Vogüé, tr. into French by Paul Antin, 2 vols. (Paris: Editions du Cerf, 1979), vol. 2, I, Prol. 9, p. 12: "... unt nonnuli quos ad amorem patriae caelestis plus exempla quam praedicamenta succendunt." Further citations are from this edition. Book, chapter, and paragraph numbers will be given in the text. The translation is mine. [13] Decarreaux, *Monks and Civilization*, 222–29.

The immediate stimulus for the emergence of the sermon exemplum was the great preaching campaigns which began in the midtwelfth century and continued well into the thirteenth. These campaigns had two sources. The more obvious and better known is the mendicant orders, the Dominicans and Franciscans, whose first and most typical institutional function was itinerant preaching, although they were also frequently licensed to hear confession. But an earlier, and surprisingly durable impetus came from the circle of Parisian clerics associated with Peter the Chanter, which included the famous preachers, Fulk of Neuilly and Jacques de Vitry.[14] The exemplum played a prominent role in both the Parisian and mendicant traditions. Jacques de Vitry was the first major compiler of sermon exempla, and most of the extant collections are Franciscan or Dominican in origin.

This shift from a monastic to a preaching context meant important changes for the exemplum's relation to its audience. The new preaching movements were tied to the newly emergent urban world. Because of their concentrated population, cities provided a convenient arena for itinerant preaching, and itinerant preachers were the Church's most logical means of reaching a new clientele. The mendicants drew their recruits from the bourgeoisie, and sometimes the urban aristocracy, and these classes became their most typical audience.[15] Indeed, in 1261 the Archbishop of Pisa went so far as to proclaim Francis the patron saint of merchants.[16] While global statements about the class status of cultural trends in the Middle Ages must always be made with caution, it seems safe to say that in the person of the itinerant preacher, the Church was usually addressing an inferior class.

The sermon exemplum will amplify the deference to institutional authority already present in the monastic tradition, and it will make increasingly abstract the participation it allows in the sacral power of such authority. This shift is reflected in the fragmented form of sermon exemplum collections, a fragmentation already evident in Cesarius: although he follows Gregory in the largest outlines of his work, his taxonomy is quite different. The *Dialogus miraculorum*, like

---

[14] John Baldwin, *Masters, Princes, and Merchants: The Social Views of Peter the Chanter and His Circle*, 2 vols. (Princeton: Princeton University Press, 1970), vol. 1, 36–39. Kemmler, *Exempla in Context*, 28–29.

[15] Barbara Rosenwein and Lester K. Little, "Social Meaning in the Monastic and Mendicant Spiritualities," *Past and Present* 63 (1974), 18–32.

[16] Rosenwein and Little, "Social Meaning," 28.

Gregory's *Dialogues*, is framed as a dialogue between an elder monk and a novice and it was, like Gregory's work, presumably intended for the edification of novices. Unlike Gregory, however, Cesarius does not set his exempla in an intermediate framework of individual *vitae*. Interestingly enough, the succession of categories correspond roughly to stages in an abstract spiritual biography: Conversion, Contrition, Confession, Temptation, Demons, Simplicity, the Blessed Virgin Mary, Visions, Sacraments of the Body and the Blood of Christ, Miracles, Death, and Eternal Reward.[17] Where the body of knowledge presented to Peter, the initiate in Gregory's *Dialogues*, was always presented through individual lives which his life might very well imitate, the knowledge presented to Cesarius's novice (himself anonymous) comes almost completely stripped of any individual origin with which he might identify: although framed by a life, that life is a generalized one consisting of abstract categories rather than incidents. In the *Dialogus miraculorum* the ecclesiastical institution which the novice is attempting to enter is clearly identified with doctrine alone, and is distinct from the narratives which form a bridge to it.

In exemplum collections intended for preachers the fiction of the life disappears completely. In some of them the categories were arranged according to some logical relationship (for example, in the *Liber exemplorum*, they are divided into "Greater Things [*De rebus superioribus*]," and "Lesser Things [*De rebus inferioribus*]"), or, more frequently as the tradition progressed, according to alphabetical order. As a further refinement, they sometimes included cross-references to other *sententiae* which a particular exemplum might illustrate.[18] These arrangements foreground the exemplum's flexibility, its amenability to a preacher's needs on a variety of occasions. This is a flexibility which sets the preacher apart from his audience even as he establishes common ground with them.

Commentary on the sermon exemplum translates this discursive advantage directly into institutional terms. Gregory's even-handed view of exemplum and precept as two equally valid ways to heaven gives way to a strict separation. The exemplum becomes the sign of the intellectual subordination of its lay audience. Bonaventura, for

---

[17] *Dialogus miraculorum*. The Latin headings are *De conversione, De contritione, De confessione, De tentatione, De daemonibus, De simplicitate, De Sancta Maria, De diversis visionibus, De sacramento corporis et sanguinis corpore Christi, De miraculis, De morientibus, De praemio mortuorum*.
[18] Bremond, *L'"exemplum"*, 60–63.

instance, recommends the exemplum for laymen because of their enjoyment of external similitudes, while the Franciscan compiler of the *Speculum laicorum* more pointedly suggests the exemplum's utility for those weak in learning and unrefined in faith (*in sciencia debiles et in fide rudes*).[19] A fourteenth-century English *Ars praedicandi* contrasts exemplum to allegory:

It will be advantageous to expound some sweet allegory and to narrate some pleasant exemplum in order that the profundity of the allegory delight the learned and the levity of the exemplum edify the simple...[20]

In none of these comments is there the dialectic which literally underpins the dialogic structure of the monastic exemplum, whereby the reader can, by emulating the exempla the exemplarist offers, achieve the exemplarist's position. There is virtually no social permeability between exemplarist and audience. There are simply two distinct groups, the clerical, (*scientes, erudites*) on one side, and the lay, (*rudes, simplices*) on the other.

The larger political significance of this distinction must be approached tentatively. Despite the truly impressive record of the medieval church established by modern intellectual and institutional historians, its cultural politics (as distinct from the slightly narrower question of its institutional politics) remains comparatively under-investigated. Recently two intellectual historians, Brian Stock and R. I. Moore, both of whom have been involved in the study of heresy, have offered Weberian models for understanding this problem. Both locate the political impetus for the Church's shifting role in medieval culture in Weberian motives of rationalization. R. I. Moore uses the model more directly. He views the Church's later medieval cultural program as driven by its need as a professional bureaucracy to seek continual expansion and vulgarization of its own administrative presence. Stock adapts Weber to his own notion of "textual communities," which he defines as "groups of people whose social activities are centered around texts, or, more precisely, around a literate interpreter of them."[21] Because religion is "the dimension of culture most accessible to the majority of people," the medieval Church after the reemergence of literacy becomes the pre-eminent

---

[19] *Le Speculum laicorum*, 1.   [20] Cited in Welter, *L'exemplum*, 77:

Secundum erit aliquam dulcem exponere allegoriam et aliquid jocundum enarrare exemplum ut eruditos delectaret allegorie profunditas et simplices edificet exempli levitas...

[21] Stock, *Implications of Literacy: Written Language and Models of Interpretation in the Eleventh and Twelfth Centuries* (Princeton: Princeton University Press), 522.

site of conflict between competing textual communities, heretical, reformist, and orthodox.[22]

These models have the advantage, as Stock puts it, of admitting no "artificial barriers between 'social' and 'religious' spheres of life," while avoiding the reductiveness of the classical Marxist base-superstructure model, which makes religion a more or less direct effect of class. Nevertheless, as might be said of Weber himself, the insistence of these authors on the internal autonomy of the religious leads them ultimately to leave the issue of social distinctions almost entirely in abeyance. This is particularly true of Stock, who concludes his discussion of the Patarene reform movement in the late eleventh century by triumphantly declaring, "The Pataria... transcended class relationships and placed conflict itself in the arena of universal morality."[23] Whatever we might say generally about this essentializing tendency in the Weberian model, the point I want to make here is that the retreat from the category of class and from the problem of external relations means this model cannot work in the case of the sermon exemplum.

As I have been arguing, the distinguishing mark of the sermon exemplum is precisely its conjointure of the internal and the external. Its narrative complexity enables it to establish common ground between clerical and lay and simultaneously maintain their distinctness. In fact, the exemplum represents a complexity in the cultural politics of the medieval Church of which neither Moore nor Stock take full account. Although their model assumes conflict, it also assumes conflict always takes place between entities which are internally coherent and undifferentiated. This model works fine in explaining either exclusion, with which Moore is primarily concerned, or inclusion, with which Stock is concerned, but it stumbles at the problem of subordination, which both includes and excludes at once. This is precisely the problem posed by the exemplum, and indeed by the cultural program of the post-Hildebrandine Church generally. It wanted both to bring the laity into closer relation to Christian ideology and to maintain its own privilege. Although even a concise discussion of the Church's cultural politics is beyond the scope of this study, I would like briefly to invoke the Gramscian notion of hegemony once again, in order to suggest that it can work on that aspect of the problem where Weberian models fail. For

---

[22] Stock, *Listening for the Text*, 123.   [23] Stock, *Implications of Literacy*, 239.

hegemony postulates a dialectical relation between the ideological and material even as it maintains their relative autonomy. In its broadest outlines the later Middle Ages illustrates such a dialectic quite neatly. By almost universal agreement among twentieth-century scholars, the hallmark of this period is consolidation both politically and ideologically. The concentration of political power into increasingly larger units, from the subjugation of allods by local lords at the manorial level to the absorption of lesser lordships by the great magnates, to the reemergence of kingship as a national force, is matched by a significant growth in the ideological reach of the Church, driven by its definitive internationalization under the supremacy of the pope. This growth was marked by the organization of the Crusades, the persecution of heretics and Jews, the preaching campaigns and changing conception of the *vita apostolica* from a primarily monastic emphasis to one that was primarily evangelical.[24] But perhaps above all, it was marked by the increasing incursion of the Church into most aspects of lay social experience. Here we might cite the growth of the ecclesiastical courts, the regulation of marriage, and especially the devotional program of the Fourth Lateran Council, which mandated that every believer receive communion and give confession at least once a year. It is generally accepted as inevitable that these two processes are complementary, and should have occurred together – so inevitable in fact that the tension between them is rarely remarked. The consolidation of political power was a process of concentration and exclusion, with more and more power passing into fewer and fewer hands. By contrast the ideological consolidation of the Church was a process of dispersion, as the Church reached out to a much wider clientele in more varied ways than it had ever done before. Moreover, the same tension between concentration and dispersion can be seen within the Church itself, inasmuch as the ideological initiatives sponsored by the papacy helped reinforce its institutional supremacy. Thus it seems reasonable to suggest that the Church's dissemination of Christian spirituality complemented contemporaneous political consolidations not by endorsing them, but precisely because it didn't. In short, in reaching out to lower-class groups it had previously ignored, the Church, as the ideological apparatus of the medieval ruling class, provided an

[24] M. D. Chenu, *Nature, Man, and Society in the Twelfth Century*, ed. and tr. Jerome Taylor and Lester K. Little (Chicago: University of Chicago Press, 1968), 207–38. See also Rosenwein and Little, "Social Meaning," 4–32.

arena apart from the political, where these previously excluded groups could share in its hegemony, or its *auctoritas*.

The sermon exemplum played an important part in this process. As it offered its lay audience entry into the authoritative discourse of church doctrine, it also held the Church apart as the source of lay empowerment. This is true even of exempla not explicitly religious in content, which deal with local lore or contemporary political events, for even they affirm the capacity of clerical discourse to appropriate and redefine the lay. In fact, such exempla account for only a small portion of the corpus; the rest, with varying degrees of specificity, are not only religious and doctrinal; they are also ecclesiological.

The most frequent topic of the sermon exemplum was the efficacy of Church ritual. Closely related to this topic are the exempla with clerical protagonists. Like the exemplum with which I opened this discussion, these focus lay spiritual aspirations in clerical figures. The most frequent topic after these is that of sins and virtues, followed by smaller groups consisting of snippets from hagiographical and classical traditions. There is also an even smaller, more miscellaneous group that touches on Christological, eschatological, or other theological issues. But the dominant theme is clearly the Church as the institutional focus of lay devotion. Both the exempla concerning Church ritual and those concerning sins and virtues should be seen as thematizing the increased engagement with the laity that occurred in the wake of the Fourth Lateran Council, and in particular with the stress on confession and penitence. In the exempla concerning ritual, the rituals most commonly explored are confession and communion, though this group also ranges widely, treating everything from excommunication to baptism, to almsgiving, and the singing of psalms.

Any global claim about the sermon exemplum must be tentative, given the current state of research in the field. Many exemplum collections remain unedited (including one of the most widely disseminated, the *Alphabetum narrationum*), while some of those that have been (such as Wright's edition of the exempla of Jacques de Vitry) are excerpts, and the study of the use, and transmission of, and interrelations between collections and individual exempla remains at a fairly elemental stage. Despite these limitations, however, enough work has been done to characterize the sermon exemplum's dominant ideological tendency in general terms. Frederick C. Tubach's *Index Exemplorum*, which was compiled from the "37 central collections available in modern print," contains plot summaries of 5400 exempla.[25] Of these more than 900 concern Church ritual, the largest single topic. Of course this number has no meaning beyond its indication of a general tendency. Tubach's Index is meant as an aid to research, not as a systematic map of the field. Nevertheless, as a general indication the figure has some value, particularly if one examines the exempla to which it refers in more detail.

The exempla concerning ritual exploit to the fullest the form's two-fold subordination of narrative and doctrine. One group corresponds to its claim that doctrine is entirely translatable into narrative terms. These focus on the material efficacy of Church forms. A second group corresponds to the claim that doctrine nevertheless transcends the very narrative form it can assume. These are the exemplum which present the capacity of ritual forms to transcend their customary incarnations. A third group combines both aspects. These deal with the power of sacred language, which they present as entirely spiritual and entirely material at once. I will examine representative instances of each group.[26]

In some exempla, sacred acts acquire such material force that they take on a power that seems almost independent of religious and moral context. Jacques de Vitry adapted from Gregory's *Dialogues* the tale of a Jew who, while making a journey, spent the night in a cemetery near the temple of Apollo. When a devil approached him, he made the sign of the Cross out of fear, and the devil, unable to harm him, returned to his companions, saying, "I met an empty vessel, that is, crossed." The others fled, and the Jew, impressed with the power of the sign, thereafter converted.[27] It is true that by the end of the tale, the sign's spirituality becomes evident, leading the Jew to Christianity, and converting the miraculous to the institutional. But at the beginning the sign is made almost as an instinctive reflex, and it takes effect even though it represents no positive belief on behalf of the one making it. It is more than a direct, outward reflection of an inner conviction: it has its own autonomous outward existence and effect.

[25] Frederic C. Tubach, *Index Exemplorum: A Handbook of Medieval Religious Tales* (Helsinki: FF Communications, 1969).
[26] The survey that follows is based exclusively on sources available in modern editions. Fortunately, although many exemplum collections remain in manuscript (see Welter, *L'exemplum*, pp. 477–502), the most basic authors and collections have been edited, either as complete texts, or excerpts.
[27] Thomas Frederick Crane, ed., *The Exempla or Illustrative Stories From the "Sermones Vulgares" of Jacques de Vitry* (London: 1890), no. 131, p. 59.

Confession exhibits similar autonomy in an exemplum concerning adultery. A servant makes love to his mistress, and his lord, suspicious, takes him to a demoniac to confirm his guilt. When his lord is momentarily diverted along the way, he hastily makes confession to a peasant, and when they reach the demoniac he is found guiltless.[28] In this exemplum, as in the one preceding, the ritual succeeds despite the doubtful motives of the person using it. Related to these two but not quite as extreme are the exempla in which those who have been devoted to the Cross, the Virgin, or a particular saint are given special protection by the object of their devotion. *The Alphabet of Tales*, a fifteenth-century English translation of the *Alphabetum narrationum*, contains the story of a thief protected from the devil for fourteen years solely on the strength of having said "Ave Maria" daily.[29] Divine intervention also protected penitents from human accusation. In an exemplum from Étienne de Bourbon, a thirteenth-century Dominican, a pregnant abbess who is to face her bishop the next day that night has her child delivered and spirited away after praying to the Virgin.[30] There are exempla which extoll the efficacy of every conceivable sort of Church practice, from alms to excommunication to paternosters to tithes. Finally, there are a number of exempla extolling the virtue of indulgences.

One of the most remarkable exemplum about confession occurs in the *Liber exemplorum*. A man who is traveling at night from one town to another sees a devil approaching him in the form of a horrible beast. He makes a circle of crosses around him with his ax, and calls on God to hear his sins:

Lord, I do not have a priest to whom I might confess my sins. I pray to you that I might discharge my sins, and not having other refuge, for the time being until I come to a priest, I confess, Lord, I have done this and this ...[31]

With each sin that is confessed a wall begins to grow around him. By the time he has finished the wall is so high that the devil cannot reach him but can only peer over it. They pass the night this way, and,

---

[28] Strange, ed., *Dialogus miraculorum*, III, 3, vol. 1, 113–14.
[29] Mary Macleod Banks, ed., *An Alphabet of Tales*, 2 vols. (London: 1904) vol. 1, no. 71, 53–54.
[30] A. Lecoy de la Marche, ed., *Anecdotes historiques, legendes et apologues tirés du recueil inedit d'Étienne de Bourbon*, (Paris: 1877) no. 135, 114–15. For variants see Frederic Tubach, *Index Exemplorum: A Handbook of Medieval Religious Tales* (Helsinki: 1969), entry 2.
[31] Little, ed., *Liber exemplorum*, no. 95, 51: "Domine, non habeo sacerdotem cui possim peccata mea confiteri. Promitto tibi quod ego dimittam peccata mea, et non habens aliud refugium cui peccata mea interim donec ad sacerdotem perveniam confiteor, Domine, inquit, hec feci et hec ..."

despite his protection, the man is so terrified he continually makes promises to God "which would have been almost impossible for anyone to fulfill."[32] The arrangement is clearly a makeshift, a point the compiler drives home when he comments, "Now you see, O Christian, what power against the devil confession must have when made to a priest, according to the rule of the Church, if this confession made to God in the middle of a field works against the devil so well."[33] This comment is surprising – for after all, how could any form of communication be preferable to a direct audience with God? – but it shows the extent to which the exemplum intends to promote the Church's institutional prerogative.[34] Indeed, throughout its presentation, the exemplum stresses the uncertainties of a direct approach to God. After the night ends, the man hurries to a confessor, and it is the confessor, Brother Adam Habe, that the compiler cites as the source of the exemplum. He approaches Brother Adam while the latter is hearing confession before preaching a sermon; the familiarity of the procedure by which he makes his makeshift confession definite contrasts sharply with the terrifying circumstances in which he initially articulated it. Even under those conditions his impulse was to avoid a direct entreaty. First, he makes the circle of crosses, which becomes a rudimentary place of worship, and then justifies his request to God by the unavailability of any priest. The miraculous wall, though it illustrates strikingly the immediate efficacy of confession, has a darker aspect. For its growth is entirely dependent on the strength of the man's penitence. When his confession is finished, his fear drives him to make impossible promises on top of it, in a desperate attempt to keep his protection increasing. The insecurity of this roofless wall with a devil peering over it stands in stark contrast to the solidity of a real church. In bringing his improvised confession to a licensed confessor, he is following the standard pattern of moving from the miraculous and revelatory to the institutional and communal, and in this case the miraculous is

---

[32] Little, ed., *Liber exemplorum*, 52: "quod quasi impossibile esset quod ab aliquo implerentur."
[33] Little, ed., *Liber exemplorum*, 52: "Nunc ergo vides, Christiane, quante virtutis est contra dyabolum vera confessio facta sacerdoti, secundum ordinem ecclesie, ubi tantum valuit contra diabolum illa confessio quam in medio campo fecit Deo."
[34] It is worth noting that this exemplum places more importance on the sheer act of confessing than did most medieval theologians, who, following Peter Lombard, held that outward confession, although obligatory, was not in itself required to obtain remission of sins. Remission of sins was obtained by inward contrition. Confession was made in order to have satisfaction imposed by the confessor and to be reconciled to the Church. See Paul Anciaux, *La theologie du sacrement de penitence au XIIe siecle* (Louvain: 1949), 275–353, 491–600, 605–06.

quite clearly no more than the means to an institutional end. As this exemplum was presented to its audience, with the improvised confession bracketed by the standard one, it offered them, in the miracle of the wall, access to the awful immediacy of divine power, but under the control of a familiar procedure. The exemplum instills confession with a vital, spontaneous force at the same time it affirms the ritual's rigid formalization. As a result, the process of formalization retains all the vitality of the miraculous in its very formulation of rigid specifics.

In the second group of exempla, ritual retains this rigid specificity, even when it has to be modified. There are many exempla in which the protagonists have died without being shriven, or without fulfilling some other obligation. Rather than some special dispensation being made for them in Heaven, they are sent back to life to fulfill their obligation on earth. *The Alphabet of Tales* contains the story of a young girl sent back for four days at mass because while alive she had slept through service.[35] Variants concerning return for confession include both those in which protagonists are at fault, and those in which they are not. An instance of the former, again from *The Alphabet of Tales*, is the woman whom St. Francis allows to return to life to confess an unconfessed sin;[36] an instance of the latter is Jacques de Vitry's story of a man who, having made confession to the devil disguised as a priest, is allowed to return to confess to a real priest.[37] In all of these cases, divine preference for the temporal machinery of the Church as the means to divine ends asserts the absolute, eternal value of Church ritual. It presents Church ritual as a symbol without any distance from the thing it symbolizes, as a form whose outward manifestation is identical to the eternal reality it represents.

Indeed, the one aspect of these exempla that might potentially be a sign of weakness is in fact a decisive sign of strength. The miraculous return to life is an improvisation necessitated by the rigidity of the ritual, which leaves it, like any other temporal procedure, at the mercy of temporal circumstance. But the divine generosity that motivates the improvisation makes this potential weakness the measure of the ritual's eternal value. It endows the ritual with a flexibility equal to its constancy. The rigidity which signifies divine power is never allowed to become a weakness in the face of temporal

---

[35] Banks, ed., *Alphabet of Tales*, no. 363, 249–50.
[36] Banks, ed., *Alphabet of Tales*, no. 331, 229–31.
[37] Crane, ed., *Jacques de Vitry*, no. 303, 127.

change. Church ritual encompasses both stability and change, so that its authority can be invoked and supported from either direction.

Flexibility is even more crucial in the case of communion, because the host, unprepossessing as a material object, is particularly subject to mundane accident. A large group of exempla concern hosts that are dropped, misplaced, or otherwise misused. The misuse is subsequently revealed through a miraculous transformation of the host's material substance. In one such exemplum from the *Liber exemplorum*, a woman hides the wafer in her shawl and places it in a box. In the middle of the night the box begins to glow and when she opens it she discovers a piece of bleeding flesh. When she brings it the next morning to her priest he discovers impressed in the flesh the same letters normally impressed in the wafer of bread.[38] In a reversal as redemptive as it is ironic, the material weakness of the host becomes its strength. The ease with which the woman steals the wafer exposes its banality, the material inconsequences of its nominally miraculous embodiment of Christ. The subsequent changes demonstrate that this banality is continually undergirded by the same transformative power that brought it into being, a power characterized by the narrative's ending as specifically textual.

The host resists the illicit act of lay appropriation that is its theft by revealing in more material terms the reality it symbolizes. Deprived of the institutional setting which enables it to represent Christ's sacrifice symbolically, it literally reenacts that sacrifice by transforming itself into a piece of bleeding flesh. This transformation demonstrates the endless capacity of Christianity's master narrative to reappropriate – quite literally, to *redeem* any institutionalized reality, no matter how banal. The material force of this narrative, textual transformation, this reenactment of the Christian Word becoming flesh once again, drives the woman back to the very institutional authority she was attempting to appropriate. She returns to the priest, whose institutional control of the Host is confirmed by the reimpression of the letters – the textual signifiers by which the Church draws an otherwise banal piece of bread into its institutional discourse.

The flexibility of Church forms is generalized in a widely disseminated exemplum concerning a bad priest. In de Vitry's version, God sends a man who has refused to receive the sacraments

[38] Little, ed., *Liber exemplorum*, no. 10, 6–7.

from unworthy priests a dream in which he feels great thirst and sees a leper drawing clear water in a vessel with a golden rope. When he approaches, the leper draws back, asking, "How can you wish to take water from a leprous hand, who scorn to accept sacraments from bad priests?"[39] The exemplum defines the relation between the bad priest and the Church by recasting it in material terms. The analogy locates within the institutional structure of the Church a form of separation imaginable only between a social structure and the material world beyond it. Just as the water in the golden vessel has a value independent of and prior to the leper who dispenses it, now the sacraments acquire an independence from the rest of the institution that holds them in place. It is certainly worth pointing out the incongruity between this exemplum and the last. In the last a sacred form is deprived of value, albeit temporarily, by being stolen from the person institutionally sanctioned to dispense it. In this exemplum, a sacred form is assigned a value independent of the person dispensing it. The incongruity is possible because in both cases the integrity of the Church is never completely exhausted either by its forms or its personnel, but, if need be, can transcend them. Of course, that is only to say that the appropriation, or redemption of the material by the spiritual, of the flesh by the Word, is an infinitely repeatable process. At any point where it rests, it may begin again; at any point where a material object or human activity has been selected to receive sacred value a similar selection can be made again. The profane can be jettisoned anew and the sacred reasserted.

Several exempla assert this capacity in aggressive renunciations of pure formalism. One may cite two of this type from de Vitry. In the first devils send a letter to negligent prelates commending them for sending so many souls to Hell.[40] In another, Bernard, asked by some Parisian clerks to settle a disputation on an abstruse, theological point, replies by putting the condemnation of Original Sin in the form of a syllogism, implying of course that this is the only question worth considering.[41] Many exempla warn that the Devil knows theology and show him preaching or hearing confession. In a particularly grisly variation on this theme, the Devil assumes the form of a good angel and tricks a hermit into killing his own father.[42]

---

[39] Crane, ed., *Jacques de Vitry*, no. 155, 68.   [40] Crane, ed., *Jacques de Vitry*, no. 2, 1.
[41] Crane, ed., *Jacques de Vitry*, no. 32, 13.
[42] Crane, ed., *Jacques de Vitry*, no. 76, 34–5. Leopold Hervieux, *Les Fabulistes Latins*, vol. 4, *Eudes de Cheriton et ses derivés* (Paris: 1896), 299. Banks, ed., *Alphabet of Tales*, no. 223, 156.

The renunciations of formalism anticipate the third group of exempla concerning ritual, which assert the materiality of authentic sacral language. Among these are the exempla which present words spoken in Church as objects, or as if their crucial quality were the fullness and distinctness of their sounds. In one, a congregation of devils attempts to drown out psalm singing with their chatter.[43] In two others, a devil collects in a sack or records on parchment idle words spoken during service.[44] In a fourth, a priest returned from the grave reports that he has seen many clerics weighed down with bundles of all the words and syllables they had not clearly pronounced during psalms.[45] This desire to give language substance was thematized less often than the desire to render material substance linguistic, but it was just as essential to the tradition. These exempla which objectify language are, in a very specific sense, about themselves. They idealize in narrative terms the social process they themselves are a part of, that is, the bringing into being of certain forms of language and language-related behavior as conventional social practice. In the very process of being understood by a lay audience such exempla accomplished what they aspired to. Not only did they, like all sermon exempla, do real institutional work, they also laid down the conditions by which that work was to be understood, conditions without which it could not have been done in the first place. They made the sacred a social actuality by convincing their audience of the linguistic and textual basis on which its material superiority to the temporal was founded. In this exemplum the durability of the written word enables it to bear an analogy the spoken word cannot.

It happened in France that a certain clerk, when he wished to confess his sins, wept so abundantly in the presence of the priest that he could not speak. The priest said to him: "My son, write down your sins, and bring them to me." And when this one had written them down and the priest had read them, he said "I want to take counsel with my superior." Opening the paper in the presence of the bishop, he found nothing but an empty sheet, and returning to the clerk, said, "Take heart, my son, your sins are forgiven you. Behold, your paper is found blank and everything is erased."[46]

---

[43] Banks, ed., *Alphabet of Tales*, no. 254, 178.

[44] Crane, ed., *Jacques de Vitry*, nos. 19 and 239, 6, 100.

[45] Lecoy de la Marche, ed., *Étienne de Bourbon*, no. 212, 184–85.

[46] Crane, ed., *Jacques de Vitry*, no. 301, 126: "Contigit in Francia quod quidam clericus, cum vellet peccata confiteri, ita copiose flebat coram sacerdote quod non poterat loqui. Cui sacerdos ait: 'Fili, scribe peccata tua et affer mihi.' Cumque ille scripsisset et sacerdos legisset ait: 'Volo habere consilium cum meo superiori.' Aperta autem carta coram

The effacement of written words from the paper serves as a material sign for the intangible process of absolution. The symbolic effacement also assigns a durability to actions which ordinarily they lack, belonging to the same transitory sphere as speech. They become identical to the written words which describe them. They, too, are symbolic, signifying evil, and they have the same distinct, unchanging identity. Once they are recounted in the proper forum, that is, to a priest in confession, they cease to exist as action, and they have become entirely superseded by the now sanctified language which describes them.

This is very much the ideal confession, and the miraculous effacement affirms the immediacy of absolution to this penitent so overcome with remorse he cannot speak. What is interesting to note is that this immediacy is nonetheless already entirely institutionalized. The tears begin in the presence of the priest, who seems to serve as a catalyst to bring the young man in touch with his own emotions. The supersession of the temporal by the sacred which concludes the exemplum in fact begins at the start. The superior presence of sacred language is simply part of the superior presence of the Church, which this exemplum affirms as the others have done.

Perhaps the most striking of the exempla concerning Church language are those in which it is degraded to the level of the charm. The following is from the *Tabula exemplorum*, a late thirteenth-century collection.

A visitor tells of a devil who told a certain holy man that there was a certain word in the Gospel which devils much feared. When the man asked him what it was, he did not want to tell. The man proposed many passages (*auctoritates*) from the Gospel, but was told none were it until at length he asked about this word, "The word made flesh," and the devil, who could not bear hearing it, cried aloud and vanished.[47]

The exemplum identifies a center, which, in the very act of demonstrating its centrality, moves off-center. The center is the Word, whose capacity to redeem the flesh so terrifies the devil he

episcopo, nil nisi cartam vacuam invenit, et reversus ad clericum, ait: 'Confide, fili, dimissa sunt peccata tua tibi, ecce carta tua vacua et omnia deleta inveni.'"

47 J. Th. Welter, ed., *La Tabula exemplorum secundum ordinem alphabeti* (Paris and Toulouse: 1926) no. 65, 20–21: "... narravit visitator de alio dyabolo qui dixit cuidam viro sancto quod erat quoddam verbum in evangelio, quod multum formidabant dyaboli. Et cum quereret ab illo quid erat, noluit sibe dicere et cum multas auctoritates de evangelio proponeret et ille diceret quod non erat illud, tandem cum quereret de illo verbo: 'Verbum caro factum,' non valens audire, clamans dyabolus disparuit."

cannot bear to hear it mentioned. And yet it is the specific fact of its being mentioned which produces the effect, rather than simply its existence, which, after all, is constant. By articulating the phrase "Word made Flesh" the holy man extends the supersession of evil by good which the act that the phrase denotes initiated, and the extension is formally identical to the original, since the original act is itself an articulation. Yet despite the formal identity, the result is different, and necessarily so. The exemplum, perilously but necessarily close to folk magic, focuses entirely on the formula's efficacy as a charm, rather than its significance as a central tenet of Christian doctrine. If that significance is clearly embedded in the tale, the lay audience is nonetheless expected to accept the charm at face value. Through this acceptance a form of folk magic would be appropriated by the Church without losing any of its magical resonance. The double status of "Word made Flesh" as charm and doctrine assigns the same essence to differing effects and insures that change bears the mark of sacral discourse. The vast distance between the two effects, the Incarnation and the charm, in fact facilitates new assertions of church prerogative. Once the identity between the two has been established, the triviality of the new imitation does not lessen its fidelity to its model.

While I would hardly argue this exemplum reveals the essence of the sermon tradition's appropriative logic, it is useful as an indication of the extent to which that logic could reach. On the one hand, the exemplum comes close to taking the Lord's name in vain, offering Christianity's central tenet as fodder for folk magic, a desacralization Christian discourse otherwise describes as blasphemous. On the other, this apparent desacralization is understood at every point as demonstrating Christianity's inexorable authority. As this instance shows, the contribution that the sermon exemplum tradition made to that authority was indefinite, uncertain, and potentially destabilizing. But for that very reason it also helped make Christian authority flexible and durable. The sermon exemplum was an important means of solidifying the ideological hegemony among the laity on the laity's own terms. From the sermon, the form spread into other clerical genres addressing the laity, most notably penitential manuals like Robert Mannyng's *Handlyng Synne*.[48] Gower and Chaucer tend to give the genre a clerical source: for Gower, the priest Genius; for

---

[48] Robert Mannyng of Brunne, *Handlyng Synne*, ed. Idelle Sullens (Binghamton: Medieval and Renaissance Texts and Studies, 1983).

Chaucer, a number of clerical speakers from the Summoner to the Monk and the Nun's Priest. The discursive concession which the narrative form of the exemplum makes to the laity, and which accounted for its ideological power, will also make it the ideal means for the vernacular appropriation of clerical authority.

CHAPTER 5

The public exemplum

The public exemplum played a crucial role in the Chaucerian adaptation of the form, one that has been largely neglected. Three central characteristics of the public exemplum distinguish it from the sermon exemplum, and the Chaucerian exemplum will draw on all three. First, the public exemplum addresses issues of lay authority. It is classicizing and political where the sermon is hagiographical and ecclesiological. For this reason the public exemplum is usually described as the classical exemplum. I have adopted the term *public* because not all of these exempla came from classical sources, including many of the most influential, such as the Donation of Constantine. Moreover, these exempla did not simply reiterate the classical, even when they did draw on classical tradition. Like its classical antecedent, the medieval public exemplum was concerned with *rei publicae*, public matters, but these were its own, contemporary public matters, not the civic virtues of some timeless *humanitas*.

Second, the public exemplum had a propensity toward the evil example, toward narratives which demonstrate the efficacy of their *sententiae* by enacting violations of them. The sermon exemplum, with its continual recourse to the miraculous tends in the other direction, toward the benevolent example, the narrative which fulfills its *sententia*, revealing it as narrative result. This rhetorical propensity of the public exemplum is simultaneously thematic, an insistence on the inherent disorder of the historical world it addresses. This insistence reaches its greatest intensity in the *De casibus* tradition – an offshoot, as I will argue, of the *Fürstenspiegel* – where human history is starkly depicted as an incessant and unerring engine of downfall. But it also characterizes the public exemplum generally. The source of authority which the public exemplum counterposes to history's inherent anarchy constitutes its third distinguishing characteristic. This source of authority is the monarch.

The development of the public exemplum is intertwined with the *Fürstenspiegel*, or Mirrors of Princes, the genre dealing with the moral instruction of princes, which originated in the early ninth century at the Carolingian court. To be sure, the two forms are by no means identical. The *Fürstenspiegel* were always more than exemplum collections. In fact, many used the exemplum only sparingly, and public exempla certainly occurred in other contexts as well. Nevertheless, the exemplum was an important rhetorical resource for the *Fürstenspiegel*. John of Salisbury's *Policraticus*, probably the most influential work in the entire tradition, was also the single most important source of public exempla in the later Middle Ages.[1] Moreover, the logic of exemplarity was written into the general rhetorical stance of the *Fürstenspiegel* as an essential condition of the genre, irrespective of the extent to which individual *Fürstenspiegel* availed themselves of the exemplum as an expository strategy.

Addressed to the prince, the *Fürstenspiegel* assumes the audience of the court. The ideal Christian prince which it holds out to this audience is an exemplary figure, concretizing in a single subject-position the moral values the audience shares. The construction of this ideal is a dynamic, paradoxical process, for the genre presents the prince not only as the exemplary source of moral order, but also as a figure in need of communal instruction. The contradiction is managed in the first instance by embodying the Prince's instruction in the voice of the Church. Until very late, *Fürstenspiegel* were always the products of clerics, who typically staged their general moral instruction as specific advice given to the prince who patronized the work. In this way, the *Fürstenspiegel* preserves the Prince's superiority to the community at large. But this maneuver does not dissipate the contradictory nature of the genre so much as it directs the contradiction more explicitly at the prince's exemplary status. For the ideal of the Christian prince is itself inherently contradictory – Christian authority defines itself as antithetical to earthly power, and yet the ideal Christian prince would be a supreme earthly power whose every act is invested with the Divine Will. Yet – and this is the crucial point – the ideological value of this ideal lies precisely in its contradiction. The *Fürstenspiegel* presents this impossible ideal as not only desirable but possible, as entirely within the reach of any monarch who adhered to its prescriptions. By simply asserting that

[1] Wilhelm Berges, *Die Fürstenspiegel des hohen and späten Mittelalters* (Stuttgart: Hiersemann Verlag, 1938), 291–92.

the ideal Christian prince is possible, the *Fürstenspiegel* invests secular monarchy with divine authority, an ideological prospect attractive to king and cleric alike. This is a possibility that is produced rhetorically, and in fact involves a double appropriation. The *Fürstenspiegel* appropriates the social position of the prince, then concretizes within it the source of moral order. But this concretization is still only a possibility; it cannot become actual until the prince adopts the identity the text has produced for him, that is to say, until he reappropriates the social position that has been appropriated from him. Both appropriations are made necessary by the very antithesis at the center of the ideal they produce. In order to propose the ideal of the Christian prince, the text has to overcome the moral anarchy of temporal existence and find within it a source of order; once that source has been defined in the prince, the prince must overcome his own sinful nature to make the ideal actual.

The antithetical nature of this ideal also insured that the very real conflicts between Church and prince, which occurred in the world outside the *Fürstenspiegel*, would not diminish their ideological complicity within it. But even in the outside world these conflicts were not entirely antithetical. Ideological disputes between royal courts and ecclesiastical primates were disputes that took place within the ruling class; very rarely did they lessen ruling class hegemony over the rest of society. For instance, few such disputes were as spectacular or as cataclysmic as Henry II's conflict with Becket; yet that conflict had very little effect on the growing institutional and juridical power the English crown acquired during his reign.[2] Indeed, to the extent these disputes clarified the boundaries of each party's sphere of influence, they strengthened ruling class hegemony, by allowing it to operate that much more smoothly. Therefore it is inaccurate, perhaps even naive to view these disputes as motivated primarily by a desire for sanctity on the side of the church, or republican sovereignty on the side of the court. They were motivated by a common desire for power – the hegemonic power of the ruling class which the two parties shared and over which each wanted to increase their own control.

This study brings to the *Fürstenspiegel* concerns substantially different from those subfields of intellectual history to whose province the genre usually falls. If the exemplarity of the *Fürstenspiegel* has to

---

[2] W. L. Warren, *Henry II* (London: Eyre Methuen, 1973), esp. 362–96 and 518–55.

this point gone unnoticed, that is because historians of medieval political thought neglect two related aspects of the texts they study – two aspects which, while distinct, tend to converge. The first is the rhetorical specificity of a given text or tradition. The second is the relation between such texts or traditions and the power dynamics of the social formation which produced them. These two aspects converge because they represent the two sides of a text's ideological status. To the extent a text is ideologically enabling, it participates in power relations. Yet it can participate in such relations only textually, that is, by virtue of its discrete rhetorical strategies.

Accounts of the *Fürstenspiegel* have ignored its rhetoric because, in accordance with the general tendency of the field, they have been less interested in its immediate historical and political significance, and much more interested in the degree to which the ideas it expressed anticipated modern constitutional thought. This tendency gives the entire field a teleological character, in which the meaning of a particular utterance is determined less by its significance to its immediate audience and more by its contribution to the ultimate emergence of the constitutional state. The development of medieval traditions of political writing becomes an exclusively intellectual drama in which the only actors are ideas, and in which the primary motivation is the purely ratiocinative desire for ever clearer solutions to logical dilemmas. The metanarrative which informs this teleology is a familiar one: it is an inflection of the medieval/humanist dichotomy. In this case the dividing line is the rediscovery of Aristotle, which enables medieval thinkers, led by the heroic intervention of Aquinas, to move away from hierocratic notions of polity, based on Augustinian assumptions, toward secular, human-centered ones. Like the more general shift from medieval theocentrism to Renaissance humanism, this shift is characteristically presented as a liberation: in Walter Ullmann's terms, a lay, egalitarian "ascending" order displaces an ecclesiastical, hierarchical "descending" one.[3] This liberation is frequently described in unabashedly teleological terms. Michael Wilks, for instance, concludes what is still the standard work on medieval ideas of sovereignty by terming the shift as one from the "Age of Faith" to the "Age of Reason."[4]

---

[3] Walter Ullmann, *Principles of Government and Politics in the Middle Ages* (London: Methuen & Co., 1961), 19–26 and *passim*.
[4] M. J. Wilks, *The Problem of Sovereignty in the Later Middle Ages* (Cambridge: Cambridge University Press, 1963), 529.

I have no quarrel with this metanarrative in its largest outlines. The rediscovery of Aristotle was obviously a crucial change, nor is there any point in minimizing the originality and power of Aquinas.[5] What should be questioned in this view, however, is the complacent sense of progress that undergirds it. It is hardly the case that Aquinas jettisons Augustine; what is presented as a liberating Aristotelian break could just as plausibly be presented as an Aristotelian redefinition. In any case the break has proven notoriously difficult to define. In practice, it has not been possible to find "hierocratic" thinkers without some crucial element of egalitarianism, nor to find "egalitarian" thinkers that do not at some point make some deference to the Church. As Wilks himself concedes, "at times the extreme papalist becomes almost indistinguishable from his most savage lay opponent."[6] It is true that even this problem can be solved in teleological terms. The confusion can be explained away simply by invoking the premodernism of all involved. Under this view, even the most "progressive" of medieval political thinkers retain retrogressive ideas, because even they have not quite arrived at the ultimate resting place that the modern "Age of Reason" will provide.

Nevertheless, it seems more reasonable to conclude that when medieval political thought embraced contradictory ideals, it did so because it valued both poles of the contradiction, not because it was striving toward some modern constitutional synthesis it had not yet found. This is particularly so when one considers that modern political thought is hardly free of contradiction, the assumptions of constitutional history notwithstanding. (One thinks, for example, of the tension between the individual and the state, the inevitability of which is an article of faith to most modern liberalism.) If we view medieval political thought as not simply a matter of ideas, but also of ideology, the contradictions can be made functional and historically specific.

As I have already suggested, in their largest outlines the ideological struggles between Church and Crown are intra-class struggles, interests within a hegemonic bloc competing for a larger share of the common interest which holds the bloc together. These struggles were real enough, but so was the vast superiority of power over the rest of

---

[5] For a concise version of the standard view, see R. A. Markus, "Two Conceptions of Political Authority: Augustine, *De Civitate Dei*, XIX, 14–15, and Some Thirteenth Century Interpretations," *The Journal of Theological History*, n.s. 16 (1965), 68–100.

[6] Wilks, *Sovereignty*, viii.

the populace which the ecclesiastical hierarchy and princely courts shared. This superiority must always be kept in mind, for it protects us from a simple binary opposition, in which hierarchy is seen as entirely on the side of the Church, and the striving for equality all on the side of the laity. As I have been arguing throughout, the Church could be hierarchical only because it was also at some level egalitarian; the nature of its commitment to hierarchy depended on how this egalitarian tendency was to be defined. Accordingly, the struggle between Church and Crown might more fruitfully be viewed as a struggle over the specific balance to be struck between hierarchy and equality, with both sides committed to different versions of both poles.

The distinctively medieval tradition concerning royal sovereignty began with Carolingian notions of sacerdotal kingship, notions which the Church quite literally produced for the Crown.[7] Although these notions are quite heavily modified as the tradition develops, they never entirely disappear. The post-Aristotelian Thomas Hoccleve can still assert the king "by wey of his office / To god I-likned is."[8] The tradition is dominated by clerics until the fourteenth century, with the result that lay spokesmen are engaging concepts thoroughly shaped by clerical thinking. This should not be surprising if we see the clerical tradition as one part of the ruling class producing conceptions of power for the other. There is no doubt this process involved an ecclesiastical appropriation of major proportions, as clerics invested pre-existent lay political forms with sacral and ecclesiological significance. There is no doubt as well that their self-awareness of their role in this redefinition led them to stress their own prominence, many of them going so far as to argue with John of Salisbury, "that the Prince is the Minister of the Priests and inferior to them" (IV, iii). But there should also be no doubt that this sacralization served the interests of lay princes as well, which is why they permitted it to happen. The laicization of the later period should therefore be seen, at least in part, as a reappropriation rather than a simple act of resistance, as the growing power of royal courts enabled them to take fuller control of the legitimating functions that had earlier been provided by the Church.

[7] Walter Ullmann, *The Carolingian Renaissance and the Idea of Kingship* (London: Methuen and Co., 1969), esp. 43–110.

[8] Thomas Hoccleve, *The Regement of Princes*, ed. Frederick J. Furnivall (London: Early English Text Society, 1897), 87, lines 2409–10. All subsequent citations are from this edition. Line numbers will be given in the text.

From this perspective even the shift from Augustine to Aristotle ceases to be entirely antithetical. The Aristotelian premise that humanity is naturally political does not of necessity exclude the Augustinian premise that coercive government is the only source of order possible in a fallen world. On the contrary, Aquinas and the thinkers who followed him used the Aristotelian premise to restate and expand the indirect affirmation implicit in the Augustinian position, the affirmation that existing political structures are God-given. For they certainly viewed the "naturalness" of human political structures to be a God-given one. In this way, the Aristotelianism which underwrites the laicization of later medieval sovereignty can be viewed, albeit paradoxically, as a final refinement of the sacralization with which the medieval tradition began.

In this paradoxical process, the *Fürstenspiegel* played a formative role. Its exemplary logic enabled it to balance the singularity of the princely ideal against the ideal's collectivity. The genre's strength consisted precisely of its rhetorical capacity to hold these contradictory tendencies in suspension. Modern scholarship's neglect of this rhetorical power is evident in the very term it uses to describe the genre. The metaphor of reflection fits perfectly the modern view of the genre as static compendia of already accepted moral ideas. Nevertheless, the metaphor of the mirror is by no means typical of the medieval works to which it is applied. Medieval *Fürstenspiegel* were rarely entitled *Speculum principum*. Much more typically their titles involved the notion of ruling or governing: *Policraticus*, *De regno*, or *De regimine principum*, the title of more than half a dozen. I retain the term *Fürstenspiegel* for convenience, but it is important to remember that the genre is neither as static nor as rigidly delimited as modern accounts would have it. Rather it is part of a larger ideological process whereby the figure of the prince becomes the autonomous focus of lay authority. In the remainder of this chapter I will sketch out the genre's role in that process. I will focus first on the two most important *Fürstenspiegel* of the later Middle Ages, John of Salisbury's *Policraticus*, and Aegidius Romanus's *De regimine principum*. Then I will look briefly at the lay appropriation of its exemplary logic in the emergence of the *De casibus* tradition.

JOHN OF SALISBURY: *POLICRATICUS*

There is no more telling instance than the *Policraticus* of the importance to medieval political thinking of rhetoric in general and the exemplum in particular. The most influential *Fürstenspiegel* of the later Middle Ages, it was also one of the period's most widely circulated exemplum collections. The exemplum provides its characteristic mode of exposition, and as I shall argue, the narrative logic that underlies the work's larger political stance. The analysis that follows will concentrate on John's characterization of the form's political parameters, and his use of exemplarity as a larger narrative logic.[9]

The *Policraticus*, subtitled *De nugis curialium et de vestigiis philosophorum* is dedicated to Thomas Becket. It was finished in 1159, while Becket was still Henry's chancellor, and John was personal secretary to Theobald, Becket's predecessor as Archbishop of Canterbury.[10] The dedication takes the form of a verse epistle entitled *Entheticus*, which opens the work. It presents Becket as a source of Christian order in the chaos of court. He is "The jewel of clerics, glory of the English / Race, the right hand of the king, and pattern / Of all good," whose function is "to cancel regal laws / That are unjust, and carry out the just / Commands of the prince who loves his country well."[11] The work is in eight books. The first three address the *nugae curialium*, satirizing the moral triviality of contemporary life at court, and

---

[9] For a comprehensive treatment of the exempla in the *Policraticus*, see Peter Van Moos's excellent study "The Use of *Exempla* in the *Policraticus* of John of Salisbury," in *The World of John of Salisbury*, ed. Michael Wilks (Oxford: Basil Blackwell, 1984), 207–61, and his recent book, *Geschicte als Topik: das rhetorische Exemplum von der Antike zur Neuzeit und die historiae im "Policraticus" Johanns von Salisbury* (Hildesheim, New York: G. Olds, 1988).

[10] For John's biography, see Christopher Brooke, "John of Salisbury and His World," in *The World of John of Salisbury*, ed. Wilks, 1–20; Hans Liebeschutz, *Mediaeval Humanism in the Life and Writings of John of Salisbury* (London: The Warburg Institute, 1950), 3–4, 8–22; and Beryl Smalley, *The Becket Conflict and the Schools* (Oxford: Basil Blackwell, 1973), 87–108.

[11] *Ioannis Saresberiensis episcopi carnotensis policratici sive de nugis curialium et vestigiis philosphorum libri VIII*, 2 vols., ed Clement C. J. Webb (Oxford: Clarendon Press, 1909), *Entheticus*: "lux cleri, gloria gentis / Anglorum, regis dextera, forma boni / ... Hic est qui regni leges cancellat iniquas / Et mandata pii principis aequa facit" (*Entheticus* vol. 1, 2). All subsequent citations are from this edition and will be given as book number, chapter number, volume number, and page number, either in the text or in the notes. The translation is from *Frivolities of Courtiers and Footprints of Philosophers*, tr. Joseph B. Pike (Minneapolis: University of Minnesota Press, 1938), 416. This is one of two partial translations of the *Policraticus*. The other is *The Statesman's Book*, tr. with an introduction by John Dickinson (New York: Russell and Russell, 1963). *The Statesman's Book* translates the central section of the work, Books IV–VI. *Frivolities of Courtiers* translates the rest. All subsequent translations are from these two works. Citations will be given as page numbers in the text.

concentrating on activities like hunting and gambling that would be more typical of lay courtiers than clerical ones. The next three, containing, in Liebeschutz's words, "most of what we may call John's political programme," advance and justify his primary claim that the prince is the minister of the priests and inferior to them.[12] The last two concern the *vestiges philosophorum* directly. After a survey of the schools of classical philosophy, John advocates the stoicism of Cicero and Boethius as more conducive to the life clerics face at court than the philosophy of Epicurus. He focuses throughout the work on the clergy as a vital organizing presence at court, transforming its chaotic power into moral order.

Such transformative power necessarily characterizes his own discourse as well, as court moralist and exemplarist. This is an essentially rhetorical aspect of the *Policraticus*, which intellectual historians have generally ignored. They have been more concerned to determine whether John should be considered hierocratic or humanist.[13] This debate is potentially endless, for both sides view these terms as distinct essences, rather than as competing tendencies which John deploys his rhetorical stance to reconcile. John is clearly hierocratic to the extent he sees the king as subordinate to the clergy. But he is also "humanist" to the extent he sees the king as subject to law. The point is that John's hierocratism is itself corporate and discursive, and his humanism is entirely Christian. The law the king obeys is divine in origin, and his subordination to the clergy is a subordination to the counsel of those whose function is to interpret that law. Their superiority to him is a specifically discursive and linguistic one. This contiguity between John's hierocratism and his humanism exposes the inadequacy of the usual view of humanism as a liberating, quasi-democratic reaction to the hierarchic excesses of the Church. John's insistence on the superiority of the clergy is an insistence on the essentially rhetorical foundations of royal power. This emphasis will pass over into the royalism of later secular writers, and it will pass over to them in large part through the exemplum.

---

[12] Liebeschutz, *John of Salisbury*, 23.

[13] The case for John as humanist was first put forward in comprehensive form by Liebeschutz, and authoritatively seconded by R. W. Southern in *Medieval Humanism* (Oxford: Basil Blackwell, 1970), 60–132. It has been largely accepted by most scholars, with two important dissenters. Walter Ullmann describes John as hierocratic in *Papal Government*, 420–26, and Beryl Smalley in *The Becket Conflict* while conceding that "John was a 'humanist' in the strict sense of being a student of 'the humanities'" (87), concludes that he was also "papalist, anti-imperialist, high church" (108).

As John's chief polemical tool, the exemplum both enforces this emphasis on the essentially rhetorical foundations of secular power and justifies it. His exempla draw on the Old Testament and the classical past in order to demonstrate that a moral order is possible in human history even in its unregenerate state. At the same time, it is only through John's Christianity that he is able to assign this order its true meaning. The nature of this order is retrospective: it inheres as much in the Christian discourse which recovers the exemplary act as it does in the act itself. In this way John offers to the court both proof that moral order can be produced within history and the rhetorical means for doing so.

John stresses the appropriating and productive power of the exemplum in a number of ways. In the prologue, he makes it clear that this power begins with the exemplum's textuality, its status as *dicta*:

The pleasure of letters, agreeable in many respects, is especially so for the reason that all inconvenience due to interval of time or space is banished, friends are brought into the presence of one another, and matters worth knowing do not remain unknown because of their separation. For arts as well had inevitably perished, law disappeared, fidelity and religion itself crumbled, and even the proper use of language had been lost, had not divine commiseration, to offset human frailty, provided mortals with the knowlege of letters.

The experience of our ancestors [*exempla maiorum*], ever incentives and aids to virtue, would never have inspired or saved a single soul, had not the loyalty, zeal, and diligence of writers triumphing over sloth transmitted them to posterity. (6)

Iocundissimus cum in multis, tum in eo maxime est litterarum fructus, quod omnium interstitiorum loci et temporis exclusa molestia, amicorum sibi invicem praesentiam exhibent, et res scitu dignas situ aboleri non patiuntur. Nam et artes perierant, evanuerant iura, fidei et totius religionis officia quaeque corruerant, ipseque recti defecerat usus eloquii, nisi in remedium infirmitatis humanae litterarum usum mortalibus divina miseratio procurasset. Exempla maiorum, quae sunt incitamenta et fomenta virtutis, nullum omnino erigerent aut servarent, nisi pia sollicitudo scriptorum et triumphatrix inertiae diligentia eadem ad posteros transmisisset. (Prol., 1, 12)

The textual enables space and time to be easily surmounted. If the *exempla maiorum* incite and aid virtue in the present, it is the present's access to the textual that enables it to be incited. This textual power the present holds over the very past which authorizes it becomes even more pronounced by the prologue's end. In discussing his use of previous authorities, John declares that not everything he says will be true. He then continues:

Since I have begun to reveal my mental secrets, I shall expose my presumption more fully. All whom I meet who are in word or deed philosophers, I deem my retainers. What is more, I claim them as my slaves, to such an extent that they in their complete subservience are to offer themselves as bulwarks in my defense against the tongues of my traducers. Yes and these I cite as my authorities. (16)

Et quia semel coepi revelare mentis archana, arrogantiam meam plenius denudabo. Omnes ergo qui michi in verbo aut opere philosophantes occurrunt, meos clientes esse arbitror, et quod maius est, michi vendico in servitutem; adeo quidem ut in traditionibus suis seipsos pro me linguis obiciant detractorum. Nam et illos laudo auctores. (Prol., 1, 16)

The attitude toward past authority in this remarkable passage is overtly, even blatantly, appropriative. Where the figure of dwarves on the shoulders of giants which John assigns to his teacher Abelard is modulated and ambiguous in its assertion of the discursive power of the present, this passage is bluntly aggressive.[14] The dependence of past exemplary acts, past *facta*, on the power of letters means not only that the present controls the past, but that one voice in the present can use that control against another. Citing authority becomes a tactical as well as constitutive act: one lays claim to the past in order to achieve an advantage in the present. As I have been arguing throughout this study, past authority's dependence on the present is an essential condition of classical and medieval notions of the term. However, this condition is rarely, if ever, expressed so baldly. For John the dependence is so complete that he hints he will not only appropriate past authorities but he will also invent imaginary ones (*auctores fictos*, I, Prol., 1, 17) if necessary.

In the middle section of the work, John proves as good as his word. He presents Book V as drawn from the *Institutio Trajani*, a work he claims was written by Plutarch for the moral instruction of Trajan. After a painstaking and thorough review of John's use of his sources, Janet Martin has concluded, to the satisfaction of most scholars, that the existence of this work is entirely John's invention.[15] What makes

---

[14] See above, 38.
[15] Martin, "John of Salisbury as Classical Scholar," in *World of John of Salisbury*, 179–201; and "John of Salisbury and the Classics," (unpub. Ph.D. diss., Harvard University, 1968). Both Max Kerner, "Zur Entstehungsgeschichte der *Institutio Traiani*," *Deutsches Archiv* 32 (1976), 558–71; and "Randbemerkungen zur *Institutio Traiani*," in *World of John of Salisbury*,

the invention particularly striking is that John assigns to Plutarch the same hierocratic argument that he makes throughout this section.

A commonwealth, according to Plutarch, is a certain body which is embodied with life by the benefit of divine favor, which acts at the prompting of the highest equity, and is ruled by what may be called the moderating power of reason. Those things which establish and implant in us the practice of religion, and transmit to us the worship of God (here I do not follow Plutarch who says "of the gods") fill the place of the soul in the body of the commonwealth. And therefore those who preside over the practice of religion should be looked up to and venerated as the soul of the body... Furthermore, since the soul is, as it were, the prince of the body, and has the rulership over the whole thereof, so those whom our author calls the prefects of religion preside over the entire body. (64)

Est autem res publica, sicut Plutarco placet, corpus quoddam quod divini muneris beneficio animatur et summae aequitatis agitur nutu et regitur quodam moderamine rationis. Ea vero quae cultum religionis in nobis instituunt et informant et Dei (ne secundum Plutarcum deorum dicam) cerimonias tradunt, vicem animae in corpore rei publicae obtinent. Illos vero, qui religionis cultui praesunt, quasi animam corporis suspicere et venerari oportet ... Porro, sicut anima totius habet corporis principatum, ita et hii, quos ille religionis praefectos vocat, toti corpori praesunt. (V, ii, 1, 282)

This passage marks the beginning of John's elaboration of the corporate fiction, about which I will say more presently. For the moment, I want to stress the pre-eminence he gives to the "prefects of religion." Despite his ostentatious correction of Plutarch ("God" instead of "gods"), this position is obviously much more medieval than antique. Martin suggests John probably intended his invention of this work as a sophisticated joke to appeal to the most learned portion of his clerical audience.[16] If so, this passage gives the joke a serious edge as well. Manufacturing an antique authority to buttress hierocratic claims was quite consistent with the Church's general strategy in its ideological assault on lay political power. What John has done here is a more localized version of the sort of ideologically-driven textual invention that produced the Donation of Constantine,

203–06; and Walter Ullmann, "John of Salisbury's *Policraticus* in the Later Middle Ages," in *Geschichtsschreibung und Geistiges Leben im Mittelalter: Festschrift für Heinz Löwe zum 65. Geburstag*, ed. Karl Hauck and Hubert Mordek (Cologne and Vienna: Böhlan Verlag, 1978), 522n, have rejected Martin's claim. But they object largely on impressionistic grounds, arguing that inventing sources would have gone against John's moral commitments. They offer no hard evidence to counter Martin's case.

16　Martin, "John of Salisbury," 196.

a story John cites elsewhere.[17] In putting his claims for the superiority of religious prefects over lay rulers in the voice of Plutarch, John has followed the polemical procedure he promised in the prologue. He has invented an authority in the past to gain an advantage in the present.

His exempla are mobilized toward the same end. He occasionally refers to his exempla as "strategems" (*strategemma, strategemmaticum*), a term he borrows from the late Roman exemplarist Frontinus.[18] Like the sermon exemplarist, he deploys his exempla with the ultimate goal of convincing a lay audience to accept the institutional authority of the Church. This goal is ultimately what grounds his appropriative stance. In the third chapter of Book IV he provides a justification for his polemical use of the exemplum which is less playful in its approach to authority than the passages I have just discussed, and which connects the exemplum both to preaching and to Christ.

Book IV concerns the Prince's relation to the law. The third chapter introduces the central claim that "the prince is the minister of the priests and inferior to them." Its first exemplum is the Donation of Constantine. After some further instances of monarchical self-sacrifice from Old Testament and post-Christian antique sources, John cites two pagan kings, Codrus and Lycurgus. Then he appeals to the example of Paul:

These examples I employ the more willingly because I find that the Apostle Paul also used them in preaching to the Athenians. That excellent preacher sought to win entrance for Jesus Christ and Him crucified into their minds by showing them by the example of many gentiles that deliverance had come through the ignominy of a cross. And he argued that this was not wont to happen save by the blood of just men and of those who bear the magistracy of a people. (12–13)

His quidem exemplis eo libentius utor, quod apostolum Paulum eisdem usum, dum Atheniensibus praedicaret, invenio. Studuit praedicator egregius Iesum Christum et hunc crucifixum sic mentibus eorum ingerere, ut per ignominiam crucis liberationem multorum exemplo gentilium provenisse doceret. Sed et ista persuasit fieri non solere nisi in sanguine iustorum et eorum qui populi gererent magistratum. (IV, iii, 1, 242–43)

[17] The Donation of Constantine comes from an eighth-century papal forgery which claimed Constantine had given the empire to Pope Sylvester after his conversion, and that Sylvester granted back to him the use of the imperial *temporalia*, to be exercised in the Church's name. The papacy used the document to support its creation of the Holy Roman Empire, and its superiority of lay princes generally. See Ullmann, *Papal Government*, 58–86.

[18] E.g., V,7, 1, 307; VIII,14, 2, 334. Cf. Van Moos, "*Exempla* in the *Policraticus*," 227–28.

Having identified self-sacrifice with *magistratum*, Paul then declared there is only one such authority to deliver all nations, "the Son of the all-powerful Father," who "holds sway over all nations and all lands" (13).[19] As John continues his summary, he focuses on Paul's exploitation of the rhetorical power of narrative. Paul uses narrative as an ideological given, a language immediately accessible to his audience, which he then translates into the language of Christian doctrine.

While he preached in this manner the ignominy of the cross to the end that the folly of the gentiles might gradually be removed, he little by little bore upward the word of faith and the tongue of his preaching till it rose to the word of God, and God's wisdom, and finally to the very throne of the divine majesty, and then, lest the virtue of the gospel, because it has revealed itself under the infirmity of the flesh, might be held cheap by the obstinacy of the Jews and the folly of the gentiles he explained the works of the Crucified One, which were further confirmed by the testimony of fame; since it was agreed among all that they could be done by none save God. But since fame frequently speaks untruth on opposite sides, fame itself was confirmed by the fact that his disciples were doing marvellous works; for at the shadow of a disciple those who were sick of any infirmity were healed. Why should I continue? The subtlety of Aristotle, the refinements of Crisippus, the snares of all the philosophers He confuted by rising from the dead. (13)

Dum ergo sic crucis ignominiam praedicaret, ut gentium paulatim evacuaretur stultitia, sensim ad Dei verbum Deique sapientiam et ipsum etiam divinae maiestatis solium, verbum fidei et linguam praedicationis evexit et, ne virtus Evangelii sub carnis infirmitate vilesceret a scandalo Iudeorum gentiumque stultitia, opera Crucifixi, quae etiam famae testimonio roborabantur, exposuit; cum apud omnes constaret quod ea non posset facere nisi Deus. Sed quia multa in utramque partem crebro fama mentitur, ipsam iuvabat famam, quod discipuli illius maiora faciebant, dum ad umbram discipuli a quacumque infirmitate sanabantur aegroti. Quid multa? Astutias Aristotilis, Crisippi acumina, omniumque philosophorum tendiculas resurgens mortuus confutabat. (IV,iii, 1, 243)

What John traces here is a series of three narrative appropriations or displacements, in which each appropriating voice progressively gives way to one which is more authoritative. John's appropriation of the classical tradition for the purpose of instructing the royal court gives way to Paul's similar appropriation for the purpose of

[19] 243: "Porro ad liberationem omnium, scilicet Iudeorum et gentium, nemo sufficiens potuit inveniri, nisi ille, cui in hereditatem datae sunt gentes, et praefinita est omnis terra possessio eius. Hunc autem alium esse non posse quam Filium omnipotentis Dei asseruit, cum praeter Deum gentes et terras omnes nemo subegerit."

converting the Athenians, which itself gives way to Christ's appropriation of human history to confute Aristotle and the rest of pagan philosophy. The crucial point, however, is that what moves this series forward is not the simple progression of authority but the very moment of appropriation, the moment when each authoritative voice emerges out of the narrative common ground.

The narrative convinces both as *dicta* and as *facta*, that is, both as authoritative utterance and as incontrovertible event. Indeed, in this series authority convinces by acquiring the incontrovertible status of an event, by becoming a fact beyond the power of language to change or withstand. The self-sacrificial acts of Codrus and Lycurgus are, both for John's audience and for Paul's, a matter of historical record. This incontrovertibility provides Paul with the basis to generalize the authority of self-sacrifice. This generalization, though evidently an induction, is ultimately authorized by the ultimate act of self-sacrifice, Christ's Crucifixion and Resurrection. That is to say, Paul's generalization is ultimately not a logical operation at all, but a simple reflection of the ultimate reality of God. His audience is referred from things it knows as fact, the account of Codrus and Lycurgus to a thing it does not know, "the word of God," the "throne of divine majesty." In learning this, however, the audience learns not only to accept the word of God as an inductive inference, but to accept it as a fact even more incontrovertible than the exemplary facts with which John began.

What John has presented here is nothing less than a narrative model of authority. He has grounded his use of exempla by appealing to the example of Paul and then grounded Paul's use of exempla by appealing to Christ. By making not simply the form of appeal, but also its ground, exemplary, John has defined Christian authority as thoroughly narrative. He has given its foundation, Christ's self-sacrifice, the same structure as narrative's most basic formal feature, the transformation of an event into a narrative utterance. The *factum* of Christ's Resurrection is also a narrative *dictum*, the irrefutable answer to all the questions of human philosophy. Moreover, this *dictum* is endlessly reiterable. It authorizes a limitless reappropriation, or, in more properly Christian terms, redemption of human history.

Armed with the example of Christ, Paul can transform the examples of Codrus and Lycurgus into vessels of Christian ideology, and following Paul, John can effect a similar transformation. Christ becomes an originary narrative voice with a limitless capacity to authorize new voices. That this voice is constituted by an act of self-sacrifice, that it speaks precisely by destroying itself, makes it remarkably similar to modern narratological models of narrative, which view narrative as constituted by a formal rupture. Beyond the *dictum* of any actual narration, narratology's "*sjuzhet*," or "narration," there is always the ideal *factum* of "*fabula*," or "story," which the *dictum* can only partially represent.[20] In John's exemplary model, Christ fulfills the role of story, the ideal *factum*.

As narratologists have convincingly argued, it is precisely the gap between *dictum* and *factum* which enables a narrative to produce its meaning. By emphasizing certain aspects of the *factum* and minimizing or eliding others the *dictum* implicitly assigns the *factum* a specific significance. Without this form of reference there can be no narrative. As Jonathan Culler explains, " If narrative is defined as the representation of a series of events, then the analyst must be able to identify these events, and they come to function as a non-discursive, non-textual given, something which exists prior to and independently of narrative presentation, and which the narrative then reports. " Culler goes on to explain that these events may in fact not actually exist, but that the narrative's analyst must treat them as if they do.[21] To this extent the narration actually produces the events it is claiming to represent: the putative existence of these events is one of the narration's rhetorical effects.

But if Christ's exemplarity anticipates the productive, rhetorical aspects of this narratological model, it also disavows narratology's residual positivism. For Christianity there can be no " non-discursive givens. " Narratology tends to treat story, the pretextual or prenarrative given, as an implacably, utterly alien force, against which the textual disruptions of the act of narrative are always ultimately futile. Christianity refuses the possibility of a pretextual given; for Christ Himself, the Word Made Flesh, though given, is also thoroughly textual. This is why as a narrative model, Christian exemplarity is always empowering. To follow Christ's example, to speak in his name, is an act of narration which disrupts a story. That story is

---

[20] On *sjuzhet* and *fabula*, see Victor Erlich, *Russian Formalism: History and Doctrine* (New Haven: Yale University Press, 1981), 239–43. The terms have been variously translated into French and English, but in my opinion the best are the terms *narration* and *story*, which Steven Cohan and Linda M. Shires use in their excellent survey *Telling Stories* (New York and London: Routledge, 1988), 52–112.

[21] Culler, "Story and Discourse in the Analysis of Narrative," in *The Pursuit of Signs: Semiotics, Literature, Deconstruction* (London and Henley: Routledge & Kegan Paul, 1981), 171.

Christ's sacrificial redemption of human history, which is always in the process of narrating itself, that is, which has already disrupted itself. In contrast to the narratological model, which continually disowns its own rhetorical power, this model explicitly recognizes the power that narrative has to produce continuity through disruption, and it names that power Christ.

It is this narrative, discursive, disruptive power which authorizes John's moral polemic against the royal court. But this power is also precisely what his polemic offers to the court. The prince who submits to Christ's example inserts himself into the unending narrative of Christian authority. Because Christ has made self-sacrifice the very engine of this narrative, the prince can submit to it and still retain his own social identity, and social privilege. He becomes Christ-like: self-sacrificial, but also self-authorizing. Here is a crucial rhetorical site where John's hierocratism and his humanism converge. His use of the classical is one of the foremost marks of his humanism. But his deployment of classical exempla to convince lay princes to become Christian serves both his humanism and his ecclesiology at once. It demonstrates that the self-sacrificial production of authority can occur from within history as well as from outside.

Though this point could be illustrated by any of the many examples of pagan virtue John cites throughout, for the sake of convenience I would like to use the two I have already mentioned, Codurus and Lycurgus, which lead into the exemplum of Paul. These stories are about royal self-sacrifice, but the sacrifice they involve is not a sacrifice to some code beyond the king. What these kings sacrifice themselves to is their own image as the sole authors of communal order. Codrus is an Athenian king about to lead his people into battle with the Dorians when he learns the oracles have declared the Dorians will be victorious so long as they do not kill him. He disguises himself, and entering the Dorian camp carrying a bundle of sticks, he provokes the Dorian soldiers until one of them kills him. Lycurgus is a Spartan who, having established a strict code of laws, sets out for Crete. Before leaving he extracts an oath from the people not to change them before he returns. In order to give the laws perpetuity, he remains permanently in exile and orders that his bones be scattered in the sea so his people will never know he has died.

Codrus surrenders the royal mantle and sacrifices his life in order to make his sovereignty secure from external threat. Lycurgus gives up day-to-day management of his realm, but in exchange receives complete fidelity to his code of laws. Like Christ's crucifixion, these sacrifices are self-generated, unconstrained, and uncalled-for acts of unlimited generosity. Though they produce law, they are exemplary rather than legislative; their authority resides entirely in their self-generated excessiveness. This is particularly clear in the case of Lycurgus, the sole author of law, who, unconstrained himself, is also the sole source of constraint.

This model of authority is entirely rhetorical, yet it is simultaneously grounded in the political superiority of the monarch. What John accomplishes here at the level of the exemplum, he also accomplishes in the overarching figure he uses to organize this middle section of the work. This figure is the metaphor of the body politic, or corporate fiction. It was one of the most fundamental and widespread of medieval political notions. Recovered for modern scholarship by Ernst Kantoriwicz's classic study, *The King's Two Bodies*, it draws an analogy between the social totality and the human body. It typically compares each social stratum to a particular body part in order to make two complementary claims: that each stratum has its own proper function and distinct identity, but that like the parts of a body all must serve a single unity, usually depicted as the head, and almost invariably identified with the prince.[22]

Though not generally considered an exemplum, this figure nevertheless has exemplary force. Like an exemplum, it concretizes communal value within a single point of view. Unlike most exempla, this figure is overtly fictive. Yet that condition in no way vitiates its exemplarity. Because, as I have been arguing, an exemplum is never purely textual, its referential fidelity to an external event is less important than its enactment of authority. What an exemplum records is the transformation of fallen historical reality into moral value, a transformation in which the exemplum itself participates. The corporate fiction effects the same transformation, generating an idealized unification of the community, then assigning that unification to a specific social position.

Moreover the corporate fiction was always articulated from a position of social superiority. Developed by the Church for the

[22] E. H. Kantoriwicz, *The King's Two Bodies: A Study in Medieval Political Theology* (Princeton: Princeton University Press, 1957). In addition to Kantoriwicz, see Tilman Struve "The Importance of the Organism in the Political Theory of John of Salisbury," in *World of John of Salisbury*, ed. Wilks, 303–17; and Struve, *Die Entwicklung der organologischen Staatsaufassung in Mittelalter* (Stuttgart: Anton Hiersemann, 1978).

prince, it embodied the entire community in a single, social position, whose political interests the Church, or, at least, the Church hierarchy, basically shared. This superiority is not simply a matter of immediate context, but was with the figure from the beginning. Its first major instance is in Livy, who describes it as a *fabula*, which the patrician Menenius Agrippa tells to an angry mob of plebians during the first Secession, or strike against conscription (494 BC).[23] The story is so successful that it convinces them to end their strike.[24] What interests Livy about the *fabula* is not so much its constitutional value, as its exemplification of the ruling class to maintain social order through the articulation of ideology.

It is not certain how explicit this dimension of the corporate fiction was in earlier medieval versions, which, after all, owe as much to the Pauline notion of *corpus Christi*, as they do to the direct influence of pagan antiquity.[25] But it was certainly explicit to John, who had access to Livy. Toward the end of his exploration of the figure (VI, 24), he retells Livy's version, characteristically recasting it in a contemporary guise, assigning it to Pope Adrian IV.[26] As in Livy the story is offered by the voice of authority in response to an attack from below. In this case the attack is not a revolt, but current complaints about the papacy, which, at the pope's request, John reports to him. John's report is remarkable for his frankness. After summarizing many accusations of rapacity and corruption made by others, John, with some qualifications, adds some of his own. Even more remarkable than this, however, is the pope's response. Not only does he laugh and commend John for his frankness and candor, but the fable he goes on to tell seems, in context, to acknowledge the legitimacy of the charges.

Adrian's version of the fable is substantially the same as Menenius Agrippa's. The members of the body, angered by the idleness of the stomach, swear to abstain from work, and after three days, become faint. Persuaded by reason, they return to their labors. "And so the stomach was acquitted, which although it is voracious and greedy of that which does not belong to it, yet seeks not for itself but for the others, who cannot be nourished if it is empty," John concludes, and then quotes Adrian's moral:

[23] The dating is traditional. See P. A. Brunt, *Social Conflicts*, 51.
[24] Titus Livius, *Ab urbe condita*, 2.32.
[25] Kantoriwicz, *King's Two Bodies*, 195; Struve, "Importance of the Organism," 304.
[26] John's knowledge of Livy probably came from Florus, a late first- or early second-century compiler of an epitome. See Martin "John of Salisbury," 185.

"And so it is, brother," he said, "if you will but observe, in the body of the commonwealth, wherein though the magistrates are most grasping, yet they accumulate not so much for themselves as for others. For if they are starved there is nought to be distributed among the members. ... Do not therefore seek to measure our oppressiveness or that of temporal princes, but attend rather to the common utility of all." (256–57)

Tale est, inquit, frater, si recte attendas, in corpore rei publicae ubi, licet plurimum appetat magistratus, non tam sibi quam aliis coacervat. Si enim exinanitus fuerit, nichil est quod membris valeat impartiri ... Noli ergo neque nostrum neque secularium principum duritiam metiri, sed omnium utilitatem attende. (VI, xxiv, 2, 72–73)

As in Livy, the threat to authority is met by a fictive deflection. Adrian denies neither his own oppressiveness, nor the oppressiveness of "temporal princes" – and the conflation is worth noting – but he uses the corporate fiction to assert that things could be no other way. In this exemplum, as in Livy's before it, narrative is literally power. By telling a story Adrian defends not only his authority but also his practical exercise of power, and its possible oppressiveness.

The corporate fiction came into the *Fürstenspiegel* via the papally sponsored ecclesiological traditions of the tenth and eleventh centuries. These traditions defined society as the *ecclesia* and made the pope its head (*caput*).[27] Though John is not the first writer to adapt it to kingship,[28] his adaptation was the first to become widely influential – so influential, in fact, that fourteenth-century canonists will credit him with its origin.[29] Following Kantoriwicz, most scholars see the import of this fiction as progressive.[30] Its stress on the organic interdependence of society's various constitutents and its projection of unity beyond the sole control any particular member, even the king, is viewed as a precursor of the modern republic.

As an indirect comment on his formal presentation of the figure at the beginning of Book V, John's return to the origin of the corporate fiction toward the end of Book VI is already enough to suggest this view may be something of an idealization. If we examine the earlier elaboration in detail, we will find that if the figure involves a

[27] Struve, *Staatsauffassung*, 87–98; Wilks, *Sovereignty*, 15–64, 455–78.
[28] Struve, "Importance of the Organism," 306.
[29] Walter Ullmann, "The Influence of John of Salisbury on Medieval Italian Jurists," *English Historical Review* 59 (1944), 384–91.
[30] For a recent, authoritative restatement of this view, see Brian Tierney, *Religion, Law, and the Growth of Constitutional Thought* 1150-1650 (Cambridge: Cambridge University Press, 1982), esp. 19–28, 80-108.

broadening in the distribution of power, it is a broadening of a very particular and limited sort. John wants royal sovereignty to include the counsel of the Church. But he assumes, and his elaboration of the figure confirms, that the fundamental social hierarchy on which medieval kingship was based should remain the same. If his scheme represents a step forward when compared to Carolingian notions of sacral kingship, or to the feudally inspired notion of the Three Estates, it is only as a rationalization of existing privilege, and certainly not as a shift in the fundamental distribution of power.[31]

In John's version of the analogy – with which he begins the fifth book, and which, as I have already mentioned, he assigns to the *Institutio Trajani* – the priests occupy the position of the soul; the prince the head; the Senate, a Romanism for the royal council, the heart; judges and administrators of provinces, the eyes, ears and tongue; courtiers, the sides; financial officers, the stomach; soldiers, the hands; and husbandmen, the feet (V,2; VI,1). Giving the priesthood the position of soul simply emphasizes the extent to which the unity of monarchy is an ideological product. It is expressed here in the overtly fictive corporeal metaphor drawn from an implicitly fictive authority. In this document royal unity is quite literally a discursive unity that John has *produced*. To make that unity bipartite, to place the priesthood at its heart is only to acknowledge an essentially ideological nature that John's very manner of presentation repeatedly exposes.

Yet John does not expose the ideological diffusion at the heart of the royal ideal in order to democratize it, and certainly not to discredit it. On the contrary, he exposes its ideological dependence in order to appropriate its power, to redefine that power as proceeding from the Church. This is a paradoxical diffusion which has as its ultimate goal centralization. Having assimilated the Church to the power of the king, John wants that power to remain concentrated, not be diffused further. The critical line of demarcation is not between the prince and the clergy, but between the royal court – understood as comprising primarily the prince and his clerical counsel – and everyone else. Though the functions of judges and

---

[31] On sacral kingship, see Walter Ullmann, *The Carolingian Renaissance and the Idea of Kingship* (London: Methuen, 1969); on the notion of the three estates, see Georges Duby, *The Three Estates: Feudal Society Imagined*, tr. Arthur Goldhammer (Chicago: Chicago University Press, 1980, rev. paperback eds., 1980, 1982, 1984). For a brief comparison between the *Policraticus* and estates ideology, see Elizabeth A. R. Brown, "Georges Duby and the Three Orders," *Viator* 17 (1986), 57, 62.

soldiers are discussed at some length, it is clear John considers them simple extensions of the prince – his eyes, ears, tongue, and hands – who are subordinate both to him and the Church.

His treatment of the rest of society – basically all those who are not members of the ruling class – is entirely perfunctory, confined almost entirely to a single chapter in Book VI (20). John defines them as the "humbler offices," all of the many ways of "sustaining life or increasing household property," which do not "pertain to the authority of the governing power."[32] Of this large and disenfranchised group,

...it applies generally to each and all of them that...they should not transgress the limits of the law, and should in all things observe constant reference to the public utility. For inferiors owe it to their superiors to provide them with service, just as the superiors in their turn owe it to their inferiors to provide them with all things needful for their protection and succor. (293–94)

Verumtamen quod generale est omnibus et singulis procuratur, ut legis scilicet limites non excedant et ad publicam utilitatem omnia referantur. Debent autem obsequium inferiora superioribus quae omnia eisdem vicissim debent necessarium subsidium providere. (59)

It is clear that "all things needful" does not include control of their own labor, since that is owed to their superiors. The public utility to which they are referred is little more than the law of their own oppression: that is, the necessity of their subordination to a hierarchy in which all sovereignty proceeds from the Church and the prince. The reciprocity of obligations is an entirely formal one which has the practical effect of reinforcing the inferiors' inferiority. They serve their superiors; in exchange the superiors allow the inferiors what they have decided is needful.

It is certainly true that John goes on to argue that "that course is to be pursued in all things which is of advantage to the humbler classes, that is to say to the multitude, for small numbers always yield to great" (*in omnibus exequenda quae humilioribus, id est multitudini, prosunt; nam paucitas semper pluribus cedit* (59)). But this comment, and

---

[32] 2, 58–59: "Pedes quidem qui humiliora exercent officia, appellantur, quorum obsequio totius rei publicae membra per terram gradiuntur. In his quidem agricolarum ratio vertitur qui terrae semper adherent sive in sationalibus sive in consitivis sive in pascuis sive in floreis agitentur. His etiam aggregantur multae species lanificii artesque mecanicae, quae in ligno ferro ere metallisque variis consistunt, serviles quoque obsecundationes et multiplices victus adquirendi vitaeque sustentandae aut rem familiarem amplificandi formae, quae nec ad praesidendi pertinent auctoritatem et universitati rei publicae usquequaque proficiunt."

a later reiteration of the reciprocity between superior and inferior with which John ends the chapter need to be understood in light of what has gone before. The "advantage of the humbler classes" will be an advantage that operates entirely within their subordinate status. Its ultimate purpose, therefore, will not be to serve them, but to make their inferiority more bearable, thereby protecting the privileges of their superiors.

Thus the reciprocity that the corporate fiction calls into being between those represented by the feet and the ruling class, represented by the rest of the body, is always weighted in favor of the ruling class. This was the fiction's purpose. It enabled medieval thinkers like John to acknowledge the radical equality, the absolute interdependence among all members of a society, and simultaneously make that acknowledgement of equality an argument for hierarchy. The corporate fiction could do this precisely because it was exemplary. It generates a point of view at once socially specific and universally available, a point of view which collapses all of its audience's divergent interests into a single unity, then names that unity the prince, or the *res publica*.

As in his exemplification of Christ, John's treatment of the corporate fiction makes public authority synonymous with the generation of narratives. These narratives are fictive to the extent that they are ideal, but it is in that very idealization that he locates their truth. Despite its valorization of unity, however, this truth is a duplicitous one. Throughout John makes the supremacy of royal authority dependent on the ideological support it derives from the Church. If the *Policraticus* offers to temporal princes an ideal of unified authority it offers even more strongly participation in that unity to the clerical counselors like his dedicatee, who no doubt made up the bulk of his immediate audience.

At the same time John's images of royal authority are sufficiently general that they would have continued to have appeal to the increasingly laicized and increasingly bureaucratic royal courts that followed John's time. It is an axiom of later medieval administrative history that as kings grew stronger and monarchy grew more centralized, they drew upon the clergy, and then increasingly the lesser nobility, to staff their administrative offices in order to distance themselves from their increasingly powerful barons.[33] That is, they

---

[33] Southern, *Medieval Humanism*, 208–12.

consolidated their power by dispersing it more widely to officers with no power base of their own. In order for this dispersion to work efficiently, administrative functions had to be more precisely delineated, and the monarch came increasingly to rely upon written records. These records in turn would eventually need to be in the vernacular rather than in Latin in order to document more precisely the specific social structures they were regulating.[34] If this need helps explain the laicization of the royal court, it also helps explain the *Policraticus*'s continuing appeal. John's exemplary model of royal authority provides a form of ideological unity which locates its own unifying power precisely in its status as rhetorical invention. That is, it makes monarchy's ideological unity a rhetorical achievement at the very moment royal political power was managing its institutional diffusion by making that diffusion textual.

The *Policraticus*'s continual influence can be attested both by the profusion of later copies and by the number of later works which draw on its storehouse of exempla. Mendicants who brought with them their affinity for the exemplum as they entered the university often used the *Policraticus* as the source for the exempla they inserted into their biblical commentaries.[35] The *Policraticus* also serves as model both in form and substance for a number of later *Fürstenspiegel* or related works. Walter Map's *De nugis curialium* obviously draws its title from John's sub-title; its parodic acceptance of life at court may indicate it was intended in part as a comic rebuttal.[36] The *De regimine principum* of Helinand de Froidment, written about 1200 for Philip Augustus is now lost, but enough excerpts remain in Vincent de Beauvais's *Speculum historiale* to demonstrate that it draws substantially on the *Policraticus*.[37] Helinand or Vincent, or both, serve as models for the Parisian tradition of *Fürstenspiegel* that begins with Guibert de Tournai, who writes *Eruditio regum et principum* for Louis IX in 1259. John is thus indirectly responsible for this later

[34] Marc Bloch, *Feudal Society*, tr. L. A. Manyon (Chicago: University of Chicago Press, 1964), v. 1, 77–78.

[35] Beryl Smalley, *English Friars and Antiquity in the Early Fourteenth Century* (Oxford: Basil Blackwell, 1960), 82.

[36] Walter Map, *De nugis curialium*, ed. and tr. M. R. James, rev. C. N. L. Brooke and R. A. B. Mynors (Oxford: Clarendon Press, 1983). Map begins: "'In time I exist, and of time I speak,' said Augustine, and added, 'What time is I know not.' In a like spirit of perplexity, I may say that in the court I exist and of the court I speak, and what the court is, God knows, I know not" (3).

[37] Berges, *Die Fürstenspiegel*, 295; Ullmann, "*Policraticus* in the Later Middle Ages," 522–23, 537–38. These excerpts can be found in J. P. Migne, *Patrologiae cursus completus, series Latinae*, 212, col. 735–96, entitled *De bono regimine principis*.

tradition.[38] The *Communiloquium* of John of Wales, not a *Fürstenspiegel*, but an exemplum collection arranged according to categories of the *sermones ad status*, draws many of its exempla from the *Policraticus*, as does the *Ludus schachorum* of Jacobus de Cessolis, one of the most widely disseminated *Fürstenspiegel* of the fourteenth- and fifteenth-centuries.[39] Nevertheless, the exemplary model of kingship that developed out of the *Fürstenspiegel* did not come from the *Policraticus* alone, though it was the single most important source. Crucial refinements were to come as well from the Parisian tradition that began a half-century later.

AEGIDIUS ROMANUS AND THE PARISIAN TRADITION

The Parisian tradition of *Fürstenspiegel* used the exemplum much less frequently than the *Policraticus*. Its mode of rhetorical presentation shifted from the adduction of exempla to the systematic distinctions of the scholastic treatise. While this shift predated Aquinas and the full recovery of Aristotle, the genre's assimilation of Aristotelian notions – beginning with Aquinas's own *De regno*, written between 1265 and 1266 for Robert, King of Cyprus, then continued about the turn of the century by Tholomeus de Lucca – gave the shift in presentation a powerful philosophical coherence.[40] The relative autonomy which medieval Aristotelianism granted to lay political structures justified an authoritative form of discourse of their own, homologous to the systematic textuality of Christian doctrine. Aristotelian notions of natural law meant lay political authority could lay claim to just such a textuality, that there was a systematic body of *sententiae* inherent to it, and that these no longer had to be

---

[38] *Le Traité eruditio regum et principum de Guibert de Tournai*, O. F. M., ed. A. de Poorter (Louvain: University of Louvain, 1914). Jean-Phillipe Genet, "General Introduction," in *Four English Political Tracts of the Later Middle Ages* (London: Royal Historical Society, 1973), xii; "Ecclesiastics and Political Theory in Late Medieval England: The End of a Monopoly," in *Church, Politics and Patronage*, ed. Dobson, 26. Ullmann, "*Policraticus* in the Later Middle Ages," 523, 538.

[39] Berges, *Die Fürstenspiegel*, 292. On the *Communiloquium*, see Smalley, *English Friars*, 51–55; and Robert Pratt, "Chaucer and the Hand that Fed Him," *Speculum* 41 (1966), 619–42. Berges does not classify the *Ludus schachorum* as a *Fürstenspiegel*, although its frame tale depicts it as a public act of instructing a tyrannical monarch. Raymond D. Di Lorenzo, "The Collection Form and the Art of Memory in the *Libellus super ludo schachorum* of Jacobus de Cessolis," *Mediaeval Studies* 35 (1973), 207–12, argues persuasively it should be considered a *Fürstenspiegel*.

[40] Berges *Die Fürstenspiegel*, 317–19; The *De Regno* is available in English as *On Kingship*, tr. Gerald B. Phelan, rev. with introduction and notes by I.Th. Eschmann (Toronto: Pontifical Institute of Mediaeval Studies, 1949).

imagined as being imposed from a Church discourse entirely outside of it. Lay princes could now conceive of themselves as consulting a set of rules specific to their sphere of power: they no longer had to depend on the constant intervention of clerics. The systematic mode of these later *Fürstenspiegel* has undoubtedly reinforced the modern tendency to assign the genre a quasi-juridical status.

Nevertheless, it is important to remember that what gets systematized is precisely the body of claims inherent in the older models of royal sovereignty. The Aristotelianism of these texts led them to define moral order as conformity to natural law. But their use of Aristotle was far from slavish, and their adaptation of his notion of natural law was, like John of Salisbury's use of the classical past, an appropriation rather than a simple recapitulation. That they accomodated natural law to Christian doctrine is a commonplace of modern medieval intellectual history; that they accomodated it just as fully to medieval power relations is less universally acknowledged. For our purposes, this accommodation can be best illustrated by an examination of the *De regimine principum* of Aegidius Romanus, the most comprehensive, most widely disseminated of the later *Fürstenspiegel*, and the most systematic in its recourse to Aristotle. The accommodation is directly relevant to our concerns for it involves exemplarity both as rhetorical maneuver and as a political ideal.

Aegidius was a university master and a student of Aquinas's.[41] He wrote the *De regimine* for Philip the Fair while Philip was still crown prince, sometime between 1277–79.[42] The *De regimine* consists of three books. The first concerns virtue in the self; the second, virtue in the household; the third, virtue in the *civitas*. Although Aegidius employs the exemplum infrequently, less than a dozen times in 300 pages, he retains the genre's larger exemplary logic at every level of his project, from his dedication to Philip the Fair, to his characterization of his own discourse, to his definition of kingship and his adaptation of Aristotle.

The dedication frames the long treatise to follow in the traditional way, as a concrete act of instruction. It engages in the traditional flattering hyperbole, with the effect of presenting Philip as already perfect in the virtues in which the work would instruct him, and connecting that perfection with "his blessed line." This reference to lineage signals an important change. Aegidius's systematic rationali-

[41] Walter Ullmann, "Boniface VIII and His Contemporary Scholarship," *The Journal of Theological Studies*, n.s. 27 (1976), 75.   [42] Berges, *Die Fürstenspiegel*, 320.

zation of lay power will focus on the interrelation between class and gender, a topic that John of Salisbury rarely mentions. As we shall see, this interrelation is crucial to the Chaucerian tradition's understanding of royal authority.

Aegidius introduces Aristotle's *Politics* in the course of the dedication, but his justification for its rationalism is utilitarian rather than moral.

The argument of the *Politics* declares that all reigns are not equally permanent, nor are particular governments measured in equal periods, for some are annual and some are for life, and indeed there are some which, through the inheritance and succession of sons, are considered in a certain way perpetual. Therefore, because as a rule all naturally resist, no violence being perpetual, whoever wishes to perpetuate his rule, in himself and his posterity, ought very much to study what might be his natural form of governing.

Clamat Politicorum sententia, omnes principatus non esse aequaliter diuturnos, nec aequali periodo singula regimina mensurari : sed aliqua sunt annualia, aliqua ad vitam, aliqua vero per haereditatem & successionem in filiis, quae quodammodo perpetua iudicantur. Cum igitur, nullum violentum esse perpetuum, fere omnia naturalia protestentur, qui in se, & in suis posterioribus filiis suum principatuum perpetuari desiderat, summopere studere debet, ut sit suum regimen naturale.[43]

The prince should wish to study the *regimen naturale* in order to perpetuate his own power. Familiarity with reason and law will enable him to overcome the inherent instability of power. Aristotle also authorizes the "naturalness" of aristocratic dominance:

For (as the Philosopher testifies), just as some are naturally servants, being strong in physical power, but lacking in intellect, so those strong in energy of mind and shrewd at ruling naturally rule.

Nam (ut testatur Philosophus) sicut est naturaliter servus, qui pollens viribus, deficit intellectu : sic vigens mentis industria, & regitiva prudentia, naturaliter dominatur. (Prol., 2)

Reason's effect on social hierarchy is entirely circular: it is a more effective, and therefore more natural, source of communal order than violent coercion, but those already in possession of the means of coercion are naturally the more reasonable. Princes like Philip who

---

[43] Egidio Colonna (Aegidius Romanus), *De regimine principum libri III*, ed. F. Hieronymum Samaritanium (Rome: Bartholomaum Zannettum, 1607; repr. Scientia Verlag Aalen, Darmstadt, 1967), Prol., 1–2. All subsequent references are to this edition. Book, part, chapter, and page numbers will be given in the text. The translations are mine.

recognize the rational basis of their own power can be acclaimed at once as "natural" rulers, and as rulers sanctified by God because the two qualities are the same. It is the natural, divinely ordained order of things that princes like Philip rule.

The synthetic interdependence Aegidius establishes in this prologue continues throughout the rest of the work. His Aristotelian exploration of kingship integrates his systematic commitment to reason and law with earlier models of kingship and with the most fundamental characteristics of medieval power relations. Kingship is periodically described as Godlike, and its authority periodically defined by the corporate fiction. Aristotelian though Aegidius's analysis of kingship is, it assumes from the outset a politically specific point of view. It conducts itself not in the interest of some universalized rational being, committed solely to the disinterested pursuit of truth, but, on the contrary, in the very specific interest of the medieval prince, and of those who share his power.

If this assumption marks the *De regimine* politically, it also makes the work incipiently narratorial, and Aegidius makes this rhetorical potential explicit in the very next chapter. This chapter is on method (*modus procendendi*) and it describes the method of the *regimine principum* as *figuralis et grossus* (I, 1, 2–5). Henri de Gauchi, who produced the contemporary translation of the *De regimine* entitled *Li Livres du gouvernement des rois*, translates the term *figuralis* as *par essample*, and though in most contexts *figuralis* would suggest allegory, in this one it does indeed seem to mean something closer to exemplarity.[44] As he introduces it, Aegidius remarks,

It should be known, therefore, that in all moral matters the method of proceeding, according to the Philosopher, is figural and broad: it is fitting in such things to penetrate figurally, because moral deeds are not completely captured in their telling.

Sciendum ergo, quod in toto morali negotio modus procedendi secundum Philosophum est figuralis & grossus: oportet enim in talibus typo & figulariter pertransire, quia gesta moralia complete sub narratione non cadunt. (I, i, 1, 2)

This certainly distinguishes *figuralis* from *sub narratione*, but it also suggests that *gesta moralia*, while not wholly narrative, are nevertheless partially so.

[44] *Li Livres du gouvernement des rois*, ed. Samuel Paul Molenaer (New York: Columbia University, 1899; rpt. AMS Press, New York, 1966), 4–6.

Whether Aegidius intended them to or not, these remarks on method summarize very neatly both the difference and ultimate similarity between the later *Fürstenspiegel* and the earlier sort typified by the *Policraticus*. Aegidius wants to penetrate (*pertransire*) the primarily narrative logic of moral examples, but the mode of penetration is itself associative and fictive, rather than purely demonstrative. As he goes on to say, the discourse of politics, like that of rhetoric, is meant to persuade, rather than demonstrate, like geometry.[45] He elaborates the distinction in a passage which, in its characterization of the process of persuasion, is reminiscent of the exemplarist's distinction between doctrine and narrative:

Since subtle reasonings tend more to illuminate the intellect, while those superficial and gross tend more to move and excite the feeling, in speculative sciences where one principally seeks the illumination of the intellect, the procedure is demonstrative and subtle; in moral matters, where one seeks rectitude of the will, that we do good, the procedure is persuasive and figural.

Cum ergo rationes subtiles magis illuminent intellectum, superficiales vero & grossae magis moveant, & inflamment affectum: in scientiis speculativis, ubi principaliter quaeritur illuminatio intellectus, procedendum est demonstrative & subtiliter in negocio morali, ubi quaeritur rectitudo voluntatis, & ut boni fiamus, procedendum est persuasive & figuraliter. (I, i, 1, 3–4)

For the exemplarist, to persuade is to narrate. For Aegidius, to persuade is to figure; as he outlines his vision of kingship, it becomes clear this figuration has the same structure as exemplification. It marks the same production of social authority through the extraordinary action of a politically dominant figure.

Aegidius builds his vision of kingship from the king's person outward. The first book treats the virtues, passions, and habits of kings as individuals. The second treats the king's management of his household. The third treats the management of the *civitas* in both peace and war. Book I opens with a general discussion of happiness. In the second part of Book I, after treating each virtue and various

---

[45] This passage casts doubt on Genet's claim that by the thirteenth century, politics was no longer associated with rhetoric ("General Introduction," xiii–xiv). Aegidius views politics as a branch of ethics, but he understands ethics as similar to rhetoric. "Geometrae igitur est non persuadere, sed demonstrare: Rhetoris vero, & Politici, non est demonstrare sed persuadere" (I, i, 1, 3). Rita Copeland has recently argued that the association between rhetoric and politics grew stronger over the course of the later Middle Ages, as the result of the laicization of rhetorical theory ("Lydgate, Hawes, and the Science of Rhetoric in the Late Middle Ages," *Modern Language Quarterly* 53 (1992), 57–82).

ancillaries to virtue separately, Aegidius discusses the four degrees of virtuous men: in ascending order, the perseverant, the continent, the temperate, and the divine (*divini*), those who are good *ultra modum humanum*. These last, he remarks, the Philosopher (that is, Aristotle) calls heroic, a term he glosses as *principans* & *dominativa* (I, ii, 32, 147). This four-fold scale is obviously related to the four dispositions to the good which he discusses in one of the opening chapters of part ii (I, ii, 4): the dispositions *perseverantia* and *continentia*, which are imperfect tendencies toward virtue; the disposition above virtue, the *virtus heroica* & *superjusta*; and the disposition between them, which is the virtues themselves. In chapter 33, he appends to the scale of virtuous men a corresponding hierarchy of virtue which he imports from Macrobius's *Somnium Scipionis*, though it ultimately derives from Plotinus.[46] There is the political order of virtue, the stage of virtues which pertains to things human and corresponds to the perserverant; the purgatory of souls (*purgatoriae animi*), which corresponds to the continent; the stage of the purged souls (*purgati animi*), which corresponds to the temperate; and the exemplary stage (*virtutes exemplares*), corresponding to the divine and the virtue that is in God himself (*in ipso deo*). The exemplary stage is the one Aegidius finds most appropriate to princes, and the one after which they should strive:

It was said above that it is not sufficient for kings and princes to be perseverant, continent and temperate, but that it is fitting for them to be in some sense divine. Therefore the virtues appropriate to them can be called exemplary because they ought to be rule and exemplar to others.

Dicebatur supra, quod Reges & Principes non sufficit esse perseverantes, continentes, & temperatos, sed decet eos quodammodo esse divinos. Virtutes ergo competentes eis, possunt exemplares dici: quia ipsi aliorum debent esse regula & exemplar. (I, ii, 33, 149)

The king is at once rule and exemplar, the model whose perfection becomes the obligatory standard for others. The conflation of these three schema establishes a hierarchy among the virtuous, and gives the notion of hierarchy an authoritative moral ground. It also connects the moral hierarchy with the political one. The example Aegidius gives of the divine man, whose heroism is *principans* and *dominativa*, is Hector. The exemplary virtue of the divine man is precisely an heroic feat. It is "superjust," above ordinary law,

---

[46] *Somnium Scipionis*, I, viii.

beyond the mode of the human. The morality such a man attains is a morality he himself produces. Once produced it becomes the rule for others: it becomes exemplary. By glossing this creative achievement as *principans* and *dominativa*, Aegidius comes close to suggesting that the production of moral order is a princely function. The prince becomes the potential author of moral law. It is true this authority is intermediate, an approach to the divine rather than divinity itself. But it is enough to place the monarch above everyone else, *ultra modum humanum*; in practical terms it gives him the same unlimited authority.

It is also true that when Aegidius makes this quasi-divine authority something to strive for, rather than a quality princes automatically possess, he assigns it more to the royal office than to the prince himself. But this simply makes the association between moral order and the existing power structure that much stronger. The association becomes stronger still when Aegidius explicitly grounds the monarch's authority in his nobility and makes nobility itself exemplary. The last part of Book I, part iv, discusses customs (*mores*); it ends with the customs of the noble, rich, and powerful. This conclusion effects a movement across Book I from ethical ideals to the habitual and practical that is itself consistent with the aim he announced in the prologue – to expose ideal principles in order to enable the Prince to rule more efficaciously. But the conclusion to Book I also definitively ties his commitment to monarchy to medieval power relations in their most regressive and fundamental form, the heritability of nobility.

His justification for heritability is remarkable both for its idealizing and its candor.

For nobility (as the second book of the Rhetoric says) is the same as the virtue of descent... The virtue ... of descent, which the Philosopher calls nobility, is nothing other than being of a certain family, or a certain line, in which from antiquity there was much power and many honors, so that it was felt to be of the nobility. Because according to the common opinion of men all things are measured monetarily, and riches are seen to be prized in whatever matter, whoever is rich, is reputed to be worthy to rule, and believed to be worthy in himself of honor and prizes. Because this is so, nobility, according to the common acceptance of men, is nothing more than old riches. Therefore, inasmuch as the nobles were rulers since long ago, and there were many honors and riches in their families, the noble heart is elevated by the example of its ancestors, so that they aspire to highness, and are magnanimous. Indeed, it is natural that the effect will always be assimilated to the cause: since sons are a certain effect of parents, it is natural for sons to imitate parents. Therefore, nobles, perceiving that there were many honors in their ancestry, and striving after challenge, that they might imitate their ancestors, affect highness, and happen to become magnanimous.

Nam nobilitas (ut dicitur 2. Rhetoricorum) idem est quod virtus generis... Virtus... generis, quam dicit Philosophus nobilitatem esse, nihil est aliud quam esse ex aliquo genere, vel ex aliqua prosapia, in qua etiam ab antiquo fuere multi principantes, & multi insignes, sic ergo sentiendum est de nobilitate. Verum quia secundum communem opinionem hominum omnia mensurantur numismate, & divitae videntur esse pretium rei cuiuslibet, ex hoc quod aliqui sunt divites, reputantur digni principari, & eo ipso creduntur esse insignes, & honore digni, quia ergo sic est, nobilitas secundum communem acceptionem hominum, nihil est aliud quam antiquatae divitiae. Quia ergo nobiles ex antiquo fuerunt praesides & in suo genere fuerunt multi insignes & divites, elevatur cor nobilium ex exemplo parentum, ut tendant in magna, & sint magnanimi. Naturale est enim, quod semper effectus vult assimilari causae: cum filii sint quidam effectus parentum, naturale est filios imitari parentes. Nobiles ergo advertentes quod in eorum genere fuerunt multi insignes, & tendentes in ardua, ut imitentur parentes, affectant magna, & contingit eos esse magnamimos. (I, iv, 5, 204)

This passage frankly concedes that nobility is an entirely arbitrary, historically contingent social formation. Its apparent inevitability is in fact entirely ideological, the product of "common opinion." The sinful human propensity to see riches as the most important thing accords to the rich the right to rule. The institution of nobility originates in this propensity, which means that, despite its presumed right to rule, and its presumed dignity, nobility means "nothing more than old riches." Yet Aegidius derives from this very arbitrariness the justification for nobility's social privilege.

The force of common opinion assures that the arbitrary association it makes between riches and the right to rule becomes an actuality. For as common opinion acts to single out the rich as noble, it also acts on the rich themselves, encouraging them to fulfill the model which it imposes on them. As time goes on the pressure grows stronger. Exalted by the example of its progenitors, the "noble heart" behaves honorably in order to imitate them. That the example being followed here is in fact an ideological fiction makes no difference. If the nobility becomes honorable through enacting this fiction, then the fiction ceases to be fictive and becomes real.

This frankly ideological reading of the public exemplum complements the more idealized one that occurs earlier, despite the obvious tensions. In the earlier one social order proceeds from the heroic activity of the exemplar. He creates it by becoming the model of virtue for the rest of the community. In this version exemplarity is an ideological form the community imposes on particular individuals. Beyond this difference, however, there is the similarity that is constituted by exemplarity itself, the presumption that social order must take an exemplary form, that communal values can have no force until they are concretized in or by a single authoritative figure. Whether the concretization is accomplished by the figure himself (as the heroic act of the divine man) or by the community (as the ideological fiction of "common opinion") is less important than its structure, its drive to specify all communal authority within a single social position. This is precisely the drive that Aegidius characterizes as exemplary, and it is this exemplary, narrative model which enables him to move from the Aristotelian ethical ideal of the heroic ruler in the first half of Book I and the more cynical, Augustinian view of political authority as an ideological stopgap with which he closes it. In both cases, the common assumption is that political authority must take a single, unitary form: it cannot be exercised except as the prerogative of a single, social position. The character of this necessity, whether it is the result of a natural dispensation – the arrangement of human beings into a hierarchy of moral competence, of which the highest is the most fit to rule – or a stopgap that evolves out of humanity's own sinfulness, seems less important than the sheer force of the necessity itself.

Indeed the affiliations between these two versions of public exemplarity could also be seen as a general affiliation between exemplarity and heritability. This commitment to heritability is worth stressing. Most immediately, it should serve as a substantial caveat to those who would view the Aristotelian impulse in later medieval thought as primarily progressive. Heritability was the oldest and most fundamental element of medieval power relations. Aegidius's overriding commitment to it insures that where his model of kingship is innovative, the innovation is motivated by conservative interests. Moreover, the self-consciously ideological nature of Aegidius's commitment to heritability is what is crucial. We cannot dismiss it as a blind prejudice, a holdover from previous tradition, which Aegidius accepts because he simply never subjects it to scrutiny. He does scrutinize it: he exposes its historical contingency, and on the basis of that contingency affirms it.

The most basic assumption here is not Aristotelian but Augustinian: that human sinfulness requires coercive government. Aegidius favors monarchy because its unity concentrates the government's coercive power. But he favors hereditary monarchy not only because heritability insures the coercion will meet the least resistance, but also because it will be least liable to abuse by the weaknesses of particular monarchs (III, ii, 5, 461–65). Appealing often to the corporate fiction, he argues that every natural body has a single ruling member – even the world itself is ruled by a single God. The essence of political authority is its concentration in a single figure: "For just as it is natural that the multitude proceeds from the one, so it is natural that all the others must be reduced to one." The best rule is the rule of a single king, which "most perfectly preserves unity" (III, ii, 4, 457–58).[47]

Like John of Salisbury, Aegidius conflates the corporate fiction with the hierarchical functionalism of estates theory. He sees the prince's duty as chief member of the social body to protect its hierarchy, arguing that he must distribute goods and honors to each according to their virtue and social rank (*virtutem et dignitatem*). Aegidius calls this hierarchy special justice (*iustitia speciali*) and declares it is as necessary for the survival of a reign as the general justice which declares all laws should sanction and prohibit evil. This special justice is what Aegidius makes comparable to the social body. The eyes must direct the feet, the feet must carry the eyes, and so forth, under the guidance of a single member (in this version, the heart) whose duty is to maintain an equilibrium (*aequalitatem*) among the different forms of service (I, ii, 11, 46–48).

This commitment to the singularity of the monarchical also underlies Aegidius's view of tyranny, which echoes the famous dictum of his teacher Aquinas, that monarchy is the best form of government and tyranny the worst.[48] Though this position may indeed be the philosophical forerunner of constitutional monarchy, as it is often claimed, it is important to see that its significance for those who articulated it was much different. Aegidius shows no interest at all in constitutional restraint. Indeed the very grounds of his view of tyranny are anti-constitutional in that they presume monarchy's virtue lies in its singularity. As he explains,

[47] Nam sicut naturale est, quod multitudo ab uno procedat: sic etaim est naturale, quod in unum aliquod reducatur ... optima est autem monarchia sive gubernatio unius Regis, eo quod ibi perfectior unitas reservetur.   [48] *On Kingship*, 23–24.

just as the rule of a king, because it is maximally united, is the most
efficacious in providing benefit, so tyranny is the most efficacious in doing
harm, because monarchy is where one rules and where power is united,
whether it be for better or worse. For if the monarchy has the right intention,
then we have a King and it is the best form of rule; through its unity of
virtues it is able to accomplish many good things. On the other hand, if it has
a perverse intention, then it is tyranny, and it is the worst, since through its
unity of power it is able to accomplish many evils.

sicut principatus Regis eo quod sit maxime unitus, est efficacissimus ad
proficiendum: sic tyrannis efficacissima ad nocendum. Monarchia enim
quia ibi dominatur unus, & est ibi virtus unita, ideo vel est optima vel est
pessima: nam si monarchia habet intentionem rectam, tunc est Rex & est
optimus principatus: quia propter unitam virtutes potest multa bona
efficere: si vero monarchia habet intentionem perversam, tunc est tyrannus
& est pessimus, quia propter suam unitatem potentiam potest multa mala
efficere. (III, ii, 7, 469)

Monarchy and tyranny are structurally identical. The difference
between *rex* and *tyrannus* turns entirely on the matter of intention. If
the monarch has *intentionem rectam*, he is *rex*; if he has *intentionem
perversam*, he is *tyrannus*. The privileging of the royal will which
informs this notion of tyranny is antithetical to modern consti-
tutionalism.

Aegidius's commitment to the existing form of medieval power
governs his adaptation of Aristotle throughout. However, his
revisions are most striking in those parts of the third book where he
engages Aristotelian notions most directly. He consistently corrects
Aristotle and the other classical authorities he cites whenever their
claims pose a threat to the medieval status quo. While Aristotle never
actually designates one form of government as most preferable,
Aegidius argues strenuously for monarchy (III, ii, 3). Where Aristotle
points out the limitations of rule by one man, Aegidius reiterates its
advantages, so long as the king seeks the common good, and consults
many advisers (III, ii, 4).[49] Where Aristotle argues for election,
Aegidius argues not only for hereditary, but indeed primogenitural
rule (III, ii, 5).[50] Where he argues that it is better to be ruled by a
good law (*optima lege*) than a good king (*optimo rege*), Aegidius points
out that this contradicts his claim elsewhere that law, being general,
fails to cover particular cases.[51] Aegidius then resolves the con-

---

[49] Although Aegidius mistakenly identifies the site of Aristotle's reservations as *Politics*, III, 7,
they actually occur in III, 15 and 16.   [50] *Politics*, III, 11.
[51] The claim that it is better to be ruled by a good law than a good king occurs in *Politics* III,
15; that law only covers general cases, in the *Ethics*, V, 10.

tradiction by claiming it applies only to written law, and that the
king, instructed by natural law, can remedy the failings of written
law (III, ii, 29). Moreover, Aegidius is continually vigilant against
the slightest suggestion of political or economic equality which his
larger engagement with classical tradition might engender. He
disputes Vegetius's claim that peasants (*agricolae*) are better fighters
than the nobility (III, iii, 5). And he spends most of the first part of
Book III disputing what, following Aristotle, he takes to be the
economic and sexual communism of Socrates, Plato, and Phaleas.[52]

The extent to which Aegidius revises Aristotle is most evident at
the very point he is most Aristotelian, in his discussion of law. To be
sure, the rediscovery of Aristotle's notion of natural law marked a key
development in medieval political thinking. As the set of founding
political principles which were fully accessible to human reason,
natural law made politics an autonomous sphere, no longer directly
dependent on the divine. I have no wish to underemphasize this
development. The notion of natural law and the systematic mode of
analysis it enables clearly allows Aegidius to distinguish royal
authority more clearly from the Church than was possible for John of
Salisbury to do. Because Aegidius accepts politics as a realm distinct
from the Church, he is free to examine the principles proper to
kingship without needing, as John did, to mediate continually
between the prince and the Church.

Nevertheless, as Althusser and his followers have pointed out,
autonomy is not necessarily independence.[53] Medieval Aristotelians
made politics autonomous, but they certainly did not dissever it from
Christian notions of authority, nor indeed from the ecclesiological
models of royal authority which developed out of it. Though Aegidius
uses natural law to stress royal autonomy, he will nevertheless define
natural law ecclesiologically, and he will mediate between law and
king by appealing to the king's exemplary power.

He makes the king subject to natural law, but this subjection is of
a very particular sort. As I have already said, it provides the king
with complete power over actual written law. Aegidius declares that
when one thinks of the king's subjection to law, one should think of
it as subjection to natural law, not as subjection to a particular
written law. It is the latter sort of law which suffers from the

---

[52] Cf. *Politics*, II, 1–7.
[53] Althusser, *Reading Capital*, 91–105; and Pierre Macherey, *A Theory of Literary Production*, tr.
Geoffrey Wall (London: Routledge and Kegan Paul, 1978), 51–53.

deficiency of being too general. The greater advantage of being ruled by a good king is that he will always remedy specific deficiencies by modifying existing written law according to the dictates of natural law. Thus, the king's subjection to natural law not only permits, but also requires his superiority to written law. For without that superiority remedying the written law's deficiencies justice would be impossible. This brings us to the ecclesiological aspect of Aegidius's notion of natural law. For that notion is Pauline as well as Aristotelian.

... natural justice offers itself immediately to the understanding; positive justice does not reveal itself immediately but is arrived at through the industry of men. And because natural laws thus offer themselves to our understanding natural justice might simply be said to be written on our hearts. For peoples which have no law by nature fashion what law is, and show the work of law to be written in their hearts.

... ius naturale prima facie se offert intellectui: Ius positivum non statim se ostendit, sed est per industriam hominum adinventum. Et quia sic se offerunt intellectui nostro naturales leges, quod est de iure naturali simpliciter dicitur esse scriptum in cordibus nostris. nam gentes quae legem non habent, naturaliter ea quae legis sunt faciunt, & ostendunt opus legis scriptum in cordibus eorum. (III, ii, 24, 519)

This language echoes Paul's defense of the gentiles in Romans:

When Gentiles who have not the law do by nature what the law requires they are a law to themselves, even though they do not have the law. They show that what the law requires is written on their hearts, while their conscience also bears witness and their conflicting thoughts accuse or perhaps excuse them on that day when according to my gospel, God judges the secrets of men by Christ Jesus. (2: 14–16)

It also recalls, somewhat less directly, Paul's use of the same metaphor to describe Divine inspiration:

You yourselves are our letter of recommendation, written on your hearts, to be known and read by all men, and you show that you are a letter from Christ, delivered by us, written not with ink but with the spirit of the Living God, not on tablets of stone but on tablets of hearts. (II Cor., 2: 2–3)

For Paul the metaphor accomplishes two contrary goals at once. He makes the Judaic tradition accessible to the Gentiles by ascribing to them a "natural" lawfulness beyond written Judaic law. However, by defining that natural lawfulness as itself a written text, he also holds out the possibility of another law every bit as codified as the

Judaic law he is rejecting. Indeed, this is the New Law of Christianity, and while he defines this law as more dynamic than the Old Law of Judaism, it nevertheless comes to justify the codification of a new priesthood. The metaphor is thus inclusive and exclusionary at once. It broadens the existing community, but it does so primarily to unify it in the single form of authority constituted by Paul's ministry.

The metaphor has a similar effect in Aegidius. By insisting that principles of political authority are available through natural reason, he makes such authority autonomous. The community can avail itself of this authority directly; the community does not have to derive it from the texts of the Church. Yet defining the authority as already written means that ultimately it retains its derivativeness. Natural law is emphatically not something the community constitutes according to its own lights. It is rather a text to be interpreted.

Moreover, unlike the biblical text, this one is entirely ideal. It can never be made public in its pure form, because it is accessible only through the written law, which imperfectly reproduces it. Accordingly, the king's subjection to this ideal is itself entirely idealized. As the coercive force which stands between natural law as ideal and the written law that is its imperfect embodiment, the king is obviously the ideal's most powerful interpreter. His putative subjection to natural law is in fact subjection to his own idealized image as its interpreter, that is, to his image as promulgator of written law.

Although Aegidius's own royalist enthusiasms were apparently cooled considerably by the face-off between Philip and Boniface VIII some quarter of a century later, his *Fürstenspiegel* helped authorize subsequent lay appropriations of the tradition. The first significant instance is Dante's *De monarchia*. Kantoriwicz's famous remark that hierocratic theory was "not even refuted by Dante; it was almost reversed" may put the matter too strongly.[54] But there is no doubt that Dante explicitly turns ecclesiological notions of monarchy against the Church in order to demonstrate that the temporal monarch derives his authority directly from God.[55] Dante's exposition is rigorously scholastic, perhaps even parodically so. Though he employs the exemplum with some frequency, the definitive lay appropriation of the public exemplum would be left to his disciple Boccaccio.

[54] Kantoriwicz, *King's Two Bodies*, 466.   [55] Dante, *Monarchy*, 91–94.

GIOVANNI BOCCACCIO: *DE CASIBUS VIRORUM ILLUSTRIUM*

The last important development in the public exemplum to precede the Chaucerian tradition was Boccaccio's *De casibus virorum illustrium*. Written in forceful, periodic Latin, this work, despite its modern neglect, was probably Boccaccio's most influential and widely circulated during the two centuries following his death. It inspired a number of translations and imitations, leading some scholars to speak, perhaps too grandiosely, of a *De casibus* tradition. This would include the Italian translation of Giuseppe Betussi, Chaucer's *Monk's Tale*, Laurence de Premierfait's *Des cas des nobles hommes et femmes*, Lydgate's *Fall of Princes*, the late fifteenth-century Spanish collection *Caida de principes*, the sixteenth-century collection, *A Mirrour for Magistrates*, and the German translation of Jacob Ziegler.[56] *A Mirrour for Magistrates* makes the connection between the *De casibus* collection and the *Fürstenspiegel* quite explicit. Similar, if less complete indications occur at earlier stages as well. Caxton refers to Boccaccio's work as *De Casu Principum* and Lydgate's very title indicates he takes monarchy to be the subject of a *De casibus* collection.[57]

The most convincing links would of course be those between the *Fürstenspiegel* and Boccaccio's work itself, and indeed, there are a number of them. The most immediately striking occurs in its opening sentence:

I was wondering how the labor of my studies might perhaps add to the benefit of the state, and many things occurred to me beyond belief, but the obscene desires of princes and rulers in general were forced upon my mind with particular energy...

Exquirenti michi quid ex labore studiorum meorum possem forsan rei publice utilitatis addere, occurrere preter creditum multa; maiori tamen conatu tamen in mentem sese ingessere principum atque presidentium ...[58]

---

[56] Vittorio Zaccaria, "Introduzione," in Giovanni Boccaccio, *De casibus virorum illustrium*, vol. 9 of *Tutte le opere di Giovanni Boccaccio*, under the general direction of Pier Giorgio Ricci and Vittorio Zaccaria, ed. Vittore Branca, 12 vols. (Milan: Arnoldo Mondadori Editore, 1983), liin.

[57] "Caxton's Prologue," in *Caxton's Malory*, ed. with intr. James W. Spisak, based on work begun by the late William Matthews (Berkeley and Los Angeles: University of California Press, 1983), v. 1, 2.

[58] Boccaccio, *De casibus*, "Prohemium," 1, pp. 8,10. All subsequent citations are from this edition. Book, chapter, and sentence numbers will be given in the text. There is in fact a partial modern translation of the *De casibus* (Louis Breuer Hall, tr., *The Fates of Illustrious Men* (New York: Frederick Ungar, 1965)), to which I have referred. Hall's approach was to

The first clause is a Ciceronian formula, from the opening of *De Oratore*, but the sentence as a whole clearly echoes Aquinas's dedication to the King of Cyprus, with which he begins *De Regno*.

As I was turning over in my mind what I might present to your Majesty as a gift at once worthy of your Royal Highness and befitting my profession and office, it seemed to me a highly appropriate offering that for a king I should write a book on kingship...

Cogitandi mihi quid offerrem regiae celsitudini dignum, meaeque professioni congruum et officio, id occurrit potissime offerendum, ut regi librum conscriberem...[59]

Boccaccio's purpose is the same, although he states it much more combatively. As he contemplates the many vices of princes, it seems to him that

Fortune led me where it desired. I seized my pen with haste to write on such men. For what is better than discoursing with all one's power in order that the errant might better be drawn back to excellence, the slothful, lulling, deadly sleep be driven out, that vices be checked and virtues extolled?

ratus eo me a fortuna deductum, quo appetabat intentio, festinus arripui calamum scripturus in tales. Nam, quid satius est quam vires omnes exponere, ut in frugem melioris vite retrahantur errantes, a desidibus sopitis letalis somnus excutiatur, vitia reprimantur et extollantur virtutes? (Pr., 2–3)

For all of his hostility, Boccaccio's announced aim is exactly that of the *Fürstenspiegel*: the moral instruction of princes.

The work even begins with a celebratory dedication to a political figure, Boccaccio's friend, the *generosus miles dominus*, Mainardo de Cavalcanti. He is not a monarch, but Boccaccio turns to him because he finds current princes, both lay and ecclesiastical, wanting. ("Dedication," 2–11) Boccaccio's oppositional stance clearly marks a departure from the previous tradition. Even as overt a polemicist as John of Salisbury is more respectful. In Book II, after declaring the habits of contemporary rulers have turned into tyranny, he seems to sanction open rebellion – indeed he makes it sacral.

simplify Boccaccio's Latin style, on the grounds that "to achieve the same effect on the modern reader that his style had on the *trecento* reader it would have been necessary to imitate, for example, Milton's style in the *Areopagitica*" (xvi). This was an unfortunate, if understandable, decision, for it leads Hall to translate so freely in some places as to paraphrase. For this reason, all the translations of this work are mine.
59 Aquinas, *On Kingship*, 2; *De Regimine Principum, Ad Regem Cypri*, ed. Joseph Mathis (Torino and Rome: Marietti, 1948), 1.

In this situation, it is a great thing to band together, take up arms, plan a trap, and oppose with force – it is a most sanctified thing, necessary above all else. When nothing else might be done, the blood of a tyrant is more pleasing to God than the host.

In hunc coniurare, arma capessare, insidias tendere vires opponere magnami est, sanctissum est et omnino necessarium, cum nulla fere sit Deo acceptior hostia tyranni sanguine. (II, v, 7)

Nevertheless, the central points of continuity he establishes between the *De casibus* and the *Fürstenspiegel* clearly show he expects his confrontational stance to be understood in relation to the previous tradition. To return to the introduction:

Nor did it frighten me to see the enormous volumes of our betters in this matter, and know these greatly surpassed my little letters in sweetness of pen and weight of *sententiae*, since I remembered that a rude voice can sometimes provoke those unmoved by thunder.

Nec me terruit maiorum nostrorum in hos ingentia vidisse volumina, et illa novisse stili suavitate et pondere sententiarum meis literulis preponenda pluriumum, cum meminerim non nunquam rudem voculam excivisse non nullos quos tonitrua movisse non poterant. (Pr. 4)

He is obviously referring to a substantial body of previous writing; given the other similarities I have already noted, the likeliest candidate has to be the *Fürstenspiegel*.[60]

The other major antecedent to the *De casibus* is Petrarch's *De viris illustribus*, from which Boccaccio's work takes its title and perhaps its general design. Nevertheless, in *De viris illustribus*, Petrarch is not centrally concerned with Fortune, which he treats in *De remediis utriusque fortune*, another widely circulated work, and his narratives are generally longer than Boccaccio's and more biographical than exemplary. The *De remediis*, on the other hand, has frequent recourse to exempla, but is only incidentally concerned with kingship. Boccaccio's achievement in *De casibus* is to bring Fortune, kingship, and the exemplum in to a single, unrelenting focus. Indeed, for most modern scholars, the work's focus is all too unrelenting. They can see in its continual insistence on the instability of Fortune, and the nearly invariable downward trajectory of each narrative it presents, nothing more than medieval didacticism of the most static variety. I would

---

[60] Pier Giorgio Ricci suggests he might particularly have had in mind the *Policraticus* and Aquinas's *De Regno* (*De casibus*, 923).

suggest, however, that this view, while clearly understandable, is also ahistorical, for what it misperceives as stasis is in fact a carefully managed tension between Boccaccio's two major antecedents. Against the stark moral horizon of Fortune, Boccaccio makes kingship entirely exemplary. This wholescale narrativization should be seen as a completion (in Harold Bloom's sense of the *tessera*) of the laicizing tendencies of the Thomistic *Fürstenspiegel* – in whose tradition Boccaccio obviously locates his work.[61] If the abstract systematizing of the Thomistic tradition gave lay authority a textuality, Boccaccio's *exempla* put that textuality into action, and insisted on its practical applicability. His return to the exemplary simultaneously refocuses the issue of monarchical authority on its actual exercise, and reestablishes narrative as the pre-eminent language of such authority. This move is reinforced by Boccaccio's other antecedent, Petrarch, who enables him to place the work as if it issued from an entirely lay tradition. There was nothing arbitrary in his choice of Petrarch. Monarchy was a topic of keen interest to Petrarch throughout his career, particularly as a means of restoring Italian political unity.[62] The same was true of Dante, as I have already noted. Both Petrarch and Dante were more strenuous in their affirmation of monarchy, but Boccaccio, though his attitude to monarchy is always ambivalent and paradoxical, returns it to its narrative ground.

The key to this shift is Fortune, which functions in the *De casibus* as both moral *sententia* and rhetorical figure. Insofar as it is a *sententia*, it maintains Boccaccio's link to the systematic discourse of the later *Fürstenspiegel*. Insofar as it is a figure, it enables him to stress the interdependence between monarchical authority and the historical realm in which it operates. Much of the scholarly resistance to the *De casibus* and its later imitations undoubtedly stems from a failure to recognize Fortune's rhetorical status. Treated simply as an abstract principle, it does indeed reduce the *De casibus* collection to repeated narrative illustrations of the same moral. Its status was more complex than that, however, as a brief reconsideration of the figure should make clear.

---

[61] Bloom defines *tessera* as the process whereby "the later poet provides what his imagination tells him would complete the otherwise 'truncated' precursor poem and poet" (*The Anxiety of Influence* (New York: Oxford University Press, 1973), 66). Cited in Spearing, *Medieval to Renaissance*, (66) who uses it to describe Lydgate's relation to Chaucer.

[62] Thomas G. Bergin, *Petrarch* (Boston: Twayne, 1970), 68–73, 81–95.

The figure's rhetorical status cannot be separated from its problematic political value. It comes to medieval culture via the *Philosophiae consolatio* of Boethius, the work to which, Richard Firth Green observes, the *De casibus* was the "narrative alter ego."[63] One of the most common works in court libraries, the *Consolatio* was introduced to the Middle Ages by Alcuin at the court of Charlemagne.[64] This courtly interest cannot be explained simply by appealing to the *Consolatio*'s cultural prestige, for it is precisely its rediscovery by the Carolingian court which initiated the accumulation of such prestige. Green suggests that its "immense popularity" stems from

the theoretical application of Boethius's experience to a situation of which all medieval rulers must have been painfully aware. No man in the Middle Ages would have needed to be convinced of the truth of the proposition that the fortunes of the world are fickle and that no position of authority is safe from unforeseen turns of fate... Boethius's work must have been read by medieval princes with a kind of personal involvement which it is perhaps difficult to conceive of today.[65]

I would like to pursue this suggestion by examining Boethius's treatment of Fortune in detail.

Boethius concentrates as much on Fortune's rhetorical instability as on its moral certitude. Lady Philosophy introduces the figure as a preliminary step, a "gentle and pleasant remedy," which, drawing on "the sweet persuasion of rhetoric," will prepare Boethius for the philosophical truths to come.[66] She describes Fortune's wheel, and then briefly adopts Fortune's persona to answer Boethius's complaint in Fortune's own voice. These devices will enable her to show him that misfortune is better than good fortune, for misfortune exposes the temporary and illusory nature of worldly goods. At this point, she can move beyond rhetorical devices and engage Boethius in philosophical exploration of the Divine Good. She uses the figure of Fortune in exactly the same way she argues the wise man should use

---

[63] Richard Firth Green, *Poets and Princepleasers: Literature and the English Court in the Late Middle Ages* (Toronto, Buffalo, London: University of Toronto Press, 1980), 145.

[64] Pierre Courcelle, *La Consolation de Philosophie dans la tradition littéraire: Antécédents et postérité de Boèce* (Paris: Études Augustiniennes, 1963), 46–47.

[65] Green, *Poets and Princepleasers*, 145–46.

[66] Boethius, *The Consolation of Philosophy*, tr. Richard Green (Indianapolis: The Bobbs-Merrill Co., 1962), II, 1, 21. All subsequent translations will be from this edition. Book, chapter, and page numbers will be given in the text.

the temporal benefits it symbolizes, as something useful only insofar as it leads to the Divine Good beyond it.

Nevertheless, the issue is never entirely transcended. Fortune's apparent injustice continues to bother Boethius, and while Philosophy gets him to see that this question is actually "the greatest of all mysteries" (involving among other things, "the simplicity of Providence, the course of Fate, unforseeable chance, divine foreknowledge and free will") she cannot ultimately resolve it, and Boethius must be content with the knowledge that the intricacies of Divine Justice are simply unavailable to the limited consciousness of human beings (II, Prol. 5–6, 89–96).

The openendedness of this conclusion leaves philosophic space for Fortune in spite of its purely figural and rhetorical status. To the extent philosophy cannot make the Divine Good intelligible in its own terms, it is thrown back on stopgaps like the figure of Fortune and her wheel. It is forced to make sense of this world from within. This indirect and rather negative acknowledgment of the autonomy of the historical is reinforced by the dialogue's dramatic context.

The misfortune for which Boethius needs consoling is political as well as personal. As a senator condemned for treason, deprived of his property and imprisoned, what he faces is expulsion from the ruling class. This is the dilemma that the *Consolatio* presented to a courtly audience, the possibility that the hegemonic power in which each member has some share can suddenly and unpredictably turn against him. If there is a political explanation to the *Consolatio*'s enduring and widespread currency at medieval courts, it is assuredly this: its dramatic situation marks the ideological limit of the internal unity of the ruling class. Fortune figures that limit, and figures it in such a way as to reduce its threat. For although the image of Fortune and her wheel speaks to the contingency of material power, it understands such contingency as absolutely random, and denies it any coherent historical specificity. It assumes an invariable baseline against which increases or losses are measured, an immutable *status quo*, which in application will turn out to be the existing class structure.

Speaking in Fortune's voice, Philosophy declares,

Here is the source of my power, the game I always play: I spin my wheel and find pleasure in raising the low to a high place and lowering those who were on top. Go up, if you like, but only on condition that you will not feel abused when my sport requires your fall. Didn't you know about my habits? Surely you had heard of Croesus, King of Lydia, who was a formidable adversary to Cyrus at one time and later suffered such reverses that he would have been burnt had he not been saved by a shower from heaven. And you must have heard how Paulus wept over the calamities suffered by Perses, King of Macedonia, whom he captured. (24)

Haec nostra vis est, hunc continuum ludum ludimus: rotam volubili orbe versamus, infima summis, summa infimis mutare gaudemus. Ascende si placet, sed ea lege, ne uti cum ludicri mei ratio poscet descendere iniuriam putes. An tu mores ignorabas meos? Nesciebas Croesum regem Lydorum Cyro paulo ante formidabilem mox deinde miserandum rogi flammis traditum misso caelitus imbre defensum? Num te praeterit Paulum Persi regis a se capti calamitatibus pias impendisse lacrimas?[67]

Like any metaphor which defines social experience as a game, this one has an aspect that is profoundly conservative. By necessity, it assumes a stable, non-ludic ground against which the play of the game can be defined as play. The balance of the passage strongly suggests that this ground is constituted by the social position of any participant the moment before he joins the game. In effect, then, the figure of Fortune's wheel posits a stable class structure to which one can always retreat. The figure further suggests one has already to be a part of the ruling class – in late Antique terms, a landowning free man – in order to get into the game in the first place. The two royal exempla Fortune cites reinforce this impression. The kind of ascent she clearly has in mind is one which begins from a certain base of social privilege and acquires more.

The *status quo* which underwrites Fortune's game also underwrites Philosophy's Stoic antidote, the internal self-possession which enables one to see through Fortune's illusions. For if we ask what exactly is possessed in this state of self-possession, we will see it can be nothing other than the equilibrium that exists in the moment before Fortune's game begins – in other words, one's social position. To suggest that some element of one's social position is innate, self-possessed, is simply to ratify the bias already built into any society ruled by an aristocracy of birth. In the figure of Fortune an aristocratic class can at once recognize the flux of historical existence, and affirm its own privilege as a locus of stability beyond such flux.

This doubleness, recognition and affirmation, is not only a function of the figure's content but is also built into its formal structure. For

---

[67] Boethius, *Philosophiae consolatio*, ed. Ludwig Bieler, *Corpus Christianorum, series latina*, 94 (Turnholt: Brepols, 1957), II, Pr. I, 9–12. All subsequent citations are from this edition. Book and chapter numbers will be given in the text.

even as the figure asserts the continual instability of historical existence, it also gives that instability a shape. To the extent that Fortune provides the instability it figures with a source, it makes it more controllable. That the figure is entirely rhetorical heightens rather than lessens such control, for it demonstrates the extent to which the instability of history can be made intelligible from within, using history's own materials. To be sure, this control is markedly minimalist. As an explanation of historical change, Fortune in fact explains very little. She is nearly featureless, beyond perfunctory indications of gender, and the threadbare metaphor of her wheel. As the putative origin of historical change, she does little more than assert that change has no logical origin. Yet even this minimalism has political value. As it reduces the logicality of change, it also reduces its desirability. The rhetorical control the figure offers an aristocratic audience gives it the confidence to act within history. The minimalist mode in which such control is defined assures the same audience that the status quo on which it rests provides a stable ground.

Boccaccio's use of the figure in the *De casibus* is as paradoxical as the figure itself. We might say he widens its scope while retaining its minimalist impulse. Because Fortune provides his central moral focus, Boccaccio in effect places the entire work within the realm of the "sweet persuasion of rhetoric," the zone which Boethius had made primarily preliminary. What Boethius was able to treat in a single book of a short, five-book work, Boccaccio expands to a full nine books of a much longer one, an expansion which literally treats all of human history from Adam and Eve to shortly before his own present, transforming that history into a long, consistent series of exemplary downfalls. At the end of the Prohemium, he declares, "I decided to use exempla to describe to them [wicked rulers] what almighty God, or – to use their language – Fortune, can and will do to those raised up."[68] It is true that this declaration distances Boccaccio from the world of the rulers he is describing, and maintains the Boethian logic which treats Fortune as an imperfect figure for God. Yet the emphasis has still shifted, and the work foregrounds Fortune throughout, despite the ultimate deference to divine authority. History becomes the pre-eminent arena for moral struggle. The opposition between Fortune and kingship establishes not only a sphere of action, but in the figurality of Fortune, a discourse specific

---

[68] Proh., 6: " ... exemplis agendum ratus sum eis describere quid Deus omnipotens, seu – ut eorum loquar more – Fortuna, in elatos possit et fecerit."

to that sphere. Indeed, as we shall see, later in the work Fortune comes to underwrite Boccaccio's own textual authority, despite the distance he announces here.

The result is a work, which, far from confirming the modern caricature of a complacent, static didacticism, is marked at every level by confrontation and conflict, from its conceptual frame to the very movement of its language. If we return once more to the Prohemium, and examine at length what I have been citing in snippets, we will see both this dynamism and the images of secular authority it generates more clearly.

I was wondering how the labor of my studies might perhaps add to the benefit of the state, and many things occurred to me beyond belief, but the obscene desires of princes and rulers in general were forced upon my mind with particular energy – along with their furious violence, their swift profligacy, their insatiable avarice, their bloodthirsty hatred, and their forceful and subtle vendettas, and the most wicked, and by far the greatest crimes. I saw that no rein might restrain these leaders from flying away with evil on all sides, and in this way oppressing all honest citizens, violating the sacred justice of laws, corrupting all virtue, and – something which is unspeakable – by abominable examples leading the souls of the multitude into impious habits. It seemed Fortune led me where it desired. I seized my pen with haste to write on such men. For what is better than discoursing with all one's power in order that the errant might better be drawn back to virtuous living, that deadly sleep be shaken from its torpid idleness, that vices be checked and virtues extolled? Nor did it frighten me to see the momentous volumes of our betters in this matter, and know these greatly surpassed my little letters in sweetness of pen and weight of *sententiae*, since I remembered that a rude voice can sometimes provoke those unmoved by thunder. With their kind permission, therefore, I will follow my impulse to speak where it leads, and perhaps my thin breath may bring stony hearts to their deliverance, or at least soften them a little.

Exquirenti michi quid ex labore studiorum meorum possem forsan rei publice utilitatis addere, occurrere preter creditum multa; maiori tamen conatu in mentem sese ingessere principum atque presidentium quorum-cunque obscene libidines, violentie truces, perdita ocia, avaritie inexplebiles, cruenta odia, ultiones armate precipitesque et longe plura scelesta facinora. Que cum ductu scelestium viderem nullo coercita freno evolantia undique, et inde honestatem omnem fedari publicam, iustitie sacratissimas leges solvi, labefactari virtutes omnes, et – quod infandum est – detestandis exemplis in mores impios ignare multitudinis ingenia trahi, ratus eo me a fortuna deductum, quo appetabat intentio, festinus arripui calamum scripturus in tales. Nam, quid satius est quam vires omnes exponere, ut in frugem melioris vite retrahantur errantes, a desidibus sopitis letalis somnus excutiatur, vitia reprimantur et extollantur virtutes? Nec me terruit maiorum nostrorum in hos ingentia vidisse volumina, et illa novisse stili suavitate et pondere sententiarum meis literulis preponenda plurimum, cum meminerim non nunquam rudem voculam excivisse non nullos quos tonitrua movisse non poterant. Bona igitur pace talium, quo inpellit dicendi impetus tendam, si forsan saxea hec corda tenui spiritu oris mei in salutem suam mollire saltem paululum queam. (Proh. 1–6)

Boccaccio addresses his audience in a relentlessly confrontational fashion; his emphatic desire to improve public life in no way mitigates his open contempt for those who engage in it. Public life is a zone of chaotic but undeniable power, to which he is continually driven back even as he is driven away. The process is played out in the very movement of his language, as his long rolling periods come back again and again to the same points. As he begins to wonder about the state he is immediately engulfed in a multitude of concerns and manages to focus on "the obscene desires of princes" only because the magnitude of its excesses forces it upon him. Each time he names one of these desires he displays the power of his language, yet each time there is another obscenity to be named, and his linguistic power gives way to the power of the thing it describes. It is precisely this ceaseless crossing of sorts that defines the chaos of political life.

As Boccaccio begins the work Fortune leads him: his moralizing is subject to the very disruptive force that moral authority should enable one to escape. What it leads him to is the *detestanda exempla* of evil princes. The obligatory force of the gerundive is precise here. These examples are *to be execrated*; they demand that reaction from the reader by virtue of their public value. Because of the prince's exemplary position his wickedness results in a general moral breakdown throughout the populace, leading "the souls of the ignorant multitude in impious habits." This view of kingship's exemplary power matches that of Aegidius Romanus. By focusing on the failure of contemporary princes to fulfill this exemplary position, he accentuates its public (as opposed to personal) dimension, thereby empowering his readership. His recognition and execration of this exemplary failure themselves constitute a source of moral order, a moral force registered by the resistant movement of the text. As this movement draws his readership in by dramatizing its own process of composition, it also gives their participation moral value.

Boccaccio engages in similar forms of dramatization throughout the collection. The work is nominally a vision, in which waves of figures from the past appear before him, sometimes engaging him in conversation, or arguing among themselves. From these he selects the stories he will tell, beginning with Adam and Eve, and ending with his own contemporaries. The number of mourners (*flentes*) or unhappy ones (*infelices*), as he describes them in the chapter headings, always greatly exceeds the number of stories that can be told, and he continually complains of the burdensomeness of the rest, as he must often drive them off, like Odysseus in the Underworld. He frequently refers to the work as if it were still being written, as if his progress through were simultaneous with that of his readers. The fable about Fortune which opens the third book is introduced as something to pass the time while he and the reader rest from the exertions of the first two books (III, Prol.). At the beginning of the fourth he observes that his examples are beginning to take effect (IV, Prol.), and at the close of the final book he asserts that he and his readers have come into port after a dangerous voyage (IX, xxvii). Even the disposition of his text seems to come to him *in medias res*. At the end of what will be the first book, he grows "weary with writing (*defatigum scribendo*)," and decides to divide the work into books in order to afford himself a brief rest (I, xix).

The collection's most frequent and most directly political mode of readerly involvement is the exempla themselves, with the universally unrelenting destruction of every monarchical figure they present. As the readers participate with Boccaccio in the process of selecting a protagonist and recounting his or her actions, and then drawing morals, they share both the protagonist's power exhibited in his or her ascent, and the more abiding power of Fortune in stripping it away. This participation in monarchical power is consistent with what I have called the class-specific appeal of the Boethian version of Fortune, with one telling difference. The plot of the *Consolatio* conceptualizes misfortune in the figure of an aristocrat oppressed by a monarch. With few exceptions, the exemplary plots of the *De casibus* figure misfortune in the downfall of the monarch himself (or herself). Thus in this work the rhetorical empowerment Fortune offers an aristocratic audience extends to narrative control of kingship itself.

The work's characterization of the dynamics of the lay tradition complements this broadening of focus. The characterization consists mainly of two colloquies which interrupt the parade of exempla.[69]

---

[69] There is also a brief exchange with Dante in Book IX (xxiii).

The first is with Fortune; the second with Petrarch. The colloquy with Fortune occurs at the beginning of Book VI. In a parodic version of Boethius's Lady Philosophy, Fortune appears to Boccaccio as a giant as ugly as Philosophy was beautiful. She disparages his work until he mollifies her by requesting her aid.

... I know that with a turn of your wheel, you can steal all from the face of the earth. I beg as a suppliant that by your grace you will favor this work which I have begun, so that my name, at present obscure, by your brilliance will become gloriously bright to posterity.

... cum te moto turbine a facie terre cuncta posse surripere noverim, queso supplex ut tua gratia ceptum secundetur opus et quod obscurum presentibus nomen meum est tuo illustratum fulgore clarum apud posteros habeatur. (VI,i,16)

This request reinforces Boccaccio's dependence on the very agent of instability his moralizing aspires to get beyond. Indeed, what Boccaccio desires to achieve through this work is the very status of *illustratus* that has been the cause of the downfalls the work chronicles. In an earlier fable, portraying the battle between Fortune and Poverty, Boccaccio had presented the standard view that Fortune could be controlled by rejecting the material prosperity she represents. The course of this conversation will suggest she can be beaten at her own game, through the linguistic power, "the sweet persuasion of rhetoric," which generates her.

In response to his request her expression softens, and smiling, she disavows the earlier fable and the traditional criticisms of her as a result of the limitations of human understanding. Then she says:

Now as if I could be fooled with lies and flattery as inexperienced little girls are often fooled, you come as a suppliant and implore my help. I know and know well what opinion you hold and what faith you have in my power. Whatever my thoughts of you might be, since I see you are not lazy and dejected in spirit, but watchful and eager for glory, directing your steps wholly toward it, but are striving onward, you have deflected my judgment and changed my plan. Now I praise your task and I praise your ability, and as long as you pursue skillfully what you have begun, my favor will not desert you, and your name and that of Certaldo will be numbered among the shining names of antiquity.

... et nunc quasi et ego, uti frequenter inexperte puellule blanditiis mendaciisque falluntur, falli possim, supplex meum exposcis subsidium. Novi et satis novi quam geras opinionem et meis in viribus habeas fidem; sed qualiscunque tibi sit mens, quoniam non inertis atque deiecti animi et glorie cupidum vigilemque totis in eam tendentem pedibus te video, sententiam flexisti meam et mutasti consilium; et cum iam ingenium opusque commendem tuum, dum solers cepta sequaris, orationi tue favor non deerit meus, quin et Certaldum tuum et tuum nomen inter clara veterum nomina numerentur ... (VI, i, 18–19)

Fortune's authority is undermined by her abrupt change of mind. She claims she cannot be manipulated like a young girl, then immediately grants Boccaccio's request. Yet he has not really flattered her, as she claims. His request for aid repeated the definition – that she was variable – that he had been offering all along. What she calls his flattery before her change of mind, and her power afterward, are really the same thing, for to recognize her variability is to recognize her power.

In that recognition lies Boccaccio's power as well. As a rhetorical figure, Fortune testifies to the ability of such a recognition to give itself shape and voice, to generate its own rhetorical narrative order. Boccaccio's connection of the figure to the question of literary reputation firmly establishes the rhetorical as a source of authority generated from within history. His subjection of his voice to hers is a subjection to another voice of his own making. More generally, to place literature under the aegis of Fortune is to place it under its own aegis, its own capacity to produce narrative order.

Having projected his own authority into the future, two books later Boccaccio puts this capacity on firmer ground with an invocation of Petrarch. In the midst of his labors he is overcome by lethargy and begins to doubt their utility. Imagining his own impending death, he decides his desire for fame is idle:

When you no longer feel momentary things, even if all of the world sings full-throated praise of no other name but yours, what honor or pleasure can you claim, being absent?

Quid ... cum nil ex momentaneis rebus amplius senties, etiam si orbis totus ore pleno nil aliud preter nomen tuum cum laude cantet, absens, honoris aut voluptatis assumnes? (VIII, i, 3)

When he finds himself nearly conquered by his despair, Petrarch appears to explain that the fame which he has just dismissed

is nevertheless a good desirable to all mortals. It is eagerly sought in many ways, but never acquired but through virtue. Whoever damns it necessarily damns the cultivation of virtue.

tanquam bonum a cunctis mortalibus exoptata est. Que cum variis perquiratur viis, non nisi per virtutem acquiritur. Quam si quis damnet, virtutis exercitium damnet necesse est. (VIII, i, 9)

Fame is a divine gift, which enables the name of merit to be carried to the end of the earth instead of perishing in darkness, where it lives on in perpetual splendor after the soul ascends to heaven. It both brings the past into the present, and constitutes the engine which drives the present into the future:

This [fame] endowed with vital strength enacts a triumph over death, of the longest earthly duration, since we mortals have nothing eternal; not without being gradually diminished by time, which gnaws away at everything, and consumed with long labor. It nourishes us with an almost continual record of the living. The most obvious demonstration of this point are those whose power is infixed in letters: Ninus, the oldest king of Assyria, among other things, the name of whose works still stands, though the ashes have disappeared; Abraham, father of the children of Israel; Moses, leader of their escape; Homer, pre-eminent poet; Aristotle, dean of the Peripatetics; most warlike Africanus; most honorable Cato; and other noble men, all of whom this same fame has brought to the present day with almost perennial greenness. Through its power, we know, praise, and honor them, and we feel great pleasure of soul, for that which they receive from us, we expect by virtue of our labors to receive from the future. Thus hopefully we anticipate future glory.

Hec, cum vitali robore predita agat ex morte triunphum, a solis longissimis seculorum spatiis, cum nil mortales habeamus eternum, sensim minuitur nec absque temporis, cuncta rodentis, labore longevo consumitur, cum a continuo fere viventium nutriatur relatu. Cuius rei evidentissimum argumentum est quod suo robore literis infixo: Ninum vetustissimum Assyriorum regem cuius, nedum alia, sed huius opere stante nomine cinis deletus est; Abraham israelitici populi patrem, Moysen fugientium ducem, Homerum vatem precipuum, Aristotilem Peripateticorum principem, Affricanum bellicosissimum, honestissimos Catones aliosque insignes viros, quos quasi perenni viridate ipsa in hodiernum usque deduxit perpetuos. Quos, ea agente, noscimus laudamus et colimus magnamque animi voluptatem sentimus, dum id quod illi suscipiunt a nobis, nos labore nostro apud futuros posse suscipere credimus; et sic futuram gloriam spirantes anticipamus. (VIII, i, 11–12)

This passage constitutes an important variation on John of Salisbury's defense of writing. It substitutes *fama* for letters as the motive force bringing the past into the present. Like John's *iocunditas litterarum*, *fama* is a divine gift, but, unlike letters, is specifically restricted to the realm of history. This force comes out of history's own inner workings: it is more directly under human control, a more purely human product. It begins with human actions, but it is no less dependent on the performative, productive power of the textual. It infixes the actions of *insignes vires* in letters, which gives those actions a greenness *quasi perenni*. But it also makes the power of the textual itself more specifically dependent on human action. *Fama* motivates not only the *insignes vires*, but also the writing which preserves them; the writers have now become important actors in their own right. *Fama* reestablishes the exchange between *facta* and *dicta* on purely historical grounds, motivated by a specifically historical interest. The *opera* of the *insignes vires* is answered by the *labor* of the lay *auctor*, propelling the present into the *futura gloria*, by virtue of that work's laborious recovery of the past.

Petrarch demonstrates the vitality of this exchange not only by his argument, but by his very appearance in the text. It makes him more than an authority, a textual principle, and insists on his historical existence as an heroic force. Boccaccio's present work is enabled by the *fama* of the past not simply as an evanescent, textual image, but by the past as a still vital force of a previous preserver of *fama*. Petrarch's textual achievement was precisely to project that force into the present, and that achievement will enable Boccaccio to project a similar force into the future. Boccaccio borrows the materiality of this exchange from the clerical versions, but he transposes it into the terms of specifically lay tradition, placing lay letters at the heart of the struggle to impose moral order on history. The *fama* which they produce at once sustains this struggle and affirms it. As the focus of moral authority within history, lay tradition enables its audience to become moral simply by reading, without necessarily requiring heroic action. Secular readership becomes a self-constituting, self-affirming moral force.

As Petrarch's remarks also make clear, the moral force represented by lay readers is also an exclusive one. The writer, he tells Boccaccio,

must act, must work and with all his power urge his skill, so that we be separated from the vulgar herd – so that, just as our predecessors through their labor benefited us, so will we, through ours, make ourselves valuable to posterity ...

agendum est, laborandum est et totis urgendum viribus ingenium, ut a vulgari segregemur grege; ut, tanquam preteriti labore suo profuere nobis, sic et nos nostro valeamus posteris ... (VIII, i, 26)

An instance of the humanist topos which distinguishes the *sapientes* from the *vulgus*, this passage demonstrates more directly than most such instances the class interest that underlies them.[70] Having established the interchangeablity between the performing and recording of heroic actions in rhetorical terms, Petrarch establishes it in class terms as well. The sheer production of a text like Boccaccio's makes one a member of the ruling class, whose power the text adumbrates. The laicization of textual authority which the *De casibus* accomplishes also establishes a political order which can claim to be constituted on purely textual terms. This was, no doubt, the final element of the *De casibus*'s political value, which accounts for its subsequent appeal in England. To a society where an expanding ruling class was converting more and more of its customary hegemony into statute law and textually recorded administrative procedure, and where the most administratively advanced monarchy in Europe was becoming an increasing locus of ideological contention, the *De casibus* projected an image of authority that was public and textual, yet also exclusive, that offered a share of such authority to all who could read it, yet reassured its readers that such shares remain the exclusive property of those above the *vulgus*.

[70] Alexander Murray, *Reason and Society in the Middle Ages* (Oxford: Clarendon Press, 1978), 239–44.

PART II

The Chaucerian tradition

CHAPTER 6

Exemplarity and the Chaucerian tradition

The exemplum was the dominant narrative genre of the Chaucerian tradition. Of its four most important works, the *Canterbury Tales*, the *Confessio Amantis*, the *Regement of Princes*, and the *Fall of Princes*, only the first is not an exemplum collection. Even that, however, is a collection of narratives which the exemplum, and the issue of exemplarity, pervades at every level. Of its twenty-four tales, at least eight and as many as twelve can be described as exempla or exemplum collections.[1] The accretion of exempla within tales – Dorigen's lamentation is one spectactular instance, Chauntecleer's defense of dreams another – is one of Chaucer's favorite rhetorical ploys. Even the tales that are not exempla in a strict generic sense, that is, the romances and the fabliaux, tend to end with moralizing explicits. The prologues return repeatedly to the opposition between moral *ernest* and narrative *game*, and the estates-satire frame implicitly makes each tale an exemplification of the social position of the character who speaks it.

In my examination of the Latin tradition I have argued that the sermon exemplum and the public exemplum formed distinct yet complementary vehicles of the Church's broad-based attempts to increase its institutional control of secular life. I will now argue that the Chaucerian tradition's dependence on the exemplum represents an appropriation, or reappropriation of the ideological authority the Church used the exemplum to promote. The Chaucerian tradition used the exemplum as the vehicle to establish its own authority. It

---

[1] One can clearly classify the *Friar's Tale*, the *Summoner's Tale*, the *Physician's Tale*, the *Pardoner's Tale*, the *Monk's Tale* (exemplum collection), the *Nun's Priest's Tale*, and the *Manciple's Tale* as exempla or exemplum collections. One could also add to the list the three pathetic tales (the *Man of Law's Tale*, the *Clerk's Tale*, and the *Prioress's Tale*), and the *Wife of Bath's Tale* on the grounds of its exemplary relation to the parodic sermon that constitutes its prologue.

draws on both strands of the Latin tradition. From the sermon exemplum it appropriates the textual authority the form had reserved to the clergy. From the public exemplum it reclaims the monarch as the source of lay political authority. This combination grounds the textual in the political but it also gives the textual a political efficacy it lacked in even the most hierocratic *Fürstenspiegel*.

While students of later Middle English literature have long recognized the exemplum's importance, they have ignored its political dimensions, even when dealing with the *Fürstenspiegel*. It is a truism among historians that the general influence of the *Fürstenspiegel* in later medieval England was negligible. As a result, where the genre's importance to the Chaucerian tradition has been recognized it has been treated largely as an apolitical exercise in learned borrowing. Berges names only two English *Fürstenspiegel* after the *Policraticus*, Peter of Blois's late twelfth-century *Dialogus cum Rege Heinrico*, and Simon Islip's mid-fourteenth-century *De speculo Regis Edwardi III*. Genet is even more restrictive, claiming only the poem by George Ashby for Edward, son of Henry VI, "qualifies entirely" to be called a *Fürstenspiegel*.[2]

The paucity of Latin *Fürstenspiegel* compiled in England only tells part of the story, however. For *Fürstenspiegel* compiled elsewhere were widely disseminated in England, especially the *Policraticus*, the *De regimine principum* of Aegidius Romanus, the *Secretum secretorum* and the *Ludus schachorum*.[3] The *De Regimine* was of particular interest to advisors of Richard II, and may well have provided an intellectual framework for his absolutist ambitions.[4] The *Secretum* inspired a large number of translations and adaptations, including Book VII of the *Confessio Amantis*, and seems to have been more popular in England than anywhere else.[5] Moreover, as Genet himself readily concedes,

---

[2] Berges, *Die Fürstenspiegel*, 71, 127–28, 293–94, 343; Genet, "General Introduction," xiv, and "Ecclesiastics and Political Theory," 32–35.

[3] For the circulation of the *Policraticus*, see Amnon Lindner, "The Knowledge of John of Salisbury in the Later Middle Ages," *Studi Medievali* 18/2 (1977), 315–66. For the *De regimine*, see R. H. Jones, *Royal Policy of Richard II: Absolutism in the Later Middle Ages* (New York: Barnes and Noble, 1973) 154–63; Green, *Poets and Princepleasers*, 141; and Genet, "Ecclesiastics and Political Theory," 32–35. On the *Secretum*, see Green, 140–42; and M. A. Manzalaoui, ed., *Secretum secretorum* (Oxford: Early English Text Society, 1977), ix-l. No comparable study exists for the *Ludus schachorum*; however the fact that the work was known by Chaucer and translated by Caxton testifies to its currency.

[4] Jones, *Royal Policy*, 154–62. It is also worth noting that a copy of the *De Regimine* may have accompanied the Ellesmere Chaucer when it was acquired by the Egerton family in the early seventeenth century. See Alix Egerton, *The Ellesmere Chaucer* (Manchester: The University Press, 1911), 6.   [5] Genet, "General Introduction," xvi.

one must also take into account the profusion of political writings in later medieval England, especially in the vernacular.[6] Indeed if one defines the *Fürstenspiegel* by its interest in kingship's public dimension, rather than by its Latinity, then one can well see these vernacular writings as the genre's greatest flowering rather than its demise. Janet Coleman argues that "works like *Richard the Redeless, Mum and the Sothsegger, Wynnere and Wastoure*" in the alliterative "complaint" tradition "can be classified *thematically* as mirrors for princes."[7] The same thing is true of the Chaucerian tradition: the *Tale of Melibee*, the *Monk's Tale*, the *Confessio Amantis*, the *Regement of Princes*, the *Fall of Princes*, even the *Clerk's Tale*, and the *Nun's Priest's Tale*, can be seen as extensions of the *Fürstenspiegel* tradition. Each of these works takes up the tradition's most fundamental ideological stance, constructing the monarch as both the subject of public instruction and the guarantor of public authority.

In so doing they were drawing on one of the most powerful political notions in the culture, whose importance can hardly be restricted to what twentieth-century scholarship has defined as the literary. One of its most striking instances occurs in the *Articles of Deposition* of Richard II. This anomalous document, which purports to be parliamentary, and to speak for the public at large, but was in fact a careful piece of stage managing by Henry Bolingbroke, was a practical instrument of the first order. Yet its most notorious article, article 33, is an almost pure recapitulation of the corporate fiction.

33. ITEM, the same King did not wish to preserve or protect the just Laws and Customs of his Reign, but to make whatever decision occured to him according to the judgment of his own will. Whenever the Laws of his Reign were explained and declared to him by the Justices and others of his Council, and according to these Laws justice for the suitors exhibited, he would say expressly with a stern and shameless countenance, that his Laws were in his mouth, and several times, in his heart, and that he himself alone was able to change or institute the Laws of his Reign ...[8]

---

[6] Genet, "General Introduction," xv-xvi, though in "Ecclesiastics and Political Theory" he suggests the English reading public "had but a limited taste for political theory as such" (34). I would suggest this claim can be sustained only if one maintains a very narrow (and probably anachronistic) view of political theory.

[7] "English Culture in the Fourteenth Century," in *Chaucer and the Italian Trecento*, ed. Piero Boitani (Cambridge: Cambridge University Press, 1983), 60.

[8] *Rotuli Parliamentorum*, ed. J. Strachey, 6 vols. (London: 1767-83), vol. 3, 419:

33. ITEM, idem Rex nolens justas Leges & Consuetudines Regni sui servare se protegere, set secundum sue arbitrium Voluntatis facere quicquid desideriis ijus occurrerrit, quandoque & frequentius quando sibi expositi & declarati fuerant Leges Regni sui per Justic' & alios de Consilio suo, & secundum Leges illas

Historians have traditionally ignored the ideological precedents of this story. They have treated it instead as a simple denunciation of tyranny, consistent with the standard constitutionalist view of the Deposition as "one more step in the transference of the centre of political gravity from ruler to people..."[9] If more recent historians have been suspicious of this sort of Whig teleology, they have still treated Article 33 as an essentially accurate depiction of Richard, even though, as Anthony Tuck concedes, there is no proof of its truth.[10] It is hard to see how there ever could be such proof, given the article's conceptual debt to the very corporate fiction it would seem to be disavowing.

At the very moment Richard voices his ostensibly discredited claim, the narrative focuses not on the specific legal results of the claim, but on his body, on what his face looked like as he spoke: "a stern and shameless countenance." This return to his body in its very physicality is both necessary and profoundly contradictory. For the story to make its case against Richard it must concede to him the very power to embody the law it accuses him of illicitly claiming. In those cases so vaguely cited here, where Richard made this claim, his voice *did* have the force of law. He was able effectively to void precedent and nullify counsel simply by announcing, according to his own *voluntas*, that he wished to do so. If the story makes Richard out as a tyrant it is not because he violated some explicitly established constitutional principle. It is because he declined to live up to the ideal of the corporate fiction. He refused to embody counsel and legal precedent in a single unifying voice: he literalized the body politic

petentibus justiciam exhiberet; Dixit expresse, voltu austero & protervo, quod Leges sue erant in ore suo, & aliquotiens in pectore suo: Et qd ipse solus posset mutare & condere Leges Regni sui...

The translation is mine.

[9] Bertie Wilkinson, *Politics and the Constitution 1307–1399*, vol. 2 of *Constitutional History of Medieval England 1216–1399*, 2 vols. (London: Longmans & Green, 1952), 298. In fairness I should say that as constitutional history has become less fashionable, more recent accounts have become less explicitly teleological. Nevertheless they still treat Richard's deposition as primarily a matter of resisting tyranny, and to this extent are guilty of a similar form of anachronism. By modern standards, all of the medieval nobility were tyrants in the sense that most of the populace lacked adequate redress against them. In this context to single out Richard's tyranny is to ignore the larger issue of class relations within which his relation to the rest of the nobility was played out. Even recent accounts do not address the issue of class, and tend to reduce Richard's "tyranny" to personal traits: according to Anthony Tuck, he was arrogant and petulant (*Crown and Nobility 1272–1461* (Oxford: Basil Blackwell, 1986), 222), to May McKisack, vindictive and possibly insane (*The Fourteenth Century* (Oxford: Clarendon Press, 1959), 496–98), to A. B. Steel, definitely on the verge of insanity (*Richard II* (Cambridge: Cambridge University Press, 1941), 278–79).

[10] Anthony Tuck, *Richard II and the English Nobility* (London: Edward Arnold, 1973), 204.

and thus revealed monarchical theory to be a metaphor – i.e., a fiction.[11]

The point of Article 33 is not to reject the corporate fiction's ideal of the king as the living embodiment of the law, but to reinstate it. Bolingbroke, the architect of the deposition wanted to replace Richard, not to alter the structure of kingship. Presenting Richard as a failed exemplar of royal authority, as a *tyrannus* in the medieval – but not the modern – sense, enabled him to present himself as an exemplar who could succeed. This narrative was a species of political power in the most material sense. For to tell this story of the royal voice was quite literally to usurp its authority. Moreover, narrative's performative power in this instance depends not simply on some purely generic property, but on a long tradition (the corporate fiction) that its performative power produced and maintained. The *Articles of Deposition* demonstrate in a particular instance what the development of the *Fürstenspiegel* suggests on a larger scale: that medieval monarchical power was dependent on discursive forms like narrative that we usually think of as literary.

For this reason, we must surely see the emergence of the Chaucerian tradition, an authoritative literary tradition in the vernacular, and the widespread cultural concern with the nature and limits of kingship as concurrent aspects of a broader establishment of lay forms of authority. Monarchist ideology was paradoxical and contradictory. As time went on the contradictions grew sharper: kingship increasingly attempted to present itself as simultaneously more representative and more absolute. In England, the emergence of an authoritative vernacular tradition associated with the royal court obviously provided an arena where kingship could be viewed as more representative. The concentration of *Fürstenspiegel*-like works within the Chaucerian tradition, in addition to the profusion of similar works outside of it made a symbolic share in monarchical power more widely available. At the same time, we must also recognize that this textual dispersion was in its very dispersiveness enacted in the name of a more ideal concentration. The singular figure of the monarch was the ideal uniting this wider audience.

Most of the vernacular works dealing with kingship are ambivalent about it – this is certainly true of all of the works we shall look at here.

---

[11] For a fuller treatment of Article 33, see my "King's Two Voices: Narrative and Power in Hoccleve's *Regement of Princes,*" in *Literary Practice and Social Change in Britain, 1380–1530,* ed. Lee Patterson (Berkeley: University of California Press, 1990), 218–26.

But that ambivalence should not immediately be read either as some form of subversion, or as some form of purely spiritual transcendence. For as we have seen, medieval ideologies of kingship were always ambivalent and contradictory, and the contradictions ran the gamut from cynical recognitions of its historical contingency to spiritual aspirations to transcend it. What I am suggesting is that the Chaucerian tradition be viewed as part of the ideology of kingship it embraced: that its contradictions are the same contradictions. I do not make this suggestion in order to "reduce" literature to the status of ideology – ideology is not a reductive category for me. Still less do I wish to suggest that the politics of kingship were entirely aestheticized. My purpose is rather to assert that kingship and the vernacular literary text were inextricably interdependent, as two complementary forms of emergent lay cultural authority. Recognizing this fact does not necessarily mean completely renouncing the distinction between political and literary authority. But it does mean acknowledging that politics and literature could come to be viewed as antithetical in the twentieth century only because at an earlier point in their historical development they were more closely related. If the Chaucerian tradition turned to the political authority of kingship so often, it was precisely because it could not take its own authority for granted. To counterbalance the textual authority of the Latin, clerical tradition from which it was attempting to break away, it needed the God-givenness of kingship as an unassailable source of social authority originating from within the lay. It did not completely sublate itself to monarchical authority. It assumed the same moral distance from the king that clerical writers had – that distance was precisely what it appropriated. From this appropriation the new tradition could establish the figure of the *auctor* as a lay, vernacular category.

Later medieval England was marked by a slight but important expansion of the ruling class. The top strata of the mercantile bourgeoisie began to acquire landed power, and the lesser gentry acquired an increasingly important voice in government, both through their participation in Parliament and their increasing dominance of the adminstration of royal justice.[12] In both of these

---

[12] The standard work on the changing composition of the nobility in later medieval England is K. B. McFarlane, *The Nobility of Later Medieval England* (Oxford: Clarendon Press, 1972). See esp. 142–76. On the fourteenth century House of Commons as "above all a gathering of lords of the manor," see R. H. Hilton, *The Decline of Serfdom in Medieval England* (London:

areas power was exercised in the name of the king, even when, as occasionally in the case of Parliament, it was exercised against his wishes. The royal bureaucracy continued to expand and began increasingly to staff itself with wealthy merchants' sons, like Chaucer, in addition to its recruitment of the lesser gentry – a tradition that extended as far back as Henry I.[13] But the retinues of lesser lords swelled as well, as their manorial business increasingly came to depend on written records, creating more opportunities for modestly born, literate men of talent than could be met by the Church, which traditionally had supplied such needs.[14] All of these changes produced a broader, more variegated ruling class, the broadest and most dynamic element of which experienced their growing power largely in the production and manipulation of texts, be they statute law, or administrative and financial record. But the textual gained a new importance as well for the older and more powerful element of the ruling class, the great barons. For their power now depended precisely on its dispersion in these new textual forms. The Chaucerian tradition, with its concentration on the public morality of kingship, would have served both elements of the newly expanded ruling class. Its emphasis on the ideological availability of monarchical authority would have been attractive to the lower stratum, while its insistence that power ultimately be concentrated in a single figure would have been attractive to the upper one. And the specific focus on kingship would have been attractive not only because so many of the newly empowered lower strata were connected to the royal bureaucracy but for another, more symbolic reason as well. The concentering of textual authority in the single figure of the king assured the whole of the ruling class that even the most exalted forms of social power could be textually dispersed yet remain singular, under the ultimate control of the figure in whose name they were dispersed.

The substantial quantity of good, recent work on the reading public in later medieval England remains divided on a central question: was that public courtly, or "middle class"?[15] The

Macmillan, 1983), 29. The lesser gentry came to dominate the administration of royal justice mainly through the institution of the office of the Justice of the Peace, which began in the fourteenth century to displace seigneurial jurisdiction. See Alan Harding, *The Law Courts of Medieval England* (London: George Allen and Unwin; New York: Barnes and Noble, 1973), 86–123.   [13] Southern, *Medieval Humanism*, 206–33.

[14] Coleman, *Medieval Readers*, 18–57; "English Culture," 38–42.

[15] The fullest statement of the courtly thesis is Green, *Poets and Princepleasers*. That of the "middle class" thesis is Coleman, *Medieval Readers*. Anne Middleton, "The Idea of Public Poetry in the Reign of Richard II," *Speculum* 53 (1979), 94–114 includes most of later

advantage of the hegemonic model I am proposing is that it allows
the answer to that question to be both. The expanding social
opportunities for the educated and literate members of the lesser
gentry and urban patriciate provided a public wide enough to
support a vernacular literary tradition. But those opportunities were
produced mainly at court by the nobility. The "middle class" this
social shift produced assumed its role precisely by entering courtly
culture and making common political cause with the nobility. Even
to describe this group as a "middle class" becomes anachronistic if
the term is given any of its modern American connotations of the
majoritarian, or average. As Janet Coleman, the most enthusiastic of
the promulgators of the "middle class" thesis, readily concedes, this
"middle class" amounted to no more than one-twentieth of the total
population, not that much larger than the nobility whose literary
values it is supposed to be overwhelming.[16] This is still, despite its
broadening function, a very elite group.

On the other hand, if it is true, as Richard Firth Green has argued,
the greater part of later medieval English literature was produced at
court, it is also true as Coleman, Strohm, Middleton and others have
argued, that it was precisely the entrance of the urban patriciate and
lesser gentry into the reading public that catalyzed the expansion of
that literature.[17] What I am proposing is that we view the Chaucerian
tradition as precisely a site of accommodation between the court, and
the sub-noble groups that were coming to share its power. As we shall
see, this negotiation will expand the already expansive paradox of
royal authority. It will also make the vernacular poet a new,
specifically lay, source of textual *auctoritas*.

This interdependence between the textual and the political justifies
including Chaucer in the tradition from which he is so often held
apart. In the discussion that follows, I will argue that Chaucer's
narrative complexity, even where it seems most purely textual, never
ceases to be political. For what he seeks is a specifically lay textuality:
his explorations of narrative complexity are always conditioned by

Middle English verse in what she terms "public poetry" (for the most part she excludes
Chaucer). This is a poetry which "speaks for bourgeois moderation" (95). Paul Strohm,
working solely on Chaucer's audience, embraces the "middle class" thesis in an early article
"Chaucer's Audience," *Literature and History*, 5 (1977), 26–41. In his recent book *Social
Chaucer*, he comes closer to Green's position, identifying Chaucer's immediate audience as
the "middle strata" constituted by the lesser officials in the "King's Affinity," but he still
stresses their independent outlook, imputing to them a "utopian" ethos, committed to
"opening up existing hierarchies" (182).   [16] *Medieval Readers*, 58.
[17] Green, *Poets and Princepleasers*, 3–4.

this political goal. I will focus on two moments in the *Canterbury Tales* where Chaucer moves from anti-clerical critique to lay affirmation, the end of Fragment III and the beginning of Fragment IV, and the end of Fragment VI and Fragment VII. This will enable us to look at the collection's one exemplum collection and five of its exempla. Seven of its ten clerical narrators are also bunched in these two places.

Like any argument based on manuscript order, this one must be made with caution.[18] But I use the sequence of these tales mainly as a useful indicator of an important conceptual relationship. Chaucer's critique of the Church always assumes an affirmation of lay authority, and his direct explorations of such authority are less detached than is usually assumed, particularly once one recognizes that for Chaucer the textual is always the political. It is true that Gower, Hoccleve, and Lydgate are all more explicit in their celebration of kingship than he is. But their affirmations also all require a textual authority that is specifically lay. Gower achieves this authority like Chaucer, via an anti-clerical critique. Hoccleve and Lydgate, both writing under the patronage of Lancastrian regimes actively seeking clerical support, are able to find their authority in the lay textuality Chaucer and Gower have already initiated.

[18] It is worth pointing out that the collocation of the *Friar's*, *Summoner's*, and *Clerk's Tales*, and Fragments VI and VII are among the most stable in all the collection's various manuscript orders. See Ralph Hannah III, "Textual Notes to the *Canterbury Tales*," in *The Riverside Chaucer*, 1121.

CHAPTER 7

Canterbury Tales (I): from preacher to prince

Most readers of the *Canterbury Tales* will agree that its opening fragment, in its movement from the *Knight's Tale* to the *Cook's Tale*, produces an unraveling of textual authority. Lee Patterson has argued convincingly that a similar movement occurs across Fragments II and III, with an important difference. The *Wife of Bath's Tale* subverts "the authoritarian orthodoxy of the Man of Law," and opens the way for the even less decorous quarrel between the Friar and the Summoner[1] – a quarrel that begins with the Friar's declaration that

> ... heere as we ryde by the weye,
> Us nedeth nat to speken but of game,
> And lete auctoritees, on Goddes name,
> To prechyng and to scoles of clergye. (III, 1274–77)

But unlike Fragment I, which ends in complete irresolution with the *Cook's Tale*, the *Summoner's Tale* closes Fragment III with a scene in the feudal court of a lord of the manor. In quitting the Friar, the anti-fraternal game played there also demonstrates the efficacy of feudal lordship. Fragment III thus restores to some extent the lay authority Fragment I had called into question.[2]

I would like to take this argument a step further. Fragment III is followed in most manuscript orders by the *Clerk's Tale*, the collection's first public exemplum, which combines an exploration of monarchical authority with a return to the genre of the *Man of Law's Tale*. This alerts us to another difference between Fragment I and Fragments II and III. The authority examined in Fragment I is feudal and chivalric; in Fragments II and III, it is clerical. If I am right to see Fragment III's restorative movement culminating in the

---

[1] Patterson, *Chaucer and the Subject of History*, 317.
[2] Patterson, *Chaucer and the Subject of History*, 317–21.

Clerk's Tale, as an affirmation of kingship, then Chaucer's purpose in calling feudal authority into question in Fragment I is to replace it with the surer form of lay authority embodied in kingship. Kingship is surer precisely because it involves a more explicit and thorough engagement with and appropriation of the clerical. In Fragment III this engagement begins in earnest with the comprehensive anti-clerical critique Chaucer uses the *Friar's* and *Summoner's Tales* to stage.

THE "FRIAR'S TALE": CHAUCER'S CRITIQUE OF THE PROPRIETARY CHURCH

The Friar's dismissal of authority is blatantly hypocritical. He can "telle a game" of the Summoner only by assuming the very sort of authoritative viewpoint he has disclaimed. The same is true of the Summoner in relation to the Friar. As each attempts to expropriate the moral high ground in order to condemn the other, each confirms the accusation of the other that his office consists of expropriating Christian authority to serve his own ends. The very fact Christian authority can be so manipulated places it beyond any particular institutional instantiation, and makes it a property of Chaucer's narrative. He stands beyond the exchange, rescuing the Church's authority from itself. While the Friar and Summoner engage in a game of narrative one-upmanship with each other, Chaucer engages in a similar game with the Church as a whole. He is less interested in their hypocrisy as a personal failing than he is in what it reveals about their institutional positions.

Like the Pardoner later on, the Friar and Summoner each represent in different ways the dispersion of Christian authority into the Church's institutional structure. Both the Friar and the Pardoner (who may also be a friar[3]) occupy positions that were primarily papal innovations. As confessors and preachers they duplicate the work already done by parochial clergy – a standard anti-fraternal charge.[4] The Friar, as a *limitour*, conducted his activities within an area defined in the first instance not by local political boundaries, but by

---

[3] See below, 192.

[4] Penn R. Szittya, *The Antifraternal Tradition in Medieval Literature* (Princeton: Princeton University Press, 1986), 45–47, 132–47, 221–25, 279–82; Yves M.-J. Congar, "Aspects ecclésiologiques de la querelle entre mendiants et séculiers dans le second moitié du xiiie siècle et le début du xive," *Archives d'histoire doctrinale et littéraire du moyen âge* 28 (1961), 54–62.

the institutional arrangements of his order – unlike Chaucer's exemplar, the Parson. Similarly, the Pardoner's fundraising is authorized by the institutional needs of the particular religious foundation which employs him, not by the spiritual needs of those whom he addresses. While the Summoner's position is not quite so alocal in character, it nevertheless depends on the most decidedly temporal of Church institutions, the ecclesiastical court. This position developed as a direct result of archidiaconal courts becoming increasingly active and sophisticated.[5] All three of these figures are comparatively late innovations, products of the international Church of the later Middle Ages, as distinguished from the older, more established and more locally oriented parochial and monastic clergy. The central institutional function of all three, at least as far as Chaucer is concerned, is to collect money, and it is a function which is delegated to them, which they do not possess authority of their own to perform. Their hypocrisy consists of performing the functions which have been delegated to them in their own interests rather than in the interests of the Church. But for that very reason, their hypocrisy exposes not simply their own moral failings, but also the vulnerability of a Church which has become so dependent on the elaboration of its institutional structures. As Gower would have it, abuses of this sort become inevitable once there "is venym schad/In holi cherche of temporal/Which medleth with the spirital" (II, 3490–92). Any attempt at institutional elaboration is bound to fail because to the extent it pursues temporal power it ceases to strive for the very spirituality which authorizes it.

Both the *Friar's Tale* and the *Summoner's Tale* draw on polemical material first produced within the Church. The *Friar's Tale* is based on a sermon exemplum which in most of its forms attacks the nobility's mistreatment of the poor. Though no source for the *Summoner's Tale* has been found, most of its incidental details, as well as both its prologue and epilogue, seem to have been drawn from the anti-fraternal tradition.[6] In appropriating this material to use against the Church, Chaucer follows the same polemical procedure as John of Salisbury. Where John appropriated classical materials to validate

---

[5] For a full account of the office of the summoner, see Thomas Hahn and Richard W. Kaeuper, "Text and Context: Chaucer's *Friar's Tale*," *Studies in the Age of Chaucer* 5 (1983), 67–109.

[6] For a full discussion and additional bibliography see Szittya, "The Friar as False Apostle: Antifraternal Exegesis and the *Summoner's Tale*," *Studies in Philology* 71 (1974), 19–46.

the clerical, Chaucer appropriates clerical materials to validate the lay. Moreover, he gives himself this advantage over his anti-clerical creations: he is concerned to analyze as well as to attack. Even as he exposes the overreaching of Church authority he makes it plausible. In the *Friar's Tale*, what is at stake is justice. The tale ends with a verdict in the form of the old woman's curse. Its irony turns on the power of this ostensibly disempowered figure to deliver damnation, the omnipotent judgment of God. In her curse the woman possesses nothing less than the power to bind and loose, the power Christ invested in the Church – albeit only momentarily. This efficacy exposes not only the sin of this individual summoner, but also the superfluity of his office. The miraculous manifestation of divine justice in the voice of an old woman stands in stark contrast to the elaborate institutionalization of the archidiaconal court, as represented by the summoner. Five of the extant analogues to the tale are sermon exempla.[7] Of the four which predate or are contemporary to Chaucer, three make the protagonist a figure of lay authority. In the first extant version, that of Cesarius of Heisterbach, he is a knight (*miles*); in the version of the English Benedictine Robert Rypon, he is a bailiff (*baillivus*); and in an exemplum in the British Library, Cotton Cleopatra D. VIII, he is a seneschal (*seneschallus*).[8] While in

---

[7] Archer Taylor, "The *Friar's Tale*," in *Sources and Analogues of Chaucer's Canterbury Tales*, ed. W. F. Bryan and Germaine Dempster (London: Routledge and Kegan Paul, 1941, reissued 1958), 269–74; and Peter Nicholson, "The Analogues of the Chaucer's *Friar's Tale*," *English Language Notes* 17(1979), 93–98. Four seem to have been earlier than or contemporary to the *Canterbury Tales* (see Nicolson, 96–97). There was also an expanded version of the narrative by the thirteenth-century Austrian poet *Der Stricker*, and a number of later analogues (see Taylor, 273).

[8] Cesarius of Heisterbach, *Die Fragment der Libri VIII miraculorum de Caesarius von Heisterbach*, ed. Aloys Meister, *Romische Quartalschrift für Christliche Alterhunskunde und für Kuntesgeschichte*, *Supplementheft* 13 (Rome, 1901), 90–91, reprinted with translation in *The Literary Context of Chaucer's Fabliaux*, ed. Larry D. Benson and Theodore M. Andersson (Indianapolis, 1971), 362–65. The Rypon exemplum is in British Library, Harley 4894, ff. 103v-104. It is summarized in G. R. Owst, *Literature and Pulpit in Medieval England*, 2nd ed. (Oxford: Blackwell, 1961) 162–63, and translated by Nicholson in "The Rypon Analogue of the *Friar's Tale*," *The Chaucer Newsletter*, 3:1 (1981), 1–2. In a claim which Janette Richardson echoes ("Explanatory Notes to the *Friar's Tale*," in *Riverside Chaucer*, 875), Nicholson declares that the Tale is "evidently not derived from Cesarius at all" ("Analogues," 95). This claim is dubious for two reasons. First, the only evidence he offers for it is the fact that in Cesarius the protagonist is aware that he is the devil's prey from the beginning, whereas in Cotton, Rypon, and Chaucer he is not. But in fact, in all three, his awareness is purposely ambiguous, and could be seen as a refinement on the earlier version of Cesarius. Second he completely ignores the continuity between Cesarius and Cotton and Rypon, which separates them from Chaucer. Not only do all three make the protagonist a layman, but all three also treat the curse – which is, after all, the core of the story – similarly. All three use the same phrase, *ex corde*, to distinguish between the earlier curses and the final one: the

Cesarius's and the Cotton version he is also an ecclesiastical functionary – an *advocatus* and a *placitator*, respectively – he does not seem to be a cleric, and his acquisition of this ecclesiastical office seems mainly intended to stress his rapaciousness. Both Rypon and Cesarius make it clear the exemplum is a warning against the expropriation of the poor.[9] In various ways, each of these versions connects the linguistic analysis implicit in the series of curses with the worldliness of the protagonist. The revelation of supernatural authority in the heartfelt curse exposes at once two kinds of formal emptiness: the emptiness of human language, and the emptiness of temporal power.

In Cesarius this analysis is at its most precise. Unlike later versions, in this version the protagonist knows from the moment the devil appears it is him the devil has come for, and he calls the devil's attention to the unheartfelt curses in the vain hope of distracting him from that purpose. This quibbling attempt at distraction neatly recapitulates the fault for which he is being damned. He treats human institutions, whether linguistic or social, as deracinated, empty forms entirely amenable to his manipulation. When he is cursed by a group of villagers as soon as they see him, and the devil exclaims, "Behold, they gave you to me from the bottom of their hearts and therefore you are mine," it comes as a direct repudiation of the protagonist's assumption that human forms can be endlessly manipulated in violation of the ultimate realities which authorize them.[10]

The irony of this ending depends on its reinvestment of supernatural meaning in the banal, quotidian act of cursing. As we have already seen, such redemption of linguistic banality was a standard tactic of the sermon exemplum.[11] In its apparent acknowledgment that Christian forms have become banal it registers the ideological power of Christian discourse: notions of the devil and damnation have become so well accepted as to be commonplace. But in its reinvestment of these forms with their original, divine force, it

devil cannot take the earlier things cursed because they are not cursed *ex corde*, while the protagonist is. In light of these continuities, I think it justifiable to set all three in equal contrast to Chaucer, as representing the same general, ecclesiastical point of view.

[9] Cesarius concludes that the exemplum should be heard by *pauperum exactores* (91), and Rypon is even more explicit, warning that *officiarii dominorum* should not be in any way greedy or harm the poor. (Cited in Owst, *Literature and Pulpit*, 163n.)

[10] *Libri VIII Miraculorum*, 91: "Ecce! isti dederunt te mihi ex intimo corde et idcirco meus es."

[11] See above, 58–63, 78–80.

ironically asserts the continual capacity of Chritian ideology to renew itself. For the ironic turn demonstrates that these forms continue to produce meaning even after they have become banal.

Though the focus on language is not quite as precise in either the Rypon or the Cotton versions, they still depend on the same irony. Like Chaucer's version, these two suppress the protagonist's awareness of his damnation until the end and focus more on his similarity with the devil. This change, however, only makes the protagonist's manipulations of social forms, still presented through his use of language, that much more egregious. While he urges the first two curses be accepted at face value, assuming language's outward forms can be manipulated however he wants them to be, the devil shows himself to be constrained by the relation between outward form and inward intent. In Cotton, the protagonist tells the devil his business is to profit from suing the poor, whether justly or unjustly. When the devil replies that he takes only what is cursed and given to the devil, the protagonist derides him, presumably for being satisfied with so little. But his derision only reveals his adoration of the temporal and immediate, and his willful denial of the supernatural. In this version, when the moment of his cursing comes, the devil asks if he had heard. "I heard," he replies, "But it is nothing to me."[12] His belief that language is purely outward form convinces him that he can disregard it at will, and the aggrieved sense of justice it here signifies.

Rypon explicitly introduces his version as illustrating the dangers of naming the devil. Against this frame, the protagonist is once again exposed as entirely unmindful of the supernatural world which sustains human forms. Like the Friar's summoner, he is unmoved when the devil identifies himself, nor does he at all comprehend the crucial distinction between them the devil draws. While he takes anything people might wish to give, the devil takes only what they wish to give with "heart and will." This dimension, of course, is precisely what Rypon's bailiff misses in the series of curses, in failing to see both that the earlier two are not heartfelt, and that the last one is.

To sum up: all three versions critique lay worldliness from the perspective of the divine and the supernatural. They present a lay protagonist whose expropriations of the poor are defined as the cynical manipulations of the immediacy of human forms, particularly

---

[12] Taylor, in *Sources and Analogues*, 272: "'audio' inquit. 'Set nichil ad me.'"

the forms of language. He is definitively punished by the miraculous reinvestment of those forms with the extrahuman force from which he had assumed he had successfully severed them.

The *Friar's Tale* celebrates the same supernatural reauthorization of human language, yet it manages to make this celebration simultaneously a critique of clerical office. Chaucer does this in the first instance by simply changing the institutional identity of the tale's protagonist. Rather than being a lay figure, or a lay figure manipulating the ecclesiastical courts for his own ends, Chaucer's protagonist is a creature of those courts. As the tale explains in explicit detail, the crimes the summoner prosecutes were all exclusive to the jurisdiction of ecclesiastical courts: witchcraft, violations of oaths or of the rules of religious observance, usury, simony, and, chiefly, adultery (III, 1304–10). Though the summoner's abuses are ultimately due to his own moral failings, it is the Church which has produced the opportunity for such abuses.

In this way, Chaucer turns the Church's own authority against it, focusing a narrative which attacks worldliness against one of the Church's own institutional innovations. If he had left the appropriation of this exemplum at that, we might have had a Langland-like denunciation, bristling with embittered satire and ridicule. Instead, however, Chaucer modulates his attack precisely by broadening it. After giving the plot a new institutional focus, he also reworks the internal logic of its linguistic analysis, implicitly but decisively shifting its articulation of Christian authority from one that favors the institutional forms of the Church to a more purely discursive affirmation of narrative.

It has often been noted that Chaucer's tale adds to earlier versions a much more developed sense of characterization and dialogue. The amplifications are usually ascribed to Chaucer's poetic mastery.[13] Without necessarily disputing the tale's aesthetic superiority, I would argue Chaucer's changes have an ideological motivation as well.[14] The tale's "masterful" characterization is conveyed mainly by its dialogue, and in this Chaucer is anticipated by the earlier versions, which dramatize the protagonist's moral status mainly through his

---

[13] As, for example, by Janette Richardson, *Blameth Nat Me: A Study of Imagery in Chaucer's Fabliaux* (The Hague: Mouton and Company, NV, 1970), 74.

[14] Though I would also point out that the analogues have an aesthetic appeal of their own. The Cesarius is particularly powerful. In its schematic compression it manages to define with precisely turned phrases the issues Chaucer develops much more leisurely.

linguistic behavior.[15] Indeed, Chaucer's revisions can all be shown to proceed from his reworking of the narrative's core, the moment of the curse.

A. C. Spearing has suggested the tale has "a more marked intellectual content" than its analogues.[16] In fact, this change makes the tale less ambiguous. In the ecclesiastical versions the interest is as much on the supernatural power of the curse as it is on the punishment of the protagonist. The curse is *ex intimo corde*; the raw expression of an emotion so violent and spontaneous, it seems beyond the speaker's conscious control. In Cesarius and Cotton, it is also communal: it is beyond the control of a single speaker, and is spoken by a group *una voce* or *unamiter*.[17] If the curse restores the balance of human justice, it does so mysteriously, by unleashing a force that is unpredictable and always beyond human control. Though the protagonist is clearly deserving of punishment, the capricious, almost arbitrary manner of the punishment threatens to eclipse his crimes. For if he is guilty, his punishment does not lie with those who curse him. Cursing, after all, is also sinful. Yet in this case, perhaps because the curse is so spontaneous, it is granted the supernatural power it would ordinarily claim only illegitimately. Rypon makes this point explicit when he interprets the exemplum to be a warning against the devil as well as against oppressing the poor.[18] Without endorsing cursing or calling on the devil as a normative means of punishment, the narrative still shows the awesome unpredictability of the retributive power sins like the protagonist's provoke.

By contrast, Chaucer disperses the mystery and moral ambiguity of the curse by having the summoner condemn himself out of his own mouth before he is cursed by the old woman. When she begs him to show his "almesse," he replies, "Nay thanne ... the foule feend me fecche / If I th'excuse, though thou shul be spilt!" (III, 1610–11) These lines bring the ironic contrast between the usual banality of

---

[15] The term is Richardson's (*Riverside Chaucer*, 875).

[16] Spearing, "The *Canterbury Tales* IV: Exemplum and Fable," in *Cambridge Chaucer Companion*, ed. Piero Boitani and Jill Mann (Cambridge: Cambridge University Press, 1988), 164.

[17] *Libri VII Miraculorum*, 91; *Sources and Analogues*, 272. The curse is also spoken *una voce* in the early fifteenth-century analogue by Basel Dominican Johannes Herolt from the collection *Promptuarium exemplorum*, cited by Taylor in *Sources and Analogues*, 271.

[18] In addition to his opening gambit, which I have already cited, Rypon's first two morals are: "First man is taught that he not name the devil out of negligence or rancor. Second that he not commend anything to him for such a commendation can perhaps be put into effect." "Primo enim docetur homo ne cum necligencia aut rancore diabolum nominet, 2°, ne sibi aliquid comendet, quia forsan talis comendacio potest sortiri effectum." Nicholson, "The Rypon Analogue," 2,1.

cursing and its miraculous fulfillment into the summoner's own voice. At the very moment he is to be damned, the summoner pronounces damnation to be his own choice. Though he intends this pronounce-ment to mean no more than his rejection of the old woman's plea, the fact that he must appeal to the very supernatural forces his whole mode of existence would deny exposes his inability to escape them. His words will frustrate his intent and regain their literal significance. The irony of this self-condemning speech-act is that its speaker actually chooses the supernatural meaning when he believes he is choosing the banal one. He choose damnation when he believes he is choosing worldly enrichment. Indeed, collapsing these choices into the ambiguity of a single phrase enables the narrative to present them as the same choice. The summoner chooses damnation in the act of choosing enrichment.

This additional twist to the terms of the narrative's central irony, the contrast between cursing's banality and the eternal damnation it ostensibly signfies, shifts its meaning. No longer is retribution visited mysteriously upon the protagonist from without. Here he chooses it. The tale makes this point even more explicit as it proceeds. After the summoner's self-cursing rejection of the old woman's pleas has moved her to curse him in return, the devil, rather than seizing upon her curse immediately, instead asks, in quasi-judicial fashion, for a clarification. "Now, Mabely, myn owene mooder deere, / Is this youre wyl in ernest that ye seye?" (III, 1626–27) Her spontaneous anger cooling slightly, she replies not with a simple reiteration of the original curse, but with a qualified declaration that could almost be taken as a statement of conditional fact: "'The devel,' quod she, 'so fecche hym er he deye, / And panne and al, but he wol hym repente!'" (III, 1628–29) Though it still has the force of a curse this restatement introduces the idea of repentance. To this extent it comes much closer to an unexceptionable observation of theological fact: if the summoner does not repent he will be damned. The summoner, of course, as firm in his denial of the eternal as ever, rejects this loophole. "Nay, olde stot, that is nat myn entente," he replies (III, 1630), and finally seals his fate.

Thus he chooses his damnation twice, once before the old woman curses him, and once after. The reiteration of this choice has the effect of making the curse seem that much more the inevitable outcome of the summoner's typical mode of behavior. Though still privileged and miraculous, the curse has now been firmly anticipated, and its terms more neutrally restated. In his moment of damnation the summoner has done little more than succumb to a commonplace of Christian justice: the sinner who does not repent is damned. Because this disregard is habitual rather than momentary, and because the summoner is behaving now no differently than he has throughout the tale, the curse becomes an inevitable fulfillment rather than a violent disruption. As a speech-act, it is as much authored by the summoner as by the old woman. His casual profanation, "the foule feend me fecche," precipitates her own, more sincerely meant curse, and the curse itself is not enacted until he refuses the chance to repent.

Chaucer also softens the curse's violent spontaneity. All reference to the heart has gone. Here and throughout the tale, he replaces the Latin *cor* with the more neutral "intent." Language is still morally grounded but less mysteriously so. Its ultimate authority is still beyond the human and certainly as ubiquitous, but it is less dark, less violent, and more predictable. When the old woman restates her curse, she introduces the notion of repentance, and explicitly ties the moment of damnation to divine authority as well as to diabolical power. In this way, Chaucer has taken his readers out of the world of the sermon exemplum, a world governed by dark, supernatural forces which are equally violent whether they are divine or diabolical, a world in which the divine can be approached or the diabolical controlled only through the Church's intercession, in which the Church's prerogative must be accepted unquestioningly precisely because it provides the only safe means through which these dark powers could be confronted. The world he brings the narrative into is one where spiritual authority is less institutional and more individuated, where at any moment believers may redeem themselves by choosing repentance. This is certainly not the Protestant world of the Elect; as Chaucer makes clear throughout the collection, repentance depends on confession. It is not even the Wycliffite world of disendowment. But it is a world in which the Church's institutional prerogatives are restricted primarily to serving the needs of the individual (lay) believer, and in which they seem to be entirely excluded from the juridical.

Even in this retreat to the individual Chaucer is dependent on ecclesiastical tradition. As Peter Nicholson points out, the motifs he adds to the end of this exemplum are themselves sermon exemplum commonplaces. There are many exempla which concern either a sinner "consigning his soul to the devil in an angry oath," or a sinner given a final chance to confess when the devil comes to take him. Indeed, both of these motifs occur liberally in the other exempla in the Cotton collection.[19] Even more important is the very logic which enables Chaucer to inject these motifs from other exempla into this one. This logic is the propensity of the sermon exemplum to define Christian spirituality linguistically and to stage its narratives as stories of linguistic behavior.

This propensity enables Chaucer to stage the summoner's evasion of Christian authority in a series of linguistic choices. The ironic ambiguity inherent in both his oath, "the foule feende me fecche," and in his impulsive dismissal of the widow's implicit offer to repent makes divine authority at once clearly available in the literal meaning of these phrases and yet hidden in the banal status they have acquired through habitual use. The narrative literally recovers this authority through the ironic working out of its own discursive logic – its *game*. Yet, paradoxically, in amplifying the tale's narrative, Chaucer makes it less ambiguous, not more so.

This is particulary true of the preliminary dialogue between the summoner and the devil, which constitutes the bulk of the new material Chaucer adds to the tale. The dialogue effects, ironically but unmistakeably, a very specific affirmation of lay justice. As he will do at the end, the summoner assumes that the language he exchanges with the devil is, like other social forms, completely under his control. He begins by identifying himself as a bailiff, in imitation of the devil's opening gambit, and eagerly enters into brotherhood with him, accepting at face value the devil's claim to have gold and silver in his chest, presumably in the belief that he will get the better of the bargain (III, 1392–1406).

When the devil reveals himself, the summoner remains unfazed. The revelation ends with the devil's pregnant declaration that he would ride "Unto the worldes ende for a preye" (III, 1454–55), but the summoner responds only to the immediate fact that he has at this moment a man's "schap" (III, 1458). The devil's explanation of his ability to change shape quickly develops into a theological explanation of his function as God's instrument in the scheme of Divine Justice. The summoner has no interest in this issue, however, and replies by once again by asking about the mechanics of the devil's ability to change shape.

---

[19] Nicholson, "Analogues," 98.

At this point the devil is even more explicit. After briefly addressing the shape-shifting question again, he warns:

> Thou wolt algates wite how we been shape;
> Thou shalt herafterward, my brother deere,
> Come there thee nedeth nat of me to leere,
> For thou shalt, by thyn owene experience,
> Konne in a chayer rede of this sentence
> Bet than Virgile, while he was on lyve,
> Or Dant also. Now lat us ryde blyve,
> For I wole holde compaignye with thee
> Til it be so that thou forsake me.　　　　　(III, 1514–22)

With this speech, the devil both warns the summoner of the danger he is in and offers him a chance to escape. But the summoner rejects the offer because he is focused entirely on what appears to him as the chance for immediate gain. Instead he reaffirms his pact of brotherhood:

> "Nay," quod this somonour, "that shal nat bityde!
> I am a yeman, knowen is ful wyde;
> My trouthe wol I holde, as in this cas.
> For though thou were the devel Sathanas,
> My trouthe wol I holde to my brother,
> As I am sworn, and ech of us til oother,
> For to be trewe brother in this cas...　　　(III, 1523–29)

He then reminds the devil that the condition of the pact was that whoever got more would share with the other, obviously still convinced that he is going to get the better part of the bargain.

The pact is of course completely delusory. Though he wishes to be, the summoner is not a yeoman. His self-deluding attempt to reinforce the oath to the devil under this false pretense is equalled by his delusion about the advantage the oath will gain him. His devotion to this oath is a hopeless attempt to impose a self-serving meaning on vacant linguistic form and impose this form on the world. His assumption that he can manipulate language in this way is consistent with the habitual self-serving manipulation of judicial forms that constitutes his whole mode of existence. It will fail for the reasons Chaucer will reveal definitively at the end of the tale, but which would have been revealed earlier had the summoner been willing to recognize them. The divine authority which weds outward linguistic form and inward intent is constantly before one and cannot be escaped. If it is true that this authority can only be manifested indirectly, it is also true its indirect, unrevealed presence is constant and unchanging.

Chaucer drives the institutional implications of this point home in the dialogue's incidental word play. At the outset the summoner accepts eagerly the opportunity the devil offers him to identify himself as a bailiff. "Artow thanne a bailly?" the Devil asks. "Ye," the summoner replies, and the Friar comments, "He dorste nat, for verray filthe and shame / Seye that he was a somonour, for the name" (III, 1392–95). The explicit declaration that the very name summoner is filthy and shameful clearly shows Chaucer's objection to this summoner is as much institutional as individual. That the summoner would prefer to be called a bailiff suggests just as clearly that Chaucer found the lay function of bailiff morally superior.[20] If so, this could only be because he finds the dispersion of power and delegation of judicial or feudal authority which both summoners and bailiffs represent more suitable and proper to the lay than it is to the ecclesiastic. Indeed, the passage suggests further that when the Church attempts to exercise such power, it can only mimic properly lay forms. Delegation of authority to serve writs or collect revenues, while legitimate within the lay, literally becomes a mockery when attempted by the Church.

The point is reinforced by the hunting imagery that pervades the tale. The summoner "evere waityng on his pray," knows lechers, adulterers, and paramours like a "dogge for the bowe" knows wounded deer. As Janette Richardson has demonstrated, the main function of this imagery is to link the rapacity of the summoner with the devil who preys upon him.[21] At the same time, this invocation of hunting, one of medieval nobility's most jealously guarded privileges, also emphasizes the summoner's burlesque of the secular. When, in the passage I cited earlier, he declares himself a yeoman in order to reinforce his oath to the devil, in imitation of the devil's own ruse, he brings the burlesque to a head. His oath is doubly delusory. In taking upon himself the improper guise of the yeoman, he is mimicking a mockery. His rapacity is an empty form, and an improper, illegitimate masquerade without any grounding in the real world.

The superiority of bailiff and yeoman to summoner is assumed rather than demonstrated. It is treated as a given, as is the properly

[20] Knight, *Geoffrey Chaucer*, 104–06.   [21] Richardson, *Blameth Nat Me*, 73–85.

lay nature of temporal power even as ecclesiastical participation in such power is attacked. The logic is indirect, but powerful. In taking the temporal status quo as a given, Chaucer does not even need to treat it particularly favorably. Indeed, making the devil a bailiff and yeoman might even suggest there was something satanic about lay power as well. But just as the devil is made to seem scrupulous and restrained in comparison to the summoner, so by extension, are lay power structures by comparison with ecclesiastical courts. And if the tale attacks the Church by strongly suggesting that its exercise of temporal power is less orderly, more rapacious, and indeed, more sinful than that of lay authorities, it more implicitly affirms lay power by suggesting that its specific institutional shape is the only shape power can effectively have in this world.

In the summoner's manipulations he can never invent new forms or devise new stratagems out of whole cloth. He is always limited to what is given. He can only attempt to appropriate temporal power in the form in which it already exists, the form given it by temporal authorities. The divinely sanctioned order he attempts to evade includes not only the subordination of this world to the next, but also the very shape which this world takes. If temporal power in the hands of lay lords is a necessary evil, in the hands of the Church it is an unnecessary one. Against the temporal sanctions of ecclesiastical justice – "Purs is the archedekenes helle" – Chaucer sets the infinitely more authoritative punishments and rewards of God: damnation and the perpetual possibility of redemption through repentance. If the Church fulfills its function by spiritually calling its believers to repentance, it should have no need for the temporal restraints that are more properly left to the laity.

Chaucer drew this view from the Church itself, from its complex of evangelical initiatives in the wake of the Fourth Lateran Council, especially the new emphasis on confession, and the homiletic interest in the exemplum. The figure of the friar best sums up these changes, and it is entirely fitting Chaucer chooses the Friar to begin his anti-clerical critique. It is not just that, along with preaching, the mendicants' most important institutional function was hearing confession and granting absolution. That privilege was certainly bitterly resented by the secular clergy, and as many scholars have pointed out, the Summoner had especial reason to resent it, since his livelihood depended on temporal punishments which absolution might make unnecessary. Precisely because its institutional authority was more directly papal, mendicant spirituality was less immediately institutional and more individuated. The mendicant was not implicated with local relations of power, and did not participate in diocesan institutional machinery. His encounters with individual believers were more variegated and wide-ranging. He did not see them in the same parish or at regularly appointed times. His mendicancy meant their financial support was less regularized, perhaps even less obligatory. When he preached to them or heard confessions it was not as the member of the local network to which they were tied materially as well as spiritually; it was rather as a representative of the Church at large. Because in effect he brought the whole Church to them, he could make their encounters with it seem less mediated, less hierarchized, less institutionalized, in fact, and more purely spiritual.

Nevertheless, as almost all scholars agree, Chaucer was no fan of the friars. If he places his first sustained attack on Church prerogative in the voice of the Friar, it is because of two tactical necessities. First, he needs to come to terms with an important source of his own authority. Second, he needs to put some distance between himself and secular clergy, where his sympathies more naturally lie, to preserve the lay specificity of his own text. Having done that, he is ready to attack the mendicants in earnest, which is what he does in the next tale.

THE ''SUMMONER'S TALE'': CHAUCER'S ANTI-FRATERNAL
CRITIQUE

It is generally acknowledged that the Summoner gets the better of his exchange with the Friar.[22] If the *Friar's Tale* is witty, the *Summoner's Tale* is, like its central event, explosively funny. The Friar scores debating points by obsessively focusing his irony on the institutional contradictions inherent in the Summoner's office. The Summoner, by contrast, is able to make the Friar look ridiculous by bringing the terms of the debate so low that the debate itself looks ridiculous. Though his invocations of institutional contradictions are in fact more extensive than the Friar's, his irony seems directed not so much at them as at the scatology with which he associates them. His prologue and tale has the structure of three successive jokes: first, the

---

[22] The best case for the Summoner's rhetorical triumph over the Friar remains Paul N. Zietlow, "In Defense of the Summoner," *The Chaucer Review*, 1 (1966), 4–19.

parodic vision of the friars in the devil's anus, then the trick Thomas plays on the tale's protagonist, and finally, the squire's scatological *jeu d'esprit*. Each punchline reiterates the same general association of friars with anal execretion, and the mass of institutional detail that surrounds them serves the same function as a straight line: simply to distract the audience until the punchline comes.

As Derek Pearsall has noted, by the end of the tale we seem to have moved into the realm of "pure comedy."[23] Yet the crowning irony of this movement into the purely comedic is that it is precisely the purity of the Summoner's comedy that enables him to get the better of his institutional rival, the Friar. The very broadness of his focus makes his narrative seem less personally motivated and more convincing. That the less direct narrative should be the more convincing, perhaps even the more authoritative, is a paradox which obviously interests Chaucer. For even less direct than the Summoner's attack on the Friar is Chaucer's attack on both of them, and through them, the institutional Church as a whole. As a closer examination of the tale will reveal, this attack is both carried out by and founded on the ironic indirection of the narrative.

Like the *Friar's Tale*, the *Summoner's Tale* is steeped in clerical lore. Most of the incidental details of the Friar's character are drawn from anti-fraternal stereotypes. Still others are drawn directly from the mendicant traditions themselves. The anecdote in the prologue is an inversion of an exemplum which first occurs in Cesarius's *Dialogus miraculorum*.[24] The three sermon exempla the friar cites in the middle of the tale (III, 2017–84) probably came from the *Communiloquium sive summa collationum* of the Franciscan John of Wales.[25] Unlike the *Friar's Tale*, however, the *Summoner's Tale* is usually considered a fabliau and not an exemplum. I consider it here as an exemplum for three reasons.

The first is its pairing with the *Friar's Tale*. Even if we take it as a fabliau, the modulation from exemplum to fabliau is precisely what

---

[23] Pearsall, *The "Canterbury Tales"* (London: George Allen and Unwin, 1985), 228.
[24] John V. Fleming, "The Summoner's Prologue: An Iconographic Adjustment," *The Chaucer Review* 2 (1967) 95–107. Cesarius's exemplum has a Cistercian monk transported to heaven where, after seeing no Cistercian anywhere is told they are hidden with the Virgin's mantle in honor of their piety. Fleming points out that the exemplum is quickly appropriated by the Dominicans, and that Martin Luther reports a Franciscan version, in which a Franciscan friar, disappointed to find no Franciscans under the mantle, is told their virtue is so perfect it cannot be hidden.
[25] Robert Pratt, "Chaucer and the Hand That Fed Him," 619–42.

is at stake in this pairing. The modulation involves the relation between moral authority and narrative *game*, the exemplum's constitutive components. Even as a fabliau, the *Summoner's Tale* will mark the limits of this relation by virtue of its response to the *Friar's Tale*. The second reason is that the tale, exemplum or not, is continually concerned with the social deployment of the genre. Its protagonist is presented throughout as an exemplarist. First, there is the quickly improvised explanation of his absence at the time of death of the couple's son (III, 1851–84). The story is like a sermon exemplum both in its assertion of a contemporary miraculous revelation, and in its use of the miracle, both of which demonstrate the sacral efficacy of a Church institution; in this case, the friar's convent. Next there are the three Biblical exempla which immediately follow (III, 1885–1917). Finally there are the three sermon exempla from a Franciscan collection, which I have already mentioned.

The third reason is that the tale has a sermon exemplum as a possible analogue, an analogue which has hitherto escaped notice. An untitled English Dominican collection from the latter half of the thirteenth century (British Museum, Royal 7.D.1.) contains an exemplum about a greedy priest who resorts to trickery in order to obtain a bequest. On his deathbed a miserly peasant loses the power of speech. The priest attending him takes down his bequests by asking him questions to which the peasant replies "Ha" if he assents, and remains silent if he does not. To the first question, "Do you wish to bequeath your soul to God after your decease, and your body to Mother Church for burial?" the peasant replies, "Ha." To the next, would he leave twenty shillings to the Church for the upkeep of its fabric, he replies, "Ha," but only after the priest squeezes his ear. To the last request, however, that he leave his treasure chest to the priest, he remains silent, even after the priest pinches him hard enough to draw blood. Finally, however, he declares in a loud voice, "O you greedy priest, by Christ's death, never shall you have as much as a farthyng of the money which is in that chest."[26]

Admittedly, this analogue seems a bit more distant than two usually cited, *La Vescie à prestre*, and "How Howleglas Deceived his

---

[26] f. 127. Summarized in Owst, *Literature and Pulpit*, 164–165. J. H. Herbert, in the *Catalogue of Romances in the Department of Manuscripts in the British Museum*, vol. 3 (London: printed by order of the Trustees, 1910) notes another occurrence of this exemplum in British Library, Harley 2851, f. 66, col. 2 (p. 499).

Ghostly Father," from *Til Eulenspiegel*.[27] It does not involve a false gift. It does, however, involve a greedy cleric at a bedside, and moreover, one who, like the Summoner's friar, depends on a linguistic ruse. While this exemplum is distant enough from the tale that it provides no useful evidence regarding the tale's source, it does demonstrate two other points which are relevant to the present discussion. First, it shows that the greedy cleric in search of bequests is a figure who could occur in exempla as well as fabliaux. Second, the fact it occurs in a Dominican collection shows that the secular/ mendicant controversy that raged within the sermon exemplum tradition as well as elsewhere could be focused on this theme.[28] Both of these facts mean not only that Chaucer might have found the source for this tale in a sermon exemplum as easily as in a fabliau, but also, more crucially, that he could have expected his audience to recognize this tale, whatever its source, as an exemplum. While the fact remains that the tale's central event is more characteristic of a fabliau than an exemplum – exempla generally turn on miracles, not scatology – we can still say, without attempting to explain away this discrepancy, that on balance the tale is more like an exemplum than a fabliau. Fabliaux, both Chaucer's and the tradition as a whole, tend to be concerned with the politics of gender and class; this tale is concerned with ecclesiology.[29] It delivers a moral evaluation of an ecclesiastical office. As we shall see, even its scatology serves this end.

Like the *Friar's Tale*, the *Summoner's Tale* begins with an exposition of its protagonist's institutional function. The friar is a preacher, a preacher whose purpose above all is to encourage contributions from his audience (III, 1709–23). His preaching is directed squarely at immediate institutional goals and the contributions no less so. They are to support his order by subsidizing either the performance of

---

[27] In *La Vescie à prestre*, a priest promises to bequeath to two greedy Jacobin Friars "something for which he would not accept a thousand marks." When they show up the next day he promises them his bladder. In the other tale Til Eulenspiegel offers his confessor as bequest a pot of turds with a little money strewn on top. Both of these tales are reprinted and translated in Andersson and Benson, *Literary Context*, 344–59, 339–40. In "Structural Models for the Fabliaux and the *Summoner's Tale* Analogues," *Fabula* 15 (1974), 103–13, Roy J. Pearcy urges, on the basis of an analysis of the "deep structure" of these narratives, that the *Summoner's Tale* has no known analogues, a view which has met with some acceptance (see, e.g., Richardson's notes to the tale in *Riverside Chaucer*, 877). I find Pearcy's argument unconvincing because it depends on a radically ahistorical and universalist notion of deep structure. [28] See Owst, *Preaching*, 71–77.

[29] It is generally acknowledged that this tale does not share the thematic concerns of Chaucer's other fabliaux: see Pearsall, "*Canterbury Tales*," 166.

trentals, or the building of convents. As blatantly self-interested as this appeal is, however, it still advances a coherent ecclesiological position.

The "hooly houses" to be built are

> Ther as divine servyce is honoured,
> Nat ther as it is wasted and devoured,
> Ne ther it nedeth nat for to be yive,
> As to possessioners, that mowen lyve,
> Thanked be God, in wele and habundance.   (III, 1719–23)

The trentals are to be sung by friars and not by "a preest joly and gay" who "syngeth nat but o masse in a day" (III, 1727–28). The friar contrasts a proprietary ecclesiology, that of "possessioners," the diocesan and monastic clergy, with his own mendicant ecclesiology, pointing out not simply the spiritual superiority of an ecclesiology based on apostolic poverty, but its institutional superiority as well. Possessioners living in "wele and habundance" are not as immediately responsive to their clientele. Priests who only sing one mass a day cannot handle the volume of trentals the friars can. The friar offers a mendicant ecclesiology based on poverty, but also on growth and speed.

Mendicancy's very commitment to poverty put it in a much stronger position to respond to a money economy than the proprietary Church. Its institutional expansion was directly driven by the money it raised, rather than depending on the acquisition of land. The beginning of this tale clearly shows that Chaucer recognized this fundamental practical strength of the mendicants. His exploration of the movement's weakness departs from this opening recognition, and retains its institutional focus throughout. This point is worth stressing because most of the scholars who have documented Chaucer's use of anti-fraternal material in this tale have been convinced his interest in it was primarily theological. Yet from the very beginning the secular/mendicant controversy was ecclesiological. Its first texts were produced in the mid-twelfth century at the University of Paris in response to administrative squabbles between secular and mendicant scholars. Throughout the subsequent incidents that make up the long history of this controversy, the institutional focus remains constant. To what rights and privileges were the mendicants entitled? Had they abused them? How were they to be limited? It is certainly true, as Penn Szittya is at pains to argue, that the mode of these debates was intensely exegetical, and they quickly developed an eschato-logical tone that became pervasive.[30] Yet surely this is to be expected in any debate conducted within an institution founded on a sacred book, which locates its institutional privilege in its power, through its exegesis of that book, to lead this world to the next. The ultimate purpose of both the exegesis and the eschatology is not to deflect the ecclesiological away from the institutional into abstract theology; precisely the opposite. Both serve either to attack the mendicants' institutional privileges or to protect them.

The anti-fraternal material Chaucer invokes in this tale draws on its central target, mendicant pretensions to the *vita apostolica*. The tale recapitulates this line of attack repeatedly, beginning with the presentation of the friar as a *penetrans domos*, who pries into every house. The phrase comes from one of anti-fraternalism's fundamental biblical texts, II Timothy 3: 1-6, where Paul uses it to describe the pseudo-apostles of the Last Days.[31] Chaucer often presents the friar's actions in violation either of an apostolic text, such as carrying a staff or travelling with a servant, or of his own apostolic claims, such as his repeated money-grubbing despite his declaration that spreading Christ's word is all his intent.[32] For all their banality, these stereotyped suggestions of hypocrisy are ultimately ecclesiological, for the mendicant pretension to the *vita apostolica* is an ecclesiological one. It centers on how Christ's apostolic mission is to be translated into institutional form.

For the mendicants, their renunciation of property was a literal reenactment of the apostolic life. It made them, in the friar's words, "werkeris of Goddes word" (III, 1937), whose exemplary status guaranteed their authority. For the secular clergy, however, this highly individuated form of authority was chaotic, and threatened the unity of the Church. In the words of William Saint Amour, the founder of the anti-fraternal tradition, it raised the possiblity of "an infinite and unfixed number of persons" wielding apostolic authority, *penetrans domos*, prying into every house, disrupting the orderly functioning of the traditional Church. Against this possibility, William posed the principle of ecclesiastical economy, which became

---

[30] Szittya, *Antifraternal Tradition*, 3-61, and *passim*. Szittya's insistence on the purely theological significance of these debates is made all the more puzzling by the illuminating connections he draws between them and their institutional context, particularly in the early chapters of the book.

[31] On *penetrans domos*, see Szittya, *Antifraternal Tradition*, 3-10, 22-23, 56-61.

[32] For other instances, see Szittya, *Antifraternal Tradition*, 239-46.

one the seculars' central arguments. Each ecclesiastical office should
have a single possessor. Just as each diocese has only one bishop, and
each archidiaconate, only one archdeacon, so each parish should
have only one "rector." Otherwise, the Church would become a
"monster with many heads."[33]

This argument is clearly a proprietary one. Where the mendicants
located apostolic authority in the faithful reenactment of the apostolic
life, their secular opponents located it in the Church's division of its
property and its assignment of one official to each administrative
unit. The wealth and abundance which, for the Summoner's friar,
makes the propertied orders slow and unresponsive is, for William of
Saint Amour and those who follow him, the source of the Church's
institutional stability. Moreover, the nature of that stability firmly
allies it to the most fundamental form of power in a feudal society, the
ownership of land. In formulating the principle of economy, the anti-
fraternalists are simply applying to the institutional structure of the
Church the same singular form of control over land that characterized feudal primogeniture. This ideological similarity makes
the anti-fraternalist position extremely easy for Chaucer to laicize.
By adapting the anti-fraternal stereotypes such as the *penetrans domos*,
he will affirm lay power as the ultimate source of Church stability.

The proprietary force which he opposes to the friar's acquisitive,
cash-hungry ecclesiology is not the propertied Church, but the laity,
represented first by the bourgeois household of Thomas and then,
definitively, by the local court. As he had done in the *Friar's Tale*,
Chaucer once again repositions the clerical material out of which he
builds his narrative to make lay power the guarantor of Christian
authority. And once again this repositioning will turn on a question
of linguistic mastery. His most persistent means for dramatizing the
friar's hypocrisy comes from another anti-fraternal stereotype, that
friars are perverters of speech. As Szittya observes, this charge
originated as an attempt to attack the friars at the center of their
power.[34] They began as preachers; that remained their most
important and most durable institutional role. As their orders grew
more established and they moved into the universities, their
production of clerical discourse provided the main impetus for the
emergence of scholasticism. In Chaucer's hands this charge enables

---

[33] *De periculis novissimorum temporum*, chapter 2, 21–28; *Collectiones*, 145, 150, 197–99. Cited in
Szittya, *Antifraternal Tradition*, 46–47, 60–61.
[34] Szittya, *Antifraternal Tradition*, 53–54.

the confrontation between lay and clerical to be staged on purely linguistic ground, where the lay can be shown to overcome the ecclesiastical at its own game.

The tale presents Friar John's acquisitiveness as a relentless linguistic onslaught:

> Yif us a busshel whete, malt, or reye,
> A Goddes kechyl, or a trype of chese,
> Or elles what yow lyst, we may nat cheese;
> A Goddes halfpeny, or a masse peny,
> Or yif us of youre brawn, if ye have eny;
> A dagon of youre blanket, leeve dame,
> Oure suster deere – lo! Heere I write youre name –
> Bacon or beef, or swich thyng as ye fynde.   (III, 1746–53)

He is never at a loss for words. When Thomas's wife seems resentful at his absence for two weeks after the death of her son, he quickly improvises the story of the miraculous revelation, and then appends three exempla. When Thomas complains that all the money he has given "diverse manere freres" (III, 1940) has not improved his health, John quickly explains it is because Thomas has scattered his gifts too widely. After rehearsing the three exempla against ire, he asks to hear Thomas's confession. When Thomas rebuffs him, he immediately replies with a request for gold.

At the beginning of this onslaught, he declares to Thomas's wife, "Glosynge is a glorious thyng, certeyn, / For lettre sleeth, so as we clerkes seyn" (III, 1793–94). In fact, as a mendicant preacher, Friar John embodies the power of glossing, and this declaration, in both its exuberance and its somewhat dubious theology, sums up his entire performance. To be strictly doctrinal, glossing is not a glorious thing. It is a stopgap, a provisional means of access to God's Word made necessary by the limitations of fallen human consciousness. The letter slays because human language can never fully contain the Divine Word. When the friar makes glossing a source of glory, he is in fact treating the letter as an end in itself rather than reading through it to the Spirit, which is the only true source of glory, and which glossing should always be striving beyond itself to attain.

The friar has neatly misinterpreted the principle that the letter kills and has come to exactly the wrong conclusion. Rather than seeing the emptiness of the letter as a sign of human degradation, a profound spiritual disadvantage to be continually struggled against, he sees it as an opportunity, a continual opportunity to produce new meanings, to escape all linguistic constraint. These new meanings, of course, will also be empty letters, since they are directed at the glory of glossing rather than the glory of God. In effect, then, the friar uses the literal emptiness of language as a justification for his equally empty manipulations of it.

Yet Chaucer, unlike his anti-fraternal sources, does not invoke the stereotype of perverted speech simply to dismiss the friars. The capacity of language for perversion interests him too much to be employed as simple mechanism of judgment. For, ironically, in this capacity for perversion also lies language's persuasive power. The friar's declaration, "glosying is a glorious thyng," does not, I think, immediately strike the reader as anti-doctrinal. What strikes the reader immediately is its good-humored exuberance. This exuberance makes the statement performative: the friar's glossing becomes glorious by declaring itself so. It is only upon reflection that the reader sees this exuberance actually contradicts the exegetical principle it invokes as justification.

One might well object that it is precisely because this exuberance is illusory that the reader responds to it – rather than the statement's anti-doctrinal substance – because the reader is operating under the same constraints of fallen human consciousness as the friar. But this objection in fact supports my, and I believe Chaucer's, point. Linguistic form, despite, or perhaps because of, its spiritual emptiness, has an effect in the world. This effect may be due to nothing more than the spiritual emptiness of the world itself, but it is still something worth exploring and explaining, particularly if, like Chaucer, one's interest in the vernacular commits one firmly to the language of this world.

Chaucer's ironic interest in the material efficacy of the letter in fact ultimately supports the exegetical principle of the letter's spiritual deadness. For even in its most hierocratic application, the principle that the letter kills makes all human language, even the most priestly, into a vernacular in relation to the Divine Word. Even at its most conservative this formula is always an invitation to break with some previously established authority. Read this way it does indeed make glossing a glorious thing, but not intrinsically, as the friar would have it. From this perspective, the friar's problem is not that he glosses too much, but that he does not gloss enough. For he is still attached to the act of glossing and the hieratic privilege it confers upon him, rather than to the spiritual authority for which that glossing should strive.

For Chaucer, unlike the clerical anti-mendicants, that authority inheres most immediately not in the institutional structures of the proprietary Church, but in the ironic recognition that all language is vernacular and insufficient, that the authority of all language always lies elsewhere. The tale will enact this recognition through a progression of glosses – that is, a progression of linguistic performances, each based on the last, in which those whose appreciation of their linguistic authority is the most ironic are the most masterful. The friar begins the series. As we have already observed, he distinguishes himself from the possessioners, whom he can outgloss, because his freedom from the limiting structures of ecclesiastical possession enables him to respond more flexibly and fully to the vernacular world, in which the Church must do its work. However, he will himself be outglossed, first by Thomas, and then by the squire. Thomas will trick him with an ambiguous promise, and the squire will definitively reinforce the humiliation with an elaborate reinterpretation of Thomas's joke.

The irony of that joke lies precisely in its radical degradation of all language to the same level of universal emptiness. Wind answers wind. The fart, as the evanescent by-product of human waste, is only the limit case of all human endeavor, which eventually fades to nothing before the eternal verities of the divine. But this is the one possibility the friar, despite his apostolic pretensions, can never concede. His institutional office commits him to the human. It is not just that he needs to convert sacerdotal language to cash; he needs to invest cash itself with some lasting sacral meaning. What enrages him is not so much the obvious and insulting difference between his fluent, learned chatter and the fart he receives in return, as their ultimate similarity. That similarity robs his language of its privilege, denying its power to invest the secular world with sacral meaning.

At the same time, the fart is not a renunciation of all meaning. Indeed, as a reply to the exegetical blandishments of the friar, it is a spectacularly parodic celebration of the glory of glossing. If Thomas is able to reduce the friar's language to the level of flatulence, by that very reduction he is able to endow flatulence with meaning. He is able to appropriate the glory of the gloss, the constant reimposition of meaning, by breaking it out of the ecclesiastical mold in which the friar ("moore we seen of Christes secree thynges, / Than burel folk" (III, 1871–72)) would imprison it. His reduction forces Friar John to confront the degraded evanescence of his own language; to that extent it is an ironic acknowledgment that all human meaning derives its authority from elsewhere.

This irony is developed more fully in the tale's conclusion, where the class status of mendicant spirituality is made explicit. That Friar John resorts to the lord of the village shows him doubly constrained by his dependence on the lay. Not only is his preaching directed at the accumulation of money, but when that endeavor is frustrated, he appeals to the very power of property which his mendicancy disavows. His claim to live outside the world is definitively defeated by this final appeal to the ultimate form of power within it, the noble landowner. Moreover, even here he is unable to accept the world's fallen state for what it is.

When he recounts the story to the lord and his household, the lady's response is mild surprise at his anger. "Is ther oght elles?" she asks, and to his challenge, "Madame ... how thynke ye herby?" she is dismissive:

> "How that me thynketh?" quod she. "So God me speede,
> I seye a cherl hath doon a cherles dede.
> What shold I seye? God lat hym nevere thee!" (III, 2205–07)

The court's superiority to the friar is marked precisely by its ironic acceptance of the anti-social, even potentially blasphemous, behavior of churls. But this ironic perspective is precisely the viewpoint the friar can never adopt. For the lower-class world of the churl is the world the friar's institutional position forces him to inhabit; it is the source of his institutional viability. His rebuke from Thomas has exposed his incapacity to manage that world. The squire's joke will demonstrate that the court, by virtue of its ironic detachment, can impose meaning on this world where the friar could not.

When the friar replies to the lady's dismissal, he apparently cannot bring himself to name the insult he has suffered:

> "Madame," quod he, "by God, I shal not lye,
> But I on oother wyse may be wreke,
> I shal disclaundre hym over al ther I speke,
> This false blasphemour that charged me
> To parte that wol nat departed be
> To every man yliche, with meschaunce!" (III, 2210–15)

The friar cannot specify the nature of the blasphemy because to specify it would be to concede it was not utterly meaningless, that it is possible to produce meaning from within the lay even at its most degraded. Quite simply, it would mean conceding his own authority, for that authority depends on the distinction between clerical and lay understood in exclusively formal terms. As one of the "infinite and unfixed number" of mendicants, who were, in the Wife of Bath's phrase, "thikke as motes in the sonne-beem" (III, 868), he cannot draw his authority from a fixed place in the traditional Church hierarchy. He draws it instead from the general distinction between clerical and lay, a distinction which for all practical purposes can only be concretely expressed in his speech, his preaching, and confessing. If his speech is not inherently privileged, if it can be reduced to the degraded status of empty wind, then his authority is gone. Describing his humiliating reception of the fart as being charged to "parte" that which will not be "departed," reasserts the privilege of his speech by making the fart merely nonsense, denying its satirical significance.

Of course, this reassertion of linguistic privilege only sets the friar up for a more definitive and humiliating denial. First the lord and then the squire play along, pretending that all that was insulting about the fart was the formal problem of how it might be divided. In this way, they can reinforce the real insult while pretending to be merely resolving the formal problem. The irony is all the more devastating in being thus presented as entirely passive, as flowing inevitably from the friar's own treatment of his insult. Under the cover of this passivity what emerges is a scathingly satirical image of the mendicant, a satirical image whose effortless good humor simply makes it that much more damning.

As Alan Levitan was the first to discover, the squire's "departyng" of the fart involves a complicated inversion of Pentecostal icon-ography, an inversion that once again parodies the mendicant's apostolic pretensions. Medieval depictions of Pentecost often pre-sented the twelve apostles seated around a wheel of fire, awaiting the descent of the Holy Spirit, an image similar to that envisioned by the squire.[35] Moreover, as Penn Szittya has recently pointed out, in descriptions of and allusions to Pentecost, the Holy Spirit is often described as *flatus*. In the Bible Pentecost is associated with *primitiae* or

---

[35] Levitan's findings were first presented in Bernard Levy, "Biblical Parody in the *Summoner's Tale*," *Tenessee Studies in Literature* 11 (1966), 45–60; and then in his own article, "The Parody of Pentecost in Chaucer's *Summoner's Tale*," *University of Toronto Quarterly* 40 (1970–71), 236–46.

first fruits. The descent of the Holy Spirit is described as *domum dei*, which makes the "departyng" of Thomas's "yifte" around the cartwheel an exact parody of the Pentecostal scenes Levitan has discovered.[36]

The exact significance of this iconographic material has been a matter of some dispute. Levitan feels it delivers "a parodic thrust at the inversion of the Holy Spirit among the corrupt friars;" Bernard S. Levy that it makes the tale a cautionary exemplum against ire. Szittya reads it as apocalyptic.[37] For other critics the departyng's broad burlesque makes any "serious" theological reading suspect.[38] Nevertheless, I would suggest that what makes these readings suspect is not their theology *per se*, but their complete (and completely unmedieval) separation of the theological from the ecclesiological. If, instead, we recognize that anti-fraternalism was predominantly an ecclesiological position, and focus on the ecclesiology implicit in this ending, we can, I believe, produce a reading which accounts both for the iconography and for the burlesque.

If the image of the friars at the cartwheel is indeed a parody of the descent of the Holy Spirit, then the churl is in the position of God, and his fart becomes the Holy Spirit. Accordingly, this means the friars are worshipping the churl's fart as a false god. But this analogy only makes graphic what has been implicit in the institutional positioning of Friar John from the beginning of the tale. He inhabits the world of churls, and is dependent on their offerings. All of his sacramental tasks are directed not at God, but at acquiring more and more of their earthly goods, especially their money. And that activity has already been defined as groping after the excretory both by the tale's central event, and by the pun on fart/farthyng, which this final image brings to fulfillment.

In urging Thomas to concentrate all his giving on Friar John's convent, the friar had asked, "What is a ferthyng worth parted in twelve?" Thomas's fart, is like his farthyng in that both are insubstantial, ephemeral, and utterly meaningless from the spiritual perspective the friar claims to represent. The friar's assumption that neither the farthyng nor the fart can be parted reflects his misplaced faith in the materiality of this world. His non-ironic, aspiritual commitment to the things of this world means that he has to keep the

---

[36] Szittya, *Antifraternal Tradition*, 232–36.
[37] Levitan, "Parody of Pentecost," 244; Levy, "Biblical Parody," 550–58; and Szittya, *Antifraternal Tradition*, 236–46.   [38] E.g., Pearsall, *"Canterbury Tales"*, 228.

two absolutely separate. He is sure the fart cannot be parted because he needs to read it as simple nonsense. He is sure the farthyng cannot be parted because he needs to read that as entirely integral, a repository of full meaning. The pun's fulfillment in the final image, which by parting the fart suggests the farthyng could be parted as well, brings these two false extremes together, suggesting once again that money is as insubstantial and malodorous morally as farting is materially. In founding their spirituality on the money of the lower classes, the friars have replaced the breath of the Holy Spirit with the empty, malodorous wind of human forms.

These ecclesiological implications do not so much constitute the burlesque of this image as gloss it. The burlesque is, indeed, "pure comedy," to cite Pearsall once again, but in this context even "pure comedy" has a political significance. For the comic, or what I have been calling the ironic, is the one thing the friar cannot allow. His commitment to the sacral fullness of his own glossing requires a suppression of the formal emptiness to which all human language is subject. The squire's *jeu d'esprit*, like the trick of Thomas's on which it depends, makes its general exposure of the emptiness of language the exposure of the friar's language in particular, for it follows the terms the friar himself set down.

Moreover, the comic advantage the Squire achieves results as much from his own social position as from his superior wit. He can both tolerate and manipulate linguistic irony because, unlike the friar, he has no commitment to making language fully sacral. He is in the better position to be ironic, and in this final irony lies his authority. As in the *Friar's Tale*, Chaucer's management of the narrative has enabled the moral exposure of a church office to be spoken from a lay perspective.

The condemnation is even less direct than it is in the *Friar's Tale*, but it is authoritative nonetheless. It may seem odd – not to mention hopelessly pedantic – to argue for the authority of a narrative perspective that is founded on flatulence. But if Thomas's fart enters the narrative as a complete breach of social decorum, it also exposes the friar's much more serious breach of the Church's sacred duty. As the squire amplifies Thomas's trick, he also accentuates both its ironic authority and its secularity.

He does not begin his conundrum before requesting a gown in exchange. When the gown is duly offered, the cultural production of the court is implicitly contrasted with that of ti.. mendicant preacher.

An item of apparel, usually a coat, was the typical mode of remuneration for the performance of a *jongleur*.[39] The language of the mendicant preacher is empty and motivated by hope of temporal gains, but it presents itself as replete with sacred import. The language of the court performance is similarly empty and similarly motivated, but in its explicit acknowledgement of these conditions it distinguishes itself from the language of the friar, and acquires an ironic authority the friar's language lacks. The squire leaves no doubt about this parallel. The friar, he says,

> ... hath to-day taught us so muche good
> With prechyng in the pulpit ther he stood,
> That I may vouche sauf, I sey for me,
> He hadde the first smel of fartes thre;
> And so wolde al his covent hardily.
> He bereth hym so faire and hoolily.   (III, 2281–86)

The rest of the court agrees, comparing the squire to Euclid and Ptolemy, in a final jab of sarcastic hyperbole. And

> Touchynge the cherl, they seyde,
>   subtiltee
> And heigh wit made hym speken as he spak;
> He nys no fool, ne no demonyak,   (III, 2290–92)

thus revealing their earlier statements to this effect were part of the put-on.

This ending rounds off Chaucer's anti-clerical attack. Having discredited the proprietary ecclesiology of the secular clergy in the *Friar's Tale*, he has now discredited the more linguistic, and more individuated ecclesiology of the mendicants. Both of these attacks, each spoken from rival clerical positions, ultimately depend on the ironic authority of the lay. The friar is able to defeat proprietary assumptions in the office of the summoner by invoking an individuated spirituality which finds its highest fulfillment in the personal piety of the lay believer. Speaking from an institutional position that is thus already discredited, the summoner is able to gainsay the friar, but only by invoking an ironic, fabliau-like perspective that

---

[39] R. Howard Bloch, *The Scandal of the Fabliaux* (Chicago and London: University of Chicago Press, 1986), 22–58.

ultimately depends on the political authority of the court. The dispute which began in ecclesiastically generated anger, or to use Chaucer's term, ire, dissolves in vernacular laughter. This laughter restores the moral equilibrium precisely by exposing the moral emptiness of the clerical offices which motivated the ire.

Nevertheless, we cannot read this restorative laughter as a return to some pure *game*. To do so would put us back in the position of the Friar, for whom *game* means the evasion of authority, and whose initiation of this sort of *game* produced the conflict with the Summoner in the first place. The laughter which closes the *Summoner's Tale* is restorative precisely because it is impure. Focused beyond itself, it is articulated from a lay, vernacular position which, because it recognizes its own impurity, is able to expose the same impurity in the clerical positions it attacks. The closure it effects is affirmative but not complacent. It establishes the lay as an authoritative site of resistance to what it regards as illegitimate extensions of Church prerogative, but its indications of its own authority still remain necessarily indirect. They will become more direct as the collection continues, but never entirely so. Nor can they. Chaucer's linguistic indirection forms the necessary condition for both his anti-clerical critique and his affirmations of lay power. It allows him to deauthorize the clerical just enough to appropriate its authority in order to reauthorize the lay. This is not a simple process. We cannot make Chaucer's assertion of lay authority the master-key to the *Canterbury Tales*. But we also cannot ignore it. It is an essential component of his irony; a *sine qua non* in fact. In the next tale, irony and affirmation are completely intertwined. The *Clerk's Tale* affirms monarchy precisely by focusing on the self-regulating power it retains even at its most excessive.

POWER AND PATHOS: THE "CLERK'S TALE"

The *Clerk's Tale* is Chaucer's first public exemplum in the *Canterbury Tales*, and the Clerk is the first ecclesiastical speaker competent to speak on public matters. Harry Bailly makes indirect note of this when he charges the Clerk to keep his rhetorical resources, his "termes," "colours," and "figures," "... in stoor til so be ye endite / Heigh style, as whan that men to kynges write" (IV, 16–18). The Clerk's textual authority must come from within the contest of narratives the collection uses to characterize lay culture. As Harry warns, "what man that is entred in a pley, / He nedes moot unto the pley assente" (IV, 10–11). The high style is a clerical style, associated with the institution Chaucer has just discredited in the previous two tales: Harry also warns the Clerk to "precheth nat, as freres doon in Lente" (IV, 12). He expects instead "som murie thyng of aventures" (IV, 15), but Chaucer has already tested that tradition in the *Knight's Tale* and found it wanting. The textual prestige he appropriates in the figure of the Clerk will enable him to locate a more satisfactory source of lay authority in the figure of the monarch.

As befits the parameters of the collection's narrative contest, he accomplishes this shift indirectly, through the improvised genre of laicized hagiography, which Robert O. Payne called "the sentimental experiment" and which R. W. Frank has more recently described as "the tales of pathos."[40] The anti-clerical critiques affirm lay authority by discrediting the Church. The tales of pathos, the *Man of Law's Tale*, the *Clerk's Tale*, the *Physician's Tale*, and the *Prioress's Tale*, offer authoritative examples of lay suffering, in which a lay figure's saint-like *passio* exerts a redemptive transformation in this world. The piety they display through their appropriation of the hagiographical is countered by their display of a moral authority that exerts itself from within the secular.[41]

All of these tales define their suffering against existing relations of power, whose legitimacy they never fully question. The *Clerk's Tale* makes this dependence explicit. Griselda, a peasant and a woman, demonstrates her moral heroism by her inexhaustible acceptance of her own subordination. This acceptance, moreover, is solicited at every point by Walter, her husband and monarch. Without his continual exercise of an entirely capricious monarchical privilege, her heroism would literally not be possible. As the interdependence demonstrates her virtue, it also demonstrates the self-regulating nature of the political position he occupies.

Older criticism of the *Clerk's Tale* stressed its fidelity to cultural, and especially Christian, authority. Newer accounts have stressed its critical self-consciousness.[42] The reading I offer here splits the

---

[40] Robert O. Payne, *The Key of Remembrance: A Study of Chaucer's Poetics* (New Haven and London: Yale University Press, 1963), 164–70; Robert Worth Frank, "The *Canterbury Tales* III: Pathos," in *Cambridge Chaucer Companion*, 143.

[41] Both Payne and Frank make the *Second Nun's Tale* part of this group, and while I agree in general I have left it out of the discussion here because it is an actual hagiography.

[42] This work includes Anne Middleton, "The Clerk and His Tale, Some Literary Contexts," *Studies in the Age of Chaucer* 2 (1980), 121–50; Judith Ferster, *Chaucer and Interpretation* (Cambridge: Cambridge University Press, 1984), 94–121; Dinshaw, *Chaucer's Sexual Poetics*,

difference, not for the sake of compromise, but because I believe even some of the newer accounts retain a reductive notion of authority. Chaucer's self-consciousness about the tale he inherits is taken to be necessarily oppositional: in one account, his version becomes a critique of the expectations of medieval audiences; in another, a rejection of Petrarch and monarchism.[43] Such oppositional readings not only underestimate the continuities between Chaucer's tale and its antecedents. They also ignore the strong affirmation implicit in the very act of retelling of a tale not otherwise known to most of his audience.

The tale first appears in the *Decameron*, as the last tale of Day 10. Petrarch translates it into Latin in a letter to Boccaccio (*Epistolae seniles* XVII, 3), and these versions serve as the basis for a number of other translations into Italian, Latin, and French. One of the French translations was Chaucer's direct antecedent, though he also consulted Petrarch. Whether he knew Boccaccio's is unknown.[44] The plot which Boccaccio presents does not vary in any substantial way in either of the subsequent versions. All three begin with some approach to the Walter figure from his dependents, include his insistence on picking his own wife, and the subsequent choice of a poor but virtuous peasant girl. In all three, she becomes an exemplary marchioness, vindicating Walter's moral perspicuity. In all three the tests are the same: the removal of first daughter, then son. There is the same staging of the sham, covertly incestuous marriage, complete with the same counterfeit papal bulls enabling a divorce. The Griselda figure is recalled in all three to supervise the wedding arrangements, and there is the same resolution. Variations among the three major versions, significant though they are, are largely confined to interpretive differences oriented around the same narrative core. If these differences reorient the narrative, they also pass it on, perpetuating the general range of ideological possibilities it implies.

132–55; Michaela Paasche Grudin, "Chaucer's *Clerk's Tale* as Political Paradox," *Studies in the Age of Chaucer* 11 (1989), 68–91; David Wallace "'Whan She Translated Was,': A Chaucerian Critique of the Petrarchan Academy," in *Literary Practice and Social Change*, 156–215; Elaine Tuttle Hansen, *Chaucer and the Fictions of Gender* (Berkeley and Los Angeles, 1992), 188–207.

43 The first is Middleton, "The Clerk and His Tale," the second, Wallace, "'Whan she translated was.'"

44 J. Burke Severs, *The Literary Relationships of Chaucer's "Clerkes Tale"* (New Haven: Yale University Press, 1942).

Moreover, the relation between interpretation and narrative forms the center of these possibilities, and all three stage this relation as a confrontation between moral and political authority. In the *Decameron*, Dioneo, the story's teller, offers it as a corrective to what he views as the idealization of previous contributions to the day's theme, "those who have performed munificent deeds." While he distinguishes Gualteri, the Walter figure, from the kings and sultans of previous versions, his focus on Gualteri's coercive power (*una matta bestialità*) assumes a political position that is monarchical in character – supreme and unconstrained.[45]

Petrarch focuses on Griselda's virtue, the exemplary value of her *feminine constanciam*, rather than Walter's brutality.[46] This shift enables a general elevation in tone, and Petrarch also adds "a lengthy description of ideal government" to the tale's opening.[47] The effect of his revisions is to redeem Walter's coercion, to show how it could produce, in the patient Griselda, a figure of moral value. He drives the point home by describing the reactions of the cultivated readers to whom he shows the tale. As David Wallace astutely argues, the reader response Petrarch describes at the end of his letter projects as his audience the Petrarchan academy, a select, learned and exclusively male group.[48] The moral authority Griselda's suffering produces out of the brutality of lay politics can sustain a lay readership comparable in learning and prestige to that of clerical tradition.

Following Severs, most scholars have seen Chaucer's treatment of the tale falling somewhere between Boccaccio's and Petrarch's.[49] In the words of Michaela Paasche Grudin, his treatment of the story "enhances, rather than softens, its paradoxical elements."[50] Like Boccaccio, he emphasizes Walter's brutality, exposing the ideological contingency of his monarchical privilege. Like Petrarch, he also accentuates the sanctity of Griselda's suffering, elevating her at one point to the status of Job (IV, 932–38). Enhancing the paradox enables him to make its terms more explicit. The very distance between Griselda's patience and Walter's privilege will ironically but

---

[45] Giovanni Boccaccio, *Decameron*, ed. Vittore Branca (Milan: Arnoldo Mondadori Editore, 1976), 992.   [46] *Epistolae seniles* XVII, 3, in *Literary Relationships*, 288.
[47] Grudin, "Political Paradox," 77.
[48] Wallace, "'Whan She Translated Was,'" 160–65.
[49] Severs, *Literary Relationships*, 233. The most notable dissenter is Wallace, "'Whan she translated was,'" who sees Chaucer undercutting Petrarch and returning to Boccaccio.
[50] "Political Paradox," 79.

inevitably demonstrate the necessity of Walter's power, as the one form of order possible in a radically fallen world.

Griselda's is the suffering of a lay heroine, enacted entirely in response to the political exigencies of monarchical power. The pathos she evokes is a specifically lay pathos, which affirms the spiritual integrity of lay existence, even as it assents to the potentially oppressive necessities of lay power. Moreover, the spiritual integrity it grants to the lay affirms the ideological character it assigns to lay power. Walter's cruelty depends throughout on his consummate manipulation of ideology. The efficacy of his cruelty is very much the efficacy of the ideological structures which sustain it. Their efficacy, in turn, enables the *Clerk's Tale* to claim for lay culture both moral and political authority.

The claim begins in the Prologue, with Chaucer's eulogy to Petrarch. This eulogy is effectively a canonization, a production of a lay *auctor*, and it establishes a pattern that Chaucer's fifteenth-century disciples will follow in canonizing him. The Clerk names Petrarch as both "worthy clerk" and "lauriat poete." (IV, 26, 31) But the emphasis lies more heavily on Petrarch as poet: the circuit of authority traced through him is distinctly unclerical. The Clerk encounters Petrarch's text not in his studies at university but through personal contact with Petrarch himself. "I wol you telle a tale which that I / Lerned at Padowe of a worthy clerk," (IV, 25–26) he declares and amplifies this emphasis on the local and historical. As "lauriat poete," Petrarch's function is defined politically. His

> ... rhetorike sweete
> Enlumyned al Ytaille of poetrie
> As Lynyan dide of philosophie,
> Or lawe, or oother art particuler ...   (IV, 32–35)

This comparison with the canon lawyer Giovanni da Lignano makes the political orientation of Petrarch's laureateship normative. The purpose of any "art particuler" is to illuminate the political community (in this case, "al Ytaille") in which it is produced. Indeed, we might recall that Petrarch himself conceived of his laureateship in political terms. In his coronation oration he describes the laurel as "equally appropriate for Caesars and poets."[51] The

---

[51] "Petrarch's Coronation Oration," in Ernest Hatch Wilkins, *Studies in the Life and Works of Petrarch* (Cambridge, MA: Medieval Academy, 1955), 310.

lament for Petrarch's death delimits his function by temporally restricting his authority to this world.

> But Deeth, that wol nat suffre us dwellen heer,
> But as it were a twynkling of an ye,
> Hem bothe hath slayn, and alle shul we dye.   (IV, 36–38)

This closing delineation of Petrarch's poetic authority clearly deflates it, consigning it to a temporal realm reduced to the "twynkling of an ye." Nevertheless, the deflation is also enabling. It carries to the logical limit the temporality of poetic authority upon which the rest of the passage insists. In this passage, poetry is not only in the temporal world, but of it. The order it brings comes out of the features of that world, personal contact and political community, rather than being imposed from the world above. The very lament carries this order onward. In mourning Petrarch's loss, Chaucer quite literally keeps his authority alive, recuperates the essentially temporal source of order Petrarch's death threatens to keep "nayled in his cheste" (IV, 29), and brings it forward into his own place and time. Accomplishing the recuperation through the Clerk foregrounds its temporality, making even the clerical learning of the Church dependent upon the secular authority Petrarch embodies.

Nevertheless, this move also acknowledges Chaucer's desire for the cultural prestige of the very clerical tradition he is attempting to displace. As such, it considerably complicates the recent readings which would make the *Clerk's Tale* constitute some sort of humanist break. Chaucer clearly sees the moral authority he uses the tale to adumbrate as appropriated from clerical tradition, and he puts it in the service of a view of political authority that is equally conservative. This is the view we have already seen in Aegidius Romanus, and Grudin is right to argue that Chaucer's depiction of Walter's authority draws on the Aristotelianism of late medieval political thought.[52] But such Aristotelianism retains essential connections to the Augustianism it replaces, and Chaucer's use of it is no exception. For all of its systematic coherence, Walter's monarchy is ultimately justified by the fallenness of the world it inhabits. Moreover, like Aegidius, Chaucer locates this coherence in the exchange between the dominance of class and that of gender, the exchange that supported feudal society from its beginnings.

[52] Grudin, "Political Paradox," 68–91.

Things could hardly be otherwise in a tale which focuses so exclusively on the relations of power in and around marriage. The opening makes Walter's marriage an entirely public affair, and stresses his monarchical status.

> A markys whilom lord was of that lond,
> As were his worthy eldres hym bifore;
> And obeisant, ay redy to his hond,
> Were alle his liges, bothe lasse and moore.
> Thus in delit he lyveth, and hath doon yoore,
> Biloved and drad, thurgh favour of Fortune,
> Bothe of his lordes and of his commune.   (IV, 68–70)

Where Chaucer speaks of "lordes" and "commune," Petrarch speaks of *familia* and *terra*. *Le Livre Griseldis*, the extant French translation closest to the *Clerk's Tale*, speaks even more blandly of *gouvernement* and *dominacion*.[53] Chaucer's revision clearly identifies Walter as a monarchical figure presiding over both an aristocracy and commons. The people's request to him to marry becomes not only a public, but almost a parliamentary event. Chaucer stresses the spokesman's representative status – "That he sholde telle hym what his peple mente" – and the request's public dimension. Walter is asked to bow his neck "under that blisful yok / Of soveraynetee, noght of servyse" (IV, 113–14).

In another addition to his sources Chaucer frames Walter's counterproposal as an explicit contract between ruler and ruled:

> For sith I shal forgoon my libertee
> At youre requeste, as evere moot I thryve,
> Ther as myn herte is set, ther wol I wyve;
> And but ye wole assente in swich manere,
> I prey yow, speketh namoore of this matere.   (IV, 171–75)

In the previous versions, the promise which Walter extracts is presented purely as the final stage in a more or less free-form bargaining process. Chaucer emphasizes the *quid pro quo* which Walter demands from a position of strength. Either the people agree to uphold his absolute sovereignty in making this choice, or the subject is closed.

---

[53] Severs, *Literary Relationships*, 254–55.

Both in its content and in the very fact of its being made, the people's request exposes the collective, rhetorical component of monarchical power. By producing an heir, a monarch stabilized the entire power structure. Walter's advisor leaves no doubt that this is why the people want a queen.

> Delivere us out of al this bisy drede,
> And taak a wyf, for hye Goddes sake!
> For if it so bifelle, as God forbede,
> That thurgh youre deeth youre lyne sholde slake,
> And that a strange successour sholde take
> Youre heritage, O wo were us alyve!
> Wherefore we pray you hastily to wyve. (IV, 134–40)

The people's initiative recalls Walter to the structural basis of his own power, and reminds him that the function of that structure was not simply to produce him, but also to produce social order, which can only be maintained if the structure is maintained.

Walter's counterproposal tacitly acknowledges his collective responsibility, but it also explicitly insists on the singularity of his own privilege. If the continuance of his line is to have the function his advisor wants it to have, it cannot become entirely collective, cannot become the prerogative of the people. For then it would lack the very condensation of sovereign authority into a single figure which primogenitural ideology identifies as the source of social stability. This is why Walter's disinterest in marriage causes such a crisis. It denies the identity between social position and personality which primogeniture assumes, and on which it depends.

We can make this argument even more historically specific. Chaucer is writing for an audience affiliated with the royal court at a time when an increasingly strong monarchy was encountering resistance from an increasingly disempowered aristocracy. Centralized monarchies emerged in the first place because there was an instability at the core of medieval aristocratic power, an instability similar to that pointed up by Walter's counterproposal. Noble primogeniture was never sufficient in itself to preserve social order. As a group, the nobility always needed the supreme power of a king to prevent its disintegration into warring factions, even if as individuals, lords always resented the constraints imposed on their power. When Walter's counterproposal attacks noble status as historically contingent – "children ofte been / Unlyk hir worthy eldres ben bifore"

(IV, 155–56) he is challenging not only his advisor's presumption of his own prerogative, but also the advisor's complacent assumption that heritability can be a self-sufficient source of social order.

From this perspective, Walter's counterproposal and his subsequent behavior can be read not simply as a reassertion of monarchical privilege but also as an affirmation of its necessity. The absolute privilege which he claims will sustain heritability even as it exposes heritability's contingent status. His arbitrary imposition of noble status on Griselda comes to seem natural, and is even sustained by God:

> ... to this newe markysesse
> God hath swich favour sent hire of his grace
> That it ne semed nat by liklynesse
> That she was born and fed in rudenesse,
> As in a cote or in an oxe-stalle,
> But norissed in an emperoures halle.   (IV, 394–99)

As a number of recent commentators have pointed out, Chaucer makes the rhetorical aspect of this transformation explicit by describing it as a translation: "Unnethe the peple hir knew for hire fairnesse / Whan she translated was in swich richesse" (IV, 384–85). Tempting though it may be to see in this metaphor a straightforward celebration of the dispersive and subversive power of language, the power ultimately celebrated is Walter's. By imputing the plasticity of language to the solid realities of class hierarchy, Chaucer demonstrates the absolute extent to which these realities are under Walter's control. Walter alone has the power to make this translation: this power comes directly from the *quid pro quo* he established in response to his advisor's request.

The grace God shows to Griselda affirms both Walter's translation and the singularity of his power: only he can intervene in the *status quo*. Like the Wife of Bath before him, Walter points out that virtue comes from God, not from blood; his actions add the additional lesson that only the select few can recognize such virtue. "The peple have no greet insight / In vertu," Chaucer observes, in explaining Walter's choice (IV, 242–43). Walter's insight shows him to be "A prudent man," fully worthy of his monarchical position. The second part of the tale ends with an idealized summation of the early days of his reign after his marriage. Griselda provides him with "Goddes pees ... at hoom" (IV, 423–24) harmonious support in public affairs, and, with the birth of a daughter, promise of an heir.

If this part of the tale establishes Walter's prudence and virtue as a ruler, then the rest of it will demonstrate how inextricable such virtue is from the singular and absolute character of the monarchical position from which it is executed. Many critics have been disturbed by this interdependence and have sought to treat Walter as a principle rather than a character. Though such readings may produce a more comfortable view of the tale, it seems to me they miss the rigor of Chaucer's political conservatism, his Augustinian conviction that in a fallen world monarchy produces social order not only in spite of, but often, even because of the moral inadequacies of the monarch. Chaucer certainly does not treat Walter as an abstraction, condemning his treatment of Griselda in the Clerk's narratorial asides which Chaucer adds to his sources.[54]

The Clerk also makes Walter fully aware of the effect of his cruelty, reminding us more than once of his pity (IV, 894, 1050). Such pity also characterizes the initial agreement with his people. Their spokesman describes their plea as made "with pitous herte" (IV, 97), and the Clerk comments that "Hir meeke preyere and hir pitous cheere / Made the markys herte han pitee" (IV, 141–42). The pity of the initial, prudent Walter cannot be separated from that of the subsequent, capricious Walter. Nor can it be separated from the pity the tale expects from his audience, the pity that Petrarch reports moved one of his cultivated readers to tears.[55] This is a pity like the sympathy Chaucer recommends to readers in the *Parson's Tale*, a downward identification which affirms the very social boundaries it crosses.

The *Clerk's Tale* makes monarchy the source of this sort of pity. No one else in the tale but Walter ever knows the whole truth until the end. Only he can appreciate Griselda's virtue fully. Chaucer insists on this singularity with an addition toward the end of the narrative stressing the instability of the people. Though initially opposed to Walter's treatment of Griselda (IV, 722–28), by the time he begins to stage the mock wedding to his daughter, they have come around to what they mistakenly perceive as his estimate of the situation.

> And thanne at erst amonges hem they seye
> That Walter was no fool, thogh that hym leste
> To change his wyf, for it was for the beste.   (IV, 985–87)

---

[54] Severs, *Literary Relationships*, 232–33.   [55] Severs, *Literary Relationships*, 288.

Though this change occurs in the previous versions, Chaucer
punctuates it with a stanza-long lamentation.

> "O stormy peple! Unsad and evere untrewe!
> Ay undiscreet and chaungynge as a fane!
> Delitynge ever in rumbul that is newe,
> For lyk the moone ay wexe ye and wane!
> Youre doom is fals, youre constance yvele preeveth;
> A ful greet fool is he that on you leeveth. "   (995–1001)

This lamentation is spoken by the "sadde folk in that citee" (IV,
1002). Chaucer is clearly drawing on the contrast between *sapientes*
and *vulgus*, the early humanist commonplace with which both
Boccaccio and Petrarch were also familiar.[56] In this case, however,
the *sapientes* are less a self-sufficient intellectual elite (like the
Petrarchan academy) than a defective version of Walter himself. He
is the only one in this situation who is completely *sapiens*. Although
these "sadde folk" recognize the inconstancy of the people, they
themselves are unaware of the extent to which Walter has that
inconstancy under control. This deployment of the commonplace
gives its intellectual elitism a specific political character. The
deployment converts its general distrust of the *vulgus* into an
endorsement of the inherent *sapientia* of the monarchy.

The inconstancy of the *vulgus* is defined primarily in linguistic and
ideological terms: their delight in the novelty of "rumbul," their
ceaseless "clappyng deere ynogh a jane," and their false "doom."
Yet Walter's ideological manipulations are no less transgressive, and,
on the face of it, no less inconstant. From the very beginning, "lust
present was al his thought." The promise he makes to his people to
take a wife is made and kept in such a way as to demonstrate his own
prerogative as it is to respond to their concerns. Having responded to
those concerns, he then uses his marriage as a platform for an
intricate, drawn-out masquerade which involves lies and deception
at every turn, culminating in the forged papal bulls that enable him
to divorce Griselda. On the face of it, what is there to distinguish
Walter's language from that of the "stormy peple"?

There can be nothing but the singularity of the social position from
which his language is uttered. For if his language continually
vacillates, his purpose never does. From start to finish his single,
constant aim is the preservation of his own social prerogative, in all

---

[56] Charlotte Morse, "Exemplary Griselda," *Studies in the Age of Chaucer* 7 (1985), 85.

its capriciousness. This very prerogative, which enables his shifting self-representations to be convincingly carried out, also provides them with an underlying continuity. Moreover, because his deceptions are based on that prerogative, they can never be entirely capricious. The test of Griselda, despite all its excesses, is never far away from the social necessities which Walter uses to make it plausible. Her translation is in fact potentially scandalous. For one conclusion that might be drawn from it is that lineage is without social value. Griselda's patient submission to Walter's testing forestalls that conclusion, for it demonstrates that the virtue which justifies her transgression of the status quo is precisely her submission to it. As Bernard Levy observes,

> the great disparity in social rank between Walter and Griselda... would tend to make the *Clerk's Tale* understandable, even on the literal level, once we recognize that Walter, the noblest lord of the land, is testing Griselda, the most humble peasant, in order to prove her worthy of complete acceptance into royal society.[57]

The fact that, as the Clerk points out, Walter has already tested her enough when he begins his cruel masquerade is less relevant than the fact that Griselda's virtue is still a threat to the social hierarchy it transcends. It is only by making the test wildly excessive that Walter can neutralize that threat, for it is only by submitting to the status quo beyond all reasonable bounds that Griselda's virtue can definitively purge itself of any possible subversive taint. Chaucer's insistence on the discursiveness of power makes it more ideologically accessible, more participatory, more widely available. But this insistence also makes power more potentially anarchic and chaotic. To forestall this possiblity, he must insist on the singularity of power as the necessary regulator of its ideological contingency. Griselda's pathos consists in the fullness of her recognition of this necessity, and her wholehearted self-sacrifice to it.

For this reason, it is precisely Walter's excessiveness that is socially productive. He justifies each new outrage by invoking the potential subversiveness of Griselda's status. Her children must be taken away and she must be banished because Walter's people object to her low birth. Even though these claims are false in this context, inherent in the social reality to which they testify is a truth so potent that it produces order even when it is falsely manipulated. Though Griselda

[57] Bernard S. Levy, "The Meanings of the *Clerk's Tale*," in *Chaucer and the Craft of Fiction*, ed. Leigh Arrathoon (Rochester, MI: Solaris Press, 1986), 403.

submits to the truth of social hierarchy under false pretenses, her continued submission enables that hierarchy, in the person of Walter, ultimately to produce the social order it promises.

Moreover, the narrative logic of the Griselda story, especially in Chaucer's version, invites us to draw the implications of this point even further. The fiction to which Griselda submits is not a fiction at all, if it is defined as Walter's patriarchal control over his own offspring. What Griselda's submission assures him is that her children belong entirely to him. She can only do that if she freely grants to him even the right to destroy them. Her total submission to his power over her as father of her children reinstates the principle of heritablity her ascension to the ruling class may have violated. Chaucer's insistence on the thoroughly ideological nature of this submission suggests that such paternal power should itself be viewed as an ideological achievement rather than as a static given – that is, as a complex discursive structure that must be continually maintained by those it empowers, rather than as a pure, unquestioned constraint they can complacently accept. If patriarchy is viewed in this way, Walter's behavior ceases to be inherently excessive, and remains excessive only in that it represents a normative patriarchal response to an anomalous challenge to its hegemony. After all, patrilineal aristocracy is excessive and violent to its very core. It consists of the reproductive control exerted over one social group – that is, women – in order to maintain power over another – the non-noble. Griselda's complete abandonment of her children restores the first sort of control, and thereby assures that her apparent challenge to the second remains entirely anomalous.

The patriarchal motive of Walter's manipulations can perhaps be best demonstrated by examining the way he chooses to end them. Though the narrative's resolution has not attracted much attention, the reason it takes the exact form it does is far from obvious. Why a sham marriage, and why a sham marriage that would be incestuous if consummated? If it were simply a matter of intensifying Griselda's humiliation, any sham would do. Nor can the prospect of incest be dismissed as merely a by-product of the narrative convenience of having the children on the scene when the truth is revealed. For surely such convenience is also dependent on the sense that Walter's outrages could continue if he wanted them to, incest serving prospectively as the next outrage. So the question remains: why does Walter stop short of incest?

In their reevaluations of Freud and Lévi Strauss, recent feminist theorists have shown that the incest taboo is as much about power as it is about morality or biology. Rather than being some essential feature of human nature, the incest taboo is the minimal ideological condition for the existence of male dominance. Without the requirement of exogamy, there would be no basis for what Gayle Rubin memorably calls "the traffic in women," the system of kinship relations enabling men to share power.[58] The sham marriage demonstrates how thoroughly Walter controls this regulating structure. His threatened violation presents the taboo as an ideological fiction to be manipulated rather than a constraint to be acceded to. Walter has no desire actually to commit incest. His interest in it is purely ideological. He simulates its possiblity to satisfy himself that his control over his daughter as an item of exchange is so complete that he could commit incest if he so desired. Such power is the real object of his desire, and the source of the tale's closure.

The tale makes it clear that this power involves more than Walter's immediate family or even his household. It involves the whole social order, including, through the sham papal bulls, the head of the Church. This detail, which occurs in all the versions of the tale, is even more striking than the sham marriage as a whole. It is striking not so much because it shows Walter stooping to counterfeiting: that seems entirely in character. It is striking because it takes entirely for granted the notion that the Church would allow itself to be used in this way. It bespeaks a clear-eyed recognition of the Church's ideological role as the regulator of patriarchal relations. As contrary as such a recognition may be to modern idealizations of medieval piety, it corresponds nicely to the realities of the medieval Church.

The Church fought long and hard to become the institutionalized regulator of marriage, a drive that began with attempts in the eighth century to extend the incest to the seventh degree of consanguinity. Its efforts did not bear fruit until the later development of primogeniture. Only the Church had the expertise and resources to maintain the written records required to protect against the more intricate possibilities of consanguinity to which primogeniture,

---

[58] Gayle Rubin,"The Traffic in Women," in *Toward an Anthropology of Women*, ed. Rayna Reiter (New York and London: Monthly Review Press, 1975), 157–210. See also Juliet Mitchell, *Psychoanalysis and Feminism* (New York: Vintage Books, 1975), 361–98; Luce Irigaray, "Women on the Market," in *This Sex Which is Not One*, tr. Catherine Porter, with Carolyn Burke (Ithaca: Cornell University Press, 1985), 170–91; and Judith Butler, *Gender Trouble* (Baltimore, Johns Hopkins University Press, 1990), 35–78.

because of its greater precision, was liable.[59] Papal dispensations for divorce, while by no means common, were nevertheless an important feature of later medieval politics, particularly among kings. They provided the means of increasing the possibility of producing the all-important male heir. The issue of such dispensations was a significant source of conflict between the French crown and the papacy.[60]

Walter's manipulation of this aspect of clerical power assumes the centrality of the Church's regulatory role in regard to marriage. It also makes his position as monarch the focus of a vast network of ideological and institutional relations, and gives him much greater control over that network than he would have had in actuality. The tale's close literally makes him the author of his own authority, in all its extent and complexity. And the tale measures the efficacy of this concluding act of self-authorization by its effect on the people.

If we return now to the moment where they show their inconstancy, we can make its politics even more specific.

> And thanne at erst amonges hem they seye
> That Walter was no fool, thogh that hym leste
> To chaunge his wyf, for it was for the beste.
> For she is fairer, as they deemen alle,
> Than is Griselde, and moore tendre of age,
> And fairer fruyt bitwene hem sholde falle,
> And moore plesant, for hire heigh lynage.   (IV, 985–91)

The people's inconstancy is defined precisely by their naive belief in the power of "heigh lynage." This is the belief about nobility that Aegidus Romanus terms *communem opinionem*, and which Walter repudiated at the beginning of the tale.[61] This wife is to be preferred because her lineage insures a more virtuous heir. They accept the papal dispensation with similar naivety: "The rude peple, as it no wonder is, / Wenden ful wel that it hadde be right so" (IV, 750–51). Their naivety consists of their failure to recognize that the public dimensions of power are ideological constructs. Walter displays his

---

[59] Christopher N. L. Brooke, *The Medieval Idea of Marriage* (Oxford: Oxford University Press, 1989), 126–43; Georges Duby, *The Knight, the Lady and the Priest: The Making of Modern Marriage in Medieval France*, tr. Barbara Bray (New York: Pantheon, 1983); *Medieval Marriage*, tr. Elborg Forster (Baltimore and London: The Johns Hopkins University Press, 1978). Duby documents the coincidence between the development of primogeniture and the sacralization of marriage (see esp. *Medieval Marriage*, 1–22), but he stresses the tensions between the lay and ecclesiastical models of marriage. Brooke points out that the eventual success of the ecclesiastical model depended on its regulation of "hereditary succession," the "central point in which the aims of the nobility and the aims of the Church coincided" (141–43).   [60] Duby, *Medieval Marriage*, 25–81.   [61] See above, 111–13.

superiority over them by his very recognition that such superiority is entirely arbitrary and contingent.

This recognition distinguishes Chaucer's audience from the *vulgus* as well. For it has followed Walter's machinations through every intricate turning; it has literally shared his ideological power in order to make the narrative cohere. It is wiser even than the *sadde folk* who condemn the *vulgus*, and it shares Walter's ideological power even more intimately. If I am right to argue that that audience came from an expanding ruling class, such an identification would have served it well. In identifying itself with Walter, the audience distinguishes itself from the masses with which an expanding ruling class always risks merging. The singularity of the monarch protects hierarchical privilege; the ideological basis of that singularity makes such privilege accessible.

Paradoxically, the identification with Walter facilitates the exemplary identification with Griselda, which the Clerk's first moral, drawn from Petrarch, requires: " that every wight, in his degree, / Sholde be constant in adversitee / As was Griselde" (IV, 1145–48). The pathos of her suffering inheres precisely in the recognition that while it was cruel and arbitrary, things could not, in this fallen world, have been any other way. She sacrifices herself to the efficacy, indeed the moral necessity, of monarchical privilege. As an exemplar to Chaucer's audience, she calls them to the same sacrifice, to the sacrifice, that is, to the source of their own ideological legitimacy. Since this legitimacy was not based solely on class, or solely on gender, but precisely on the interrelation between the two, the identification with Griselda would theoretically have been attractive to the women in Chaucer's audience as well as the men. For the entire audience, the rigor of Griselda's suffering was ameliorated by their discursive participation in the monarchical authority to which that suffering was devoted. While Griselda's pathos and Walter's power must be kept distinct in order for the tale to work, the distinction itself is a discursive and ideological projection, and the recognition of their interdependence is the ultimate source of the tale's authority.

Even the playful morals that follow the first one support this recognition. When the Clerk dismisses Griselda and "hire pacience" as dead and buried in Italy (IV, 1177–78), and then flirts with the Wife of Bath, he steps back from his exemplum, and acknowledges it as a textual and ideological construct. But such constructedness also characterizes the very form of authority against which Griselda's exemplarity was defined. The Clerk's acknowledgment only reinforces his discursive control over her exemplarity. The irony of these morals returns us to the playfulness of the narrative contest and the specifically lay discourse out of which the *Clerk's Tale*'s authority emerged. When Chaucer resumes his exploration of monarchical authority at the end of Fragment VII, he combines it with a fuller affirmation of the authority of lay narrative.

CHAPTER 8

Canterbury Tales (II): from preaching to poetry

In the *Pardoner's Prologue and Tale* critique becomes affirmation. Chaucer returns to the anti-clericalism, and especially the anti-fraternalism of the *Friar's* and *Summoner's Tales*, but here he makes them the platform for a more general adumbration of the moral authority of narrative. The Pardoner clearly identifies himself as a mendicant, who "wol preche and begge in sondry lands" (VI, 443).[1] Modeled on the anti-fraternal *Faus Semblant* from the *Romance of the Rose*, he draws many of his characteristics from the anti-fraternal tradition: his itineracy, his threat to the secular clergy (in the person of the local parson (I, 701-06)), his hypocritical avarice, his sharp practices, and most of all his translation of spiritual values into commodities.[2] For all of that, Chaucer seems more interested in moving past his specific institutional position to the larger issue of the general relation between the doctrinal and the lay, an issue which the Pardoner enables him to stage in starkly discursive terms.[3] This shift to the discursive continues in the next fragment, particularly at its end where Chaucer simultaneously examines the specificities of lay political authority. The final tale of Fragment VII, the *Nun's Priest's Tale* has sometimes been taken as the ultimate expression of Chaucer's commitment to the autonomy of poetic discourse. My purpose in this chapter is to show that even that commitment is thoroughly intertwined with a laicist politics.

[1] Marie P. Hamilton, "The Credentials of Chaucer's Pardoner," *Journal of English and Germanic Philology* 40 (1941), 48–72, argued that the Pardoner was an Augustinian canon because Chaucer tells us he is from Rouncivalle, which, she points out, was run by the canons regular of St. Augustine. In the face of the explicit evidence the text offers that the Pardoner was a friar, this conclusion seems unjustified on the basis of a single, oblique reference.

[2] For a good, concise discussion of the relation between the Pardoner and *Faus Semblant*, see David Lawton, *Chaucer's Narrators* (Cambridge: D. S. Brewer, 1985), 25–31.

[3] Cf. Aers, *Chaucer, Langland and the Creative Imagination*, 74–91; and A. L. Kellogg and L. A. Haselmayer, "Chaucer's Satire and the Pardoner," *PMLA* 66 (1951), 251–77.

THE "PARDONER'S PROLOGUE AND TALE": THE AFFIRMATIONS OF ANTI-CLERICALISM

As a narrative figure entirely circumscribed by his tale's doctrinal moral, *Radix malorum est Cupiditas*, the Pardoner demonstrates this moral precisely by violating it.

> I preche of no thyng but for coveityse.
> Therfore my theme is yet, and evere was,
> *Radix malorum est Cupiditas.*
> Thus kan I preche agayn that same vice
> Which that I use, and that is avarice.   (VI, 424–28)

The Pardoner depends on the precept's ideological authority in order to violate it. As a result, he can never escape it, no matter how outrageous his violations. If *cupiditas* can corrupt even those licensed to preach against it, then the extremity of its influence justifies doctrine's identification of it as the *radix malorum*. Had Chaucer left matters here, the Pardoner would serve as no more than another anti-clerical exemplification of the distinction between sacral authority and clerical position. But Chaucer moves beyond this largely negative stance by bestowing upon narrative the same internal integrity his anti-clerical critique grants to the discourse of doctrine. Moreover, the tension between clerical voice and doctrine which circumscribes this prologue circumscribes the tale as well.

The Pardoner ends the prologue and introduces the tale by declaring, "though myself be a ful vicious man, / A moral tale yet I yow telle kan, / Which I am wont to preche for to wynne" (VI, 459–61). If the *Pardoner's Tale* is fully moral despite its teller's complete immorality that can only mean its authority inheres entirely within its discursive integrity as narrative. It acquires the same potential for the expression of authority as the expository discourse of doctrine, and thereby strengthens the authoritative pretensions of vernacular poetry. Distinguishing doctrinal authority from institutional position and defining such authority as almost exclusively textual makes it as available to the poet as it is to the preacher. Giving narrative a similar status gives the poet an edge.

Chaucer explicitly marks this affirmation of narrative as a reappropriation of a lay form appropriated by the Church. For among the Pardoner's abuses he implicates the clerical control of narrative that was the central feature of the sermon exemplum.

Immediately after declaring avarice is the only purpose of his preaching, the Pardoner reports,

> Thanne telle I hem ensamples many oon
> Of olde stories longe tyme agoon.
> For lewed peple loven tales olde;
> Swiche thynges kan they wel reporte and holde. (VI, 435–38)

These lines repeat almost verbatim one of the fundamental claims of clerical commentary on the sermon exemplum, namely, that narrative is a subordinate form characteristic of lay culture and open to clerical exploitation.[4] Placing this claim in the Pardoner's mouth exposes its institutional bias, and implicitly suggests an alternative understanding of narrative. If an exemplum's authority is not something installed in it by the preacher who appropriates it, then its authority must inhere at least in part in the narrative itself. In the reading to follow I will argue Chaucer equates this inherent authority with precisely the capacity of narrative the Pardoner so memorably embodies: its generation of subject positions. In the prologue, this equation is conveyed by the Pardoner's self-dramatizing confessions. In the tale, it is conveyed by the personification of Death – the metaphor on which the narrative turns. Like Benjamin's storyteller, in the *Pardoner's Tale*, Chaucer "has borrowed his authority from death."[5] As we shall see, his understanding of this authority not only differs from a modern understanding like Benjamin's, but may also help explain where the difference comes from. The paradoxical authority Chaucer finds in both prologue and tale will give him the chance to celebrate fully the performative power which narrative's generation of subject positions implies.

My focus on the affirmations of the *Pardoner's Prologue and Tale* runs counter to the dominant strain in its critical history, which dates back to Kittredge. This strain reads the Pardoner as a figure of despair. The general orientation of my reading nevertheless owes a great deal to this tradition's latest expressions, the explorations of the Pardoner's subjectivity by Carolyn Dinshaw, H. Marshall Leicester, and Lee Patterson.[6] Despite their considerable differences from each other, all

---

4 See above, 66–67.
5 Walter Benjamin, "The Storyteller," in *Illuminations*, ed. Hannah Arendt, tr. Harry Zohn (New York: Schocken, 1969), 94.
6 Dinshaw, *Chaucer's Sexual Poetics*, 156–84; H. Marshall Leicester, *The Disenchanted Self: Representing the Subject in the "Canterbury Tales"* (Berkeley, Los Angeles and Oxford: University of California Press, 1990), 35–64, 161–94; Patterson, *Chaucer and the Subject of History*, 367–421.

of these readings significantly redefine the fascination the Pardoner's despair has exerted on modern Chaucerians. By concentrating on his subjectivity, they show the Pardoner defines his character precisely by revealing its constructedness. His frank and thoroughgoing manipulation of the discursive principles that define his existence produce a perverse recognition: how thoroughly all sense of selfhood is socially and linguistically constructed.

Consistent with the Kittredgean tradition they illuminate, these readings all remain on what we might call the psychological side of subjectivity. To one extent or another, they identify with the Pardoner, and even as they define the sources of his subjectivity, they locate their interest in him in his perverse resistance. For Dinshaw, this is the resistance of the fetishist to the renunciation of bodily plenitude required by both Christian doctrine and male sexual identity. For Leicester, it is the disenchanted subject's resistance to God. For Patterson, it is the resistance of an authentic despair against the "inauthentic language of confession."[7] I want to focus instead on the other side of subjectivity: what the prologue and tale's production of the Pardoner as subject tells us about the nature of the cultural authority that produces him.[8] They suggest that such authority is generative, extensive and extremely efficacious, that its power is proximate to the dynamics of narration, and that this proximity affirms the moral competence and integrity of vernacular poetry.

I do not mean to suggest this affirmative aspect of the prologue and tale represents its ultimate meaning, to which the Pardoner's despair can be reduced. But I do maintain this aspect is as irreducible as the other. No account of his despair can ever fully account for the energy of his preaching: "Myne handes and my tonge goon so yerne / That it is joye to se my bisynesse" (VI, 398–99). This discursive energy clearly engages Chaucer and is clearly meant to engage us. David Lawton may be right to argue this energy reflects "the lurid unreality of a life of sin that rushes headlong to death."[9] But in the prologue Chaucer focuses on the social power of this ostensible unreality, rather than its ultimate spiritual result, which he takes for granted. The Pardoner depicts the social space through which he moves as continually transfigured by structures of ideology and language.

---

[7] Patterson, *Chaucer and the Subject of History*, 373.
[8] Cf. Knapp, *Chaucer and the Social Contest*, 81. For another reading of the tale's ecclesiology with a slightly different emphasis, see Aers, *Chaucer, Langland and the Creative Imagination*, 89–106.   [9] Lawton, *Chaucer's Narrators*, 24.

When he arrives,

> First I pronounce whennes that I come,
> And thanne my bulles shewe I, alle and some.
> Oure lige lordes seel on my patente.
> That shewe I first, my body to warente,
> That no man be so boold, ne preest ne clerk,
> Me to destourbe of Cristes hooly werk.
> And after that thanne telle I forth my tales;
> Bulles of popes and of cardynales,
> Of patriarkes and bishopes I shewe,
> And in Latyn I speke a wordes fewe
> To saffron with my predicacioun
> And for to stire hem to devocioun.   (VI, 335–46)

The bulls, the texts the Pardoner carries, define his social position down to his very body. Their warranting not only protects his body, but gives it material efficacy it would not otherwise have, establishing his authority as a preacher. This passage is at pains to show the social dynamism of such authority, its constant interchange between the textual and the material. The Pardoner brandishes his documents as a flurry of unrelated pieces of parchment. Like the Latin with which he "saffrons" his preaching, these disconnected bits of discourse exercise material power even in their disconnectedness, a power that can only come from an internal self-generating logic.

His deployment of relics works in similar fashion. A relic is semiotic by its very nature, being a part which signifies an absent whole.[10] In one sense, an authentic relic is a pure signified, a sign which immediately and transparently signifies itself. However, even an authentic relic must by definition refer to an absent unity (the spirituality of the saint to which it belonged). Even in its purity as signified, it is still signifier. In this sense, the false relic, which is entirely discursive, pure signifier without signified, simply represents the limit case of a semiotic instability which characterizes all relics. To what extent is the power of even the authentic relic discursive rather than substantial? To what extent does even the authentic relic, like the Pardoner's body, derive its value from its location in the textual network of an institutional discourse? Does the relic represent the power of such a discourse to transform the material objects, rather than the capacity of certain privileged material objects to represent

---

[10] My analysis of the Pardoner's relics is heavily indebted to Dinshaw (*Chaucer's Sexual Poetics*, 160–78), who compares them to the partial object of the fetishist.

themselves? These were matters of explicit concern to later Church thinkers, and the Pardoner's relics bring them into sharp focus.[11] They come with complicated instructions and requirements. The sheep bone must be dipped in well water that is then variously applied to tongues, drunk, or made into soup, depending on the ill it is to heal. These instructions give the relics an entirely technical status, establish their sacral power by taking it for granted. Their wholly discursive origins are disguised by the production of still more discourse (VI, 350-71).

However, both the bulls and the relics are only props. The prologue's ultimate confirmation of the discursive energy of doctrinal authority is the Pardoner himself. His contradictory confessional stance as the liar revealing the truth about his lies cannot finally be separated from his joy at his discursive "bisyness." The frankness of his confession is in part an entirely amoral appreciation of doctrine's sheer ideological efficacy, an appreciation, that is, of its production of his voice. The authority embodied in *Radix malorum est Cupiditas* both requires and disclaims the production of such a voice. The principle obviously disclaims the *cupiditas* it names as the *radix malorum*. Nevertheless, in the very act of so naming it, the principle expects violation: its whole point is to give such violation the particular name of *cupiditas*. The Pardoner unites these two tendencies as a narrative voice that speaks the principle in order to violate it, and whose violations continually affirm it. In so doing, however, he only takes to its limit a tension already inherent. *Radix malorum est Cupiditas* demands performance and expects performance to fall short. As a metonym for all Christian doctrine, it is in continual retreat from the world it governs, and must depend on mediations it can never entirely acknowledge. The figure of the Pardoner suggests such mediations approach the condition of narrative. His tale confirms this suggestion more explicitly.

The tale is divided into two parts. The second, the tale proper, as it is usually called, is an exemplum derived from a very common folktale (Aarne-Thompson 763[12]). It is preceded by a section of moralizing close enough to a sermon in form that some critics have argued it should be viewed in those terms.[13] There is no need,

[11] See Stock, *Interpreting Literacy*, 244–59.

[12] Antti Aarne, *The Types of the Folk-Tale: A Classification and Bibliography*, tr. and enlarged by Stith Thompson (Helsinki: FF Communications, 1928), 121.

[13] The best recent case has been put by Robert P. Merrix, "Sermon Structure in the *Pardoner's Tale*," *Chaucer Review* 17 (1982), 35–49. See also the cogent objections of Siegfried Wenzel,

however, to make the correspondence that exact. The similarity
enables Chaucer to continue his examination of the Pardoner's
sermonizing; the sermonizing's contiguity to the narrative reinforces
the comparability of the two Chaucer has already established in the
prologue. We find the same fascination here with the performative
energy of clerical discourse, this time focused even more on its
internal dynamics. The sermonizing emerges incidentally, as the
Pardoner is in the process of establishing the tale's setting, and it
addresses not one sin but a cluster of them – blasphemy, gluttony,
drunkenness, and gambling – as if the complex reality of sin always
remains to some extent beyond the penitential taxonomy which
preachers apply to it. Like the formula *Radix malorum est Cupiditas*,
here the categories of sin require and produce narrative confirmation,
each category generating a series of exempla before giving way to the
next. Penitential categories are presented performatively, as a
language continually in motion, in need of continual reimposition on
a refractory reality.

The issue of linguistic performance also dictates the internal
relations between the categories. Although the Pardoner declares
they are all "annexed to glotonye" (VI, 482), his discussion both
begins and ends with blasphemy, in the specific form of swearing
oaths. The curious collocation of oaths and gluttony has a good deal
of traditional warrant, as R. F. Yeager has discovered, from the
strand of penitential writing that begins with the *Somme-le-Roi* of
Frère Lorens. Lorens classifies both blasphemy and gluttony under
"Sins of the Mouth."[14] The justification for the collocation may
indeed derive, as Yeager argues, from a passage in Matthew (15:11)
where Christ discusses both sins, although Christ's purpose in that
passage seems to be to differentiate rather than unite them.[15] But the
context in which the *Pardoner's Tale* places the collocation provides a
rationale which is considerably more specific. An oath is performative
language at its most transgressive. Annexing blasphemous oaths to
gluttony emphasizes the materiality of speech, its active participation
in the same fallen world as food and drink. Framing the bodily "sins
of the mouth," gluttony and inebriation, with the linguistic one
suggests that all sin is linguistic to the extent that it involves the

"Chaucer and the Language of Contemporary Preaching," *Studies in Philology* 73 (1976),
138–40.
[14] R. F. Yeager, "Aspects of Gluttony in Chaucer and Gower," *Philological Quarterly* 81 (1984),
48–53. [15] Yeager, "Aspects of Gluttony," 53–54.

imposition on the world of a fallen, humanly constructed system of value.

The tale proper will demonstrate the dependence of such performative impositions on the very divinity they violate. This dependence clusters around death, the narrative's main focus. As the limit to human systems of value, death is the boundary which separates them from divine authority. In the narrative's exploration of death's liminality, it will find the source of its own discursive authority, an authority which consists precisely of the inescapability of the divine. The three rioters are "perverse *imitatores Dei*," in Lee Patterson's memorable phrase: their quest to slay death is no more than a perverted desire for the redemptive power of Christ, which their habitual oathtaking abjures. Oaths initiate the quest, and linguistically return them to this redemptive power.

> Togidres han thise thre hir trouthes plight
> To lyve and dyen ech of hem for oother,
> As though he were his owene ybore brother.
> And up they stirte, al dronken in this rage,
> And forth they goon towardes that village
> Of which the taverner spoke biforn.
> And many a grisly ooth thanne han they sworn,
> And Cristes blessed body they torente –
> Deeth shal be deed, if that they may him hente! (VI, 702–09)

This characterization of the oath actually reiterates the characterization already given at the beginning of the tale, where the rending is explicitly identified with the Crucifixion.

> Hir othes been so grete and so dampnable
> That it is grisly for to heere hem swere.
> Oure blissed Lordes body they totere –
> Hem thoughte that Jewes rente hym noght ynough –
>   (VI, 472–75)

The assertion that these oaths reenact the dismemberment of the Crucifixion is a graphic insistence both that the human world is immediately dependent on the divine, and that the nature of that dependency is linguistic. The goal of the quest is simply the goal of Christ's Redemption, "Death shal be deed," restated as an oath. The scope of these sinners' power is so limited that at their most blasphemous, they can do no more than attempt to usurp the work Christ is already doing. Initiating the quest means establishing a social contract: the three "plight" their "trouthes" to live and die for the others as if they were brothers. Insofar as this brotherhood is secured by their oaths, it is secured by the dismemberment of Christ. The equation makes the mutilated body of Christ the ground of sinful human associations. But this only recapitulates humanity's most sacred form of association: Christian communion: "'Take, eat; this is my body.' And he took a cup, and when he had given thanks, he gave it to them, saying, 'Drink of it all of you; for this is my blood of the covenant, which is poured out for many for the forgiveness of sins'" (Matthew, 26: 26–28).

As Jonathan Dollimore has recently demonstrated, perversion always assumes proximity.[16] The similarities between the three rioters and the Christian *caritas* they parody are so close we might well ask where the difference lies. It clearly involves the distinction between the Letter and the Spirit. The rioters' inability to interpret personifications of Death symbolizes their spiritual blindness. Ironic characterization through carnal exegesis was a staple of later medieval literature, as three decades of Patristic criticism have taught us. Nevertheless, it is important that we recognize in this case that the spiritual/literal distinction cannot be mapped directly onto a distinction between doctrinal discourse and narrative. For the personification of Death is a feature of the doctrinal which it never entirely moves beyond. As R. A. Shoaf has pointed out, it is characteristically expressed in the apostrophe from Hosea, "O death I will be thy death," whose speaking voice is taken to be Christ.[17] Like most apostrophes, this one works by extending subjectivity to inanimate entities like Death.[18] It distinguishes itself from human apostrophes in that it is able to sustain the extension. Christ will actually confer personhood upon Death to the extent that at the Last Judgment he will kill it. But this is a difference in the effect of the linguistic performance, not a difference in its structure. Even when Christ makes Death's subjectivity actual, his performance has the same shape as a human apostrophe: it still imposes subjectivity on an inanimate entity. By this production of a subject position it retains its affinities to narrative.

The difference between the rioters and Christ, then, is not that

---

[16] Jonathan Dollimore, *Sexual Dissidence: Augustine to Wilde, Freud to Foucalt* (Oxford: Clarendon, 1991), esp. 103–30.

[17] R. A. Shoaf, *Dante, Chaucer and the Currency of the Word* (Norman: Pilgrim Books, 1983), 220 and 274, n. 18. Cf. Patterson, *Chaucer and the Subject of History*, 402.

[18] Jonathan Culler, *The Pursuit of Signs: Semiotics, Literature, Deconstruction* (Ithaca: Cornell University Press, 1981) 135–54.

their carnality mires them in narrative while he speaks a spiritual language that is entirely non-narrative. It is that he tells a better story than they do. The nature of this difference is crucial, for it denies clerical tradition the discursive advantage it was wont to claim in its dealings with the laity, especially in regard to the exemplum. If doctrinal discourse shares the characteristics of a discourse like narrative that is generally associated with the lay, then the clergy can no longer claim ideological supremacy solely on the basis of its discursive forms. Paradoxical as it may seem, the structural similarity between clerical discourse and narrative Chaucer establishes here is actually a condition for the distinction between doctrine and narrative on which he insists in the *Parson's Tale*.[19] Placing doctrinal authority beyond all discursive genres requires stripping clerical tradition of its discursive privilege. Accordingly, the moral authority this tale achieves it achieves narratively.

It begins by making as plausible as it will later make damnable the rioters' misapprehension of the personification of Death. Ian Bishop has suggested that "Death is the only character in the tale who is completely individualized," and indeed, the tale's irony depends precisely on the extent to which the reader finds compelling the possibility that Death is not only a personification but a person.[20] The rioters derive the personification from the young boy who informs them of the demise of their "old felawe."

> Ther cam a privee theef men clepeth Deeth,
> That in this contree al the peple sleeth,
> And with his spere he smoot his herte atwo,
> And wente his wey withouten wordes mo.   (VI, 675–78)

The personification is no mere whim, but an expression of the figural capacities inherent in language, a capacity evident even in the banality of everyday usage. The Death we are concerned with here is not death considered in itself, but death as human beings have named it, as "men clepeth" it. The personification of Death as a privy thief, smiting wordlessly with his spear, is a plausible extension of this figural capacity of human language to name what it cannot fully comprehend.

There is no doubt that the rioters' misapprehension is meant to signify the mental incoherence to which their perpetual drunkenness has reduced them. It may even be that the taverner's intervention,

[19] See above, 14–15.
[20] Ian Bishop, "The Narrative Art of the *Pardoner's Tale*," *Medium Aevum* 36 (1967), 18.

which, in the lines immediately following, plays out the boy's personification further, is to be taken as an act of toying with this drunken incoherence. "The child seith sooth," he assures them, adding that death must have his "habitacioun" in the "greet village" a mile hence, for he has slain so many there this year (VI, 685–91). Nevertheless, even as a sign of drunkenness, the misapprehension rests on the personification's original plausibility. It dramatizes language's figural power to transgress its own limits and makes that power specifically narrative, by linking it to narrative's endless capacity to produce new points of view. The tale will reveal the narrative the rioters think to tell (their quest which kills Death) to be part of a stronger narrative announced by the Old Man. Their ironic position in this narrative keeps blasphemy and narrating proximate, and the Old Man will distinguish the two precisely on the basis of this proximity.

When he directs the rioters to the pot of gold, he revalues their personification, opening up the figurality they assume they have closed down. This opening up only works, however, because he can close it down again, because the performative power of his refiguration is greater than that of theirs. The figural equation that he establishes between the term *Death* and the pot of gold is metaphoric and metonymic at the same time. It is metaphoric because it involves a relation of similarity. Within Christian ideology – and especially in the fragment *Radix malorum est Cupiditas* which governs this tale – a pot of gold is synonymous with spiritual death. The equation is metonymic because its actual enactment in the narrative involves relations of contiguity. The pot of gold does not directly enforce the death of the three rioters. It is merely the catalyst for the deaths they themselves cause. Indeed, it is precisely because the pot of gold is not the direct cause of death that the old man's equation of it with death is so convincing. Like the moral it is based on, the metaphoric prolepsis can be confirmed by the metonymic enactment of death because the prolepsis does not forcibly impose itself on the course of the narrative. It merely anticipates the event which arises inevitably out of the inherent logic of the narrative sequence.

This logic gives the prolepsis a power entirely analogous to personification. It demonstrates the Old Man's power over the subjectivity of the rioters. When they demand he tell them where Death is, their carnality enables him to make the equation between Death and the pot of gold. It is as if he is saying to them, "Because you read human existence so carnally, a pot of gold will mean your death. You will destroy each other to possess it." Their attempt to make Death a character in their narrative enables the Old Man to make them characters in his. This reversal produces moral authority in a thoroughly narrative manner, demonstrating the possibility of articulating such authority from within human history using history's own materials.

The point can be confirmed by comparing Chaucer's treatment of the tale with its analogues. He makes two changes. In the analogues, the speaker who identifies the pot of gold as death is typically Christ himself.[21] Chaucer not only changes Christ into the old man, but also incorporates the prolepsis into the causal chain leading up to the dénouement. In the analogues Christ merely describes the gold as death to his disciples, who then witness the validity of the equation when another group of characters happen upon it independently. In Chaucer's version, the Old Man's characterization of the pot of gold is also what leads the rioters to it. These changes should be seen as refinements of a tradition that is already quite ideologically specific. The metaphoric comparability between death and the pot of gold only makes sense within the framework of the Christian belief that the wealth of this world can bring spiritual death. The metonymic connection, though ultimately no less figural or ideologically motivated, is a good deal less specific. It alone constitutes the folktale type. The prolepsis is a specifically Christian addition.

Like the analogues, Chaucer's version imposes a Christian frame on the folktale archetype, but unlike them, he makes the Christian moral emerge from within. The old man, no longer the voice of divine authority, speaks from the accumulated experiential authority of old age. In so doing, he demonstrates that the spiritual death of worldly things is evident from within the world; it is not entirely dependent on Divine Revelation. The causal role Chaucer assigns the old man recovers the autonomy of the folktale motif, while investing it with Christian authority. The motif is a paradox: the quest whose achievement destroys the communal bonds which established it. The paradox suggests that human community is founded as much on struggle as it is on concord, that the pot of gold, in its concrete embodiment of the human power to produce social forms, embodies not commonalty *per se*, but a common site of conflict. Chaucer's

21 Bryan and Dempster, *Sources and Analogues*, 415–38.

version can acknowledge the constitutive role conflict plays in producing social forms and yet find in that very acknowledgment a mode of authority that transcends it.

Death operates throughout the *Pardoner's Tale* as a product of figuration, as the result of the imposition on the world of discursive and ideological values. The death that comes to the three rioters is a death which they produce, albeit not under conditions entirely of their own choosing. From the moment of the oath onwards the death that comes to them depends on their efforts, and in particular on their manipulations of the discursive framework they all share. If this permeability between death and human forms of collectivity provides the tale with the vantage point from which it can gesture beyond itself, it also provides a model of narrative which is authoritative precisely because it is collective. As the textual form appropriate to the vernacular and the secular, narrative provides the collective means whereby its audience can affirm access to cultural authority on its own terms.

Chaucer's dependence on the figure of Death for access to such authority clearly bespeaks a profound conviction in the reality of Christian redemption. But it also bespeaks an equally strong belief in the performative power of narrative figuration. If modern scholarship has been slow to detect this conviction in the *Pardoner's Tale*, it is because modern literary thought takes death *literally*, often as the literal fact *par excellence*. Peter Brooks's psychoanalytic theory of narrative provides a representative instance. Following Benjamin, he argues that "the narrative must tend toward its end, must seek illumination in its own death."[22] Death becomes a terminal boundary which is absolute. By contrast, the death which authorizes the narrative of the *Pardoner's Tale* is not a terminal boundary, but a figural possibility which underwrites the narrative from start to finish, framing its logic and providing an essential element of its motivation. Moreover, what it figures is not the actual limit of narrative, but narrative's capacity to figure such limits. The difference is instructive. Formulations like Brooks's suppress the figural and social aspects which the term *death*, like any other piece of language, must contain. They produce models of narrative in which the social is superseded by the biological. Brooks compares narrative to the Freudian death-wish, the biological organism's individual

---

[22] Brooks, *Reading for the Plot*, 103.

struggle to "die the right death."[23] But human death is never purely biological. It is also irreducibly social, and not just when it comes in the form of execution or battle fatality.

The *Pardoner's Prologue* and *Tale* insists on this collective aspect, which it grounds in Christian redemption, but which it articulates against clerical tradition in the name of the vernacular. Is it not possible that the modern biologism exemplified by Brooks is a later stage in the same process? His literal reading of Death gives literature the authority of natural science, modernity's ultimate self-authorizing discourse. All of the pathos with which modernity connects literature with death may be the price it willingly pays for such exalted authority. This would mean that Death's figural value for modernity lies precisely in its literality, and would explain why the affirmation that figuration involves seems so hidden.

Lacking a strong model of vernacular literary authority, Chaucer could not afford the same luxury. His dependence on Christian authority is out in the open, and his appropriation of it no less so. The violent argument between the Pardoner and the Host at the tale's conclusion returns to the anti-clericalism of the tale's prologue and conflates it with the ambiguities surrounding his sexuality first raised in the *General Prologue*. This conflict exposes instabilities which the Knight's intercession does not succeed in defusing.[24] Nevertheless, I cannot agree that the result of this destabilization is a turning away "from a poetics that engages with the fallible, mediate letter of human language."[25] On the contrary, the tale's affirmation of the authority of narrative anticipates the three tales at the end of the next fragment, *Melibee*, the *Monk's Tale*, and the *Nun's Priest's Tale*, which constitute Chaucer's most sustained reflection on lay authority. For all of its excess, the Pardoner's approach to Harry Bailly recapitulates the breakdown in clerical authority similar to that which occurs in the *Summoner's Tale*, and the Knight plays the same restorative role as the Lord's court. The tale's affirmation of narrative remains intact, and provides lay authority with a textual dimension that underwrites the political dimension Chaucer locates in the figure of the monarch.

[23] Brooks, *Reading for the Plot*, 107.
[24] The fullest reading of these instabilities is Dinshaw's (*Chaucer's Sexual Poetics*), 168–84.
[25] Dinshaw, *Chaucer's Sexual Poetics*, 181–83.

CHAUCER'S *FÜRSTENSPIEGEL*: THE "TALE OF MELIBEE" AND
THE "MONK'S TALE"

Fragment VII constitutes a remarkable reproduction in miniature of
the Canterbury collection's generic economy. It contains a fabliau, a
tale of pathos, an abortive and parodic romance, a prose treatise, a
miniature exemplum collection, and an exemplum in the form of a
beast fable. It is even more striking that the fragment's movement
through these genres proceeds from the *game* of the fabliau to the
exemplum's earnest engagement with *moralitee*. This movement runs
counter to the one seen within earlier fragments, which begin with a
sententious genre, then devolve into more ludic ones.[26] At the same
time this movement within Fragment VII from *game* to *ernest* is
analogous to that of the collection as a whole, whose tale-telling
impulse gives way to the spirituality of pilgrimage and the closure of
the *Parson's Tale.*

The morality toward which Fragment VII moves is an exemplary
one which adumbrates a model of lay authority in both social and
textual terms. Its social focus is the figure of the monarch, around
which *Melibee,* the *Monk's Tale,* and the *Nun's Priest's Tale* all center
in various ways. But that focus depends on the moral authority of the
narrative discourse that produces it, and each of these tales will make
their affirmation of kingship inseparable from their affirmation of
narrative. Taken together, the *Tale of Melibee* and the *Monk's Tale*
constitute Chaucer's direct engagement with the *Fürstenspiegel.* Each
represent one of the two complementary strands of the later tradition.
The *Tale of Melibee,* whose connection to the *Fürstenspiegel* has only
recently been recognized, follows the neo-Aristotelian strand in its
adumbration of a specifically lay system of textual authority for
political action.[27] The *Monk's Tale* represents the drive toward
narrative embodied in Boccaccio's *De casibus.* But, as we shall see, the
model of authority *Melibee* offers is no less exemplary, and it
distinguishes itself from its neo-Aristotelian relatives by its insistence
on the narrative structure of its authority. Carrying through both
tales, this emphasis will lead to the more indirect but more global
affirmations of the *Nun's Priest's Tale.*

It may seem odd to view narrative as an important category in the

---

[26] See above, 105–06.
[27] Lee Patterson, "'What Man Artow?': Authorial Self-Definition in the *Tale of Sir Thopas,*
and the *Tale of Melibee,*" *Studies in the Age of Chaucer* 11 (1989), 139.

Tale of Melibee, when the prevailing view is that as a narrative, the tale is entirely negligible. It is true that the events the narrative documents can be summarized in a few sentences. Sophie, the daughter of a rich man, Melibee, is gravely wounded by his enemies. After calling an assembly of advisors who recommend he take revenge, he is convinced by his wife Prudence to disregard this suggestion and let her speak to his enemies. She convinces them to put themselves at his mercy, then convinces him to forgive them. These events are entirely dwarfed by the exhaustive compilation of authoritative citations which mandate them. It is also true that the *Tale of Melibee* is a close translation of the early fourteenth-century *Le Livre de Melibeé et de Dame Prudence* by Renaud de Louens, itself an abbreviated version of *Liber consolationis et consilii* of Albertanus of Brescia.[28] These two circumstances make the authority of these citations seem doubly given, first as commonplaces, second as the preponderant part of a translated text. The Tale fits easily into the modern stereotype of medieval didacticism, as the simple reiteration of accepted truths. Most commentators have trouble believing Chaucer took the tale very seriously, although the older notion that he intended it parodically has increasingly been rejected.[29] As I have been arguing throughout this study, the trouble with such views is that they take medieval authority much too simplistically. Its most salient feature was not its inevitable givenness, but precisely its need for continual reenactment. Translation was one form of such reenactment, which most medieval writers viewed not solely as submission to previous authority, but precisely as a means of appropriating it.[30] The production and acceptance of *counseil* was another. The *Tale of Melibee* defines and explores both of these forms of reiteration in narrative terms, translation in its characterization of Chaucer's own voice, *counseil* both in its production by Prudence and its acceptance by Melibee, and in the exemplary transformation that acceptance will effect in his social position. Indeed the very movement from Chaucer's voice in the frame tale to Prudence as the voice of textual authority in the tale, to the authoritative trans-

[28] J. Burke Severs, "The *Tale of Melibeus*," in *Sources and Analogues*, 560–614.
[29] Nevertheless, this view still has a remarkable vitality. See, for example, Daniel Kempton, "Chaucer's Tale of Melibee: 'A Litel Thyng in Prose'," *Genre* 21 (1988), 263–78.
[30] Rita Copeland, "Rhetoric and Vernacular Translation in the Middle Ages," *Studies in the Age of Chaucer* 9 (1987), 62–66; and *Rhetoric, Hermeneutics and Translation in the Middle Ages* (Cambridge: Cambridge University Press, 1991).

formation of Melibee's own subjectivity is a movement toward ever greater specificity that could itself be described as narrative. Chaucer's presentation of his own voice as constituted by the translation of authority is a gesture that should be taken seriously, but not as a cultural given that defeats analysis. Its cultural significance is precisely what must be interrogated and analyzed. We have already seen how, in his description of Griselda's transformation, Chaucer uses the notion of *translatio* to indicate the discursive aspects of social power. Here, in the headlink to the *Melibee*, his characterization of translation as a discursive practice emphasizes its sociocultural concreteness.

He concludes the headlink by stressing the fidelity of his *sentence*:

> ... though I nat the same wordes seye
> As ye han herd, yet to yow alle I preye
> Blameth me nat; for as in my sentence,
> Shul ye nowher fynden difference
> Fro the sentence of this tretys lyte
> After the which this murye tale I write.
> And therfore herkneth what that I shal seye,
> And lat me tellen al my tale, I preye.   (VII, 959–66)

Paradoxically, the very direction of his audience's attention past his translation to the *sentence* of the work being translated, returns them to his actual act of writing.[31] The importance of his *sentence* demands their attention to his utterance, "this murye tale I write," in all its linguistic particularity. Even if the "I" in "I shal seye" is constituted entirely by the repetition of a past authority, the very act of repetition

---

[31] I am here taking the phrase "this tretys lyte" to imply a comparison between Chaucer's version and the French version he translated, in contrast to the scholarly tradition that began with Albert H. Hartung's unpublished dissertation on the tale ("A Study of the Textual Affiliations of Chaucer's Melibeus Considered in Relation to the French Source" (Lehigh University, 1957)), which understands the comparison implied to be between this version and an earlier one by Chaucer, perhaps written for Richard II. (For a brief discussion and further bibliography, see Patterson, "'What Man Artow?'," 117–25.) Despite the widespread acceptance of this reading, I find it unconvincing. In the first place, medieval poems frequently circulated in differing versions. Even if there were an earlier version of this tale, why would Chaucer have felt it necessary to apologize for the variation? In the second, this reading posits differences between the putative variants which are impossible to square with the relation between this text and the French antecedent. As it exists in the *Canterbury Tales*, Melibee is a very faithful translation – extraordinarily so by medieval standards. If we accept the notion of an earlier version by Chaucer sufficiently different from this one as to require explanation, we are in effect claiming that first he did a loose translation, then did a much closer one, and then explained this reversion to close translation by affirming the right of the translator to vary from his original.

produces a difference of crucial importance. This difference can acknowledge itself only in denial, only in its striving to submerge itself in the *sentence* of the text it repeats, but even this denial makes a difference. Chaucer implicity affirms the difference in the profusion of the first-person singular in the last three lines: "this murye tale I write," "what that I shal seye," "And lat me tellen al my tale, I preye." The poet as *auctor* is a translator, whose textual authority inheres in his own active self-effacement before the *sentence* he transmits. It is precisely this self-effacement which constitutes the poet's authority, and which enables him to give past authority his own name. Deferral to the past is simultaneously a means of appropriating it.

Moreover, Chaucer has from the beginning of the discussion characterized this deferral in a manner that effects an even more striking appropriation. He compares his translation from one vernacular to another to the activities of the most authoritative writers who have ever lived, the Evangelists Matthew, Mark, Luke and John:

> ... ye woot that every Evaungelist
> That telleth us the peyne of Jhesu Crist
> Ne seith nat alle thyng as his felawe dooth;
> But natheless hir sentence is al sooth,
> And alle acorden as in hire sentence,
> Al be ther in hir tellyng difference. (VII, 943–48)

Deferral to an antecedent characterizes these writers no less than it does Chaucer. Their authority inheres ultimately in their *sentence*; the "difference" in their "tellyng" makes their texts as variable and dependent as his. For this "tellyng" is also indispensable to their authority: it is this "tellyng," for all its variablity, which brings the Divine Word to humanity. In similar fashion, the value of Chaucer's text lies precisely in its difference, in its *translatio* of its own authoritative *sentence* into a new language for a new audience. Like John of Salisbury's *jocundatis litterarum*, it literally brings the past into the present, smoothing over the gap between the two.[32]

Chaucer's implicit insistence on the importance of his "tellyng" is matched by an equally implicit insistence on the narrative status of that telling. He describes *Melibee* as a "tale" three times in the prologue. Although, as I have already noted, the narrative is

---

[32] See above, 90–91.

relatively poor in what narratologists call event, event is only one aspect of plot. The other, equally essential aspect is agency.[33] In this aspect *Melibee* is much richer, to modern tastes excessively so. It tells the story of taking counsel – of preparing to cause an event, of becoming an agent. If it seems to break the process into such incremental stages, like some interminable series of freeze-frames, so that it ceases to be intelligible as a coherent process, we would do well to remember that this too is part of the ideal of authority it promulgates. By presenting every step in the exercise of such power as enabled by the citation of authority, it demonstrates with even greater specificity than the neo-Aristotelian *Fürstenspiegel* that lay authority has a systematic textuality proper to it.

Counseil becomes another form of *translatio*. Bringing past texts to bear on the course of present action, it translates them from their authoritative Latin into the vernacular, and from the written to the oral. Whatever the excesses in the tale's exhaustive compilation of past texts, it is nevertheless entirely oriented around the problem of taking action. Although the events the narrative records seem dwarfed by the authorities, it is the events which provide the essential precondition to their compilation. The compilation is never an end in itself. Each citation is directed by the action under consideration, which determines both its selection and its application. The overall frame which the string of events provides, skeletal though it is, is the basis for the richer aspect of the plot, the secondary movements in the giving and receiving of counsel. Most of the citations occur during the course of Prudence's dialogue with Melibee. The narrative movement of this dialogue, in which Melibee is brought grudgingly to Prudence's point of view, resisting her citations with his own, demonstrates both the dependence of lay political power on textual authority and its resistance to it. The intricacy with which the tale traces out this dynamic of imposition and resistance is precisely what accounts for the narrative's dilatory expanse.

The entrance of textual authority into history is always mediated through specific political interests: "Thanne shaltow considere of what roote is engendred the matiere of thy conseil and what fruyt it may conceyve and engendre," Prudence warns Melibee (VII, 1208). Much of the narrative is given over to demonstrating the many ways in which counsel which seems authoritative in itself can be manipu-

---

[33] For a good, concise discussion, see Cohan and Shires, *Telling Stories*, 52–82.

lated by counselors to serve their own ends, or misinterpreted by the one counseled. It can be divided into three sections. In the first, VII, 967–1050, in response to the attack on his daughter, Melibee calls an assembly of his counselors, who advise him to make war and exact vengeance. In the second, VII, 1051–1725, Prudence meticulously reexamines the context and content of the assembly's advice, eventually convincing Melibee it were better to forgive his enemies than to wreak vengeance upon them. In the third, VII, 1726–1888, she seeks out his enemies and brings them to be reconciled. The third serves to demonstrate the efficacy of the laborious interpretive operations Prudence lays out in the second.

First, Prudence explains from whom one should take counsel: from God, from oneself, and from a small group of one's wisest, eldest, and most tested friends (VII, 1115–71). One should not take counsel from fools, flatterers, enemies reconciled, servants, drunks, "wikked folk," or "yong folk" (VII, 1172–990). Then she explains how counsel should be examined. One should clarify one's goals and reveal them honestly to one's counselors, ascertain their counsel, and then consider what effects their suggestions will have (VII, 1200–22). After this, she reexamines the assembly's advice, pointing out to Melibee that he has continually neglected to discriminate among the motives of his counselors, and that he has let his own anger cloud his judgment of the good advice he did receive. Rather than calling a few counselors, he called a "greet multitude." He indicated beforehand which way he was himself inclined, encouraging the majority to tell him what he had already made clear he wanted to hear. He failed to make "division" between his counselors, casting the words of his wisest and oldest "in an hochepot" with all the rest. This meant foolish advice was inevitable, for there are always more fools than wise men – in large assemblies, "fooles han the maistrye" (VII, 1236–60). Because he was himself so eager for vengeance, he misinterpreted the surgeons' advice to cure by contraries, assuming the contrary of war is more war, when it is in fact peace; he brushed aside the advice of old and wise counselors not to proceed hastily; and he decided on war without considering any of the consequences.

As Stephen Knight has accurately observed, the *Tale of Melibee* is a "serious and thoughtful address to the powerful on how to save their power."[34] This address defines power in profoundly con-

---

[34] *Geoffrey Chaucer*, 139.

servative terms, precisely as something to be saved. The conception of power assumed throughout this long middle section of the tale defines it as God-given, and always already in place, best preserved when least disturbed. Such is the conviction that motivates all of Prudence's advice, which is aimed at minimizing disturbance, at preserving the status quo exactly as it is. If Melibee restrains himself from violence and avoids all challenge to the divinely ordained status quo, it will sustain him.

Thanne dame Prudence discovered al hir wyl to him and seyde, / "I conseille yow," quod she "aboven alle thynges, that ye make pees betwene God and yow, / and beth reconsiled unto hym and to his grace. / For, as I have seyd yow heer biforn, God hath suffred yow to have this tribulacioun and disese for youre synnes. / And if ye do as I sey yow, God wol sende youre adversaries unto yow / and maken hem fallen at youre feet, redy to do youre wyl and youre comandementz. (VII, 1713–18)

God exerts a force within the social structure, such that if Melibee reconciles himself to it, if he denies his own interests in favour of it, it preserves his interest intact. In this paradoxical conception of power, stablity lies in an equilibrium with God, an equilibrium which sin has put just beyond reach, but to which it is possible to return not only in the next life, but in this one too. The tale characterizes this God-given stability as both textual and past. Prudence's counsels to patience and passivity are buttressed by the texts of classical and Christian authorities, venerable both for their wisdom and for their antiquity. Yet this past can be made continuous with the present, to the present's benefit. If Melibee strives to submerge the present in the past, and submerge his will in God's, his power returns all the more firmly guaranteed. Submerging the present in the textual past brings it more firmly under control.

The paradox can be made politically and historically specific. Submitting power to a system of texts also describes the rule of law as it was coming to be defined in later medieval England, with the substantial growth in statute law and the consolidation of seigneurial jurisdictions under the Crown.[35] Despite Prudence's continual warnings about sin, her dialogue with Melibee is more directly about two competing forms of justice. The first is vengeance, which Melibee and his advisors advocate. The second is an adjudicatory ideal, which

---

[35] Harding, *Law Courts*, 86–123.

Prudence advocates. Vengeance is a chivalric ideal and recalls the world of romance which Chaucer has just burlesqued in the *Tale of Sir Thopas*. The adjudicatory ideal is much closer to neo-Aristotelian notions of the systematic character of natural law, and corresponds to the changes in English justice I have just mentioned. When Prudence urges Melibee to leave punishment to "the juge that hath the jurisdiccion" (VII, 1442), she is asking him to understand his political power within this new context, in which justice is not the right of every lord, but is exercised by specially designated agents in a unified, abstract system that applies to all. It is true, of course, that the critique of vengeance was a feature of the *Liber consolationis*, and was even more prominent there than in either Renaud or Chaucer. But that fact lessens its contemporary significance for Chaucer only if we reject his broadened notion of *translatio*. The rejection of vengeance was an innovation of late medieval jurisprudence. Even if Renaud and Chaucer had done no more than reiterate it, they would have still been contributing to its dissemination. That is, they would have been engaging in precisely the sort of reiteration that Chaucer celebrates in the headlink's emphasis on *tellyng*. In fact, they did more. Renaud composed his translation for the Duke of Burgundy at a time when his barons had risen against him. He makes Albertanus's advocacy of adjudicatory justice specifically monarchist.[36] Chaucer recapitulates this monarchism, and slightly amplifies it, while bringing it to a new audience.

The submission to royal authority implicit in Melibee's relinquishing of the ideal of vengeance will paradoxically make a share of that authority available to him. Characterized by Prudence as nonsovereign before he makes this change, he afterward acquires a power just as clearly characterized by the sovereignty to which he has submitted. At the urging of Prudence, his enemies arrive at his court.

Thanne Melibee took hem up fro the ground ful benignely, / and receyved hire obligaciouns and hir boondes by hire othes upon hire pledges and borwes, / and assigned hem a certayn day to retourne unto his court / for to accept and receyve the sentence and juggement that Melibee wolde comande to be doon on hem by the causes aforeseyd. (VII, 1827–30)

Melibee has become judge, the very power to whom Prudence restricted the right of vengeance. His submission to her judicial

---

[36] James M. Powell, *Albertanus of Brescia: The Pursuit of Happiness in the Early Thirteenth Century* (Philadelphia: University of Pennsylvania Press, 1992), 74–89, 124–25.

scheme has issued in control of it. He apparently even has the regal right of disinheritance and exile, though Prudence persuades him not to use it. In this final portion of the tale, Chaucer's otherwise strict translation loosens up slightly. His changes emphasize Melibee's newly acquired sovereignty. In Renaud's version, the adversaries' petition is shorter and less politically marked:

nous nous offrons a vous, appareilliez d'obeïr a tous voz commandemens, et vous prions a genoulz et en lermes que vous ayez de nous pitié et misericorde.[37]

Chaucer expands this to:

we submytten us to the excellence and benignitee of youre gracious lordshipe, / and been redy to obeie to alle youre comandementz, / bisekynge yow that of youre merciable pitee ye wol considere oure grete repentaunce and low submyssioun / and graunten us foryevenesse of oure outrageous trespas and offense. / For wel we knowe that youre liberal grace and mercy strecchen hem ferther into goodnesse then doon oure outrageouse giltes and trespas into wikkednesse, / al be it that cursedly and dampnablely we han agilt agayn youre heigh lordshipe. (VII, 1821–25)

Not only does Chaucer draw out the moment of submission, making the adversaries more abject and obsequious than in Renaud, but he also explicitly marks it twice as a submission to Melibee's *lordshipe*.

This acquisition of sovereign status is implicit and figural, nor can it ever move beyond that indefinite state. Sovereign power is something Melibee can acquire only in renouncing. It is offered to him by the abject submission of his adversaries, but the very moral logic which motivates their submission depends on his renunciation of the power they offer him. His assumption of it is entirely symbolic. Here is the tale's paradox in its final and narrowest instantiation. Political power and textual authority can never be fully coincident, for authority is ultimately always dependent on the power it authorizes. The tale's resolution articulates this dependence in a specifically narrative fashion. The enactment of the body of authority so extravagantly cited depends on two voluntary renunciations of power, first, that of Melibee's enemies, then second, that of Melibee himself. The two are complementary: they form a narrative economy. Were there only the first renunciation, with Melibee taking whatever punitive compensation the law allowed him, we might have a non-

[37] Bryan and Dempster, *Sources and Analogues*, 612.

narrative resolution, with the systematic body of past authority imposing its own internal coherence on the narrative. In point of fact, however, this renunciation is made not toward the law, but toward Melibee himself. As the adversaries declare, "we submytten us to the excellence benignitee of youre gracious lordshipe." Their submission to him in fact places the entire transaction beyond the purview of the law, for it invests him with a sovereign power he does not otherwise possess. This investment is narrative and exemplary, in that it concentrates a collective interest in a single subject position. When Melibee refuses to accept the sovereignty he has been offered, thereby paradoxically showing himself worthy of it, he exposes this narrative dynamic even more fully. For his refusal is a deferral of the subject position the narrative has just assigned to him, a deferral which draws on and demonstrates narrative's capacity to generate new subject positions and transform existing ones. Chaucer's final deflection toward narrative enables him to retain its ideological power as a specifically lay discourse, while still laying claim to the systematic, neo-Aristotelian textual authority inherent in the body of citations the tale assembles. Having brought that authority into the collection and having assigned it to his own voice, Chaucer completes his engagement with the *Fürstenspiegel* in the next tale, where he turns to the public exemplum in its most purely narrative form.

The *Monk's Tale* is a miniature exemplum collection, a reworking of Boccaccio's *De casibus*. Its miniaturization foregrounds the compression already built into the genre, making the tale as much an analysis of the genre as an instance of it – an exemplum of the exemplary impulse, as it were.[38] Chaucer eliminates Boccaccio's subsidiary moral reflections, focusing on Fortune alone as the sole *sentence*. As a result, the narratives in the *Monk's Tale* are more unrelentingly isomorphic than those in the *De casibus*. They replay again and again, with swift, unerring precision, the fall from prosperity to ruin, presided over by a single moral principle, a principle which consists of little more than the generalization of that fall.

This is the negative exemplum in its most distilled form. The rhetorical distance between its narrative and its *sentence* consists literally of history's moral incompleteness. The tale also enacts this incompleteness in the interruption that constitutes its conclusion.

---

[38] Cf. Peter Godman, "Chaucer and Boccaccio's Latin Works," in *Chaucer and the Italian Trecento*, ed. Boitano: "Where Chaucer's narrative is compressed, Boccaccio's is slow and calm" (271).

The interruption figures the disjunction between textual authority and political power in the Knight's resistance to the Monk's moralizing. Chaucer's frame tale enables him to give this tension a direct institutional context, and the contextualization means the tale's analysis of the exemplum includes an analysis of its political value. The face-off between the Monk and the Knight, the pilgrimage's highest ranking representatives of the first two estates, recapitulates the public exemplum's alignment as it was received by lay poets like Chaucer. The public exemplum was moral counsel spoken by the Church to the nobility. Like the *De casibus*, the *Monk's Tale* makes both positions available to a lay audience, but unlike Boccaccio's work, its identification of textual authority with the voice of the Church makes its appropriation more explicit.

Nowhere in Chaucer studies has the postmodern return to history had a more dramatic effect than in the consideration of this tale. Until the last decade it was almost universally despised, taken to be an immature work marked by monotonous, simplistic moralizing, and a hypocritical speaker with a materialistic, nihilist, or even hedonistic world view.[39] If not dismissed outright, its simplistic moralizing and the fractured narratives were interpreted as exposing the Monk's moral failings and his unsophisticated, un-Boethian conception of Fortune.[40] By contrast, the three most important recent expositors of the tale, Peter Godman, Renate Haas, and Winthrop Wetherbee have declared it "a modest *tour de force*," "a brilliant response to the most advanced literary philosophical discussions of the age," and "a landmark in medieval literary history."[41] Concentrating on the Zenobia exemplum, Godman stresses the care and complexity of Chaucer's adaptation of Boccaccio. Haas and Wetherbee both see the tale as an engagement with ancient tragedy: Haas asserts the tale makes Chaucer "the first poet to experiment with tragedy in the vernacular."[42] I share these critics' enthusiasm and their commitment to viewing the tale in relation to the specific late medieval traditions it engages. The earlier criticism was less

---

[39] Jack B. Oruch, "Chaucer's Worldly Monk," *Criticism* 8 (1966), 280–88.

[40] R. E. Kaske, "The Knight's Interruption of the *Monk's Tale*," *ELH* 24 (1957), 261.

[41] Godman, "Chaucer and Boccaccio's Latin Works," 281; Renate Haas, "Chaucer's *Monk's Tale*: An Ingenious Criticism of Early Humanist Conceptions of Tragedy," *Humanistica Lovaniensia* 36 (1987), 44; Winthrop Wetherbee, "The Context of the *Monk's Tale*," in *Language and Style in English Literature: Essays in Honour of Michio Masui*, ed. Michio Kawai (Hiroshima: The English Research Association of Hiroshima, 1991), 159.

[42] Haas, "*Monk's Tale*," 44.

concerned with reading the tale than with finding reasons not to read it, precisely because of the challenge it poses to both the the modernist ideal of an anti-didactic Chaucer, and the more general modern conviction that narrative and didacticism are antithetical.[43]

These earlier accounts dismissed the tale on two grounds. The first was its early date. The second was the claim that Chaucer uses it solely to repudiate its teller. The first claim is easily disposed of – a clear case of aesthetic preference masquerading as a judgment of philological fact. Scholars posited an early date of composition because they felt the tale so obviously unworthy of Chaucer's maturity. In fact, there is no other evidence to support this view. The tale is firmly embedded in the collection with both prologue and epilogue. There are no insurmountable textual inconsistencies, and it is linked thematically to the tales around it, while its teller clearly fits the frame tale dramatically. What is even more striking is the one piece of hard chronological evidence that we do have – one more than we have for most of the tales. On its face this evidence suggests a later date rather than an earlier one. Among the so-called Modern Instances (VII, 2375–2462), there is the stanza on Bernabo Visconti, lord of Milan, which could not have been written before his death in 1385, or during the same period when the Canterbury collection was being composed. Yet even this fact has not deterred those favoring an earlier date. They have simply constructed the unlikely hypothesis that the Modern Instances, or at the very least this episode, were later interpolations made when Chaucer placed the tale in the collection. Why he would have bothered tinkering with a tale so obviously beneath his talents is a question which never gets addressed. The force of the preference for an earlier date can be gauged by a remark F. N. Robinson makes in the notes to his edition, a remark which the editors of the *Riverside Chaucer* have let stand. Describing the view of Tatlock, one of the few to oppose the early date, he declares that Tatlock "gives no decisive reason in support of the late date."[44]

---

[43] It is interesting to note that the one earlier critic who approved of the *Monk's Tale*, D. W. Robertson ("Chaucerian Tragedy," *ELH* 19 (1952), 1–37), also found it to be without intrinsic interest, and used it as a flat gloss on a text he accepted as intrinsically more complex, *Troilus and Criseyde*.

[44] *Riverside Chaucer*, 929. The argument has been made most recently by M. C. Seymour in "Chaucer's Early Poem *De Casibus Virorum Illustrium*," *Chaucer Review* 24 (1989) 162–65. Seymour adds the imaginative suggestion that the tale "once existed as an independent poem in a booklet of, say, fourteen quarto leaves (more if illustrated by a cycle of miniatures)," but he offers no hard evidence to support it. His principal argument for an

Robinson is so sure the tale is early that he cannot see that the burden of proof lies on him, and not on Tatlock.

The matter of the tale's relation to its teller cannot be settled quite so easily, for the collection itself demands the tales be read as defining their teller. The *General Prologue* portrays the Monk as the quintessential worldly cleric, whose worldliness is an entirely plausible result of his office as *outridere*. He fits the general terms of Chaucer's anti-clerical critique, and it is reasonable to expect his moral failings to be reflected in his tale. The problem is that the directness with which most critics have attempted to impose this relation seems designed only to screen Chaucer from the tale. The tale is always on the verge of being unauthored: its internal structure is solely the product of the Monk and the exemplary tradition he represents, replicated by Chaucer for the express purpose of repudiating it. The question of Chaucer's own investment in the tale never arises because that is precisely the question this line of argument is trying to make moot. And here is where this strategy of dismissal breaks down, exposing its own failure to confront the complex specificity of the tale it wishes to present as an instance of pure mystification. To the extent that the tale characterizes the Monk, it ceases to be mystification, and the dilemma the Monk poses becomes as much a matter of his discourse as of his behavior. No coherent analysis of this text can use the teller to escape the discursive specificity of the tale.

In fact, as I hope to show, Chaucer's commitment to this tale goes well beyond this minimal condition. He is much more interested in the moral authority of the tale than the moral failings of the teller, and he takes these as illustrating the necessary political conditions which accompany the public exemplum's actual articulation. Haas fruitfully suggests that it is the very undecidability of Fortune, the tale's central figure, that constitutes its moral value. She cites the early *trecento* humanist Mussato, who "hoped that" the "representation of the fickleness of Fortune would guide people towards a kind of Stoic *ataraxia*," an ethical detachment and freedom from passion.[45] In my view, however, she vitiates the force of this insight by construing it as antithetical to Christianity. Her commitment to the medieval/humanist opposition leads her to define the late medieval revival of tragedy as a complete break with Christian authority – at

---

early date remains aesthetic: he cites "its avoidance of Boethian complexity" and "both the uneven structure and comparatively flat narrative line" (164).

[45] Haas, "*Monk's Tale*," 55.

one point she even refers to the revivers as "the avant-garde."[46] While this framework enables her to rescue the tale (precisely as an avant-gardist "experiment"), it also makes the teller's relation to the tale even more problematic: the Monk does not make a very convincing avant-gardist.[47]

Haas recognizes this problem, and argues that the Monk should be viewed as a "sham humanist" whom Chaucer implicitly pits against the real humanist Petrarch, in order to show the risks which the humanist celebration of tragedy entailed. While ingenious, this explanation is not very convincing historically. As always, the problem with the medieval/humanist opposition is that the poles are always defined so antithetically that the transition between the two proves impossible to locate within a specific historical context. In order for Chaucer's audience to recognize the Monk's version of tragedy as a sham, they must already be familiar with the Latin humanist tradition which preceded it. But if that is true, then Chaucer's distinction as "the first poet to experiment with tragedy in the vernacular" becomes rather hollow. The vernacular audience to which he brings tragedy is already conversant with it. Once again, the tale's specificity is avoided. Indeed, Haas's actual reading of the tale consists largely of the traditional catalog of its narrative shortcomings – all ascribed, in the traditional manner, to Chaucer's desire to ironize the Monk.

All indications, however, are that the tale did have an important impact on the subsequent vernacular tradition, so despite her reading of the Monk, Haas is right to insist on the tale's innovative effect. It was among Chaucer's most popular tales in the fifteenth century, and it introduces the *De casibus* tradition to England. Its importance can be explained more convincingly if, as I have been suggesting throughout this study, we view the medieval/humanist dichotomy as underlaid by the more historically and politically specific opposition between the clerical and lay. For the humanists Haas cites are also Christian. Their concern, and Chaucer's, was not to break away from the Christian to the purely human (whatever that might be), but to establish the authority of the lay within the general system of Christian belief they shared with the rest of their society. Appropriation, not subversion, best describes their approach to clerical authority and tradition. If we read the *Monk's Tale* under that rubric,

[46] Haas, "*Monk's Tale*," 57.
[47] For another view, see Wetherbee, "The Context of the *Monk's Tale*," 161–77.

it becomes possible to account for both Chaucer's affirmation of the tale, and his anti-clerical critique of its teller.

The textual authority Chaucer grants to the Monk is synonymous with the spiritual authority he has granted to the Church all along. It is the authority of the moralist to provide spiritual correction. What he denies the Monk is what he has denied to clerical figures all along: temporal institutional power. In demonstrating the Monk's textual authority, Chaucer affirms Christian authority, but at a level beyond its embodiment in the Church's institutional power. The clear break he maintains between the Monk as moralist and the Monk as monastic officer enables him to reinforce the separation between textual authority and temporal power – one of the central themes of the tale. It also reinforces his assertion of the necessity that the Church continually resist its own institutional prerogatives.

The Monk's ecclesiastical identity is exclusively a feature of his social existence; it leaves no direct mark on his text. His exempla are not in any sense directed toward some institutional result. There is no effort to entice his audience into the cloister, or into some other closer relation to the Church. He simply confronts them again and again with the negativity of their own position. This empty textual authority translates into a curious kind of superiority. Chaucerians have long recognized the deliberate contrast in the portraits of the General Prologue between the Knight and the knightly pretensions of the Monk (his fondness for hunting, good food, and fine clothes.)[48] This contrast deepens the context for the confrontation between Knight and Monk which ends the tale.

While the Monk's pretensions ultimately represent a personal moral failing, they are also an occupational hazard, and in a curious way, an occupational benefit. They demonstrate the radical difference between the institutional function of the Church and that of the nobility. As an "outridere" (I, 166), the overseer of monastic property, the Monk has privileges similar to those of temporal lordship but without similar responsibilities. It is precisely because he can play at being knightly that he can enjoy his hunting and feasting more thoroughly than a real knight could, and that he can seem more knightly in the dignity of his appearance than the Knight himself. Coming directly from his battles to the pilgrimage, the Knight is

---

[48] See for example, Kaske, "The Knight's Interruption," 254–57; and Kurt Ollson, "Grammar, Manhood, and Tears: The Curiosity of Chaucer's Monk," *Modern Philology* 76 (1978), 1–17.

outfitted in armor "al bismotered" (I, 76). The Monk, on the other hand, shielded from such direct confrontation with the violence political responsibilities incur, is "a lord full fat" (I, 200) with "bootes souple" and a "hors in greet estaat" (I, 203). Even in the temporal sphere the Monk's privileges are greater than the Knight's because his institution is more immediately bound to God. Yet that is precisely why the institution is obliged to keep those privileges at a minimum. The privileges came to it as the result of its sanctity, yet they continually threaten to contaminate the very sanctity to which they are a tribute. Nowhere was this paradox more marked than in the case of the monastic orders. Established as retreats from the temporal world, their reputation for sanctity would inevitably attract bequests of land. Since in a feudal society land is material power in its most concrete and durable form, an order's very success in escaping the world inevitably brought it back into the world at its worldliest.[49] When Chaucer makes his Monk both moralist and outrider, he articulates the Church's dilemma in its broadest terms.

The Monk combines in one character two forms of confrontation between Church and the world: the legitimate role of moral correction, and the less legitimate role of self-interested proprietor that inevitably accompanies it. If the Church stays cloistered it remains morally pure, but fails in its obligation to correct society at large. And yet spiritual authority differs so radically from the secular political power it must correct, that as soon as the Church moves into the world, chances are it will be contaminated. Chaucer's insistence on this contamination accomplishes two things. As it asserts the need for the Church continually to resist its own prerogatives, it also clears a space for the lay moralist. Since spiritual authority differs so radically from political power it cannot be coincident with any institutional form, even the divinely sanctioned forms of the Church. Its very otherness makes it as available to the lay as to the clerical.

Chaucer's insistence on the radical otherness of moral authority also helps account for readings which see the tale as un-Boethian. His commitment to the incompleteness of the temporal leads him to stress Fortune's indiscriminacy, to present her as Boethius argued she appears most immediately to the philosophically unsophisticated. In this he follows Boccaccio, isolating the same tension to which Boethius gave more cursory treatment. And like Boccaccio, he in no way

---

[49] Cf. Georges Duby, *The Chivalrous Society*, tr. Cynthia Postan (Berkeley and Los Angeles: University of California Press, 1980), 4.

intends his depiction as un-Boethian, as the manner in which he introduces it makes clear.[50] The definition of tragedy which he puts in the mouth of the Monk comes directly from a gloss in his translation of *The Consolation of Philosophy*. The gloss occurs in Lady Philosophy's opening discussion of Fortune, and it reads:

Tragedye is to seyn a dite of prosperitee for a tyme, that endeth in wrecchidnesse. (*Boece*, II, Pr. 2, 70–73)

The Monk's definition, though somewhat expanded, is nearly identical:

Tragedie is to seyn a certeyn storie,
As olde bookes maken us memorie,
Of hym that stood in greet prosperitee,
And is yfallen out of heigh degree
Into myserie, and endeth wrecchedly.   (VII, 1973–77)

That Chaucer bothers to insert the gloss indicates he views Fortune as a serious literary problem.[51] While his definition may be simplistic by modern critical standards, there is kind of brutality to it that makes it compelling. The simplicity of the fall from high degree also gives it an immediate universality which becomes the surest sign of the Monk's discursive authority. The Monk processes each narrative swiftly and unerringly, inexorably reducing them all to the same lesson, clearly demonstrating an ability to make all human history fit one pattern. (Though he tells only seventeen exempla, he claims to have a hundred in his cell, and that is probably the one point on which his credibility has never been questioned.)

He begins the tale at dead center, repeating the definition already given in the prologue:

I wol biwaille in manere of tragedie,
The harm of hem that stoode in heigh degree,
And fillen so that ther nas no remedie
To brynge hem out of hir adversitee.
For certein, whan that Fortune list to flee,
Ther may no man the cours of hire withholde.
Lat no man truste on blynd prosperitee;
Be war by thise ensamples trewe and olde.   (VII, 1991–98)

These lines provide the single *sententia* for all the exempla to follow and yet their authority is purely negative. Nothing is recuperated;

---

[50] See also Haas, "*Monk's Tale*," 54–57; and Douglas L. Lepley, "The Monk's Boethian Tale," *Chaucer Review* 12 (1978), 162–70.

[51] For a fuller discussion see A. J. Minnis, *Chaucer and Pagan Antiquity* (Cambridge: Cambridge University Press, 1982), p. 26.

their insistence on the irreversibility of the tragic downfall makes narrativity itself suspect. The fall becomes the normative form of change. Indeed, the first exemplum will present its archetype. Where Boccaccio had begun with Adam and Eve, Chaucer extends the universalization of Fortune still further, and begins with Lucifer. Many critics have complained about this opening gambit, seeing it as confirmation of the Monk's narrative incompetence. Fortune is conventionally restricted to human history; it clearly does not apply to Lucifer's fall. Still, the figure is only an improvisation, even as regards human history. While this extension may literally be improper, the figure's explanatory value does not reside in its literal propriety.

Moreover, the Monk frames the story with disclaimers:

> At Lucifer, though he an angel were
> And nat a man, at hym wol I bigynne,
> For though Fortune may noon angel dere,
> From heigh degree yet fel he for his synne
> Doun into helle, where he yet is inne.　　(VII, 1999–2003)

Lucifer's story is structurally identical to the tragedies that follow, and his fall brings the Fall as a form of change (or perhaps even change *tout court*) into the world. It necessitated the creation of Adam and Eve, and when they succumbed to his temptation, change was specifically introduced into human history as well. The structural identity remains as the only evidence available in purely temporal terms of the cosmic link between Lucifer's fall and the process of human history. The story cannot provide the Monk with the central authority of an origin, but that is precisely its point. It distills the figural authority of Fortune to an irreducible doubleness, confirming at once its universality and its incompleteness.

Doubleness is also the tale's most salient structural feature. As Robert Burlin has shown, the exempla are arranged in pairs:

After Lucifer and Adam, the great originals, come the two strong men betrayed by women, followed by two royal idolators. The order is interrupted when the imperial pair, Zenobia and Nero, are separated to introduce some modern instances, the two betrayed Peters and two imprisoned Italian nobles. But the sequence concludes with two powerful enemies of the Hebrews, and the "grete conquerors two," Caesar and Alexander, leaving Croesus to find his dreaming mate in Chauntecleer.[52]

[52] Robert B. Burlin, *Chaucerian Fiction* (Princeton: Princeton University Press, 1977), 189.

The reason for this scheme is partly stylistic – it allows Chaucer to give the impression of random extemporaneous composition without really relinquishing control – but even at the stylistic level it has thematic significance. Because it is not immediately evident, the scheme can create in readers of the tale the impression of a definite structure just beyond their grasp, similar to the way in which, on a more rigorous epistemological plane, the figure Fortune is expected to awaken knowledge of the moral order beyond her. (The same effect is achieved by the ending of the tale, which is presented as an interruption, even though the redefinition of tragedy (VII, 2761–66) would have provided a suitable conclusion.) The binary structure has a more overriding significance as well. It diminishes the uniqueness of each protagonist and makes the Monk's already obvious interventions even more so. As heroism becomes repeatable, its status as *factum* becomes more clearly *dictum*. The range of the Monk's discursive moralizing is such that it extends beyond the general imposition of the same ending to fuse with the specifics of each narrative. The narrative function of *facta* within the exemplum becomes indistinguishable from their discursive function as *dicta* within the Monk's moral argument. As narratives, the exempla have almost no middle; there is little plot development. After a state of high degree has been sufficiently delineated, it gives way almost instantaneously to wretchedness. The Monk's moral point is that wretchedness is the true name of prosperity, as it is of any earthly condition. By eliminating the intervening process of decline, he makes the equivalence that much more emphatic. This nearly instantaneous exchange of wretched ending for prosperous beginning is at once narrative and argumentative – narrative inasmuch as it is unexpected, and argumentative inasmuch as it is definitional, motivated by an inevitable moral logic.

At the end of the tale of Hercules, the Monk observes,

> Beth war, for whan that Fortune list to glose,
> Thanne wayteth she her man to overthrowe
> By swich a wey as he wolde leest suppose.   (VII, 2140–42)

Fortune is a gloss, the exchange of one discursive term for another, that manifests itself as unpredictably and disruptively as possible. Like Boccaccio, the Monk has given Fortune a voice, or more precisely, *he has made her disruptiveness discursive*. That is, he has constructed a narrative field where disruption, narrative's characteristic assertion of its own autonomy, becomes the sign of discursive control without ceasing to be narrative.

From the start the Monk's narratives present themselves as the products of interpretive intervention. Without exception each opens in the mode of summary, defining in superlatives the initial prosperity and power of the protagonist. Of Adam, for example, the Monk says, "Hadde nevere worldly man so heigh degree" (VII, 2011); of Cenobia, "no wight passed hire in hardynesse, / Ne in lignage; ne in oother gentilesse" (VII, 2250–51). Often the paradox is even more pointed: the protagonist's superlative status is defined precisely by its resistance to definition. Of Nabugodonosor the Monk says,

> The myghty trone, the precious tresor,
> The glorious ceptre, and roial magestee
> That hadde the kyng Nabugodonosor
> With tonge unnethe may discryved bee.   (VII, 2143–46)

As the grammatical form of all three of these passages indicates, the superlative status of good Fortune is a negative one, which can be defined only by comparison to the status of others. The Monk deprives his protagonists of their heroism in two respects. First he confers what status they have by definition, rather than allowing them to earn it in the course of the narrative. Second, what he confers lacks positive force. This formal strategy anticipates the lesson that good Fortune is in no way a possession of those blessed with it.

The intervention implicit in the beginnings achieves its fullest prominence in the endings. The endings underline Fortune's disruptive power by depicting misfortune at its most invasive. With two exceptions, all the protagonists suffer downfalls initiated in their own households, and which often directly attack their bodies (for example, Hercules's poison shirt, Nabugodonosor's metamorphosis, Antiochus's accidental flaying, and Caesar's stabbing). The focus on the gruesome and intimate detail of each downfall demonstrates by its specificity the thoroughness of Fortune's domination of human existence. She deprives the most powerful of people even of the simple control of their own bodies. The complete loss of personal autonomy drives home the essential uncontrollability of political power.

This is the moral certainty which the Monk presents to the Knight, and which the Knight resists. Most critics have assumed that the Knight, in interrupting the Monk, speaks for Chaucer, delivering the final verdict on a thoroughly incompetent storyteller. However, if we assume, as I have been arguing, that Chaucer takes this tale seriously, the significance of the interruption becomes more complicated. The Knight's main justification – that sometimes a man in poor estate grows fortunate (VII, 2775–76) – seems like Pollyannaish special pleading. The accession of a poor man to rich estate only further confirms the essential instability that the Monk has argued defines human history. On this point, the cultural authorities, medieval and humanist alike, are on the Monk's side, and not the Knight's. The Knight's resistance itself is a characteristic instance of that instability, for it is nothing less than the resistance of political power to textual authority.

While this opposition is implicit in every aspect of the tale, the Monk also explicitly thematizes it. Obstinacy in the face of wise counsel figures in four of his exempla: Nabugodonosor, Balthasar, Nero, and Croesus. These four exempla anticipate the Knight's rejection of the Monk, and vindicate him in advance. Two of the three counselors, Daniel and Seneca, commanded considerably more moral authority than the Monk and still were subjected to far harsher treatment by those they advised. Nero forces Seneca to bleed to death, "By cause Nero hadde of hym swich drede, / For he fro vices wolde hym ay chastise" (VII, 2504–05), and Nabugodonsor gelds Daniel. The gelding of Daniel is particularly significant in this context, for unlike the story of Seneca's murder, which was widely disseminated in the Middle Ages, this detail has been found in only one other extant source.[53] Chaucer's inclusion of it here shows he was especially concerned to assert that material or physical inferiority in no way impugns a moralist's authority. Daniel is subject to the same kind of bodily violation that afflicts most of the Monk's protagonists, but as the voice of moral authority he keeps speaking, returning in the exemplum immediately following to read the writing on the wall for Balthasar.

At the same time, the Knight's interruption affirms for Chaucer's lay audience its ultimate control of textual authority. The interruption completes the appropriation of the Monk's voice, for it offers that audience both his authority and the power to resist it. As an analysis of the public exemplum, the *Monk's Tale* affirms narrative's authority in its very incompletion. Indeed, the tale's incompletion is a fitting culmination to the compression that has

[53] Dudley R. Johnson, "The Biblical Characters of Chaucer's Monk," *Publication of the Modern Languages Association* 66 (1951), 834–35.

governed it throughout. The speed with which it invokes one historical catastrophe, imposes a kind of moral order, invokes another, and imposes the same order once again, lends both urgency and power to the project of producing moral authority from within history. Like the *De casibus*, the *Monk's Tale* fictively puts its reader in the position of counsel to its predominantly monarchical protagonists. Its devaluation of their heroism and its narrative compression make the reader's position that much more powerful. This power is figural, to be sure, but it is figural within a cultural conjuncture where the textual authorized the political. The appeal of the *Monk's Tale* for Chaucer's public and his immediate posterity lies here, in the cultural authority it offered them through the lay language of narrative.

Moreover, this model of narrative authority is not that distant from our own. In fact, one might plausibly argue that the modern resistance to the *Monk's Tale*, and the *De casibus* genre as a whole is the result not of an unbreachable historical difference, but, on the contrary, of a similarity too close for comfort. The late medieval notion of Fortune does not seem very far distant from the tendency in post-Enlightenment literary history that Paul de Man describes as irony. He argues that

the target [of ironical texts] is very often the claim to speak about human matters as if they were facts of history. It is a historical fact that irony becomes increasingly conscious itself in the course of demonstrating the impossibility of our being historical.[54]

Irony for de Man is the master-trope of demystification, and the guarantor of literary authenticity. Like the figure of Fortune, the authority of this trope is founded on its self-conscious exposure of the incompleteness of history. De Man is entirely candid about the theological provenance of his view of authenticity, explicitly ac-knowledging the dependence of his ironic conception of history on the Christian notion of the Fall. As the passage I have just quoted indicates, he locates the difference between the two in irony's ever-increasing self-consciousness – a radically paradoxical claim, not simply because it is a self-consciousness of its own emptiness, but because the very notion of emptiness beggars the authorizing, authenticating force of the notion of increase. Like the majority of post-Enlightenment thinkers, de Man believes, as deeply and firmly as any medieval thinkers believed in God, that the present knows

---

[54] Paul de Man, *Blindness and Insight* (Minneapolis: University of Minnesota Press, 1983), 211.

more than the past, simply by virtue of being the present. This conviction enables him to accept the idea of the Fall without the idea of Redemption, and to do so quite complacently, with no fear at all of incoherence.

Indeed, such presentism makes the denial of Redemption heroic; the advantage that modernity claims over Christianity is precisely its clear-eyed, self-conscious capacity to face the fallenness of history on its own, without any need to appeal to the notion of a Redeemer. Nevertheless, the simple fact is that the Fall *is* an incoherent notion without the notion of Redemption, and if one manages to stand outside modernity's myth of progress for just a moment, one begins to wonder at its fierce attachment to such a major fragment of the very Christianity it claims to demystify and leave behind. What the example of the *De casibus* tradition suggests is that the rejection of Christianity's redemptive aspect is not so much a heroic self-denial, as a paradoxical, but crucial appropriation. Modernity, and deconstructive postmodernity after it, want to retain the notion of the Fall without the Redemption, precisely because it undergirds the authenticating originality of their own ironic, dystopic self-consciousness. The ostensibly unique extent of their discovery of "the impossibility of... being historical" covertly authorizes the numerous historical and political commitments they still retain, just as the *De casibus* tradition's assertion of the impossibility of history in the figure of Fortune enabled it to authorize the interests of lay culture.

In de Man's case, his repression of political commitments is too notorious to require comment here, and in any case, that is not really the sort of repression I have in mind. It is easy to see why the ideal of political exculpation which the impossibility of history affords would have attracted someone like de Man, but it is more important in my view to see that the repression such ideals involve operates at a cultural level well beyond that of the personal guilty secret. From the Italian Futurists to Heidegger, to Pound and Eliot, avant-gardist thinking has had more constitutive and more overt ties to reactionary politics. Its debts to Christianity have been an embarrassment precisely because they expose the extent to which a self-conscious rejection of history can undergird ideological affirmations. The "humanist" moment represented by the *De casibus* tradition is particularly embarrassing because it exposes the extent to which the very desacralization of the Fall began much earlier than modernity. Furthermore, the specific example of Chaucer shows how deeply even irony, the master-trope modernity claims as somehow especially its own, was implicated in this process, and how it too can, through its very indirections, and its vertiginous self-consciousness, define and adumbrate political interests. With this in mind, I turn now to the *Nun's Priest's Tale*, where Chaucer's irony is at its most affirmative.

THE *NUN'S PRIEST'S TALE*: THE AUTHORITY OF FABLE

It is not the least of this tale's ironies that it provides exactly the sort of narrative the Knight wanted from the Monk. The story of Chauntecleer is the story of misfortune returned to prosperity, a point the Nun's Priest drives home by remarking just before Chauntecleer makes his escape, "Lo, how Fortune turneth sodeynly / The hope and pryde eek of hir enemy!" (VII, 3403–04). Instructed by Harry Bailly to "Telle us swich thyng as may oure hertes glade" (VII, 2811), the Nun's Priest offers his tale directly into the breach between the Monk and the Knight. Its ironic reversal of the reversals of Fortune will produce a fictive resolution of the opposition between the textual authority and political power which those two figures embody.

The tale can be both fiction and resolution because it is a fable. As Cicero defines it, a fable is neither the truth nor like the truth.[55] As an overtly false discourse, one which continually and ostentatiously declares its falsity even as it produces a coherent narrative, the fable allows a maximum of discursive play to be combined with a maximum of discursive control. Its overt falsity prevents its play from ever being completely subversive, for its play always defers to an external standard of truth. At the same time, its falsity prevents the deferral from ever being direct. A fable is a text without a past, a text whose indirect relation to authority means it must be written entirely in the secular language of the present. The ironic resolution the tale offers lay power will be a resolution achieved through the logic of narrative at its most fictive.

A beast fable could also be an exemplum. The genre comes to Chaucer as a long-established site of ideological conflict betweeen the clerical and the lay. The genre descended to the Middle Ages through the monastic preservation of Aesop's fables. Within the monasteries it gave rise to clerical satires such as *Ysengrimus* and the

---

[55] *De inventione*, I, xix.

Speculum stultorum. Adapted by *conteurs* for the nobility of twelfth-
century France it led eventually to the corrosively anti-clerical and
anti-monarchical *Roman de Renart* and its successors.[56] But the
Renardian fable was reappropriated as sermon exempla by preachers
like Odo of Cheriton, who made the fables exempla by assigning
them allegorical doctrinal morals. Chaucer locates the very boundary
between the beast fable and sermon exemplum by proclaiming it has
a doctrinal moral, yet failing to make such a moral explicit.

> But ye that holden this tale a folye,
> As of a fox, or of a cok and hen,
> Taketh the moralite, goode men.
> For Seint Paul seith that al that writen is,
> To oure doctrine it is ywrite, ywis;
> Taketh the fruyt, and lat the chaf be stille.   (VII, 3438–43)

This passage has become one of the most notable cruxes in the
entire collection, a crux notable not merely for its difficulty, but also
for its comparatively recent vintage. It dates back only to the 1950s,
when after passing five and a half centuries as a largely unremarked
portion of the Chaucer canon, the *Nun's Priest Tale* abruptly became
the quintessential Chaucerian text. As the tale which "fittingly serves
to cap all of Chaucer's poetry," its ending provided a central site of
conflict in the debate between patristic and formalist approaches.[57] It
fit perfectly the tropological terms on which the debate characteristically turned: was Chaucer to be read allegorically or ironically?[58] Patristic scholars, taking literally the parting injunction to

---

[56] On the politics of Renardian fable, see John Flinn, "Littérature bourgeoise et *Le Roman de
Renart*," in *Aspects of the Medieval Animal Epic: Proceedings of the International Conference, Louvain,
May 15–17, 1972*, ed. E. Rombauts and A. Welkenhuysen (Louvain/Leuven: Leuven
University Press; The Hague: Martinus Nijhoff, 1975), 11–23.

[57] Charles Muscatine, *Chaucer and the French Tradition* (Berkeley: University of California Press,
1957), 238.

[58] Cf. Knight, *Geoffrey Chaucer*, 1. I list here only the most important contributions to this
debate. For a comprehensive critical history of the tale, see Derek Pearsall, ed., *The Nun's
Priest's Tale*, vol. 2, pt 9 of *A Variorum Edition of the Works of Geoffrey Chaucer*, ed. Pearsall
(Norman: University of Oklahoma Press, 1984), 30–81. From the patristic perspective:
Mortimer Donovan, "The *moralite* of the Nun's Priest's Sermon," *Journal of English Germanic
Philology* 52 (1953), 493–508; Charles Dahlberg, "Chaucer's Cock and Fox," *Journal of
English and Germanic Philology* 53 (1954), 277–90; D. W. Robertson, *A Preface to Chaucer*
(Princeton: Princeton University Press, 1959), 251–52; Bernard F. Huppé, *A Reading of the
Canterbury Tales*, rev. ed. (Albany: State University of New York Press, 1967), 174–84;
Bernard S. Levy and George R. Adams, "Chauntecleer's Paradise Lost and Regained,"
Mediaeval Studies 29 (1967), 178–92. Donovan and Dahlberg lay out the general lines of the
argument, and marshall an impressive array of evidence from theological sources. Donovan
identifies the cock with the preacher and the fox with the devil, while Dahlberg introduces

"Takyth the fruyt and lat the chaf be stille," read the tale as an allegory for some doctrinal metanarrative, such as the Fall. Formalists, on the other hand, read the injunction ironically, insisting with E. Talbot Donaldson, that "the fruit of the tale is its chaff."[59] The field has moved beyond this controversy, and post-structuralist literary theory, beginning with Paul de Man, has deconstructed the tropological opposition between allegory and irony on which it turned.[60] Allegory is no longer seen as the univocal, pre-determined reiteration of prior tradition that both sides of the patristic/formalist debate viewed it as. Instead, like irony it is seen as a sign explicitly structured by reference to a previous sign. While irony demystifies the anterior sign, allegory reiterates it, but only by acknowledging the temporal distance separating the two. Both figures, in de Man's words, "are...linked in their common discovery of a truly temporal predicament."[61]

This common connection makes it difficult if not impossible to oppose the two figures on the basis of their relation to previous tradition – allegory as entirely reiterative, and irony as entirely subversive. Even the most faithful allegorical reference necessarily acknowledges the temporal gap between it and the sign to which it refers. Even the most corrosive irony necessarily depends on the very sign it demystifies to give it meaning. One can assume neither, as patristic critics had, that allegory automatically governs a text's

additional evidence that associates the fox with the friars. Robertson produces iconographic support for the argument and Huppe and Levy and Adams broaden its focus, seeing the tale as an allegorical reworking of the Fall. Judson Boyce Allen, "The Ironic Fruyt: Chauntecleer as Figura," *Studies in Philology* 66 (1969), 25–35, also derives his evidence from theological sources, but argues Chaucer's use of them was ironic, that Chauntecleer fails to live up to his exegetical models. The formalist reading begins with Muscatine, *Chaucer and the French Tradition*. Muscatine concludes his account this way: "Unlike fable, the *Nun's Priest's Tale* does not so much make true and solemn assertions about life as it tests truths and tries out solemnities" (242). Recapitulating this line of argument in various ways have been E. Talbot Donaldson, ed., *Chaucer's Poetry* (New York: Ronald Press, 1958), 940–44; Stephen Manning, "The Nun's Priest's Morality and the Medieval Attitude toward Fables," *Journal of English and Germanic Philology* 59 (1960): 403–16; Stanley Fish, "*The Nun's Priest's Tale* and Its Analogues," *College Literature Association Journal* 5 (1962), 223–38; Jill Mann, "The *Speculum Stultorum* and the *Nun's Priest's Tale*," *Chaucer Review* 9 (1975), 262–82; A. Paul Shallers, "The 'Nun's Priest's Tale': An Ironic Exemplum," *ELH* 42 (1975), 319–37; Alfred David, *The Strumpet Muse: Art and Morals in Chaucer's Poetry* (Bloomington: Indiana University Press, 1976), 223–31; Donald R. Howard, *The Idea of the Canterbury Tales* (Berkeley: University of California Press, 1976), 280–307; Burlin, *Chaucerian Fiction*, 229–37.

[59] E. Talbot Donaldson, *Speaking of Chaucer* (New York: Norton, 1970), 150.

[60] Paul de Man, "The Rhetoric of Temporality" in *Blindness and Insight: Essays in the Rhetoric of Contemporary Criticism*, 187–228. For a fuller application of de Man's argument to this tale see my "The Authority of Fable: Allegory and Irony in the *Nun's Priest's Tale*," in *Exemplaria* I (1989), 43–51.   [61] de Man, "Rhetoric," 222.

ambiguities, nor, as formalists had, that irony automatically subverts
a text's allegorical aspirations.

In hindsight it is possible to see how the fascination patristic
scholars had for this tale clearly illustrates Derek Pearsall's observation that

this approach to medieval literature is the product of particular crisis in
modern culture, in this case the crisis of the orthodox conscience, which,
finding itself outflanked on every side by what are seen as unsavory
developments in modern society, finds consolation in a dogmatic interpretation of the literature of the past.[62]

In its battle with modernism, patristic exegesis thought it had in this
tale clear proof that the irony modernism prized so highly depended
on a stable system of belief one could only approach allegorically.[63]
But a similar observation might be made of formalist readings of the
tale as well. The final lines compress the issue of Christian textuality
into six scant lines. To show Chaucer was undercutting it would
clearly illustrate the formalist conviction that he was a poet first and
a Christian second, and the broader conviction that poetic form
transcends history. This is essentially a modernist debate, with both
sides assuming the stereotypical view of past authority as static and
uncontested. For one side it is a lost ideal to be lamented; for the other
a mystification to escape. I do not think we should simply dismiss the
debate out of hand as anachronistic and ephemeral. But I do think we
should see that its terms, indebted as they are to the concerns of
modernism, are by no means inevitable. The commitment of both
sides to the same stereotype of medieval authority has meant most
interpretive energy has focused on the meaning of the ending and
comparatively little has been exerted on the tale's narrative as
narrative.

If we focus our energies there we will find the crucial opposition in
this tale is indeed between the exemplary and the fabulous rather
than the allegorical and ironic. The former dichotomy subtends and
frames the latter. To be sure both allegory and irony are nearly
ubiquitous in the tale. But that is because both are important
components of the moralized fable, the beast fable in its exemplary
form. Therefore, their operation is secondary to the tale's melding of
the exemplary and the fabulous. Both the exemplum and the fable
are similar in that both defer to the authority of the past in such a way

[62] Pearsall, "Canterbury Tales," 318.
[63] On patristic exegesis's battle with modernism see Patterson, Negotiating the Past, 26–39.

as to stress the importance of its reenactment in the present. In fact, the fable takes this emphasis to a figural limit, for its reenactments are entirely fictive. That is, they are purely *dicta*, and purely human *dicta*, with no grounding as *facta*. To this extent, they affirm the purely intrinsic authority of human language. Even the most aggressively doctrinal moralized fable tacitly affirms this authority as a necessary condition of its own intelligibility. By finding divine authority in purely human language with no connection to Holy Writ, it must concede such authority is intrinsic to language in its very humanness. This paradoxical notion of authority is similar to that which John of Salisbury articulates when he claims the right to make up his own.

The tale is more directly indebted to another of John's notions of authority. The concluding claim that all writing is doctrinal does indeed originate with Paul (Romans 2: 28–29), as the Nun's Priest declares, but in Paul it applies only to the writings of the Old Testament. John is the first to make it apply to all writing.[64] This claim cannot be viewed as a simple proposition. It is the invocation of a practice of textual appropriation, whose meaning varies in accordance with the interest which motivates it. To restate the problem in slightly different terms, the claim that all writing is doctrinal never stands by itself. It is always made in order to authorize other claims. Paul makes it in order to appropriate the authority of Judaic law for his fledgling group of non-Judaic Christians. John of Salisbury makes it in order to appropriate lay traditions. And Chaucer makes it in order to reappropriate the authority John's appropriation implicitly grants the lay.

Moreover, by applying this principle of appropriation to a fable, Chaucer takes it to the furthest reaches of lay discourse, capturing for his text the figural power of Christian exegesis traditionally reserved for the recuperation of the Divine.[65] That he doesn't name the doctrinal moral he claims for his text marks a crucial difference between it and the moralized fables on which it is patterned. It is certainly true that it is possible to go back to the narrative and apply to it equivalences gleaned from commentaries, other moralized fables, or bestiaries, where the Cock represents the priesthood, or mankind, for example, and the fox represents the devil. But that is only because these equivalences are made explicit in such texts, so that the clerical moralizers who compiled them realized the doctrinal

---

[64] *Policraticus*, III, viii.
[65] For a fuller discussion, see "The Authority of Fable," 49–55.

could not be taken for granted, but had to be continually rearticulated and reimposed. Chaucer's refusal to make the doctrinal
authority he claims explicit is a difference that cannot be ignored.
Indeed, it is from this difference that the tale draws its ideological
power.

The doctrinal warrant it claims remains continually deferred. The
deferral enables it both to draw authority from the clerical, and to
maintain its lay specificity. To the extent the tale needs a single,
global moral, the deferral provides it: all writing is doctrinal. This
claim occurs at the very end of the tale; it is connected, albeit
tenuously, to the narrative; and it is more global than the series of
practical morals which immediately precede it. In short, it is
everything a reader might reasonably expect in a moral. If it has
seemed incomplete or ironic to previous scholarship, that is because
previous scholars have failed to recognize that the authorizing power
of the claim that all writing is doctrinal lies precisely in its openendedness.

Viewing the tale's ending in this way, as an authorizing strategy,
enables us to move beyond it to the specificities of the narrative. That
narrative is very much a story about the authority of utterance: who
has it, where it comes from, and how it is maintained. As is
appropriate in a tale which will proclaim all writing to be subsumed
under a single authority, authority in this narrative has a single
shape. It is patriarchal and monarchical; its position is occupied by
Chauntecleer. This position will constrain utterance throughout the
tale, though the continual tendency of most utterances – Pertelote's,
the fox's, and even Chauntecleer's – is away from it. Chauntecleer is
threatened throughout by the discourse of his subordinates, first by
Pertelote's dismissal of dreams, and then by the fox's flattery.
Moreover, it is his own utterance that nearly does him in: crowing at
the wrong time is what enables the fox to capture him. Despite this
continual movement away from the authoritative position in which
Chauntecleer begins, by the end the narrative has returned him to it.

It may seem a bit ludicrous to speak of Chauntecleer as patriarchal
and monarchical, so I should stress that I am not describing his
"character" so much as I am describing the position that character
occupies in the narrative. It is true Chauntecleer is nothing more
than a talking rooster. Yet one makes sense of a beast fable in the first
instance not by appealing to zoology, but by appealing to the social
categories the narrative imposes on its animal characters. Chaucer

makes Chauntecleer the voice of authority in the barnyard community he inhabits, and he qualifies that authority as male and royal.
Thinking of a rooster as a royal obviously involves ironic displacements that Chaucer exploits at every opportunity. Nevertheless, the
position Chauntecleer occupies continues to structure the narrative
even as the narrative demonstrates his comic inappropriateness to it.
Authority as male and royal is the status quo from which the
narrative begins and to which it returns.

The narrative is in two parts: the dream debate, where Chauntecleer's authority as male is threatened by the female discourse of
Pertelote, and the capture, where his authority as ruler is almost
destroyed by the flattery of the fox.[66] Both parts are drawn from the
Renardian tradition and from one of its forerunners, Marie de
France's *Fables*. In previous versions the tale is a single, continuous
whole. Chaucer bifurcates it by making two changes in the previous
versions. First, he shifts the role of protagonist from Renart to
Chauntecleer (changing Renart's name to Russell in the process to
emphasize the shift). Second, he makes Chauntecleer's dream the
occasion for dramatizing two opposite modes of reading, male and
female. The narrative is thus broken up into two discrete assaults on
a single discursive authority embodied in Chauntecleer, with the first
assault the ostensible precondition for the second.

By initially locating Chauntecleer's authority in his superiority to
Pertelote, Chaucer gives the tale, as Sheila Delany has argued, a
more decidedly misogynist cast than its predecessors.[67] The reason for
this shift becomes clearer if we consider the differences between
Chaucer's audience and the audience for the Renardian tradition
from which the tale is appropriated. The Renardian tradition was
produced for the lesser provincial French nobility of the 12th and
13th centuries, a subclass with an embattled relation to the reigning
social forces of Church and Crown.[68] Continually pressured by the
growing hegemony of the French and British monarchies, and the
growing international hegemony of the Church, it found an ironic
legitimation in the incessant anti-monarchical and anti-clerical
machinations of the outlaw Renart. Renart's machinations, his
engins, are discursive ruses which consist of initially acceding to the

---

[66] In what follows, I rely heavily on Robert A. Pratt, "Three Old French Sources of the
Nonnes Preestes Tale," *Speculum* 47 (1972): 422–44, 646–68. What I have called the
"capture" Pratt calls the "fable."
[67] Sheila Delany, "'*Mulier est hominis confusio*': Chaucer's Anti-popular *Nun's Priest's Tale*,"
Mosaic 17 (1984), 1–8.   [68] J. F. Flinn, "Littérature bourgeoise."

royal authority of Noble the Lion, or the spiritual authority of a series of ecclesiastical figures, then renouncing them as soon as he is safely beyond their reach, usually in his impregnable castle Maupertius. (In Branche I, for example, called to Noble's court to account for his crimes, he publicly repents and dons the attire of a pilgrim. Once he is safely out of the court, though not out of earshot, he tears off his clothing and reviles Noble and the Church in the most corrosive terms.)

Chauntecleer's discourse can often be as flagrantly self-interested as Renart's, but it is always under greater constraint. Renart's falsity is inventive; he is literally a plotter, a spinner of false tales, a fabulist. Chauntecleer is only an interpreter – of the heavens, of dreams, of previous textual authority. His misstatements are misreadings, not fictions invented out of whole cloth. He speaks to Chaucer's broader ruling-class audience, which instead of being excluded from ruling-class power, is offered access to it precisely as political authority to be discursively defined. Chauntecleer's status as an interpreter enables him to become for this audience a figure of authority rather than an outlaw.

At the same time the social authority which Chauntecleer fictively represents already has particular social characteristics. If he is to represent this authority convincingly, even in fictional terms, he must in some way share its characteristics. This helps explain why Chaucer defines Chauntecleer's interpretive power as sexual power. As I have already suggested, sexual dominance was the *sine qua non* of noble power in the Middle Ages, for the later medieval nobility was constituted primarily by primogeniture. Defining Chauntecleer's authority in terms of his maleness gives Chaucer's audience access to noble power through its most basic and therefore broadest constituent. Introduced against the background of the widow's "narwe cotage" and her straitened circumstances, Chauntecleer is a hyperbolic masculine splendor. His comb is redder than coral, his bill black as jet, his claws whiter than the lily, his legs azure, and his body like burnished gold. Holding seven hens "in his governaunce," he is a fecund source of male power in a female world impoverished precisely by its lack of a man.

This male power is epitomized in his peerless crowing.

> ... she hadde a cok, hight Chauntecleer.
> In al the land, of crowyng nas his peer.
> His voys was murier than the murie orgon

On messe-days that in the chirche gon.
Wel sikerer was his crowyng in his logge
Than is a clokke or an abbey orlogge.
By nature he knew ech ascencioun
Of the equynoxial in thilke toun;
For whan degrees fiftene weren ascended,
Thanne crew he that it myghte nat been amended.

(VII, 2849–58)

In the figure of Chauntecleer's crowing Chaucer has translated the dilemma of the *Nun's Priest's Tale* to its narrowest compass. On the one hand, the crowing is nothing more than the instinctive behavior of a rooster. On the other, Chaucer presents it as an act of interpretation, making it a tiny allegory for lay discourse – for discourse, that is, that derives its authority from without. Chauntecleer's reading of equinoxial ascensions translates a cosmic text into the terms of human time. If his crowing is more certain than such interpretive machines as clocks or horologes, that is because of the fidelity with which he reproduces his text. In "Whan fiftene degrees weren ascended / Thanne crew he," "Thanne" follows "whan" with an immediacy that has an almost logical force: the instant Chauntecleer sees the sun rise to the proper point, he declares the beginning of day to the community.

The immediacy of his crowing reinforces the etymological sense of his name: Chauntecleer, the clear singer, whose transparent voice contains nothing but the external reality which authorizes it. At the same time, the crowing never ceases to be crowing, that is, never ceases to be the completely inarticulate noise of an animal. But this doubleness enhances the force of the allegory rather than defeating it. Chauntecleer's crowing works as a model of lay discourse because it is both faithful to external authority and irreducibly distant from it.

The combination of these two characteristics, fidelity and referential distance are also what enable the model to structure the rest of the narrative. Chauntecleer's position can be threatened because its authority is not inherent. He is open to temptation. Pertelote will tempt him to evade the prophetic authority of his dream, and the fox will tempt him to evade the authority of the heavens by crowing blindly. Yet he can restore himself through the same sort of evasion, flattering the fox as the fox had flattered him. Chauntecleer's authority can practice evasion because like all lay authority, it is secondary and derivative, evasive in its very essence.

This propensity is dramatized first in the dream debate, where it is increasingly linked to Chauntecleer's gender. The debate begins with a challenge to his masculinity. When he retells his frightening dream, Pertelote mocks his fear. Like D. W. Robertson's Wife of Bath, Pertelote is a carnal reader. Citing Cato, she dismisses dreams as mere symptoms of indigestion and offers Chauntecleer a laxative. He responds to this provocation with an exposition of the authority of dreams that is staggering by contrast. To Pertelote's single authority, he cites three exempla, a life of Saint Kenelm, Macrobius's *Dream of Scipio*, the Book of Daniel, the story of Joseph from the Book of Exodus, and the stories of Croesus and Andromache. His defense is at once authoritative and evasive: authoritative because it treats the issue of dreams correctly, and evasive because that is the wrong question. Instead of considering the implications of his dream, he is distracted by Pertelote into demonstrating his sexual superiority. When the debate concludes, and he leaves his perch to feather Pertelote twenty times, and tread her "eke as ofte," he is simply duplicating bodily the subjugation that has already taken place discursively.[69]

Moreover, despite its carnality, even this evasion begins with an act of interpretation. Chauntecleer concludes his exposition of dreams and announces his desire for love-play by mistranslating a Latin authority:

> Now let us speke of myrthe, and stynte al this.
> Madame Pertelote, so have I blis,
> Of o thyng God hath sent me large grace;
> For whan I se the beautee of youre face,
> Ye been so scarlet reed aboute youre yen,
> It maketh al my drede for to dyen;
> For al so siker as *In principio*,
> *Mulier est hominis confusio* –
> Madame, the sentence of this Latyn is,
> "Woman is mannes joye and al his blis"...   (VII, 3157–66)

Mulier est hominis confusio is the beginning of a sardonic definition of woman so widely circulated in the Middle Ages that Susan Kavanaugh, in her notes to the tale, calls it "almost proverbial."[70] As given in the *Speculum historiale* of Vincent of Beauvais, the complete definition runs as follows:

---

[69] Ian Bishop, "*The Nun's Priest's Tale* and the Liberal Arts," *Review of English Studies*, n.s. 30 (1979): 266.   [70] *Riverside Chaucer*, 939.

What is woman? The confusion of man. An insatiable beast. A continual trouble. An unceasing battle. The wreck of the continent man. A human slave.[71]

Chaucer's deployment of the definition makes its irony double-edged. On the one hand, it serves as an ironic summation of the entire first half of the tale: what has been presented is the confusion of a male by a female. Yet for that very reason the ultimate target of the definition is not Chauntecleer but Pertelote. To the extent that Chauntecleer's invocation and mistranslation of the definition undercut his pretension to authority, they also illustrate the definition's essential truth. Chauntecleer is a figure of ridicule at this point not because he has not resisted Pertelote, but because he has not resisted her enough. He chooses to luxuriate in the superiority of his position rather than confront the threat posed to that position which his dream foretells.

It should be noted as well that Chaucer presents this evasion in very precise terms as a breakdown between sacral and lay authority. When Chauntecleer claims that the proposition *Mulier est hominis confusio* is "also siker as *In principio*," he is presenting it as a second *Verbum*; that is, he is presenting it as a truth as certain and originary as *In principio erat verbum*, or *In principio creavit Deus caelum et terram*. Yet *Mulier est hominis confusio* can never have the stability of the Divine Word because it expresses not stability but confusion. The confusion extends even to the manner in which the Divine Word is here invoked. The fact that the abbreviated phrase *In principio* can stand for either the opening of John, or the opening of Genesis, or both at once, is a sign of its vulgarization. The repetition of these sentences had for Chaucer's audience become such a regular part of everyday routine, that their sacral authority had become overlaid by the sheer fact of their continual reiteration.

From this perspective, Chauntecleer's mistranslation is simply a more extreme case of the inevitable loss that marks the passage from the sacral to the lay. The lay translation of the sacral will always be a mistranslation: while Chauntecleer's mistranslation may expose the contradiction of his position, it does not invalidate his authority. Since laicization never fully commands the authority it claims, the simple fact of Chauntecleer's pretension is not less significant than its

---

[71] XI, 71. Cited in Carleton Brown, "Mulier est Hominis Confusio", *Modern Language Notes* 35 (1920), 479–82.

failures. Chaucer clearly expects his audience to find Chauntecleer's exuberance appealing even as he undercuts it. The conclusion of the dream debate is a triumph of what one critic has inelegantly but accurately called Chauntecleer's "cockiness."[72] If his dream threatens to displace him from his authoritative position, the energy which he devotes to subjugating Pertelote reinforces his position even if it fails to meet the threat. Perhaps it is for this reason that Chaucer twice calls him royal in the last ten lines of this half of the tale.

> Real he was, he was namoore aferd.
> He fethered Pertelote twenty tyme,
> And trad hire eke as ofte er it was pryme.
>
> ...
>
> Thus roial, as a prince is in his halle,
> Leve I this Chauntecleer in his pasture,
> And after wol I telle his aventure. (VII, 3176–78, 3184–86)

The note of triumph in these lines is hyperbolic and ironic in the extreme; it is triumphal nonetheless.

Moreover, the hyperbole looks ahead to the actual moment of crisis, which is staged more straightforwardly as the crisis of a prince. Flattery was for the Middle Ages a predominantly political problem; making the fox a flatterer casts Chauntecleer in the role of a prince or a great lord, about to be trapped in the discursive exchange of his own court. *Renart le Contrefait*, Chaucer's most immediate extant source for the tale, opens with a scene at the court of Noble the Lion in which Renart plays the flatterer.[73] Behind this Renardian topos lies the didactic tradition of the *Fürstenspiegel*, a point the Nun's Priest emphasizes by pausing to warn "ye lordes" that "many a fals flatour / Is in youre courtes" (VII, 3325–26). John of Salisbury presents flattery (*adulatoria*) as one of the chief means by which courtiers manipulate the power of their superiors, and the foremost agency of the *concupiscentia* which destroys the public welfare. He makes flattery the cause of Rome's decline, claiming that its end (*finis*) is the destruction of liberty and the promotion of tyranny.[74] Such theoretical discussions frequently found practical issue in accusations of bad counsel, one of the commonest, and probably one of the safest, ways to complain about a medieval king. This line of attack was used

---

[72] Shallers, "*The Nun's Priest's Tale*," 332.
[73] *Le Roman de Renart le Contrefait*, ed. Gaston Raynaud and Henri Lemaitre (1914; repr., Geneva: Slatkine Reprints, 1975), 5–9, lines 415–788.
[74] *Policraticus*, III, iv-x; VIII, xvii.

consistently against Richard II almost from the moment he began to rule on his own in 1380 to his deposition in 1399. The most serious threat before 1399 came in exactly this form in the Merciless Parliament of 1389. The thirty-nine charges offered by the Lords Appellant, though actually directed against Richard's concentration of royal power within his household, were framed entirely as an attempt to protect him from the encroachment of his personal advisors.[75]

In both theory and practice, the concept of flattery often served the same function it does in this tale: to stake out a zone of completely degraded, completely false discourse against which more authoritative political discourse could be defined. As the flatterer, the fox is able to displace Chauntecleer by convincing him that political authority could be self-contained and inherent. He ingratiates himself by praising the inherent beauty of Chauntecleer's voice and linking it to "my lorde youre fader." When he asks, "konne ye youre fader countrefete?" (VII, 3321) he is tempting Chauntecleer to claim a place in the artificially inflated patrilineage he has just constructed.

Though both characters will continue to communicate in the degraded language of flattery throughout this scene, they do so under severe discursive constraint. The fox must flatter Chauntecleer by appealing to his lineage: he cannot imagine a new form of power; he can only manipulate the proper form. Similarly, the only difference between the authorized and unauthorized versions of Chauntecleer's crowing is a negative one: in the unauthorized version he closes his eyes. Moreover, the authority Chauntecleer abdicates remains ironically present throughout the scene in the form of the resultant anarchy.

In a social world where authority has a single shape, the displacement of Chauntecleer can have no other result but anarchy. The pursuit that follows his capture draws every member of his community, including the bees who swarm from their hive, away from their accustomed places. Chaucer compares the mob first to fiends in hell and then to the English Rising of 1381.

> So hydous was the noyse – a, benedicitee! –
> Certes, he Jakke Straw and his meynee
> Ne made nevere shoutes half so shrille
> Whan that they wolden any Flemyng kille,
> As thilke day was maad upon the fox. (VII, 3393–97)

[75] Anthony Tuck, *Richard II and the English Nobility* (London: Edward Arnold, 1973), 122–23.

The reference to Jack Straw, a leader in the Rising, is one of very few topical allusions in the *Canterbury Tales*. It is usually dismissed as a curiosity, but viewed in relation to Chauntecleer's ruse immediately following it acquires a somewhat larger significance.

> This cok, that lay upon the foxes bak,
> In al his drede unto the fox he spak,
> And seyde, "Sire, if that I were as ye,
> Yet sholde I seyn, as wys God helpe me,
> 'Turneth agayn, ye proude cherles alle!
> A verray pestilence upon yow falle!
> Now I am come unto the wodes syde;
> Maugree youre heed, the cok shal heere abyde.'"
>
> (VII, 3405–12)

When Chauntecleer suggests the fox address this anarchic mob as proud churls, and command them to turn back he tempts the fox to speak with the authority of a prince. The turning point in the Rising occurred when Richard, then twelve years old, went to negotiate with the rebels massed at Smithfield and convinced them to disperse. Most of the chroniclers, irrespective of their general view of Richard, portray his role in the Rising as that of the sole authoritative voice, decisively pacifying an anarchic mob through the sheer assertion of his privileged position in public discourse. The fullest example of this view is Walsingham's. After Wat Tyler is mortally wounded during negotiations and a riot seems imminent,

the king with marvellous presence of mind and courage for so young a man, spurred his horse towards the commons and rode around them, saying "What are you doing? Surely you do not wish to fire on your own king? Do not attack me and do not regret the death of that traitor and ruffian. For I will be your king, your captain and your leader. Follow me into that field where you can have all things you would like to ask for."

The mob follows him to a nearby open field, "before they had fully decided whether they ought to kill the king or be quiet and return home," where they are easily surrounded by an armed band hastily summoned by the mayor of London.[76]

In effect, Chauntecleer invites the fox to make the same gesture as Richard – to restore order through the power of his voice. True to his character as flatterer, the fox cannot resist the prospect of completing his appropriation of Chauntecleer's authority. The attempt to

---

[76] Thomas Walsingham, *Historia Anglicana*, I, 456–67, excerpted and tr. in *The Peasants' Revolt of 1381*, ed. R. B. Dobson (London: Macmillan, 1970), 178–79.

complete the appropriation immediately exposes its momentary and illusory character. As soon as the fox opens his mouth to speak Chauntecleer escapes, and the power he had apparently appropriated disappears.

It is a final irony that Chauntecleer must resort to flattery in order to escape the Flatterer. Like the other ironies in this tale, however, this one also serves the status quo which structures the narrative. While the fox's flattery simply misconstrues the authority Chauntecleer represents, and has no other aim than anarchy, the effect of Chauntecleer's flattery is restorative. It forces the fox to face the impossibility of any form of authority other then the one he would destroy, and ultimately returns Chauntecleer's world to the position of stability from which the narrative began. Chauntecleer's descent into the language of flattery is justified by the authority he represents. Chauntecleer's descent is also Chaucer's: this final act of flattery – this final ungrounded linguistic figuration – is necessary to secure the coherence of Chaucer's narrative. It is only fitting that a narrative which aspires to achieve the stability of Christian authority through the detour of fable should turn on an instance of linguistic evasion. Like Chauntecleer's, Chaucer's discourse is authoritative in its very evasions, its competence enabled by an antecedent structure it steadfastly resists.

Chaucer never relinquishes the shifting, contradictory space between the allegorical and the ironic, for the contradictions which constrain his authority are the very conditions which make it possible. Never fully exemplary, the tale is always more than fable. Its comic protagonist is a monarchical figure, whose authority is defined as the textual, interpretive transmission of a law beyond himself, whose power is upheld by that authority, even when he transgresses it. This reconciliation between textual authority and political power is fictive yet crucial. It has been implied from the beginning in Chaucer's many affirmations of narrative, which continually assume narrative can produce authority from within its own discursive logic; that is, fictively. From this perspective, the tale's modernist elevation is justified. It "epitomizes the *Canterbury Tales*" in that the authority of narrative, which is everywhere else assumed, and frequently demonstrated, is here given its broadest range.[77] That this authority never becomes entirely explicit, nor receives much notice from Chaucer's

[77] Muscatine, *Chaucer and the French Tradition*, 238.

immediate posterity, fits perfectly its indirect, ironic role. Chaucer's more direct claims of authority still depend on it. It is precisely because his explorations of narrative are so thorough that he is able to reclaim it as a medium of lay authority. By extension, the authority he assumes for the fifteenth century can be traced to these explorations as well. Chaucer's ironic, self-conscious awareness of narrative's textual complexity, far from being an aspect of his poetry that eluded the fifteenth century, was one of the preconditions for everything it did.

CHAPTER 9

Bad examples: Gower's Confessio Amantis

My account of Chaucer as a poet profoundly engaged with the source and nature of his moral authority clearly necessitates a reevaluation of his contemporary John Gower. Modern scholars have generally distinguished the two on the basis of Gower's interest in morality, which, they have felt, Chaucer did not share. If this account ignores a good deal of what happens in Chaucer's own poetry, it also ignores his view of Gower. It was Chaucer, after all, who first described him as the "moral Gower", even if that honorific was to become "the very stick" by which his later reputation "was to be beaten,"[1] as Derek Pearsall has recently observed. As the post-Romantic aversion to didacticism hardened into modernist dogma, so did Gower's marginalization, on the grounds of his status as a moralist. This marginalization has persisted despite his considerable rehabilitation in other respects in the last three decades. The early work of Derek Pearsall and John Burrow helped expand the appreciation of Gower's narrative artistry which began with C. S. Lewis.[2] More recently, R. F. Yeager has devoted a book-length study to Gower's poetics, and a number of critics have called attention to his abilities as an ironist.[3]

---

[1] Derek Pearsall, "The Gower Tradition," in Gower's "Confessio Amantis": Responses and Reassessments, ed. A. J. Minnis (Cambridge: D. S. Brewer, 1983), 179–97, esp. 179–80 and 194–95. The essays in the recent collection Chaucer and Gower: Difference, Mutuality, Exchange, ed. R. F. Yeager (Victoria, BC: English Literary Studies, 1991) explore the complexities of the relations between the two poets with a depth and subtlety that has not been achieved before. Nevertheless, in my opinion most of the contributors still overestimate the differences.

[2] C. S. Lewis, The Allegory of Love: A Study in Medieval Tradition (Oxford: Oxford University Press, 1936), 198–222; Pearsall, "Gower's Narrative Art," PMLA 81 (1966) 475–84; Burrow, Ricardian Poetry, 29–32, 83–85.

[3] R. F. Yeager, John Gower's Poetic: The Search for a New Arion (Cambridge: D. S. Brewer, 1990); David Hiscoe, "The Ovidian Comic Strategy of Gower's Confessio Amantis," Philological Quarterly 64 (1985), 367–85; Linda Barney Burke, "Genial Gower: Laughter in the Confessio Amantis," and James Dean, "Gather Ye Rosebuds: Gower's Comic Reply to Jean de Meun," both in John Gower: Recent Readings, ed. R. F. Yeager (Kalamazoo: Medieval Institute Publications, 1984), 139–63, and 21–37.

John Fisher, Patrick Gallacher, Masayoshi Itô, and Russell Peck have all stressed the subtlety and unity of Gower's philosophical and moral outlook.[4] Nevertheless, Gower studies during this period has not been successful in its oft-declared goal of moving Gower out from under Chaucer's shadow. In my opinion, this is because the field has been too reluctant to challenge the modernist antithesis between poetry and morality upon which the invidious comparison to Chaucer depends. Gower is interested in poetry as a form of moralizing, to be sure, but he is just as interested in moralizing as a form of poetry, that is, as a rhetorical project. Michael D. Kuczynski has recently suggested that the *Confessio Amantis* is an exercise in "medieval metaethics – the branch of moral philosophy concerned with the nature of moral language."[5] Whatever the justice of the modern term "metaethics" as applied to medieval moral philosophy, Kuczynski points to a fact that even Gower's supporters have not sufficiently appreciated. Gower is every bit as searching and self-conscious about poetic language as Chaucer. The desire to consign him to the status of Chaucer's foil has everything to do with the persistence of modernist ideals of poetic authority, and very little to do with Gower's actual status in the literary culture of later medieval England.

For that status we could do worse than return to Chaucer's other explicit engagement with Gower's work, the playful allusion to the *Confessio Amantis* in the Introduction to the *Man of Law's Tale*. The Man of Law speaks censoriously "Of thilke wikke ensample of Canacee ... / Or ellis of Tyro Appollonius," two tales prominent in the *Confessio*; he declares no "swiche unkynde abhomynacions" will be found in Chaucer's *oeuvre* (II, 78, 81, 86–89). For nearly two

---

[4] John H. Fisher, *John Gower: Moral Philosopher and Friend of Chaucer* (New York: New York University Press, 1964); Patrick Gallacher, *Love, the Word, and Mercury: A Reading of John Gower's "Confessio Amantis"* (Albuquerque: University of New Mexico Press, 1975); Masayoshi Itô, *John Gower: Medieval Poet* (Tokyo: Shinozaki Shorin, 1976); Russell A. Peck *Kingship and Common Profit in Gower's "Confessio Amantis"* (Carbondale and Edwardsville: Southern Illinois Press, 1978). This brief summary by no means exhausts recent work on Gower. For a more comprehensive bibliography, see R. F. Yeager, "The Poetry of John Gower: Important Studies, 1960–1983," in *Fifteenth-Century Studies*, ed. R. F. Yeager (Hamden: Archon Books, 1984), 3–28; and John H. Fisher, R. Wayne Hamm, Peter Beidler, and R. F. Yeager, "John Gower" in *A Manual of the Writings in Middle English 1050–1500*, ed. Albert E. Hartung (Hamden: Connecticut Academy of Arts and Sciences, 1986), vol. 7. See also Peter Nicholson, *An Annotated Index to the Commentary on Gower's "Confessio Amantis"* (Binghamton: Medieval and Renaissance Texts and Studies, 1989).

[5] Michael D. Kuczynski, "Gower's Metaethics," in *Recent Readings*, ed. Yeager, 189.

hundred years, these lines were cited as evidence of a feud between the two poets.[6] While most scholars now view that possibility as apocryphal, considerable ingenuity has nevertheless been devoted to making these lines into some form of put-down of Gower's didacticism. For if taken at face value, they would seem to make Chaucer the prude, and Gower the fearless challenger of convention. However, if we reject the modernist antithesis between poetry and morality that makes such ingenuity necessary, it becomes easier to take these lines at face value, and that is exactly what I propose to do.

They are playful to be sure: they are spoken by a character given to self-inflation, and form part of a discussion in which Chaucer aims for self-deprecation through hyperbole. Its pretext is that the Man of Law will have difficulty finding a tale to tell because Chaucer has told them all: "And if he have noght seyd hem, leve brother, / In o book, he hath seyd hem in another" (II, 51–52). Nevertheless, within this playfulness, the term "wikke ensample" points to a significant difference between the two poets within their shared project. Chaucer does avoid fully confronting incest, even where he implicitly raises the issue.[7] And although he also uses wicked examples, he tends to treat them decorously, as illustrating the downturn of Fortune, or as the foil for the suffering of a figure like Griselda. Gower, by contrast, displays in the *Confessio Amantis* a taste for the lurid that might make Stephen King squeamish – not only incest, but adultery, rape, infanticide, parricide, beheadings, mutilations, and all other manner of violence and brutality, up to and including the story of Rosamund, the queen who murders her husband Albinus, after he serves her wine in a goblet made from the top of her father's skull (I, 2459–2646).

This taste for the lurid is only the more spectacular aspect of Gower's general predisposition toward explicitness. Where Chaucer claims moral authority more indirectly, for the most part discrediting clerical tradition and then speaking its authority in his own voice, Gower combines anti-clerical critique with a more explicit celebration of lay political authority. Such explicitness requires a more searching exploration of the disorder against which lay authority is directed. In this sense Chaucer's implicitness actually keeps lay

---

[6] Fisher, *John Gower*, 1–36; Carolyn Dinshaw, "Rivalry, Rape and Manhood: Gower and Chaucer," in *Gower and Chaucer*, ed. Yeager, 130–34. Dinshaw argues that eighteenth- and nineteenth-century scholars constructed the feud as part of an attempt to gender Chaucer's literary authority as male.

[7] See Dinshaw, "Chaucer's Sexual Poetics," 88–112; and 187–88 above.

poetic authority closer to the clerical authority it displaces, although
we only recognize this fact with difficulty. For Chaucer's appropriation of Christian authority remains much closer to our own, to
that translation of Christian transcendence hidden in modernity's
continuing conviction that the literary is defined by a fundamental
disjunction with the historical. Gower's explicit connection of poetic
authority to the authority of kingship has made his didacticism more
prominent to modern readers, but it has also obscured for those same
readers the extent to which this version of authority depends on the
wicked, or negative example, and all the self-conscious exploration of
narrative which that requires.

SIMULATING THE VOICE OF GOD (I): THE ANTI-CLERICAL CRITIQUE

The *Confessio Amantis* presents itself as an exemplum collection,
announcing its dependence on the form more directly than does the
Canterbury Tales. Nevertheless, Gower's vernacular appropriation is
every bit as complex as Chaucer's. He draws on the Latin tradition
in both its sermon-exemplum and the public-exemplum forms, and
effects the combination by drawing on a number of other laicizing
traditions at the same time. First, there is the same penitential
tradition that Chaucer draws on in the *Parson's Tale*, which Gower
draws upon even more fully. The *Confessio Amantis* disposes its
exempla according to the penitential framework of the Seven Deadly
Sins and their subcategories, specifically recalling *Handlyng Synne*, a
text where the penitential and sermon exemplum traditions converge.[8] Yet the penitential framework itself emerges in a dialogue
between Gower, in the persona of *Amans*, and his confessor, Genius,
the priest of love. As exempla embedded in a dialogue, this
arrangement recalls the monastic tradition of Gregory and Cesarius
of Heisterbach, but the priesthood of Genius is a specific legacy of the
School of Chartres, which comes to Gower through the *Romance of the
Rose*.

This crossing and recrossing of the boundary between the clerical
and lay poses an interpretive problem whose dimensions have not yet
been sufficiently acknowledged. Is Genius primarily a priest whose

---

[8] Cf. D. W. Robertson, "The Cultural Tradition of *Handlyng Synne*," *Speculum* 22 (1947),
162–85.

sententiae can be taken more or less at face value, and whom Gower uses to establish a systematic, harmonious moral vision? Or is he primarily an embodiment of the erotic, who appropriates the penitential tradition to endow secular love with spiritual authority? Whether we accept the first alternative, as many recent Gower scholars have, or follow C. S. Lewis and accept the second, we have still left unexplained the figural complexity which impels us to the choice in the first place. This difficulty characterizes the poem at every level of specificity. Gower breaks the penitential frame with Book VII, which he presents as a compact *Fürstenspiegel,* and for which Genius frankly acknowledges he lacks the proper discursive authority. The eighth book, which, according to the usual taxonomy should deal with lechery, focuses on incest instead. At a more local level, as many commentators have observed, the poem's exempla frequently fail to fit the *sententiae* Genius assigns to them.[9] Gower's detractors have traditionally assigned these apparent inconsistencies to his incompetence as a poet. More recent accounts have resisted such broad impositions of anachronistic standards of poetic competence, and have frequently provided philosophical justification for Gower's rhetorical disjunctions, rightly arguing, for example, that Book VII is central to moral concerns that run throughout the poem.[10] Nevertheless, the very justice of these accounts threatens to obscure the rhetorical disjunction they are intended to explain. Book VII *is* a disruption of the penitential frame, and a rather spectacular one at that. Like the other disruptions, it should not be dismissed, but it should not be explained away either. Any attempt to impose a single, unified vision on the poem belies its actual rhetorical complexity.

It seems more promising to take this fascination with disruption as itself part of the poem's point. For it enables Gower to justify both the need for lay authority generally, and the specifically textual dimension with which poetry provides such authority. To the extent moral disorder characterizes the Church, it demonstrates the need for the sort of order provided by the king. But to the extent such disorder also afflicts kingship, it demonstrates the indispensability of the moral correction that comes from the poet. In the opening sections of the poem, from the Prologue to the end of Book II, Gower is especially

---

[9] For example, see Pearsall, "Gower's Narrative Art," *PMLA,* 475–84.

[10] Fisher, *Gower;* Peck, *Kingship and Common Profit;* Gallacher, *Love, the Word, and Mercury.*

concerned to demonstrate the necessity of lay authority by means of anti-clerical critique. But he is just as concerned to demonstrate the irreducibly double nature of such authority, the interdependence between poet and prince, and the extent to which the prince's authority is always discursively constructed.

There are two prologues to this poem: the one properly so called, and the first two hundred odd lines of Book I, which establish the frame tale at the court of Venus, and introduce both Genius and Amans as confessor and confessant. Together, the two prologues sketch out Gower's indictment of clerical authority and the form of lay authority he offers in its place. Two tales at the end of Book II, Boniface, and the Donation of Constantine, recapitulate this critique in narrative terms.

The Prologue contains both an estates-satire and a dedication to a royal figure – Richard II in the first recension, and Henry Boling-broke in the second. It begins and ends with affirmations of the authority of poetry. The beginning recapitulates John of Salisbury's opening to the *Policraticus*.

> Of hem that writen ous tofore
> The bokes duelle, and we therfore
> Ben tawht of that was write tho:
> Forthi good is that we also
> In oure tyme among ous hiere
> Do wryte of newe som matiere,
> Essampled of these olde wyse
> So that it myhte in such a wyse,
> Whan we ben dede and elleswhere,
> Beleve to the worldes eere
> In tyme comende after this.   (Prol., 1–10)

In this passage's broadest outlines Gower simply repeats John's position: writing has the power to convey authority from the past to the present. But he gives this notion a distinctly laicist cast, coming close to the position which Boccaccio, in the *persona* of Petrarch, stakes out in Book VIII of the *De casibus*.[11] The line "Essampled of these olde wyse," can mean either "drawing *exempla* from these old books," as indeed the *Confessio Amantis* does, almost exclusively, or "following the example of older writers." To the extent the first meaning applies, Gower repeats John. But to the extent he also

---

[11] See 131–33 above.

implies the second meaning, he is foregrounding the exemplary authority of the new vernacular tradition itself, and the importance of its powers of transmission.

This new form of authority provides a decisive counterpoint to the depiction of contemporary decline which occupies much of the Prologue. Following the usual conceit of the estates-satire, Gower argues throughout that the present is in a state of moral crisis unknown in the past. But he also suggests, more implicitly, that the older forms of sustaining moral authority are now less efficacious than they once were. He continually holds out the possibility that the new form of authority he is proposing, this "bok" in "oure englissh," in which "fewe men endite," which goes "the middel weie ... / Somewhat of lust, somewhat of lore," can succeed where the others have failed (Prol., 16–23). The suggestion is made tentatively and almost apologetically. He has taken on this task because someone has to:

> If noman write hou that it stode,
> The pris of hem that weren goode
> Scholde, as who seith, a gret partie
> Be lost ... (Prol., 41–44)

The authority of the past now lies with him, a "burel," or lay "clerk" (Prol., 52), and his status as lay clerk makes the political contours of his "middel weie" clearer. Gower intends nothing less than a clericalization of the vernacular, the production of a lay textuality with an authority separate from but analogous to the Latin traditions of the Church.

His account of the Three Estates emphasizes the collapse of clerical authority. He spends at least three times as many lines on its failings as he does on the failings of the other two estates: 305 to 99 lines for temporal rulers and a scant 29 lines for the commons. Like Chaucer, he defines the Church's role as an exemplary one, and condemns the present Church for being more interested in temporal and institutional advantage than in serving as the "Mirour of ensamplerie," as it did in its earlier days. Anticipating the critique that will come later, he accuses the Church of coveting the temporal sword (242), of perverting the "tresor of the benefice" to its own avaricious purposes (314–20), and of involving itself in military adventures (243–77), and he presents the papal schism as the inevitable outcome of these failures (329–95).

In addition to being briefer, the accounts of the other two estates are less overt in assigning blame. Instead they dwell on the current lack of harmony and its dangers. In contrast to "the tyme passed," when "The privilege of regalie / Was sauf, and al the baronie / Worschiped was in his astat," now "the regnes ben divided" (Prol., 93–135). The commons, lacking leadership, are a barrel broken loose of its moorings or a stream overflowing its banks: "Where lawe lacketh, errour groweth" (Prol., 499–513). The solution is good counsel. Since every region ("climat") is subject to "blind fortune" the only hope for order is that

> ... the pouer
> Of hem that ben the worldes guides
> With good consail on alle sides
> Be kept upriht in such a wyse,
> That hate breke noght thassise
> Of love, which is al the chief
> To kepe a regne out of mischief.   (Prol., 144–50)

In the absence of a reliable clergy, such counsel must come from "burel" clerks like Gower, and the rest of the prologue affirms the importance of lay textual authority.

This is true even of the two dedications. Normally the occasion for the compiler of a *Fürstenspiegel* to display his dependence on the prince he is advising, these dedications tend to show the opposite, both in their content, and by the very fact there are two of them. Despite the attention the alternate dedications have long attracted, this is a point which is frequently missed. Most discussion has been concerned with what the dedications indicated, if anything, about Gower's own factional allegiances: more recent scholars being eager to clear Gower of the charge of political opportunism levelled at him by a hostile nineteenth century. Yet if it were possible to retain essentially the same poem, while changing the dedicatee, then it must be the case that Gower was more concerned with the general public and institutional aspect of kingship, and less interested, at this level of generality at any rate, with any particular king. These dedications place the *Confessio Amantis* in the tradition of the *Fürstenspiegel* as an act of public instruction. Their alternation should alert us to the fact Gower stresses the discursive construction of the monarch even more than the Latin *Fürstenspiegel* had. The substance of the dedications confirms this fact.

The dedication to Henry is brief and perfunctory. Although Gower substitutes a passage with the same number of lines as the longer dedication to Richard which he drops, only twelve of them address Henry. The rest provide an opportunity to expand the opening discussion on the importance of writing (Prol., 24–80). The dedication to Richard, while complimentary, comes nowhere near the flowery hyperbole that usually characterizes royal dedications. The setting is equally striking. Richard's charge to Gower does not occur at court, the nerve center of a monarch's sovereignty. It occurs instead on the much more indefinite space of the Thames river, where Richard's barge, though presumably grand, is one vessel among many, and he is only the current player in a much larger scheme of national destiny.

> As it bifel upon a tyde,
> As thing which scholde tho betyde, –
> Under the toun of newe Troye,
> Which tok of Brut his ferste joye,
> In Temse whan it was flowende
> As I be bote cam rowende,
> So as fortune hir tyme sette,
> My liege lord par chaunce I mette;
> And so befel, as I cam nyh,
> Out of my bot, whan he me syh,
> He bad me come in to his barge.   (Prol., *35–*45)

Gower goes out of his way to underline the incidental nature of this direction from Richard. He uses the word "bifel" twice in the space of ten lines, and the analogous formulae "as fortune hir tyme sette" and "par chaunce" twice in the space of two. The description of London as "the toun of newe Troye," and the citation of the eponymous Brut put this chance encounter on an epic footing – and indeed reactivate the Plantagenet connnection to Arthurian legend that goes back to Henry II – but they also diminish Richard's personal importance, and place the encounter more firmly in the realm of vernacular poetry.

The aquatic setting also anticipates the poetic domain of Arion, the figure with whom the Prologue ends. Arion was a seventh-century Greek poet, none of whose work survives. Sometimes credited with the invention of the dithyramb, his significance derives mainly from the myths that came to cluster around him. Ovid recounts these briefly in the *Fasti*, where Gower found them. Arion's most salient

characteristic was his power to defuse conflict through his song. As
Gower puts it, he sets the hind at peace with the lion, the wolf with
the sheep, the hare with the hound, and the lord with the commons
(Prol., 1053–67). Once, after having been cast overboard on a sea
journey, he avoided drowning by taming a dolphin and riding it
ashore.[12]

Gower invokes Arion after a discussion of Nebuchadnezzar's
Dream, which gives the estates-satire motif of current crisis the
dimensions of an apocalypse:

> And now to loke on every side,
> A man may se the world divide,
> The werres ben so general
> Among the cristene overal,
> That every man now secheth wreche...   (Prol. 895–99)

In his dream, Nebuchadnezzar sees a figure with a head and neck of
gold, an upper torso of silver, stomach and thighs of brass, legs of
steel, and feet of a mixture of steel and earth. Gower reinterprets
Daniel's explanation of the dream as a prophetic projection of a
universal history of decline, with each metal corresponding to
succeeding ages, each less worthy than the one before. He concludes
in the present.

> Thapostel writ unto ous alle
> And seith upon ous is falle
> Thende of the world; so may we knowe,
> This ymage is nyh overthrowe,
> Be which this world was signified,
> That whilom was so magnefied,
> And now is old and fieble and vil,
> Ful of meschief and of peril,
> And stant divided ek also
> Lich to the feet that were so,
> As I tolde of the Statue above.   (Prol., 881–91)

Ostensibly sacral, this view of secular history makes the current crisis
the last stage in an inevitable process of historical decline. Yet Gower
follows this view with the supplication for a new Arion. As the
representative at once of poetry and the pre-sacral authority of the
classical, Arion stands in stark contrast to Daniel, an exegetical and

---

[12] Yeager, *Gower's Poetic*, 238–39.

clerical figure drawn out of biblical tradition. Where clerical tradition can offer only a vision of secular decay, Arion raises the possibility of social harmony effected from within human history by the power of poetry.

This claim begins as a supplication: "Bot wolde god that now were on / An other such as Arion" (Prol., 1053–54). The supplication is a compressed version of Gower's central project. The deference it pays to God undercuts the deference he just paid to Daniel. For what it requests is a poet rather than a clerical exegete. If Daniel's clerical authority can no longer come from the Church, which Gower has already demonstrated is morally bankrupt, then it must come from the Arion-like texts of "burel" clerks like Gower. His "middel weie" will have the "lore" of clerical traditions, and the "lust" of vernacular poetry.

The poetic and the clerical are identified even more thoroughly in the *de facto* second prologue, the frame tale that opens Book One. In the Prologue proper, Gower repeatedly defines the current crisis with the observation "love is falle into discord," with "love" here meaning *caritas*, the Christian love that binds the human community together in the name of God. But Love is also *fin'amors*, the grand theme of vernacular poetry generally and of this poem in particular, as its title, *Confessio Amantis*, announces. The title has already drawn this theme into clerical discourse and Gower will literalize the connection in the penitential taxonomy he uses to organize his exempla. At the same time, the frame tale which introduces this taxonomy insists on love as *fin'amors*. Assuming the traditional, not to say hackneyed, role of a suffering lover, Gower recounts his vision of Venus's court, where he is directed to Genius, whom Venus identifies as both her priest and clerk (I, 193, 96).

Genius is the perfect figure for Gower's clericalization. Initially a Roman deity appropriated by the School of Chartres in its project of extending Christian modes of exegesis to the natural world, in Jean de Meun's continuation of the *Roman de la Rose*, he becomes the ironic proponent of *fin'amors*. It may well be, as Denise Baker has argued, that Gower's Genius marks a return to the more straightforwardly moralistic Genius of the Chartrians, but if so, the return gives the moralizing a decidedly lay turn.[13] In the *Confessio Amantis*,

---

[13] Denise Baker, "The Priesthood of Genius: A Study of the Medieval Tradition," *Speculum* 44 (1969), 568–84.

Genius is not only a Roman deity become a priest, but also a clerk moralizing stories retold in the vernacular, drawn largely from classical tradition, focusing largely on issues of lay power. While his power will frequently offer critiques of *fin'amors* – sometimes quite brutal ones – he insists at the outset not only that the lay world of power relations that *fin'amors* assumes cannot be avoided, but also that one is obligated to make moral order of it. He writes of his "woful care" because

> ... in good feith this wolde I rede,
> That every man ensample take
> Of wisdom which him is betake,
> And that he wot of good aprise
> To teche it forth, for such emprise
> Is forto preise; and therfore I
> Woll wryte and schewe al openly
> How love and I togedre mette,
> Wherof the world ensample fette
> Mai after this, whan I am go,
> Of thilke unsely jolif wo,
> Whos reule stant out of the weie,
> Nou glad and nou gladnesse aweie,
> And yet it may noght be withstonde
> For oght that men may understonde.   (I, 78–92)

This passage recapitulates the exemplary version of lay tradition he offers in the prologue. Out of human experiences like love, which "may noght be withstonde," it is possible to derive exemplary "wisdom," which one is then obligated to pass on ("teche it forth"). This wisdom has obligatory authority, but hovers uncertainly between the clerical and lay – like Genius himself. As the poem unfolds, Genius solidifies this uncertain "middel weie" with a thorough exploration of the authorizing power of kingship.

Kingship, even in the broad sense in which I am using it here, does not provide the collection's central focus with the same predictability and regularity as it does in the *De casibus* collection. Nevertheless, it recurs continually, and Gower's interest in its discursive aspect enables one to draw even the stories not explicity addressed to kingship into its orbit, by virtue of their concern with the relations between language and political and institutional position. There are a number of tales in the first two books which explore how monarchical and other forms of political and institutional authority both enable and are defined by the performative power of language: all of the extended tales in Book I, Mundus and Paulina, The Trojan Horse, the Tale of Florent, The Trump of Death, Albinus and Rosemond, Nebuchadnezzar's Punishment, and the Tale of the Three Questions; and most of those in Book II, Demetrius and Perseaunt, The False Bachelor, Boniface, and The Donation of Constantine.[14] The most important of these for our purposes are the last two, which Gower clearly intends to be read as a pair. As I have already mentioned, The Donation of Constantine began as a ninth-century forgery, which the papacy employed as the historical authority for their claims of temporal supremacy over the monarchy. It enters the *Fürstenspiegel* with the *Policraticus*. Ultimately, Lorenzo da Valla will expose it as a forgery in 1440.[15] What is striking, however, is that lay resistance to the story's ideological claims can be documented as much as two and one-half centuries earlier. Walther von der Vogelweide, a German court poet in the time of Frederick II, the most vigorous of early imperial resisters to papal claims of universal sovereignty, makes the story the subject of a lyric, but concentrates on the angelic prophecy he adds to it. After Constantine gives the imperial temporalia to Sylvester an angel is heard on high, declaring, "Alas, alas, three times alas! Once Christianity stood in proper splendor, but now a gift works its poison, and the honey is turned to gall. The world will bitterly regret it."[16] Walther accepts the story's authenticity, but he attacks its symbolic value and its *sententia*. The angelic prophecy he adds changes a tale that the papacy used to demonstrate lay deference to clerical power into a demonstration that such claims of institutional superiority marked instead the clergy's moral collapse: "The clergy wish to pervert the

---

[14] One might also include the Tale of Constance, which Winthrop Wetherbee reads as focusing on social values ("Constance and the World in Chaucer and Gower," in *Recent Readings*, ed. Yeager, 65–93).

[15] Lorenzo Valla, *De falso credita et ementita Constantini Donatione*, ed. W. Setz (Weimar: H. Böhlaus, 1976).

[16] Walther von der Vogelweide, *Werke*, ed. Joerg Schaefer (Darmstadt: Wissenschaftliche Buchgesellschaft, 1972), 96, p. 250, ll. 5–9:

> "owê, owê, zem dritten wê!
> ê stuont diu kristenheit mit zühten schône.
> Der ist nû ein gift gevallen,
> ir honec ist worden zeiner gallen,
> daz wirt der werlt her nâch vil leit."

Gift is a pun: it can mean either "gift" or "poison."

virtuous laity."[17] This revision is entirely consistent with the view of the Church Gower adumbrates in his prologue, and thus he retains Walther's addition to the story.

The form this royalist resistance takes is as worthy of note as its substance. For this angelic intervention, which is added to the tale some four centuries after its inception, is no less fictional than the tale itself. Walther was obviously aware of this fact, but the story's ideological value clearly interested him more than the question of its absolute veracity. The same thing was probably true for Gower as well, since both the laicist and the papalist versions of the tale would have been available to him. This point should be stressed, for it provides a concrete illustration of the ideological power that I have been arguing both sides in the papalist/royalist debate granted to narrative as narrative, that is, as a linguistic and discursive construction. The royalists in this debate were less concerned to reject clerical authority than they were to redefine it. The lay version of the Donation suggests that its proponents were happy to have the Church retain its institutional identity and ideological authority. They just wanted these things redefined as more purely spiritual.

Gower's pairing of the Donation with the tale of Boniface VIII, and his reinterpretation of that tale itself, makes his a particularly extreme version of the royalist position. Boniface VIII was the author of the bull *Unam sanctam*, which most ecclesiastical historians view as the high-water mark of papalist assertions. Directed at Philip the Fair, it declared that "temporal authority" should be "subject to the spiritual power."[18] Though Gower's tale unaccountably renames Philip "Lowyz," it follows Philip's general view of the affair, claiming that Boniface demanded "Lowyz" pay him feudal homage.[19] But it also focuses mainly on an event unmentioned in any contemporary records of the affair: the ruse Boniface uses to make himself pope.

After the death of Nicholas III, Celestine, a recluse, is named pope. A cardinal who has long coveted the papal throne contrives with a "clergoun" of "his lignage" to trick Celestin into abdicating.

---

[17] Walther, *Werke*, 253, l. 14: "Die pfaffen wellent leien reht verkêren".

[18] Brian Tierney, *The Crisis of Church and State 1050–1300 (with selected documents)* (Englewood Cliffs, NJ: Prentice Hall, 1980), 189.

[19]
> Ayein Lowyz the king of France
> He tok querelle of his oultrage,
> And seide he scholde don hommage
> Unto the cherche bodily.   (II, 2966–69)

He tells the clergoun to sneak into Celestin's bed-chamber with a
brass speaking-trumpet, and

> ... take riht good kepe,
> Whan that the Pope is fast aslepe
> And that non other man be nyh;
> And thanne that thou be so slyh
> Thurghout the Trompe into his Ere,
> Fro heven as thogh a vois it were,
> To soune of such prolacioun
> That he his meditacioun
> Therof mai take and understonde,
> As thogh it were of goddes sonde.
> And in this wise thou schalt seie,
> That he do thilke astat aweie
> Of Pope, in which he stant honoured,
> So schal his Soule be socoured
> Of thilke worschipe ate laste
> In heven which shal ever laste.   (II, 2869–84)

Convinced that his abdication is "goddes wille," Celestin asks the
Consistory if such an action would be lawful. While all the other
cardinals are surprised and silent, the plotter

> Al openly with wordes pleine
> Seith, if the Pope wolde ordeigne
> That ther be such a lawe wroght,
> Than mihte he cesse, and elles noght.   (II, 2919–22)

On his "Papal Autorite," Celestin issues such a decree, and then
resigns. The plotter replaces him and takes the name Boniface.
Driven both by pride and envy, Boniface openly brags about his ruse,
then picks the quarrel with Louis.

If Boniface is a boastful usurper, Louis is the very model of a lawful
king. "Conseiled ... of his Barnage," he declares with them,

> ... that the Papacie
> Thei wolde honoure and magnefie
> In al that evere is spirital;
> Bot thilke Pride temporal
> Of Boneface in his persone,
> Ayein that ilke wrong al one
> Thei wolde stonden in debat: (II, 2983, 2985–91)

And Gower underlines the distinction between man and office:

And thus the man and noght the stat
The Frensche schopen be her miht
To grieve ...   (II, 2992–94)

The tale presents this, Boniface's final usurping gambit as the
consequence of two previous usurpations: his usurpation of Celestine,
and his originary usurpation of the *vox Dei*. Of the three, the original
one is obviously the most striking. It implies an anti-papalism and an
anti-clericalism that would be difficult to overstate. Gower makes
Boniface's assertions of papal privilege tantamount to the cynical act
of blasphemy that gained him the papacy in the first place.

Nor does Gower indict Boniface alone. For he presents Boniface's
usurpations as no more than the culmination of the process of moral
degradation that originated in the intermixing of temporal and
spiritual of Constantine's Donation. As Patrick Gallacher observes,
Boniface's blasphemous fabrication of the voice of God anticipates in
form as well as fulfilling in substance the angelic prophecy which ends
the Tale of Constantine and Silvester to follow.[20] In the face of this
blasphemy even the uncorrupted elements of the Church are entirely
ineffectual. Celestine's simple faith undoes him, for it never occurs to
him that God's voice could be fabricated. The other cardinals, who
chose Celestine in a manner "that wolden save / The forme of lawe"
(II, 2811–12), are outmaneuvered as well. The fabrication of God's
voice speaks directly to the source of Church authority – if God's
voice can be convincingly fabricated, then what guarantee can the
Church give that what it binds on earth shall be so bound in heaven,
and what it looses shall be loosed there? Gower not only associates
papal assertions of temporal power with this ultimate blasphemy, he
also demonstrates, in the process of making the association, that there
is nothing in the Church's institutional structure to contain or
regulate it.

Yet it would be wrong to see Gower as simply the complacent or
naive moralist aghast at a Church gone so wrong. He is clearly as
fascinated by the Church's power to fabricate divine authority as he
is appalled by it. If this story suggests that "Papal autorite" may be
entirely discursive, and therefore contingent and arbitrary to an
almost unlimited degree, it also suggests the ideological power such
authority can wield, however contingent. Gower is intensely inter-

20 Gallacher, *Love, the Word, and Mercury*, 123.

ested in the power human beings can wield over the divine figures to whom they ascribe ultimate authority. He has already explored the problem in a less focused way in Mundus and Paulina, in which a Roman "bachelor" seduces a virtuous matron by impersonating a God. He will return to it as he moves into the sustained consideration of kingship of Book VII.

In this tale all that constrains Boniface's self-generating *auctoritas* is Lowys's royal *potestas*. This *potestas* inheres in both the king's military power and in the feudal relations which enable him to manage it.

> ... And fell ther was a kniht,
> Sire Guilliam de Langharet,
> Which was upon this cause set;
> And therupon he tok a route
> Of men of Armes and rod oute,
> So longe and in a wayt he lay,
> That he aspide upon a day
> The Pope was at Avinoun,
> And scholde ryde out of the toun
> Unto Pontsorge, the which is
> A Castell in Provence of his.   (II, 2994–3004)

The narrative moves crisply back and forth between the sheer contingency of historical events and the specificity of political relations. Gower introduces "Sire Guillam de Langharet" in purely contingent terms: "And fell ther was a kniht," yet then immediately identifies him more definitely than any of the other principals in the story, Boniface, whose pre-papal identity is never disclosed, the misnamed "Lowys," or the anonymous *clergoun*. Guillam is further specified by his royal mission, which he accomplishes by assembling a "route," then lying in wait for Boniface to happen by.

The specificity of Boniface's movements, from Avignon to Pontsorge, his castle in Provence, underline his entanglement in the world of temporal relations, where he will always be at the mercy of Louis and his emissaries. Indeed Gower foregrounds this disadvantage from the start. Boniface's ruse depends on the "clergoun ... of his lignage." In order to accomplish his institutional goals within the Church, Boniface must have recourse to the very network of lay power relations he will try to claim should be subordinate to him. His capture in Guillam's ambush demonstrates such claims had been empty all along. Ambush represents the power of historical contingency turned to military advantage, the efficacy of feudal relations in the most material terms possible. Boniface simply has no means to manage contingency in that way. By contrast, Guilliam's feudal *potestas* never ceases to be lawful and orderly.

"We pleigne noght ayein the Pope," he tells Boniface,

> For thilke name is honourable,
> Bot thou, which hast be deceivable
> And tricherous in al thi werk,
> Thou Bonefas, thou proude clerk,
> Misledere of the Papacie,
> Thi false bodi schal abye
> And soffre that it hath deserved.			(II, 3016–23)

The retainer acts not for himself but in the name of his king ("*We pleigne noghte*"). In spite of its brute force, the corporate *potestas* he wields can be exerted with such orderly precision that it seizes the pope's body, yet leaves his office intact. Set against such precision, any clerical encroachment, no matter how far-reaching, must ultimately disintegrate under the weight of its own self-delusion. In the tale's final image, a starving Boniface devours his own hands while imprisoned in a French tower. As Russell Peck observes, this final image suggests the ultimately self-destructive character of clerical depredations on temporal *potestas*.[21] But it also suggests something even more general about the nature of clerical power. Entirely derived from and dependent on the divine, it has no material specificity of its own. Any attempt to act in its own interest in temporal matters will always be necessarily self-destructive and self-devouring.

This anti-clericalism, while extreme, is not finally anti-ecclesi-astical. Like Chaucer, Gower disenfranchises clerical power by making it entirely spiritual. The tale insists throughout on the unassailable authority of clerical office in all things spiritual. It simply restricts the spiritual to a realm entirely separate from the structures of lay power. At the same time, Gower will continue to build the fascination this tale shows for the power of sovereign figures to appropriate divine authority to their own needs. Where ideological power marked the limit of moral degradation when exercised by a clerical figure like Boniface, it will be shown in lay contexts as a necessary adjunct to kingship's more material powers. Before he does

21 Peck, *Kingship and Common Profit*, 73.

this, however, Gower will need to adumbrate more clearly kingship's internal orderliness. For this purpose he turns to the Tale of Constantine and Silvester.

Critics of the *Confessio* have frequently cited this tale as one of Gower's best.[22] While most comment on its politics in passing, no one has explored them in detail. Such an exploration is crucial. It will not only enable us to replace Gower the unreflective moralist with Gower the sophisticated political thinker, it will also show how fully narrative Gower's political sophistication actually is – that is, how much his political vision depends on his subtle manipulation of narrative detail.

In the figure of Constantine, Gower draws on one of the richest and most powerful symbols in the discourse of medieval politics. Amnon Linder is probably right to argue that Constantine's legendary conversion to Christianity had the status of a foundation myth.[23] As an historically authentic figure embodying the seamless interweaving of the clerical and the monarchical, of *auctoritas* and *potestas*, Constantine was important to both sides in the institutional struggles between the papacy and lay monarchy. The myth of Constantine actually consisted of two partially contradictory traditions. The first, which originates with Eusebius, relates his conversion to his dream before the battle of Milvain Bridge, in which he saw a banner bearing the Cross and heard the words, "By this sign you shall conquer." This tradition generated the legend of the True Cross, and a variety of other hagiographical and reliquary customs.[24] The other tradition originates with the *Vita Sancti Silvestri*. The version Gower draws upon, it relates Constantine's conversion to a miraculous cure for leprosy effected by Sylvester's baptism. It gives rise in the eighth century to the *Constitutio Constantini*, which purports to be the gift to Silvester from the grateful Constantine of the temporalia of the Empire. From the Carolingian period to the Investiture Crisis and beyond, the papacy will draw upon this story again and again to justify its institutional prerogatives.[25] By the twelfth century, lay resistance had generated the counter-version first articulated by

---

[22] This view begins with Macaulay, in an article he wrote in 1908 for the *The Cambridge History of English Literature* (v. 2, 174). Cited in Nicholson, *Annotated Index*, 209.

[23] Amnon Linder, "Ecclesia and Synagoga in the Medieval Myth of Constantine the Great," *Revue Belge de Philologie et d'Histoire* 54 (1976), 1019–23.

[24] Amnon Linder, "The Myth of Constantine the Great in the West: Sources and Hagiographic Commemoration," *Studi Medievali*, 3rd ser., XVI (1975), 43–98.

[25] Ullmann, *Growth of Papal Government*, 57–102 and *passim*.

Walther von Vogelweide. Dante, Langland, and Wycliff are among the anti-clerical writers who repeat this version of the story.[26] Dante even anticipates Gower in associating it with Boniface.

Most of these writers, however, mention only this part of the story, and none of them, including Walther, tell it with anywhere near the detail that Gower does. He has clearly returned to the hagiographical tradition, though we are unlikely to be able to pinpoint an exact source until the immensely complicated textual history of the *Vita S. Silvestri* is untangled – there are extant versions in at least 300 manuscripts.[27] A heavily hierocratic work, the *Vita S. Silvestri* treats Constantine's conversion as marking the Church's triumphant conquest of the Roman state. It takes his leprosy as divine punishment for his persecution of Christians, and it rehearses in great detail both the many constitutional changes by which he made Christianity the state religion, and the impromptu assembly of the Roman people where they renounce their paganism. Its undoubted high point comes at the moment of the Donation, where Constantine in floods of tears prostrates himself before Sylvester, renouncing his crimes against the Church.

By contrast, Gower makes Constantine himself the focus of the story, an exemplar of monarchy's endlessly productive tension between hierarchy and community. He changes Constantine from a infidel persecutor redeemed, like Paul on the road to Damascus, to a type of the virtuous pagan miraculously granted enlightenment. Omitting any mention of divine retribution, he makes Constantine's leprosy a moral revelation that anticipates the lesson of Christian charity Constantine will learn from Sylvester. After he is stricken with leprosy, his "grete clerkes" decide he can only be cured by bathing in the blood of infants (II, 3198–3215). He decrees that all children below the age of seven be assembled at his palace, but the spectacle of so many nursing mothers in tearful horror prevents him from going through with the plan. Reminding himself that

[26] Dante, *Inferno*, xix, 52–117; Langland, *Piers Plowman*, B-Text, XV, 557–61 (ed. George Kane and E. Talbot Donaldson, rev. ed. (London: Athlone Press, and Berkeley: University of California Press, 1988)) and C-Text, XVII, 220–24 (ed. Derek Pearsall (London: Edward Arnold, 1978)); see Mildred Jochums, "The Legend of the Voice from Heaven," *Notes and Queries*, 209 (1964), 44–47. For Wycliff, see Jochums, 45, and Hudson, *Premature Reformation*, 330, 335.

[27] Macaulay suggests the *Legenda Aurea* was Gower's source, but in fact his version is much closer to that recorded by Bonino Mombrizio, a Renaissance compiler of hagiography from monastic sources, in *Sanctuarium, seu Vitae Sanctorum*, 2 vols. (Milan, before 1480, reprinted in Paris, 1910), vol. 2, 508–31. I use Mombrizio's version here as the basis of comparison.

The povere child is bore als able
To vertu as the kinges Sone;
...
He sih also the grete mone,
Of that the Modres were unglade,
And of the wo the children made,
Wherof that al his herte tendreth,
And such pite withinne engendreth,
That him was levere forto chese
His oghne bodi forto lese,
Than se so gret a moerdre wroght
Upon the blod which gulteth noght.
Thus for the pite which he tok
Alle othre leches he forsok,
And put him out of aventure
Al only into goddes cure;
And seith, "Who that woll maister be,
He mot be servant to pite."   (II, 3258–59, 3286–3300)

Constantine's conversion begins from within the temporal and the
social, with the engendering of "pite" within his own heart. His
recognition of the moral equality of all humanity is enabled by the
spectacle of gross social inequality he has before him, and cannot be
divided from it. Constantine apparently had no qualms about mass
infanticide in the abstract; it is only when brought face to face with
the actuality of the deed that he relents. Confronting the absoluteness
of his prerogative in its most horrific degree encourages him,
voluntarily and spontaneously, to restrain it. It is as if monarchical
power, in its supreme amorality, stimulates from its possessor an
irresistable need for moral order. This ethical, entirely secular
conversion constitutes Gower's first example of monarchy's inherently self-regulating character, the paradoxical but inevitable
logic whereby absolute prerogative produces its own self-generated
restraint. This idea governs much of Book VII.[28]

Constantine's pity is of the same sort we have already seen in the
Parson's Tale, and the *Clerk's Tale*: a downward identification that
reinforces the very class boundaries it crosses. Christianity makes this
reinforcement even stronger. As it intensifies the identification, it
lessens the sacrifice that the identification requires. Before Christ's
miraculous intercession, Constantine's refusal of infanticide still

[28] See below, 282–91.

leaves him with leprosy. His conversion to Christianity enables him to maintain his identification with those he rules, and still achieve the benefit his unconstrained prerogative promised him. Saint Peter and Saint Paul appear to him in a dream that night, and tell him "for thou hast served / Pite, thou has pite deserved" (II, 3339–40). They send him to Sylvester to be baptized, which cures his leprosy. As the universal agency of pity, divine authority enters the social to empower monarchical self-restraint, removing any material cost such self-restraint has to pay. When, at a more abstract level, Sylvester teaches Constantine the basic tenets of Christian history, and the ultimate equality of all humanity before God on the day of judgment, he literally provides Constantine with a space outside the social to which his pity can always be deferred.

Gower confines the Church to this role throughout the narrative. Constantine's ethical conversion at the beginning of the tale fully anticipates the doctrinal instruction that accompanies his miraculous cure; the angelic prophesy at the end entirely restricts the Church to the spiritual sphere from which such instruction draws its authority. He also foregrounds the moral integrity of the secular in the metonymic associations that surround the miraculous moment of baptism. In the *Vita S. Silvestri*, Constantine meets the assembly of mothers and infants on the way to the Capitol, where the bath is to take place. Gower changes the meeting-place to his palace, where the baptism also takes place. He specifies this narrative economizing further by making the baptism occur in the very "vessel which for blod / Was mad" (II, 3445–46). The *Vita* also turns on a comparison between the two immersions, but it emphasizes contrast rather than continuity. It treats Constantine's prospective bath in blood as an embodiment of pagan polity, based on no more than the brutality of bloodletting, which it contrasts to the Christian commonwealth, based on the *caritas* of Christ's sacrifice, memorialized in the redemptive cleansing of baptism. "[Sylvester] will show you the piscina of pity" (*ipse tibi piscinam pietatis ostendet*), Peter and Paul tell Constantine in his dream, implicitly distinguishing this piscina from the one the narrative earlier imagined as filled with blood.[29] By explicitly making these two piscinae the same, Gower foregrounds Christianity's dependence on material reality, and anticipates the concluding prophesy, which assumes that only the temporal power

---

[29] Mombrizio, *Sanctuarium*, II, 511, 510.

can safely enact moral order. Thus this prophecy marks for him not only the moral collapse of the Church, but something of an abdication on the part of Constantine, for all his exemplarity. In ceding his *temporalia* to the Church, he gives up the power which, as this exemplum has just demonstrated, only someone in his position can manage. This abdication will make necessary the reassertion of royal privilege which occurs in the Tale of Boniface, and for which Gower will argue more systematically in Book VII. Before he does that, however, he will use the intervening books to distinguish monarchy from other forms of lay authority.

SIMULATING THE VOICE OF GOD (II): THE CRITIQUE OF ROMANCE

Incongruous as it may seem, given his pious reputation, Gower will avail himself twice more of the motif of simulating divine voices: first in the Tale of Nectanabus, and then in his version of Lycurgus and His Laws. Slightly less audacious than the Tale of Boniface, these tales are nevertheless located at crucial points in a sustained meditation of the contingencies of cultural authority, of which the anti-clerical critique forms only the first part. For Gower, all of cultural authority depends on institutional and discursive processes of historical construction. Authority must be maintained, and largely produced, from within history. When he arrives at his systematic affirmation of kingship in Book VII, he does so not because he has found the one source of authority which is natural and given. On the contrary, what he values in kingship is that in a world where all authority is necessarily contingent and constructed, kingship provides the form in which it can be maintained most efficiently. Accordingly, he follows his critique of the Church with a critique of courtly love and the chivalric ideals attached to it.

Having established the parity between lay and clerical authority, Gower seems eager to distance such lay authority from the chivalric values in which medieval romance traditionally located it. The four books between II and VII are nominally devoted to Wrath, Sloth, Avarice, and Gluttony. While they do not focus exclusively on courtly love, love stories dominate them and nearly all the stories of famous lovers Gower recounts he recounts in this broad middle section of the poem: Pyramus and Thisbe, Phoebus and Daphne,

Aeneas and Dido, Ulysses and Penelope, Pygmalion, Demephon and Phyllis, Ceix and Alcione, Iphis and Araxarathen, Mars and Venus, Jason and Medea, and Theseus and Ariadne.

Students of Gower have long recognized his critical view of romance. They have tended, however, to read it as an effort to bring courtly love more closely into line with Christian doctrine.[30] This reading underestimates the force and extent of Gower's critique, and completely ignores his anti-clericalism. In fact, as we shall see, Gower will interrupt the critique in Book V for an account of the world's religions that will include a recapitulation of his attack on the Church – as if he were making sure it had not been forgotten. I have no desire to impugn Gower's piety, nor to suggest this poem is anti-Christian. But it must be recognized that piety has little to do with the project of this poem, despite its Christianity. If purely religious sentiment enters the poem at all, it enters on terms that are mainly political : as a suspicion of all forms of human authority – lay as well as clerical – so profound that it out-Augustines Augustine. Such suspicions certainly provide the motive for the critique of romance. Gower's objection to romance is that it insufficiently recognizes its own contingencies.

In Book IV Genius offers a discussion of *gentilesse* distinctly reminiscent of the definition of *nobilitas* Aegidius Romanus offers in *De regimine principum* :

> The grounde, Mi Sone, forto seche
> Upon this diffinicion,
> The worldes constitucion
> Hath set the name of gentilesse
> Upon the fortune of richesse
> Which of long time is falle in age.   (IV, 2204–09)

Just as Aegidius does in the case of *nobilitas*, Genius acknowledges the contingent, ideological status of *gentilesse*, ascribing its meaning to the "worldes constitucion," which has assigned the term to ancient "richesse." Genius makes this acknowledgment even more un-equivocally than Aegidius does, concluding after another fifty lines, "So wot I nothing after kinde / Where I mai gentilesse finde" – that is, there is nothing natural or inevitable about the category. Yet he will recuperate the term by making it an internal virtue achievable

---

[30] For a recent, well-argued version of this position, which also incorporates an account of its history, see Yeager, *Gower's Poetic*, especially 230–79.

by whoever "wole in his degree/Travaile so as it belongeth" (IV, 2292–93). Having disappeared as something given in the natural order of things, the social privilege *gentilesse* describes returns as an ideological value produced by human labor. This labor begins with the acceptance of one's degree. Like Aegidius, Gower debunks the class privilege of nobility precisely so as to put it on a more authoritative footing. Rejecting any simplistic notion of nobility as some direct expression of the natural order of things, both writers make it an artificially constructed value whose efficacy lies precisely in the effort it draws forth from those who construct it.

Gower accepts – indeed, insists on – the necessity and efficacy of the class and gender distinctions upon which romance rests. But he wants to understand those distinctions in terms less evanescent than the negational and utopian gestures which the romance characteristically employs. In the transgressive erotic relationships that define romance, *gentilesse* displays itself most emphatically in the impossible pursuit of a love it cannot have. That is to say, romance makes *gentilesse* knowable precisely by the magnitude of its failure, by its incapacity to bend historical necessity to its own control. The adventurous, competitive spirit that drives the romance hero toward his forbidden love can never finish until it confronts the chivalric community that both gives that spirit meaning and forbids its full expression, and either the hero or the community, or both, are destroyed. Gower will defuse the dilemma by insisting on the radical contingency of both erotic desire and the ideological limits which constrain it.

The most obvious and notorious means by which Gower achieves this demystification is his focus on incest. Book III opens with "thilke wikke ensample" of Canace and Machaire. Introducing his consideration of *fin'amors* in this way undercuts at once its pretence to spirituality. If courtly love is to be defined by its transgressiveness, it cannot distinguish itself in any absolute sense from the transgressions of incest, which cannot be so easily spiritualized. Gower will make this scandalous similarity explicit in the poem's final book by substituting incest for the more conventional sin of lechery. He conveys the similarity here by presenting their erotic relations as if they were entirely typical courtly lovers.

> Whan kinde assaileth the corage
> With love and doth him forto bowe,
> That he no reson can allowe,

Bot halt the lawes of nature:
For whom that love hath under cure,
As he is blind himself, riht so
He makth his client blind also.
...
And so it fell hem ate laste,
That this Machaire with Canace
Whan thei were in a prive place,
Cupide bad hem ferst to kesse,
And after sche which is Maistresse
In kinde and techeth every lif
Withoute lawe positif,
Of which sche takth nomaner charge,
Bot kepth hire lawes al at large,
Nature, tok him into lore
And tawht hem so, that overmore
Sche hath hem in such wise daunted,
That thei were, as who seith, enchaunted.

(III, 155–60, 166–78)

This grim parody, with its concomitant reduction of love at court to sheer natural urge, does no more than take to its literal limit the sheer random contingency figured by Cupid's blindness. If we read this figure to the letter, then it is entirely possible that he could bring both brother and sister together, even though this is a possibility so scandalous that romance, for all its celebrations of the forbidden, finds literally unthinkable. By presenting incest in the vocabulary of courtly love, Gower finds the social constraint romance can never transgress, and upon which its idealizations depend. The assault on the orderly structures of lineage which Canace and Machaire have begun becomes complete when their father, King Eolus, discovers their crime. He orders that Canace throw herself on a sword and has her baby left in the forest to be devoured by beasts. Gower uses her death-scene as the occasion of another parody. As she is dying, she writes to Machaire, who has already fled:

O thou my sorwe and my gladnesse,
O thou myn hele and my siknesse,
O my wanhope and al my trust,
O my desese and al my lust,
O thou my wele, o thou myn wo,
O thou my love, o thou my hate,
For thee mot I be ded algate.   (III, 279–86)

This is the oxymoronic language of the suffering courtly lover, except that here, the suffering lover's hyperbolic death becomes a literal one. In a conventional romance context this series of oxymoronic apostrophes would convey, by its transgression of logical categories, the delight forbidden desire takes in its own transgressiveness. Here, however, the oxymorons convey a desire so transgressive as to have become literally unspeakable, and this literalization makes the conventional transgressions of romance seem like cheap thrills indeed.

Gower's reduction of eros to incest, is only one in a number of ironic strategies he uses in this book. In Pyramus and Thisbe he turns Ovid's decorous treatment of the lovers' double suicide into a grisly parody of the sexual act. In the *Metamorphoses* (IV, 55–166), Pyramus stabs himself and withdraws the sword so that when Thisbe falls on it their blood mingles. In this poem, however, Pyramus sets the pommel in the ground and impales himself to the hilt (III, 1443–49). Then Thisbe throws herself on top.

> Hire love in armes sche embraseth,
> Hire oghne deth and so pourchaseth
> That now sche wepte and nou sche kiste,
> Til ate laste, er sche it wiste,
> So gret a sorwe is to hire falle,
> Which overgoth hire wittes alle.
> As sche which mihte it noght asterte,
> The swerdes point ayein hire herte
> Sche sette, and fell doun therupon,
> Wherof that sche was ded anon:
> And thus bothe on o swerd bledende
> Thei weren founde ded liggende.   (III, 1483–94)

In Ovid's version the sword's figuration of phallic desire remains indirect enough that each lover's death retains the aura of a tragic sacrifice. Gower transforms Ovid's images into an ungainly shish kebab: " ... thus both on o swerd bledende / The were founde ded liggende." The corporeal realities which underlie these lovers' sacrifices return all too literally, undercutting any claim the story might make on behalf of the spirituality of the erotic.

The longest tale in Book III is that of Orestes. Classifying it as an example of Homicide, Genius is mainly interested in it as a story of justifiable retribution. However, he begins it as the story of adulterous love between Climestre and Egistus. Although their love occurs at

court, he characterizes it as an act of cuckoldry in the reductive terms
that bespeak the world of the fabliau rather than that of the romance:

> An old sawe is, "Who that is slyh
> In place where he mai be nyh
> He makth the ferre Lieve loth":
> Of love and thus fulofte it goth.
> Ther while Agamenon batailleth
> To winne Troie, and it assaileth,
> Fro home and was long time ferr,
> Egistus drowh his qweene nerr,
> And with the leiser which he hadde,
> This ladi at his wille he ladde   (III, 1899–1908)

This "old sawe" reduces erotic attachment to sheer physical
proximity. In fact, this is the same proverb Chaucer's Miller uses to
explain Alisoun's preference for Nicholas over Absolon (I, 3392–93).
The demystification of courtly love continues in Book IV. Aeneas
and Dido, and Ulysses and Penelope are offered as examples of
Lachesse, the "ferste point of slowthe" (IV, 3,). In the case of Aeneas
and Dido this classification is particularly striking. Gower completely
suppresses any mention of Aeneas's sacred destiny taking him to
Italy, at least partially against his will. In Gower's version he simply
leaves, and his refusal to return is purely inertial. When Dido writes
to him, pleading for his return,

> ... he, which hadde hise thoghtes feinte
> Towardes love and full of Slowthe,
> His time lette, and that was rowthe ...   (IV, 118–20)

This anomalous revision seems at first glance to confirm the frequent
complaint that Gower's penitential taxonomy does violence to the
tales he imposes it on. Yet in this case, that violence is precisely the
point: it demonstrates the interpretive and discursive power to which
Gower is laying claim. First, to read sloth as the motive force
underlying this tale is to deny point-blank the priority which the tale,
both in its originary versions of Virgil and Ovid, and in most of their
medieval reworkings, assigns to erotic desire. If Aeneas's great
passion can give way so easily to sheer laziness, it cannot have such
all-encompassing power after all. Second, the very fact the tale can be
reinterpreted in this manner demonstrates the extent to which the
desire the tale traditionally celebrates is itself discursively con-

structed. Gower makes this point quietly but effectively toward the beginning of the tale.

> ... Dido sche was hote;
> Which loveth Eneas so hote
> Upon the wordes whiche he seide,
> That al hire herte on him sche leide
> And dede al holi what he wolde. (IV, 87–91)

Dido's hot love is, in the first instances, produced by and directed at "the wordes whiche he seide." The differences in desire which separate them is possible because desire is always triangulated through language.

If desire is discursively constructed, it is also regulable, a point which the next tale, Ulysses and Penelope, seems designed to make. Penelope sends a letter to Troy imploring Ulysses to hurry home to rescue her from the press of suitors. As soon as Ulysses can, he hurries home:

> He made non delaiement,
> Bot goth him home in alle hihe
> When that he fond to fore his yhe
> His worthi wif in good astat ... (IV, 226–29)

The separation of lovers is a problem as easily solved as this. The note of matter-of-fact, self-satisfied domesticity which ends this tale, suggests, in contrast to the tale immediately preceding, that erotic desire is entirely manageable within the social constraints imposed on it both by marriage and political position.

The next story, Pygmalion, continues Gower's exploration of the constructed and contingent nature of desire. But it also raises for the first time the substantive issue of Venus's role as the sign of desire's contingent constructions. As the Goddess to whom Gower's Amans nominally makes his confession, Venus also nominally delimits the authority of his text, restricting it to the subordinate realm of secular poetry. His examination of her discursive status will enable him to evade this limit and lay claim to a moral authority that rivals that of clerical texts. As an archetypal illustration of the male power to construct its own object of desire, the Pygmalion story demonstrates, in Genius's *sententia*, "That word mai worche above kinde" (IV, 439). Desire becomes *almost* entirely a discursive projection, which literally produces the material body it pursues.

Yet what lies in that *almost* is the paradoxical essence of the authority Gower seeks. For as he strives after and, indeed, celebrates his poetic authority as a self-generating textual construct, he is also searching through this very celebration for some extra-textual ground. Pygmalion constructs his wife-to-be in every detail: all Venus does is breathe life into her and even that is the result largely of his effort rather than Venus's: "of his penance / He made such continuance / Fro dai to nyht, and preith so longe, / That his priere is underfonge / Which Venus of hire grace herde" (IV, 415–19). As ground which validates Pygmalion's projections, Venus is almost entirely passive, nearly as responsive to his will as the wife he has molded. Yet for all its featurelessness and passivity, Venus's validation is the *sine qua non* upon which all Pygmalion's assertions depend.

This view of divinity enables Gower to have his authority both ways. On the one hand, he can present power as discursively constructed and pursue the process of its construction in all its variability. On the other, he can return any time in the course of his explorations to an extra-textual divine ground, and this ground will authorize the givenness and naturalness of dominant forms of aristocratic power, not in their substance but precisely in their constructedness. Indeed, after the frank acknowledgment constituted by this tale, most of Book IV is given over to assertions of the efficacy of chivalric values, albeit on demystified terms. Genius offers a defense of the traditional chivalric notion that lovers should prove themselves in battle, punctuated by a series of exempla of "Prouesce" (IV, 1615–2199), followed immediately by the discussion of Gentilesse. The book ends with the tale of Iphis and Araxarathen, which Gower recasts from "a tale designed to encourage women to yield to their lovers' desires into one which criticizes men for despairing."[31]

The danger for Gower's view of authority is not that it is too rigid and complacent to accomodate the complex mass of historical complexity he treats in his narratives. On the contrary, the danger is that it will become too flexible. Books V and VI are concerned with the problem of idolatry, or authority as constructed rather than received. Since Book V treats Avarice and Book VI, Gluttony, the two deadly sins constituted by excessive interest in external, material

---

[31] Nicolette Stasko, "The Tale of Iphis and Araxarathen," in *John Gower's Transformations in the "Confessio Amantis"*, ed. Peter G. Beidler (Washington, DC: University Press of America, 1982), 54.

objects, Gower is able to weave his larger problem through the poem's penitential schema quite successfully. Book V is dominated by a long discussion of the historical variety of religious belief, which Gower, following in part the *Vita Barlaam et Josaphat* divides into five categories, the beliefs of the Chaldeans, the Egyptians, the Greeks, the Jews, and the Christians. Framed by two stories in which Venus figures prominently, Vulcan and Venus (V, 635–725), and Paris and Helen (V, 7195–590), this "very ill-advised digression" puzzled and annoyed Macaulay:

if the question of false gods was to be raised at all, it ought to have come in as an explanation of Venus and Cupid, in the first book. Many stories have been told... which required the explanation as much as [Vulcan and Venus], and the awkwardness of putting it all into the mouth of the priest of Venus is inexcusable. (vol. 2, 515)

Nevertheless, this awkwardness may be exactly Gower's point. If my reading of his view of authority is correct, then he would have a much more modulated sense of Venus's falsity than Macaulay's rather prim, late-Victorian sensibility would allow. What Gower wants to find is the extent to which the construction of divine authority can itself be divinely authorized. He wants to assert that a pagan god retains textual authority despite its falsity.

After exploring the falsity of other beliefs, Genius ends his discussion of Christianity with an attack on the *Slouth of Prelacie* that asserts that even Christianity is not proof against idolatry.

> Bot every Prelat holde his See
> With al such ese as he mai gete
> Of lusti drinke and lusti mete,
> Wherof the bodi fat and full
> Is unto gostli labour dull
> And slowh to handle thilke plowh.
> Bot elles we ben swifte ynowh
> Toward the worldes Avarice;
> And that is as a sacrifice,
> Which, after that thapostel seith,
> Is openly ayein the feith
> Unto thidoles yove and granted ... (V, 1944–55)

Accusing the clergy of idolatry at once recapitulates the critiques of the Prologue and the Tale of Boniface and clears some space for an even more complicated one. If even Christian authority can be converted into an idol, then idolatry is not simply a matter of the propositional content of a religious belief. It also depends on how the belief is received and maintained. If a true belief can be maintained in a false manner, as Christian belief clearly has by the prelates Genius denounces, then it must also be possible that a false belief can be maintained in a true manner, that is, in a manner that will lead it beyond itself and toward truth. This seems to be how Gower thinks of his use of Venus in these middle books, as a metonym for lay poetry. Despite her falsity, Venus can lead the poetry she authorizes toward truth.

In the tale which occasions the digression on religion, Venus, as a character in the narrative, enacts the very uncontrolability of erotic desire she personifies as a deity. Vulcan, infuriated by her infidelities with Mars, entraps the two in bed with strong chains he has made. His success turns to failure, however, for when the other Gods discover them bound in bed, they ridicule Vulcan for a cuckold. This tale associates Venus with a power beyond human social constraint, understood in its broadest terms. Vulcan speaks both for the power of craft and artifice and for the rectitude of institutional constraints like marriage, in whose interest such craft is deployed. To the extent the tale characterizes the nature of Venus's authority, it characterizes that authority as precisely that which escapes the human and the social. As her confessant, then, Gower's *persona* Amans moves beyond the idolatrous Christian prelates, who define their own authority entirely in terms of their institutional positions.

The story of Paris and Helen, the final tale of Book V, rounds out this assertion of Venus's authority precisely by indicating its incompleteness. Drawing on *Le Roman de Troie*, Gower places both the lovers' first meeting and the subsequent abduction in the Temple of Venus. The location of the meeting produces a paradox which Gower exploits by classifying the tale under the rubric of Sacrilege. In this version of the story, Paris goes to Greece expressly because Venus has promised that there he will meet and marry the most beautiful woman in the world. As he seizes Helen, she is in the middle of a prayer to Venus's image. That Venus allows her own rites to become the pretext for abduction suggests she is a divinity for whom sacrilege is the characteristic *modus operandi*. In order to fulfill her promise to Paris, she must make a sham of Helen's prayer. She sacrifices her ritual, the set of formal rules which should undergird her every transaction with humanity, and her temple, the privileged locale which activates the rules, for the contingent needs of one particular utterance. She fulfills her promise to Paris by falsifying the more general divine authority under whose auspices the promise was made. Her divine authority is thus by nature incomplete, and must accomplish its ends by ruse and indirection. Yet Gower deploys her indirection in his text so as to validate his own reliance on her. It is Genius, her priest, who tells this tale. In his explicit exposure of Paris's sacrilege, he implicitly exposes the sacrilegious status of his own authority, and in so doing indicates his capacity to see beyond it. Accordingly, it is fitting that he should periodically break out of his own pagan discourse to speak Christian truth, however awkward later readers have found such moments. As a figure, like Venus, for Gower's own authority, he demonstrates the capacity of lay poetry to generate from within its own limitations an authority that transcends them.

Nevertheless, even this vindication of his own authority is not sufficient for Gower. The final prologomena to his *Fürstenspiegel* in Book VII is the Tale of Nectanabus, one of the longest in the entire collection, and the last extended tale in Book VI. After a relatively brief treatment of Gluttony *per se*, Genius modulates into a long discussion of magic. Magic will enable him to characterize the paradox of lay authority even more precisely than he has to this point. For a late medieval thinker like Gower the dividing line between magic and orthodox Christian practice was much less precise than even the sometimes fuzzy boundary between Christian and pagan notions of divinity. Many forms of medieval magic were learned and textual. As astrology and alchemy they shaded ambiguously into legitimate scientific belief. Moreover, magic, like Christianity, is above all a set of semiotic practices: it involves supplications of supernatural forces not always easily distinguishable from the sacral supplications of prayer.[32] But magic seeks to put these forces at human disposal, rather than to serve them. It raises, in all its ambiguity and complexity, the question of how authority is constructed from within history.

Nectanabus, a sorcerer and Egyptian king, is the legendary father of Alexander the Great, who uses his magical powers to impregnate

[32] To confirm the semiotic status of magic in medieval thought, one need go no further than Augustine's *De doctrina Christiana*, which discusses various forms of late antique magic among its treatment of conventional signs in the second book. For a good, concise discussion of medieval magic that is particularly strong on its ambiguous relation to religion, see Richard Kieckhefer, *Magic in the Middle Ages* (Cambridge: Cambridge University Press, 1989).

Olimpias, Philip of Macedonia's queen. Having foreseen through sorcery the coming of enemies he could not defeat, Nectanabus flees to Macedonia. He arrives while Philip is away, beholds Olimpias during a procession and immediately falls in love with her. When she notices him as a stranger and asks to see him, he tells her he is a "clerk," with a message he can give her only in private. As soon as that is arranged he tells her that the Libyan god Amos wants to beget of her a son "Which with his swerd schal winne and gete / The wyde world in lengthe and brede" (VI, 1936–37). To convince her fully he sends her a dream "thurgh the craft of Artemage" (VI, 1957), in which Amos appears to her first in the form of a dragon, and then takes the form of a man to make love to her. The next night Nectanabus is able to make love to Olimpias himself by repeating this performance in person. Afterwards, he sends a dream to Philip out on his campaign, which the clerk Amphion interprets as meaning "A god hath leie be thi wif, / And gete a Sone, which schal winne / The world and al that is withinne" (VI, 2164–66). For good measure, once Philip has returned, Nectanabus also appears before the court, once again in the form of a dragon, and embraces the queen.

While Alexander grows up, Nectanabus serves as one of his teachers. One night while they are on a tower so that Nectanabus can explain the astrological influences of the stars, Alexander asks if he can predict his own death. He replies, "Or fortune is aweie / And every sterre hath lost his wone, / Or elles of myn oghne Sone / I schal be slain, I mai noght fle" (VI, 2302–05). Thinking, "Hierof this olde dotard lieth," Alexander impulsively shoves him off the tower, and then says,

> ... "Ly doun there apart:
> Wherof nou serveth al thin art?
> Thou knewe alle othre mennes chance
> And of thiself hast ignorance:
> That thou hast seid amonges alle
> Of thi persone, is noght befalle."   (VII, 2307, 2311–16)

As he is dying, Nectanabus replies by telling Alexander the whole story of his conception.

This outlandish account of Alexander's paternity both concludes the critique of romance, and introduces the miniature *Fürstenspiegel* of Book VII. Genius will claim to be reproducing the pseudo-Aristotelian *Secretum secretorum*. While Book VII does not draw from that work as systematically as Genius implies it does, the connections are not inconsiderable either.[33] Most important is the ideological status that the *Secretum* held for later medieval culture, which believed it was written for Alexander by Aristotle. This belief – that antiquity's greatest philosopher would have devoted himself to producing a *Fürstenspiegel* for its greatest conqueror – suggests the conviction that royal power not only desired secular wisdom but needed it. Prefacing his own expression of this conviction with the legend of Alexander's birth enables Gower to explore to their fullest the relations between the ideological and political aspects of lay authority.

The transgressive, scandalous status the legend assigns to this birth cannot easily be overemphasized. Nectanabus's sorcery not only expropriates Philip's patriarchal and dynastic prerogative, but it also expropriates divine prerogative as well. One can push the point even further: Nectanabus's claim to bring a message from a God who would beget a human son of a mortal woman, parodies the Annunciation. Yet, in spite of the multiple transgression, Olimpias

> ... conceived
> The worthiest of alle kiththe,
> Which evere was tofore or siththe
> Of conqueste and chivalerie;
> So that thurgh guile and Sorcerie
> Ther was that noble knyht begunne,
> Which al the world hath after wunne.   (VI, 2086–92)

In these lines Gower makes explicit what is implicit throughout the tale. Alexander's superlative status as "the worthiest of all kiththe," the "noble knyht ... which al the world hath ... wunne" is enabled by a direct violation of the patrilineal relations the categories *kiththe* and *noble* claim to regulate. Nectanabus's constitutive violation of these categories suggests that the categories are themselves constituted by transgression. This is especially so because Gower doubly marks Nectanabus's violation as a usurpation of divine prerogative: first, as an act of sorcery, and second, as an act of sorcery that specifically consists of impersonating a god. In this way he presents aristocratic power not only as transgressive, but as transgressively self-authorizing. It is Nectanabus, not the gods, who predicts

---

[33] M. A. Manzalouai, "'Noght in the Registre of Venus': Gower's English Mirror for Princes," in *Medieval Studies for J. A. W. Bennett*, ed. P. L. Heyworth (Oxford: Clarendon Press, 1981), 162–80.

Alexander will be the greatest conqueror the world has ever seen, and does this mainly as a means to sleeping with Olimpias. Yet for all its manifest invention, the prediction comes true. Indeed, its coming true ratifies the power of patriarchy in a curious way, but not as an orderly transmission of aristocratic rule from one generation to the next by an entirely biological process of paternity. Instead, Alexander's fulfillment of Nectanabus's ersatz prophecy, ratifies patriarchy as a transgressive projection of power that is as much discursive as it is biological.

Gower underlines this through the content of the dream Nectanabus sends to Philip. Philip sees Amos sleeping with his queen:

> Whan he up fro the queene aros,
> Tok forth a ring, wherinne a ston
> Was set, and grave therupon
> A Sonne, in which, whan he cam nyh,
> A leoun with a swerd he sih;
> And with that priente, as he tho mette,
> Upon the queenes wombe he sette
> A Seal, and goth him forth his weie.   (VI, 2144–51)

This version of the conception makes it not so much an insemination as a textualization. Alexander becomes a projection of Nectanabus's power, which he literally imprints on Olimpias.

Despite its obliquity, this semiotic characterization of the genesis of aristocratic power moves a step beyond Aegidius. Its paradoxical tensions are consistent enough to enable Gower to move past the virtues of chivalry to those of monarchy from within chivalry itself. For if aristocratic power is not merely contingent but also transgressive, its continual transgressiveness provides the force which regulates its contingency. Nectanabus's magical usurpation of the divine is defeated by the same form of lay monarchical power that defeated Boniface's blasphemous usurpation of it, except that here power is entirely arbitrary and capricious. The absolute control Alexander has over his subjects enables him to push Nectanabus off a tower for no other reason than to test his ability as soothsayer. Such capriciousness is entirely consistent with the transgressive paternity that brought Alexander into being, and yet the arbitrariness of the second action corrects the arbitrariness of the first. It is precisely because the transgressive language of Nectanabus's prophecy had the power to make itself real in the person of Alexander that his linguistic power must ultimately succumb to the material power it produced. At the same time this surrender is regulative, for it is Nectanabus's language that calls forth Alexander's reaction, both in terms of the narrative as a whole and of this particular event.

For in killing Nectanabus Alexander reacts directly to Nectanabus's language, and yet the reaction has power because its relation to the content of those words is oblique. Alexander misunderstands the prediction and brings it to fruition by misunderstanding it – indeed by mistakenly thinking he can defeat it. Like Nectanabus before him, Alexander seeks to turn his power to his own immediate interest, yet that transgression turns out to correct the transgressiveness in which his power originated. Once again, we have a characterization of power not unlike that in the Pygmalion story, where power is sustained by divine authority precisely through its oblique and indirect relation to such authority. Genius makes this point explicit both at the beginning and the end of the tale. He introduces the tale by saying,

> The hihe creatour of thinges,
> Which is the king of alle kinges,
> Ful many a wonder worldes chance
> Let slyden under his suffrance;
> Ther wot noman the cause why,
> Bot he the which is almyhty.
> And that was proved whilom thus,
> Whan that the king Nectanabus ...
> Out of his oghne lond he fledde ... (VI, 1789–96, 1803)

And he concludes,

> And thus Nectanabus aboghte
> The Sorcerie which he wroghte:
> Thogh he upon the creatures
> Thurgh his carectes and figures
> The maistrie and the pouer hadde,
> His creatour to noght him ladde ... (VI, 2337–42)

Divine authority works in this tale precisely by allowing itself to be manipulated. It controls Nectanabus by making him think he is controlling it. And it allows his ultimate defeat to come from within history, as the inevitably transgressive outcome of his own transgressive power. By pushing the oblique relation between divine authority and temporal power to this extreme, Gower is able to authorize lay power precisely in its transgressive coerciveness. For it is precisely the self-regulating structure of that transgressiveness that Gower takes as divine authorization. Lay power is by its very nature contingent and incomplete. But for Gower its continual reassertions of its contingency and incompletion produce a self-regulation that is continually able to point beyond that incompletion. Alexander comes to maturity by parricide, exposing the hoax of his own lineage and the moral incompleteness of aristocratic privilege, while with this tale, Genius moves through the incompletion conferred upon him by his divinity to the higher moral competence of Book VII. Thus, Book VII comes as a rupture, but a rupture authorized precisely by the incompletion of the lay realm it disrupts.

SIMULATION AS AUTHORITY: BOOK VII, GOWER'S *FÜRSTENSPIEGEL*

The kingship Book VII celebrates is no less contingent than *gentilesse*, but it is better able to manage its contingency. The king is part of the nobility, but as the guarantor of its privilege, he is also distinct from it. The power he draws directly from class relations is less significant than the power he draws from his obligation (and right) to maintain them. In this way, even at its most material his power is more ideological and discursive than the noble power on which it depends. Such discursiveness provides the basis of Gower's affirmations. He will press it to its limit in order to assert the distinctiveness of royal authority, and its self-sufficiency with respect to the relations of material power from which it emerges. These relations can never be escaped entirely, since ultimately they provide royal power with its purpose. Gower minimizes kingship's dependence on them by treating them in their most generalizable state. Class dominance is restricted to royal prerogative, the single hierarchy that guarantees all the others. But, as I have already argued a number of times, in an aristocratic society, the hierarchy of class presupposes that of gender. Even royal authority cannot escape this necessity – a point Gower seems intent on demonstrating when he uses the story of Alexander's nativity as the transition to his *Fürstenspiegel*.

Amans initiates the digression of Book VII by asking to learn "Hou Alisandre was betawht / To Aristotle ... / Of al that to a king belongeth" (VI, 2411–13). If this request moves the poem out of the realm of Eros and into the "scoles of Philosophie," where Genius's authority is uncertain, it also frames philosophy as a political undertaking in the broadest sense. It defines Aristotle, history's most authoritative philospher, as instructor of Alexander, its most powerful monarch. Moreover, as it makes philosophy political, it also makes politics and, specifically kingship, philosophical. Amans asks for nothing less than entrance into the philosophical discourse which authorizes royal power.

Such entrance as Genius provides, he provides in largely narrative terms. Book VII divides Philosophy into three parts: *Theorique*, *Rethorique*, and *Practique*. Discussion of the first, which is subdivided into *Theologie*, *Phisique*, *Mathematique*, and includes digressions on the Four Elements and the Four Complexions, or humors, occupies lines 61–1506. After a brief treatment of rhetoric (1507–1640), he turns to *Practique*, which occupies the remainder and bulk (1641–5438 – over two-thirds) of the book. Following Aegidius Romanus, he subdivides this category into *Etique*, *Iconomique*, and *Policie*.[34] *Etique*, "Hou that a king himself schal reule ... / Of good livinge in his persone" (VII, 1654, 1657), is equivalent to Book I of the *De regimine*; Genius disposes of this topic in eighteen lines (1651–68). *Iconomique*, how a king should manage his family and household, is equivalent to Book II of the *De regimine*. Genius's treatment of this topic is even briefer: ten lines (1669–78). He focuses mainly on *Policie*, the equivalent to Book III of the *De Regimine*. Unlike Aegidius, however, who largely follows Aristotle's *Politics* in concerning himself with comparing monarchy to other forms of government, Genius construes *Policie* in exclusively personal and exemplary terms. He subdivides it into Truth, Liberality, Justice, Pity, and Chastity, a scheme loosely borrowed from the *Secretum secretorum*. He accurately describes each of these as "virtues." Three of them, Liberality, Pity, and Chastity, clearly refer on their face to the king's personal behavior. The other two, though they might theoretically be understood as institutional qualities, are also defined here as effects of the king's personal behavior.

The king thus stands as the exemplary figure at the center of Genius's exposition of Philosophy. He is constrained by Philosophy's wisdom, but the constraint is one he takes on of his own accord, which has force only by virtue of his voluntary submission to it. Book VII

---

[34] Both A. J. Minnis, "'Moral Gower' and Medieval Literary Theory" in *Responses and Reassessments*, ed. Yeager, 71–72; and Wilhelm Kleineke, *Englische Fürstenspiegel vom Policraticus Johanns von Salisbury bis zum Basilikon Doron König Jakobs I* (Halle: Niemeyer, 1937) have commented upon this correspondence.

offers Amans discursive participation in this exemplary power, and
through Amans, Gower's audience, whom he pictures as largely
courtly, though not exclusively so. What this audience shares is an
interest in the *status quo*, which royal power will protect.

In his definition of *Practique* Genius remarks,

> Thurgh hih pourveied ordinance
> A king schal sette in governance
> His Realme, and that is Policie,
> Which longeth unto Regalie
> In time of werre, in time of pes,
> To worschipe and to good encress
> Of clerk, of kniht and of Marchant,
> And so forth of the remenant
> Of al the comun poeple aboute ...
> And though thei ben noght alle like,
> Yit natheles, hou so it falle,
> O lawe mot governe hem alle,
> Or that thei lese or that thei winne,
> After thastat that thei ben inne. (VII, 1681–89, 1694–98)

The universality of royal law inheres in its protection of the hierarchy
of social estates, the maintenance of the relations of power that
constitute the *status quo*. In this way, Gower recuperates the lineal
prerogatives he had interrogated in his long critique of the chivalric
tradition. They are now assumed to be of interest to others who hold
property, such as merchants, but the emphasis is still on the lineal,
"thastat." This attenuation of this principle is the condition of its
recuperation.

The same thing is true of the gender relations upon which lineal
principles depend, as the first exemplum in the section makes clear.
It occurs under the heading Truth, the first point of *Policie*. Entitled
King, Wine, Woman, and Truth, it is built around successive answers
to a riddle. Each answer seems progressively to diminish royal power,
until the end of the exemplum, where it is recuperated all the more
emphatically. Daires, the Sultan of Persia, who came to his empire
through "wisdom and hih prudence / Mor than for eny reverence /
Of his lignage" (VII, 1787–89), offers a reward to three trusted
counselors for the best answer to this question: which is strongest,
Wine, Woman, or King? The first advisor argues for the king,
because "The pouer of a king stant so, / That he the lawes
overpasseth" (VII, 1838–39). The second argues for wine, claiming

that it "be weie of kinde / Is thing which mai the hertes binde / Well more than regalie" (VII, 1869–71). The third counselor, Zoroabel, begins by arguing for women, since "The king and the vinour also / Of wommen comen bothe tuo" (VII, 1875–76). They also control the power of love, a point he illustrates by offering two exempla.

The first involves Apemen, a young woman who ruled the emperor Cyrus through his infatuation for her. The second is the story of Alcestis, which Gower imports into this tale from Ovid. Alcestis saves her dying husband Duke Ametus by convincing Minerva to allow her to take on his disease and die in his stead. "So," Zoroabel concludes,

> ... mai a man be reson taste,
> Hou next after the god above
> The trouthe of wommen and the love,
> In whom that alle grace is founde,
> Is myhtiest upon this grounde
> And most behovely manyfold.   (VII, 1944–49)

However, this conclusion leads him to expand the grounds of the question in a way that approaches a rebuke. Truth, he suggests, is mightier than any of the alternatives Daires originally offered.

> The trouthe is schameles ate ende,
> Bot what thing that is troutheles,
> It mai noght wel be schameles,
> And schame hindreth every wyht:
> So proveth it, ther is no myht
> Withoute trouthe in no degre.   (VII, 1964–69)

Truth was not one of the alternatives Daires proposed, but it is so clearly superior to the rest that it threatens to trivialize the problem and Daires's reputation as a deep thinker along with it.

Nevertheless, both the substance and the immediate context of this claim ultimately recuperate the royal power they initially put in question. If Zoroabel challenges the basis of Daires's riddle, Daires is the one who ultimately makes Zoroabel's challenge good, for he adjudicates and rewards the superiority of Zoroabel's response. In this sense he can claim as much responsibility for the challenge as Zoroabel himself can. Daires established the conditions of the riddle, and maintains the general climate at court which rewards virtue.

Moreover, there is a subtle continuity in the way each of the competing answers defines power that returns it readily to the actual existing relations of power between Daires as monarch and his counselors as dependents. For each of the successive answers involves an overpassing similar to that articulated in the first answer as the king's overpassing of law. Wine and women can force men to overpass law as well, and more effectively. Nevertheless, the power of woman is exemplified most definitively not by the coquetry of Apemen, but by the sacrifice of Alcestis. Indeed, this act is more extravagant, more *lawless*, than the acts of a tyrant, drunkard, or coquette, but it differs in that its excess is directed inward; that is, the excess manifests itself as pure constraint. To what is that constraint directed? Ultimately to the status quo. Alcestis dies in order that "hir lord" may live. She preserves the power structure she inhabits by destroying herself. The power to overpass the law, then, is strongest when directed back toward it. The successive answers of the riddle, even as they lead away from kingship, end with an exercise of power which serves the royal interest. Truth becomes performative, and what it performs is the feat of internal constraint, the constant return, that is, to the givenness of the world in which human beings find themselves. Submitting himself to the judgment of his advisors, putting his material resources at their disposal, Daires is rewarded with a lesson which legitimates even as it challenges the givenness of his position, and names as truth the performative self-restraint which perpetuates his power.

Throughout the discussion that follows, Gower continually presents monarchy as a form of exemplary self-restraint whose overriding purpose is maintaining first its own privilege and then the privilege of those who share his power. After this demonstration as "the ground ... / Of every kinges regiment" (VII, 1980–81). Genius moves onto Largesse, whose imperative is to "yive riht to the lignages / In partinge of here heritages / And ek of al here other good" (VII, 2007–09). Defining this virtue as Largesse rather than Justice enables Gower both to affirm hereditary rights, and to make them the product not of their own givenness, but of the king's sovereign generosity. This, in turn, will enable him to define Justice in similar terms, not as the protection of existing rights secured by correspondence to external standards and regularized institutional procedures, but as the king's gift. The gift comes in part from the king's own voluntary restraint of his awesome, potentially absolute power, and in part from his willingness to unleash that power on those of his judges who do not follow his example.

One of the most striking exempla in this section is that of Cambyses, the Persian king who has a lawless judge flayed alive. He then orders that the dead man's skin be nailed to the seat his son and successor will sit on, as a cautionary reminder. In this tale, the rule of law becomes identical to the king's unlimited capacity to carry out punishments in its name. Gower follows this exemplum with the Tale of Lycurgus (VII, 2917–3028), his final treatment of the simulation of divine authority. Lycurgus, having developed a code of stringent laws, hits upon a ruse to insure that they are obeyed. He tells his people that the laws are entirely the invention of Mercury, whom he must now go to consult. He makes them promise to observe the laws until he gets back. Then, "after that he was ago, / He schop him nevere to be founde" (VII, 3002–03), insuring the laws would have force in perpetuity. This tale was well disseminated in the later Middle Ages, owing largely to the influence of the *Policraticus*, where we have already seen it.[35] John takes the story from Justinus, the author of a first-century epitome, but completely represses the ruse, which for Justinus had been one of its most important elements. Justinus leaves no doubt Lycurgus is feigning divine authority to advance a political purpose. He remarks that Lycurgus makes Apollo the author of the laws in the expectation that religious awe would overcome the tedium of compliance (*ut consuescendi taedium metus religionis vincat*).[36] That this interpretation of the story was not Justinus's alone can be confirmed by glancing at Valerius Maximus, who places a shorter version under the heading *Qui religionem simulaverent* (I, II, ext. 3). Some exemplarists following John returned to Justinus and restored Apollo, but still ignored the significance of Lycurgus's simulation. The *Gesta Romanorum*, for instance, mentions Apollo but leaves the ruse almost completely implicit. It then moralizes Lycurgus as Christ, bringer of divine law, erasing the ruse altogether.[37]

By contrast, Gower, who changes Apollo to Mercury, makes the ruse the center of his tale. Although he gives Lycurgus pious

---

[35] See above 97.   [36] Justinus, *Epitoma historiarum Phillipicarum*, III, 3.

[37] *Gesta Romanorum*, ed. Hermann Oesterley (Berlin: Weidmannsche Buchhandlung, 1872), L. 169, 557. Unfortunately many of Gower's modern expositors have retained this view of the tale. Gallacher (*Love, the Word, and Mercury*), for instance, seems as taken in by Lycurgus's ruse as Lycurgus expected his people to be. He takes Lycurgus's speech entirely at face value: "in it Lycurgus formally recognizes and acknowledges Mercury as the source of his legal inspiration" (119). Similarly, the ersatz mission to consult with the god is the result of an actual "divine message" (119), and the people's agreement to Lycurgus's terms constitutes "an anagnorisis, a movement from ignorance to knowledge in regard to the divine authority of their ruler" (120).

intentions, he leaves no doubt that what the intentions aim at is deception. When Lycurgus sees the benefit of his laws,

> He, which for evere wolde plese
> The hihe god, whos thonk he soghte,
> A wonder thing thanne him bethoghte,
> And schop if that it myhte be,
> Hou that his lawe in the cite
> Mihte afterward for evere laste
> And therupon his wit he caste
> What thing him were best to feigne,
> That he his pourpos myhte atteigne.   (VII, 2940–48)

The feigning he decides upon takes the form of a speech he makes to a "Parlement" (VII, 2949) he assembles. In twelve lines he manages to assert three times that his laws were made by Mercury.

> The lawe which I tok on honde,
> Was altogedre of goddes sonde
> And nothing of myn oghne wit;
> So mot it nede endure yit,
> And schal do lengere if ye wile.
> For I wol telle you the skile;
> The god Mercurius and no man
> He hath me tawht al that I can
> Of suche lawes as I made,
> Wherof that ye ben alle glade;
> It was the god and nothing I,
> Which dede al this...   (VII, 2961–72)

Nor is it the repetition alone that carries the point. The laws came "altogedre" from divine decree and not at all from Lycurgus's "oghne wit." It was no human being but Mercury who taught him all he knows about them. The god did everything and he did nothing.

As Lycurgus emphasizes the divine source of his authority, Gower emphasizes his fabrication of it. The emphasis suggests Gower himself returned to Justinus, though not enough is known either about Gower's reading habits or the availability of Justinus to be able to say for certain. What is clear is that he did not get the idea from the clerical tradition descending from John of Salisbury, and his revision of this tradition returns to Justinus in spirit if not in fact.[38] Indeed, in

---

[38] The other works in this tradition besides the *Gesta Romanorum* are the *Summa praedicantium* of John Bromyard (L, 3, 8); the *Communoloquium* (I, 3, 4); and the *Ludus schachorum* (II, 4). The first two do not mention Apollo. The last one does, and is much closer in detail and emphasis to Justinus, but adds a change of its own, which does not occur in Gower. See below, 316–17.

some ways Gower is more extreme than Justinus. In Justinus, Lycurgus does not speak, and, as we have just seen, it is the speech which enables Gower to emphasize the ruse. Moreover, the speech dominates the tale. The other versions, including John of Salisbury's, detail the mechanics of Lycurgus's self-imposed exile, his residence in Crete, and his command that his bones be scattered in the sea after his death. Gower merely notes tersely, "He schop him nevere to be founde" (VII, 3003).

In Lycurgus's ruse authority and monarchy converge in a paradoxical manner that asserts at once their unity and their distinctness. He achieves authority by faking it, but his faking has the same result that an actual divine intervention would have had. Gower's ascription of a Christian-like piety to this act, Lycurgus's constant desire to please the "hihe god," intensifies the paradox but does not remove it. On the contrary, the ascription suggests actual divinity is so far beyond social existence that it will sanction even fakery, so long as the fakery enforces social constraint. The ideological power this view of authority gives to monarchs is limitless, even if it does not come cheaply.

Lycurgus exchanges day-to-day control of his state for an intellectual control which is absolute. Self-sacrificial but entirely sovereign, he is Christ-like, and is, perhaps even more than Constantine, Gower's ideal monarch.[39] Yet it is important to recognize he is only *like* Christ, *pace* the *Gesta Romanorum*: his sacrifice is not finally salvific. He actually achieves his power from the gap between monarchy and the divinity he simulates. The simulation only empowers him because he is not divine. And because he is not divine, he is exemplary. His manipulation asserts not so much the sheer credulity of his people as their endless responsiveness to the initiatives of a self-producing, self-regulating monarch. Although he leaves, he never leaves. His sovereignty not only continues in force, but the self-imposed exile makes it absolute. No less a simulator than Boniface or Nectanabus, he achieves lasting authority because his simulation is exercised from a social position where power and self-restraint are synonymous. Because he draws his power from his

---

[39] This point has frequently been made before, albeit on the basis of a much different reading of the tale. See Fisher, *John Gower*, 202–03; and Peck, *Kingship and Common Profit*, 148–49. Nicholson (*Annotated Index*, 461) also cites Ethel Street, "John Gower," *London Mercury* 24 (1931), 230–42, and Edwart Weber, *John Gower: Dichter einer ethisch-politischen Reformation*, 101.

embodiment of the *status quo*, the monarch grows more powerful as his self-restraint makes that embodiment purer. This peculiar form his power takes makes his simulations self-policing.

Gower will make the same point in grimmer terms in his version of the Phalarean Bull, which occurs in the next section. This is the section on Pity, and placing the story here might seem odd, were it not for the equation Gower is intent on making between royal self-restraint and power. Through the exercise of pity, the king submits himself to the needs of his kingdom, but he does so always as an act of sovereign, unconstrained generosity, which Gower continually compares to Divine Grace. Indeed, in the opening lines of this section, he makes the two identical.

> It nedeth noght that I delate
> ... the vertu of Pite,
> Thurgh which the hihe mageste
> Was stered, whan his Sone alyhte,
> And in pite the world to rihte
> Tok of the Maide fleissh and blod.
> Pite was cause of thilke good,
> Wherof that we ben alle save ...   (VII, 3103, 3107–3113)

The monarch's quasi-salvific self-restraint founds the lay polity in the same way Christ's sacrifice founds the *societas Christiana*, but Gower emphasizes the sacrificial aspect of such restraint less than the power it produces. He retells the Tale of Codrus, another exemplum from the *Policraticus*, which John of Salisbury had placed just before the story of Lycurgus, as one of the exempla Paul used in preaching to the Athenians.[40] However, in most of the other exempla in this section what Gower stresses is pity's political and ideological efficacy. Sometimes its efficacy results from Divine intervention, as in the Jew and the Pagan (VII, 3207*–3360*),[41] and sometimes it results from the exemplary force of a monarch's act, as in Pompeius and the King of Armenia. Gower repeatedly makes it clear that royal pity has unrestricted royal prerogative as its precondition. In a brief exemplum concerning a condemned knight's plea to Alexander for clemency, Alexander reminds the knight his decisions are beyond appeal: "Non is above me" (VII, 3173*). In the knight's reply, he will enable Alexander to grant his appeal, precisely by making clemency an act that demonstrates Alexander's omnipotence, rather

---

[40] See above, 97–98.   [41] Neither this tale or the next are in all manuscripts.

than curtailing it. "Fro thy lordschipe appele I nought, / But fro thy wraththe in al my thought / To thy pitee stant myn appeel" (VII, 3175*-77*). The last few exempla, drawn mainly from the Old Testament, take pity to comprehend the direct exertion of force of arms. By punishing those who deserve punishing, the king takes pity on the rest of the realm. Gower uses the example of Gideon to illustrate the necessity of just war, and the examples of Saul and Agag, and David and Joab, to illustrate the necessity of executing those who deserve executing (VII, 3627–3890).

The Phalarean Bull occurs in the middle (VII, 3295–3337), sandwiched between two other exempla concerning monarchical cruelty. In the other two cruelty leads to the monarch's downfall. Here, however, the monarch is affirmed in spite of, or perhaps even because of, his cruelty. This exemplum reprises on a smaller scale one of Chaucer's central ideas in the *Clerk's Tale* (where pity also plays an important role); that kingship is so singular as the form social order must inevitably take that even bad kings produce order. The story originates with Ovid, and is briefly recounted by Dante in *Inferno* XVII. Gower probably drew it from Godrey of Viterbo's *Pantheon*. He mistakes Phalaris's name to be Siculus, apparently by mistranslating Phalaris Siculus. Siculus is a pitiless tyrant. His counselor Berillus presents him with a brass bull within which victims are roasted alive. The machine's construction is such that it makes all their cries of pain sound like the bellowing of a bull, depriving victims not only of their lives but also of their voices and denying all meaning to their resistance. It invalidates even their experience of their oppression, for the only language they have for expressing that experience has already been prescribed by their oppressor. His control over their language is as absolute as his control over their bodies. However, the first victim becomes Berillus himself.

In this exemplum, monarchy becomes so dominant that it is literally the only form in which power can be represented or articulated. While Berillus's cruelty is punished, Siculus's cruelty is accepted as a given, the inevitability which both calls Berillus's forth and then punishes it. In this exchange of cruelty Siculus trumps Berillus, but in so doing, he corrects the excess Berillus represents. In this way, the exemplum's narrative denouement recapitulates the absolute royal dominance the bull figures emblematically. Monarchy inevitably produces social order, because it is the only form order can take.

The final point of *Policie* is chastity. After the suggestions of divinity and absolute prerogative that circulate through the sections on justice and pity, this conclusion may seem a bit of a retreat. The ideal of chastity definitely requires submission to an external constraint, and Genius's recommendation of it recalls the king from the limitless zone of judicial and political action, where restraint is self-generated, to the more restricted arena of sexuality, where his actions must conform to external moral standards. Yet this retreat, if it is one, is not so great as it first appears to be. We should be wary of judgments that depend on that very modern distinction between the public and the private. As feminism has taught us, sexuality always involves power, and that is especially true in aristocratic societies where class status depends largely on birth.

Making the king's sexuality a matter of public policy reaffirms his person as the locus of public order. Gower magnifies the claim by comparing the king's chastity to that of the clergy.

> Bot yit a kinges hihe astat,
> Which of his ordre as a prelat
> Shal ben enoignt and seintefied.
> He mot be more magnefied
> For dignete of his corone,
> Than scholde an other low persone,
> Which is noght of so hih emprise. (VII, 4245–51)

This evocation of royal prelacy delivers the sanctification of lay authority Gower has been seeking throughout the poem. He has played chivalric values off against the Latin traditions of the Church. As the final magnification of kingship, chastity enables him to move beyond the evanescent spirituality of *fin'amors*, to a form of personal authority that approaches the solidity of the clerical, but which, by virtue of its location in the king, remains resolutely lay.

As Genius remarks shortly after this passage, this ideal is also exemplary. Aristotle warned Alexander that while he should enjoy the beauty of women, "forto gladen his corage," he should also

> ... set an essamplaire,
> His bodi so to guide and reule,
> That he ne passe noght the reule,
> Whereof that he himself beguile. (VII, 4259, 4262–65)

The self-regulated body of the monarch can become an exemplary force drawing together the rest of the court. Moreover this exemplarity is precisely what enables a king to move beyond the chivalric realm of *fin'amors*. It gives his body, and by extension, his personal superiority, an entirely discursive force, which nevertheless remains his property, subject to his agency. In effect, chastity enables him to embody the *status quo* at precisely the point where class and gender, its two fundamental determinants, intersect. By respecting his female subjects' right to their own bodies, the king also respects the lineal rights of their husbands and fathers. Gower's exploration of this virtue concentrates first on the former, but will move quickly to include the latter as well.

If the king becomes unchaste, it is because he "beguiles" himself, not because he is beguiled by women. Since men are socially sanctioned to pursue women (VII, 4284–91), they must be viewed as the instigators of their own passions.

> For if a man himself excite
> To drenche, and wol it noght forbere,
> The water schal no blame bere.
> What mai the gold, thogh men coveite?
> If that a man wol love streite,
> The womman hath him nothing bounde;
> If he his oghne herte wounde,
> Sche mai noght lette the folie... (VII, 4276–83)

This insistence that a man in love wounds his own heart flatly contradicts the conceit of Cupid's bow, that cornerstone of courtly love, which depicts the courtly lover as a passive sufferer. Once love becomes the product of the male lover, it becomes entirely amenable to his own regulation. This final dismissal of the hyperbolic discourse of romance leads to a final articulation of the more balanced discourse of royal authority, although it comes in a characteristically negative fashion. Gower illustrates chastity mainly by wicked exempla from Roman history, the stories of Lucrece and Virginia.

These stories enable him to orient the ideal of chastity around class as well as gender. They also raise the specter of deposition, as Genius will explicitly acknowledge. But he does so in a distorted fashion which eliminates any hint of republicanism. While the invocation of deposition acknowledges monarchy's dependence on public support, the elimination of republicanism insures that kingship remains the inevitable form social order must take.

The repression of republicanism begins in Gower's version of Lucrece, which does not mention deposition, and completely de-

emphasizes the aftermath of her suicide, disposing of it summarily in
seven lines:

> And al the toun began to crie,
> "Awey, awey the tirannie
> Of lecherie and covoitise!"
> And ate laste in such a wise
> The fader in the same while
> Forth with his Sone thei exile,
> And taken betre governance.   (VII, 5117–23)

Genius completely neglects the transition from the old Roman
kingdom to the Republic, which for Livy is the central meaning of
this incident. The reference to "betre governance" is so vague that it
is possible to read the "comun clamour" against "the tirannie" as
directed solely against the personal excesses of Tarquin and Aruns,
and not against the structure they represent.

Gower prefaces the story of Lucrece with the tale of Tarquin's
perfidious conquest of Gabii, which he takes from Ovid. Tarquin's
son, whom Gower names as Aruns (in Ovid and Livy he is Sextus),
secretly wounds himself, then convinces the Gabians his father has
sent him into exile. Once he has gained their confidence, he stealthily
beheads their princes, on his father's orders, leaving the city
completely defenseless to his father's attack. These actions are so
reprehensible that when Tarquin offers a sacrifice in thanks to
Apollo, it is rejected. In his rejection Apollo declares cryptically that
these wrongs will be avenged by the first of those present to kiss his
mother. Brutus, the leader-to-be of the republican insurgency, whom
the text continually describes as a "knyht," falls immediately to the
ground to kiss "his mother," the earth (VII, 4735–53). In this way,
Gower ties the two exempla together, and makes Lucrece's rape the
final instance of Tarquin's more general "covoitise," his continual
infringement on the prerogatives of his knights. His downfall affirms
the centrality of this obligation, but it does so entirely within a
monarchical framework.

Gower withholds explicit mention of deposition until the end of the
Virginia story, where it can have no republican overtones. Macaulay
unaccountably claims, "Gower follows Livy, or some account drawn
from Livy, without material alteration" (vol. 3, 535). In fact, he
completely changes the tale's political setting, transforming Appius
Claudius into a king, and Virginius, who was a plebeian in Livy, into
a knight. This change at once makes the story more immediately

applicable to the subject of Book VII, and dehistoricizes Livy. Livy presents the Virginia story as one of a series of rapes or captures which each mark an important constitutional shift in the history of the city. Gower makes the story a flat analogue of the Lucrece exemplum, depriving it of any larger significance in the development of Rome, and dedicating it entirely to his exploration of the exemplary significance of royal sexuality.

He does present the process of deposition in more detail here. After beheading his daughter, Virginius returns to camp, "ther as the pouer was / Of Rome," who all swear to return to the city and "stonde be the riht" (VII, 5265–81). The king's "prive tricherie" (VII, 5287) becomes known, and

> Thurgh comun conseil of hem alle
> Thei have here wrongfull king deposed,
> And hem in whom it was supposed
> The conseil stod of his ledinge
> Be lawe unto the dom thei bringe,
> Wher thei receiven the penance
> That longeth to such governance.   (VII, 5294–5300)

This passage asserts monarchy's public obligations, but it does so in terms which clearly recall the personal logic of the corporate fiction. The king is he "in whom it was supposed / The conseil stod of his leding": he is obligated to embody the common interest of his "conseil," but he is obligated to do so on his own initiative, by "his ledinge," not in response to legal restraint. There is no republicanism here. The king is deposed, just as Richard will be, for his failure to embody the common interest – a common interest which some lines earlier has been defined as the patriarchal privileges of his knighthood. When the "pouer of Rome" decide to return to the city, they declare

> For thus stant every mannes lif
> In jeupartie for his wif
> Or for his dowhter, if thei be
> Passende an other of beaute.   (VII, 5273–76)

We could say that Appius fails to maintain the moral obligations that accrue to him personally as part of his unconstrained royal prerogatives. But we come closer to Gower's position if we say that he fails to make the exchange Lycurgus makes – self-restraint for power. It is not just that he doesn't live up to his obligations. He fails to recognize that the obligations themselves are the product of his monarchical position. He fails to take control of the exemplary authority only a king can produce and misses the opportunity to produce it not only in his realm, but in the very regulation of his body.

These negative exempla end Gower's consideration of kingship in a way that affirms both its public dependence and the absolute singularity of its authority. In fact, it makes the two synonymous. The image of the self-regulated royal body informs both of these narratives, but its force is necessarily implicit, brought to them by Gower's readers with his guidance. To that extent royal self-regulation comes from them and they share its power. This may be another reason for ending with chastity. Bringing royal authority back to the body gives the ideological connection between Gower's readers and his royal exempla material force. For chastity is a virtue they can all exercise in a way they could not with the first four. Moreover, it could empower them in the same way it empowers the monarch, to whatever extent they share an interest in the *status quo* he protects. By protecting the sanctity of marriage they protect the balance between class and gender relations on which the distribution of power depends.[42]

The poem's final book, with its substitution of incest for lechery, reinforces this materialistic, political view of marriage. The opening discussion treats the incest taboo as contingent and historically specific, making it largely a post-Christian phenomenon identified with the regulatory apparatus of canon law.[43] The bulk of the book is devoted to one exemplum, the other story to which the Man of Law objected, Apollonius of Tyre. However, this is not a wicked example in the way I have been using the term; instead, it is a story of royal forbearance rewarded. Persecuted by an incestuous father whose secret he has has discovered, betrayed at various points on his

---

[42] This would hold for female as well as male readers, though obviously the exemplary identification would be more attractive to men. Since the figure of the chaste king protects class as well as gender privilege, it would make itself available to aristocratic women, who would be invited to accept gender subordination in exchange for class privilege.

[43] Cf. VIII, 140–47:

> [The Hebrews] ...
> For evere kepten thilke usance [i.e., incestuous union among cousins]
> Most comunly, til Crist was bore.
> Bot afterward it was forbore
> Amonges ous that ben baptized;
> For of the lawe canonized
> The Pope hath bede to the men,
> That non schal wedden of his ken
> Ne the seconde ne the thridde.

wanderings, and beset by natural calamities, Apollonius eventually ascends to the throne, recovers the wife and daughter he had thought both lost, and acquires his father-in-law's kingdom as well. R. F. Yeager suggests the tale is an "exemplary *summa*," in which all of the sins of the previous books are encountered and overcome.[44] Whether a reading this encyclopedic can be sustained or not, it is clear that Apollonius's hard-won triumphs fulfill the opportunity left empty at the end of Book VII: moral order established by the struggle of an exemplary monarch against fierce resistance.

The affirmations of this ending are not complacent ones, any more than complacency marks Gower's project as a whole. If he views moral order as achievable within history, he also views it as coming at a great cost in a form that requires heroic effort to maintain. That form is kingship, which he explicitly and systematically identifies as the only form in which moral order can be achieved. This affirmation provides a point of certainty, to be sure, but one that is constantly under siege. For Gower arrives at the certainty from his profound distrust of all forms of human authority, rather than from some spontaneous and pious veneration of monarchy. His differences with Chaucer have been entirely overstated. Can we really say, for example, that Book VIII, with its clear-eyed analysis of incest, and its account of the long-suffering Apollonius is a more conservative and complacent ending than the *Parson's Tale*? Chaucer's certainties tend to be expressed in religious terms, Gower's in political ones. If modern readers have too often neglected Chaucer's dependence on the clerical traditions he resists, they have also neglected Gower's systematic recognition of the contradictions surrounding the political structures he affirms. But Gower's explicit engagement with the political was no less important in the establishment of the Chaucerian tradition than Chaucer's reappropriation and redefinition of clerical tradition. As the fifteenth century put the tradition in place, it gave the tradition Chaucer's name, and made him its authoritative source. In so doing, however, they drew just as heavily on the more explicitly political models of authority developed by Gower.

[44] Yeager, *Gower's Poetic*, 218.

CHAPTER 10

The Chaucerian tradition in the fifteenth century

One of the premises of this study has been that narratives depend on readers, and that this dependence is not only a formal property but also an historical condition. It may well be that Chaucer's innovations justify the ascription of his name to the tradition both he and Gower initiate. But it must not be forgotten that that ascription was not his accomplishment, but that of his fifteenth-century successors. In this chapter I examine the exemplum collections of the two most important of these successors, Thomas Hoccleve, and John Lydgate. I argue that they constitute not a regression, as they are conventionally viewed, but a consolidation. The most significant difference between Hoccleve and Lydgate and Gower and Chaucer, is that the later poets largely abandon the anti-clericalism that so marks the work of the earlier ones. This shift is not a matter of some simple resurgence of piety (in any case it is hard to imagine a poet more pious than Chaucer in his pious moments). It can be explained as a confluence of historical circumstances directly related to the politics of the emergent lay tradition. First, the Lancastrian royal court was becoming increasingly anxious about clerical orthodoxy, in the face of a growing Lollard threat. Second, lacking clear dynastic legitimacy, it needed ideological support from the Church that the Plantagenets had not. Third, this second circumstance drove it to seek ideological legitimacy as well in patronage of the new vernacular tradition, a legitimacy which did not exist until Chaucer and Gower produced it. As long as we recognize the political basis of Chaucer and Gower's anti-clericalism, we can also recognize the political reasons Hoccleve and Lydgate had to abandon it. With a specifically lay source of vernacular authority already available there wasn't the same need for direct appropriation from the Church. Hoccleve and Lydgate could meet the needs of their Lancastrian patrons by making lay legitimation and clerical legitimation compatible. As we shall see, however, their reconciliation with clerical tradition occurs entirely on the restricted ground the anti-clericalism of Chaucer and Gower laid out. Their main emphasis is to solidify the shape of lay authority, connecting its political aspect specifically to the Lancastrians, and its textual aspect specifically to Chaucer. In the modern metanarrative of canonical authority, the ultimate *auctor* is Homer, the origin of Western literature. It has been the considerable accomplishment of twentieth-century classical scholarship to demonstrate that Homer's authority is more accurately understood as the product of a complex, continually self-elaborating tradition, than as the solitary achievement of a single, sovereign consciousness. We should not be surprised to find the authority of Chaucer, the first English *auctor* – England's Homer, as the Renaissance described him – similarly constituted.[1]

THE KING'S TWO VOICES : HOCCLEVE'S *REGEMENT OF PRINCES*

Until quite recently, Thomas Hoccleve (*c.* 1368–*c.* 1437) has been virtually ignored by modern scholarship, despite the evidence of his contemporary significance. The *Regement of Princes*, his most important work, survives in approximately forty-five manuscripts, suggesting its dissemination was comparable to that of *Piers Plowman* and the *Confessio Amantis*. This would have made its circulation much wider than that of the *Pearl* poems, and other later Middle English texts which have attracted far more attention. Indeed, its extant copies are significantly outnumbered by those of only one Middle English poem, the *Canterbury Tales*.

The recent interest in Hoccleve has centered largely on his use of autobiography.[2] In this account of the *Regement*, I want to broaden that approach to a concern with subjectivity, and to stress its political dimensions. Hoccleve was Chaucer's first major disciple; in the

---

[1] Alice Miskimmin, *The Renaissance Chaucer* (New Haven: Yale University Press, 1975), 9, 241.

[2] John Burrow, "Autobiographical Poetry in the Middle Ages," *Proceedings of the British Academy* 68 (1982) 389–412; and "Hoccleve 'Series': Experience and Books," in *Fifteenth-Century Studies*, ed. R. F. Yeager (Hamden: Archon Books, 1984), 259–73; Albrecht Classen, *Die Autobiographische Lyrik des Europäischen Spätmittelalters* (Amsterdam, Atlanta: Rodopi, 1991), 211–67; Penelope B. R. Doob, *Nebuchadnezzar's Children* (New Haven: Yale, 1974), 208–31; D. C. Greetham, "Self-Referential Artifacts: Hoccleve's *Persona* as a Literary Device," *Modern Philology* 86 (1989), 242–51; Douglas J. McMillan, "The Single Most Popular of Thomas Hoccleve's Poems: *The Regement of Princes*," *Neuphilologische Mitteilungen* 89 (1988), 63–71. Spearing, *Medieval to Renaissance*, 110–20.

Regement he connects the problem of narrative authority to that of narrative voice even more tightly than the master does, and his interest in autobiography is always colored by that connection. The *Regement* was a public poem, and one of the most important public poems of its time. Any autobiographical approach which does not come to terms with that fact distorts the significance of the very autobiographical impulse it claims to explain. Hoccleve was a very public poet: during the course of his career he received or sought the patronage of Henry V, his brothers Humphrey and Edward, the Treasurer, Lord Furnivall, the Chancellor, Sir Henry Soner, and the Countess of Westmoreland, to name only the most notable.[3] He may be English literature's "first chronicler of private worries," but neither the chronicle nor the worries themselves ever ceased to be public.[4] His autobiographical turns are decidedly not the expressions of some unitary private self in a pre-social or pre-ideological state. They are continually framed both by his position at court as a Clerk of the Privy Seal, and by the traditions he draws upon to articulate them. Although there has been some effort to distance Hoccleve from many of the postmodern concerns he anticipates,[5] the fact is his approach to autobiography is quite similar to postmodern views of the self as a nexus of social and ideological forces. Nowhere is this truer than in the *Regement of Princes*.

The *Regement* was written between 1410 and 1412 for the future Henry V.[6] It is both an exemplum collection, and as its title announces, a *Fürstenspiegel*. It has a long, autobiographical prologue that accounts for over a third (2016 lines of 5463) of its total length. In the course of describing Hoccleve's financial worries, the Prologue will enable him to stage the *Fürstenspiegel* to follow as a begging poem. While preoccupied with these worries, he meets a beggar. When he tells the beggar he cannot get his annuity paid regularly, the beggar, after some philosophical advice about the virtue of poverty and the

---

[3] William Mathews, "Thomas Hoccleve," in *A Manual of the Writings in Middle English 1050–1500*, ed. Albert E. Hartung, 7 vols. (New Haven: Connecticut Academy of Arts and Sciences, 1972), vol. 3, 747.   [4] Burrow, "Hoccleve's 'Series,'" 268.
[5] Burrow, "Hoccleve's 'Series,'" 260.
[6] Since the work is addressed to Henry as the Prince of Wales, it would have to have been written before March 21, 1413, the date of his coronation. Its allusion in the Prologue to the March 1, 1410 execution of the Lollard John Badby places it after that date. Furnivall (*Hoccleve's Works: I. The Minor Works* (London: published for the Early English Text Society by Kegan Paul, Trench Trübner & Co., 1892), xiii) settles on 1412 because the Court Rolls seem to indicate an interruption in Hoccleve's annuity in that year. This date, however, depends on a strictly literal reading of the poem's begging stance.

instability of Fortune, suggest that in exchange for Prince Henry's intervention, Hoccleve translate some "tretice / Groundid on his [i.e., Henry's] estates holsumnesse," that is, a *Fürstenspiegel*.[7]

The begging poem was a comparatively late genre, emerging in France in the fourteenth century.[8] It presupposes a court in transition from the personal to the bureaucratic, one sufficiently bureaucratized that petitions for small sums of money have become routine, but still sufficiently invested in the personal to want to see the granting of such petitions as the whimsical response to a *jeu d'esprit*. The begging poem postulates a royal will which acts entirely at its own pleasure, and thus stands as a striking counterpoise to the didactic presumptions of the *Fürstenspiegel*. At the same time, yoking the two genres together simply underlines a tension between moral constraint and royal freedom that I have been arguing was already long established within the *Fürstenspiegel* itself. Hoccleve's recourse to autobiography will enable him to foreground this tension in a novel way.

As a minor lay official, Hoccleve had neither the institutional prestige of the Church, nor even the comparative independence of writers like Boccaccio and Gower, to bolster his pretension to offer moral counsel to a prince on whom he was soon to be entirely dependent. But authority was a problem for Henry too. His father had never succeeded in making the constitutional basis of his title entirely coherent. Henry IV had faced revolts in 1400 and 1402, and by 1410, his ailments had forced him to leave the overseeing of the kingdom to councillors who were openly feuding with the Prince.[9] Against this background the *Regement of Princes* can be seen as a direct attempt to secure the continuity of Lancastrian rule. In fact, it was the first of many ideological projects Henry V sponsored to confirm his legitimacy.[10] By addressing a *Fürstenspiegel* to the future Henry V, Hoccleve effectively settles the question of dynastic rights by treating it as if it were already settled. He reinforces the point by scattering through the poem favourable invocations of the Prince's patrimony: his father, the king (816–26, 1835, 3347–67), his grandfather, John of Gaunt (3347–67), and his great-grandfather, Henry of Lancaster

---

[7] Thomas Hoccleve, *Regement of Princes*, ed. Frederick J. Furnivall (London: 1897), 71, lines 1949–50. All subsequent citations are from this edition and will hereafter be given in the text.   [8] A. C. Spearing, *Medieval to Renaissance*, 111.

[9] McFarlane, *Lancastrian Kings*, 106–112. See also David Lawton, "Dullness and the Fifteenth Century," *ELH* 54 (1987), 776–77, who reads the situation somewhat differently.

[10] For a brief account, see G. L. Harriss, "Introduction: The Exemplar of Kingship," in *Henry V: The Practices of Kingship*, ed. Harriss (Oxford: Oxford University Press, 1985), 1–29.

(2647–53). This rhetorical representation of Henry as dynastically legitimate with a long, honorable patrimony, and about to receive a *Fürstenspiegel*, can appropriately be described as a narrative positioning. It is narrative because it historicizes. It not only locates the *persona* it produces within a pre-existent social totality, but also produces the *persona* precisely by so locating it. Yet this positioning is also curiously self-generated, whether we view it from Hoccleve's standpoint or from Henry's. The authority of such narrative self-generation is the main concern of the poem's Prologue, and the ulterior motive behind its recourse to autobiography.

Largely a dialogue between Hoccleve and the beggar who is in many ways Hoccleve's alter-ego, the Prologue defines the problem of authority as a problem of voice. As I have already remarked, narrative's generation of voice links it to ideology and the generation of subject-positions.[11] As an intersection between language and selfhood that never ceases to be linguistic, voice gives narrative its strongest claim to be reproducing the real.[12] The Prologue's focus on voice returns to one of the central features of the Canterbury collection: Chaucer's claim to be reproducing the voice of others. Like Chaucer, Hoccleve uses the exchange between narrative voice and social position to complicate the problem of authority. But he will also make such complications themselves authorizing, and this too is like Chaucer. Hoccleve presents his autobiography as an exemplification of the mutability of Fortune. Through the series of cross-identifications involved in the generation and exchange of the Prologue's narrative voices, he will produce two sources of authority which provide a means of transcending Fortune, the vernacular poetic authority embodied in Chaucer, and the political authority embodied in Henry.

These shifts in narrative voice are as daring as anything that can be found in Chaucer, and Hoccleve opens with a particularly audacious maneuver. "Musyng upon the restles bisynesse / Which that this troubly world hath ay on honde," the poet spends a sleepless night at the Chester Inn (1–7). His reflections on the "brotylnesse" of Fortune (15–21) quickly become generalized:

> Me fel to mynde how that, not long ago,
> ffortunes strok doun threst estaat royal
> Into myscheef; and I took heed also
> Of many anothir lord that had a fall... (22–25)

---

[11] See above, 30–36.   [12] Cf. Genette, *Narrative Discourse*, 86–87.

Hoccleve derives the justification for this explicit comparison between his estate and that of the deposed Richard from the exemplary logic of the *De casibus* tradition. The spectacle of a king's fall holds a lesson for his subjects by requiring them to put themselves in his place, to recognize that the Fortune which punished him can punish them even more easily. Nevertheless, this logic tends to be an implicit one. Making it this explicit would be presumptuous even if the comparison did not raise other questions as well, which it does with a vengeance. Indeed, this allusion to the deposition would seem to cast serious doubt on Hoccleve's entire project. Is he sympathizing with Richard? Is he presenting Richard as an unwitting victim of Fortune, when the Lancastrian position assumed that Richard brought his fate entirely upon himself? Doesn't this recollection of the uncertainty of Richard's position call attention to the fragility of Henry's? Fortune, it would seem, levels all distinctions and invalidates all political authority. For it not only makes Hoccleve and Richard indistinguishable, it also makes Henry and Richard indistinguishable, and denies the Prince the very authority which Hoccleve in writing this poem expects to ascribe to him.

Hoccleve solves this problem by exacerbating it. The exemplary logic which produces the identification with Richard depends on narrative's capacity to move between subject positions. Hoccleve preserves the distinctions this opening calls into question by pushing the process onward and generating another narrative voice, that of the beggar. The beggar is Hoccleve's alter-ego in both public and personal terms. He anticipates Hoccleve's beggarly position in relation to Henry; indeed, Hoccleve assumes that position at his suggestion. He also echoes Hoccleve's confessional *persona*. He tells his own autobiography, and its explanation of how he became a beggar recalls, in its portrayal of a youth misspent in taverns, *La Male Regle*, Hoccleve's account of his own misspent youth. At the same time, the beggar's very alterity gives him an authority Hoccleve cannot claim in his own voice. As this alterity clears the narrative space Hoccleve needs to achieve his own authority, it also justifies such authority's self-generation. It demonstrates narrative can produce moral authority out of its own internal logic.

The beggar enters the Prologue as an authority very much narratively constituted. Despite its long philosophic pedigree in both classical and medieval tradition, the dialogue is always narrative, even if only incipiently so. Hoccleve foregrounds the dialogue's narrative dimension through both the continual interchange between the autobiographical and philosophical, and through the continual exploitation of the irregularities and discontinuities of colloquial speech. As authoritative interlocutor, the beggar's antecedent is Gower's Genius, and the diverse allegorical tradition of similar figures. He acts for much of the dialogue like a confessor, prompting Hoccleve to reveal his state of mind, interrogating him about his beliefs and habits and offering him moral counsel. But the beggar also offers his own confession, and what gives his counsel authority is not some allegorical status, but his own exemplification of the efficacy of such counsel. He can recommend the virtue of poverty as a defense against Fortune because his own experience demonstrates it.

The two encounter each other in an open field where Hoccleve goes to wander after his restless night. When Hoccleve does not respond to his greeting, the beggar shakes him out of his day-dreaming, and despite Hoccleve's repeated desire to be left alone, urges him to tell his troubles. Warning that despair can lead one to heresy, the beggar recounts the Lollard John Badby's denial of Transubstantiation, and his subsequent execution. After Hoccleve responds by assuring the beggar he is not a Lollard, the beggar warns Hoccleve not to despise his counsel because of the poverty of his attire. This leads to a long attack on dressing above one's station, followed by the beggar's autobiography and then Hoccleve's explanation of his financial worries. After a series of exchanges in which the beggar explains the virtues of Poverty and Hoccleve resists, Hoccleve insists on his need to support his wife, and the beggar, once he determines Hoccleve has married for love and not lust or money, suggests he approach Prince Henry.

The attacks on Lollardy and contemporary dress may seem digressive. In fact, both are aimed against the kind of presumption which the Prologue's opening threatened, and which the beggar was brought into the poem to defuse. As the beggar presents it, Lollardry aspires to appropriate the doctrinal privileges of the clergy. Dressing above one's station is obviously an attempt to appropriate the social privileges of lordship. Having established these two parameters of social order, the beggar can proceed to deal with Hoccleve's problem more directly. He stands before Hoccleve as proof positive that poverty cannot only be endured but can bring with it virtue. The "povert" which followed his wasted youth is "þe glas and þe merour / In whiche I se my god, my savyour" (690–91). His exemplary authority is all the more convincing for the fact that he never sought it. As a young man his only interest was the tavern. In a stanza which explicitly recalls the *Pardoner's Tale*, he declares,

> Whan folk wel rulyd dressyd hem to bedde,
> In tyme due by rede of nature,
> To þe taverne quykly I me spedde,
> And pleyde at dees while þe nyghte wolde endure.
> Þere, þe former of every creature
> Dismembred y with oþes grete, & rente
> Lyme for lyme, or þat I þennes wente. (624–30)

Like the Pardoner's rioters, he set out to destroy the source of all authority (through *speech*), and like them ends by affirming it, although in less violent fashion. That he survives his fall affirms as well the availability of such authority within temporal existence on temporal terms. The authority he offers to Hoccleve is an authority Hoccleve can offer in turn to Henry to stabilize the anarchic chaos in which the poem began.

The beggar's suggestion of an appeal to Henry through the composition of a *Fürstenspiegel* will solve Hoccleve's financial problem at the same time it strengthens a threatened "estaat royal." There is nothing coincidental about the connection. For the solution to both problems assumes the possiblity of moral authority that comes from outside historical existence, but is fully recognizable within it. This point is confirmed by the indirect and apparently casual manner in which the solution is introduced. The beggar speaks:

> "O my good sone, wolt þou yit algate
> Despeired be? nay, sone, lat be þat!
> Þou schalt as blyve entre in-to þe yate
> Of þi comfort. now telle on pleyn and plat:
> My lord þe prince, knowyth he þe nat?
> If þat þou stonde in his benevolence,
> He may be salue un-to þin indigence.
>
> "No man bet, next his fadir, our lord lige."
> "Yis, fadir, he is my good gracious lord."
> "Wel sone, þan wole I me oblige, –
> And god of heuen vouch I to record, –
> Þat if þou wolt be ful of myn accord,
> Thow schalt no cause haue more þus to muse,
> But heuynesse voide, and it refuse.
>
> "Syn he þi good lord is, I am ful seur
> His grace to þe schal nat be denyed;

Þou wost wele, he benying is and demeur
To sue vnto; naght is his goost maistried
With daunger, but his hert is ful applied
To graunte, and nat þe needy werne his grace;
To hym pursue, and þi releef purchace." (1828–48)

This suggestion comes much more easily via the beggar than it would have had it been made in Hoccleve's own voice. The beggar's praise of Prince Henry would have had the appearance of crass flattery had it been addressed to Henry directly by Hoccleve. But because it arises in the course of a conversation where the Prince is not present, it acquires the givenness of an objective truth. When the beggar off-handedly concludes, "No man bet, next his fadir," his very off-handedness increases the impression that Henry's virtue is a matter of both lineage, and simple common knowledge, both now standing beyond any possible dispute.

Hoccleve links this assertion of Henry's virtue to the granting of his suit, leaving the onus of proof deftly and almost imperceptibly on Henry, but making such proof, by the very imperceptibility of the link, a matter of course. The suit is at once a test of Henry's generosity and a ratification of his future. For as Hoccleve's projected redeemer, Henry becomes a moral force standing outside the cycle of Fortune, impervious to the instabilities that undid Richard.

The beggar enforces this impression with the specific suggestion, which comes a bit later, that the appeal take the form of a *Fürstenspiegel*:

"looke if þou fynde canst fynde any tretice
Groundid on his estates holsumnesse;
Swych thing translate, and unto his hynesse
As humbely as þat þou canst, present." (1949–52)

Hoccleve will appeal not simply to Henry's grace, but to his presumed enthusiasm for moral instruction. The beggar precedes this final suggestion with a warning against flattery: "But of a thyng be wel waar in al wise, / On flaterie þat þou þe nat founde," adding that advisors are afraid to tell their lords the truth, and instead, "thei stryuen who best rynge shal þe belle / Of fals plesance" (1912–13, 29–30). Lords are so continually surrounded by such flattery that it is impossible for them to learn their true condition, and therefore the greatest service Hoccleve can perform for Henry is to tell him the truth (1933–46).

The beggar so firmly associates pleasant news with flattery that the measure of the truth becomes virtually its unpleasantness to princely ears. As a form of speech that is purely false, flattery functions as a degraded other in relation to the authoritative claims of both the dialogue with the beggar and the imminent address to the Prince. For flattery also involves movement between points of view, but a movement which does not acknowledge itself as such. The flatterer assumes the point of view he takes to be his lord's, and speaks in the voice the lord wants to hear. But he never admits the shift has occurred. By contrast, Hoccleve's audacity and presumption becomes a sign of his integrity, and paradoxically, of his respect for the very social distinctions his narrative shifts are continually breaching. At this point the narrative frame for Hoccleve's authority has been fully articulated, providing the Prince with moral grounds for granting his suit. By accepting the *Fürstenspiegel* Hoccleve offers, the Prince will demonstrate that he is a ruler who prefers the truth to flattery – a virtue with which, of course, the beggar has already endowed him. The beggar's intervention transforms a self-interested petition into a fully moral exchange between a model ruler and a loyal subject. In return for moral instruction, Henry will award an annuity, not as mere compensation, but as a sign of his devotion to morality. This entirely authoritative exchange is the product of the Prologue's narrative transformations, transformations which move between social positions precisely as a way of demonstrating the integrity such positions necessarily retain. Like the voice of any narrative figure, the beggar's is at once his author's and his own, but Hoccleve intensifies the effect of this resemblance in difference precisely by identifying this voice as a beggar's. This diffuses the begging position from which he himself speaks, making it more general. Generalizing the position of beggar enables him to present it favorably. The beggar resembles Hoccleve in that both are beggars; he differs from Hoccleve in that Hoccleve is his social superior. This difference means that when he speaks to Hoccleve, and through Hoccleve to Prince Henry, both Hoccleve and the Prince are now in the same position: social superiors being addressed by a subordinate.

Yet their shared difference in relation to the beggar will ultimately affirm their difference from each other, and certify the autonomous space from which Hoccleve speaks. When the beggar first offers his assistance Hoccleve scoffs at his infirmity and meager appearance, concluding that "it moste be a greter man of myght / þan þat þou art, þat scholde me releve" (176–77). In the long dialogue that follows, as the beggar breaks down Hoccleve's resistance he implicitly breaks down the Prince's as well. When he suggests the appeal to the Prince at the end of the dialogue, the suggestion comes as if it were completely external. The considerable presumption involved in both begging poems and _Fürstenspiegel_ is diffused, for the suggestion that two are in fact one is made by a figure who has just demonstrated the independent moral authority beggars can possess.

A similar observation might be made about the generic shift the addition of the beggar to the Prologue effects. Its production of authority out of shifts in narrative voice can be seen as an extension of the begging poem's central ploy, the construction of a conceit whose intricacy will distract attention from the crassness of the request. The implication is that what the prince pays for is the elegance of the poetic structure: a begging poem always pays its patron the compliment of making him the arbiter of poetic value. In the _Regement of Princes_, the poetic structure is also a moral one. By being a _Fürstenspiegel_ and begging poem at once, it defines Henry as the repository of moral as well as poetic value. This combination allows Henry to have it both ways. Accepting the _Regement_ as a begging poem will certify his moral rectitude; acceding to it as a _Fürstenspiegel_ will not diminish his social authority.

By the same token, acknowledging his dependence will not compromise Hoccleve either. His narrative insistence on the social location of his text reinforces his authority because he has made narrative intrinsically authoritative. As the dialogue with the beggar shifts to a dialogue with the Prince, Hoccleve maintains the same complex dynamic of identity and distinction. He addresses Henry in the language of compliment, confident that such language now carries moral weight.

> Hye and noble prince excellent,
> My lord the prince, o my lord gracious,
> I, humble servant and obedient
> Unto your estate hye & glorious,
> Of whiche I am full tendir & full ielous,
> Me recomaunde unto your worthynesse,
> With hert entier, and spirite of mekenesse.
>
> Right humbly axyng of you the license,
> That with my penne I may to you declare
> (So as that kan my wittes innocence,)
> Myne inward wille that thursteth the welefare

Of your persone; and elles be I bare
Of blisse, whan þat the colde stroke of deth
My lyfe hath quenched, & me byraft my breth.   (2017–30)

Like any good dedication to a *Fürstenspiegel*, this one is flowery and obsequious, so flowery and obsequious, in fact, one tends not to notice that its subject is almost entirely Hoccleve. The first line is devoted entirely to the Prince; while the second is devoted mainly to him, the twice repeated "my" takes on a decidedly personal cast in retrospect, as the focus shifts from the Prince to Hoccleve's devotion to him. By the final lines, where Hoccleve effectively makes the "license" to declare this devotion the condition of his own salvation, he has defined his own identity precisely by its complete subordination to the "persone" of the Prince. This paradoxical definition gives his identity solidity and integrity even if it is primarily negative. These two stanzas are so full of his will to subordinate himself, that they very nearly eclipse the identity of the very Prince to whom he would be subordinated. In its crossing of social boundaries, this process of identification is much the same as the comparison with Richard which opened the Prologue. Yet here the insistence on subordination means the identification with the Prince must ultimately affirm his distinctness.

As the very ornateness of these introductory lines make clear, direct address does not simply locate a *persona* but constitutes it as well. Hoccleve is not simply addressing a prince all of whose attributes are immediately available outside the text, but a prince whom he makes high, noble, and excellent by so addressing. To the extent this *persona* is perceived as simply Hoccleve's invention, the project fails. The elaborate, and elaborately self-abnegating request for "license" acknowledges the inventiveness and simultaneously subsumes it under the sign of the real Henry, even if his personhood is signified mainly by the excessive subordination he invites.

Hoccleve keeps his moral instruction in the second person, maintaining the fiction of Henry's personal presence throughout the poem. Some of the extant manuscripts take the fiction a step further still, inserting between the text of the Prologue and the text of the Proem, at the very point where Hoccleve begins to address Henry directly, an illustration in which a small, kneeling poet presents his book to a larger standing figure wearing a crown.[13] Hoccleve cannot

---

[13] There are three of them, from two different scribal traditions, all in the British Library: Arundel 38, Harley 4866, and Royal 17.D.vi. See M. C. Seymour, "Manuscripts of

assert his own independent moral authority without simultaneously reiterating his status as a dependent addressing a prince. His authority is always dependent on the central fiction of Henry's presence, just as that fiction itself depends on the poem's auto-biographical dramatization of Hoccleve's speaking voice. This frame personalizes the other side, the moralist's side, of the exemplary conceptions of royal authority Hoccleve inherits from the *Fürsten-spiegel* tradition.

The poem proper is divided into fifteen sections with an envoy. The first four deal with the royal *voluntas*: royal dignity, the coronation oath, justice, and the observance of the laws. Next are five personal virtues: pity, mercy, patience, chastity, and magnanimity. After three on the management of wealth and two on counsel, there is a concluding section on peace. The emphasis throughout is on the power of the royal example, the social order that Henry will produce by assuming these virtues. Upon occasion Hoccleve explicitly invokes Henry's absolute freedom, making his acceptance of moral constraint an act of grace:

> Who-so þat in hye dignite is sette,
> And may do grevous wrong & cruelte,
> If he for-bere hem, to commend is bette,
> And gretter shal his mede and meryte be ...   (2843-46)

But even where this freedom is not made explicit, the aspect of Henry's personal moral restraint Hoccleve stresses most is the awe and respect it will arouse in his subjects. When moral restraint meets royal power, the result is social control, and the moral shades into the ideological.

The transaction is most evident where the personal and political are hardest to distinguish: royal speech. The discussion of coronation oaths returns this issue to a *locus classicus* of medieval tradition. The coronation oath was a symbolic instrument for finessing the ambigu-ities surrounding the problem of royal prerogative. In taking the oath, a monarch voluntarily constrains his own prerogative to the laws of his predecessors. Thus the oath was a ceremonial recognition of the practical constraint on royal prerogative which nonetheless left it theoretically absolute. Hoccleve trades on this ambiguity by stressing the performative aspect of oath-keeping, its prescription of internal consistency rather than its assertion of simple conformity to an external standard.

> And syn a kyng, by wey of his office,
> To god I-likned is, as in manere,
> And god is trouthe itself, þan may the vice
> Of untrouthe, naght in a kyng appeere,
> If his office schal to god referre.
> A besy tonge bringeth in swiche wit,
> He þat by word naght gilteþ, is perfit.
>
> A! lord, what it is fair and honurable,
> A kyng from mochil speche him refreyne;
> It sitte him ben of wordes mesurable,
> ffor mochil clap wole his estate desteyne.
> If he his tonge with mesures reyne
> Governe, than his honur it conserveth.   (2409–21)

To what extent is the God-like king "trouthe itself"? Obviously, royal speech is not absolutely performative in the way of divine speech; it cannot call truth into being simply by articulating it. And yet Hoccleve strongly implies that so long as "untrouthe" is avoided, royal speech may become God-like.

In this paradoxical formulation royal speech is performative within certain bounds, bounds which become clearer as the passage proceeds. The advice against speaking too often follows directly the warning against "untrouthe," as if the two were equivalent. To view royal speech as capable of excess is to assume that royal prerogative is safest when least evident, as if ultimately it were incapable of justifying itself in purely linguistic terms. It is to assume a status quo that operates best when least observed. "For mochil clap wole his estate destayne": a king who speaks too much is likely to expose himself as no more in control of language than its other users.

A king can control his estate by controlling his tongue; the status quo provides the reference point against which "untrouthe" is to be judged. Royal speech becomes performative precisely by not seeking to be, by always seeking to submerge its effects in its preservation of royal power. It is as if the ideal of royal speech were silence. This is the reason kingship always needs another voice, like Hoccleve's. Justification spoken in another voice will always make royal authority seem to be a power beyond language, which it must always be in order to be justified at all.

Moreover, Hoccleve meets this need with more than his own voice. His celebration of Henry finds its necessary counterpart in his canonization of Chaucer. As a figure more historically and linguistically continuous with Hoccleve than those of classical or clerical tradition, Chaucer provides a source of lay textual authority from within the very political community Hoccleve is attempting to solidify. Following the pattern Chaucer himself established in his eulogy to Petrarch in the *Prologue to the Clerk's Tale*, Hoccleve consistently locates Chaucer's authority biographically.[14] There are three discussions of Chaucer, all following essentially the same pattern. First is a celebration of Chaucer's authority, then a lament for his death, and, in the last two, a prayer that he rest in peace. In several of the manuscripts this final invocation is accompanied by a portrait. The portrait in British Library, Harley 4866 (leaf 91) is the earliest known of Chaucer and is probably the source of most later portraits, including the equestrian portrait of the Ellesmere manuscript.[15] This fact, though it may seem no more than a charming bit of antiquarianism, signals a crucial change. It signals an increasing historicization of discursive authority, an increasing desire to locate authority within a personage historically and linguistically immediate.

This exercise in canonization provides a particularly concrete illustration of A. C. Spearing's observation that Chaucer invents "the possibility of a history of English poetry."[16] Hoccleve takes the model of lay poetic authority that Chaucer provides in his eulogy to Petrarch and applies it to Chaucer himself. The Clerk learned the Griselda story from Petrarch personally; Hoccleve's first two eulogies personalize Chaucer's authority in similar fashion. The first occurs in the Prologue directly after he agrees to write the *Regement* (1958–81), and begins with the regret that Chaucer is not available to lend "consail and reed" (1960). The second occurs in the discussion of his sources (2052–135), where he makes it clear his access to these authorities, meager though it is ("Simple is my goost, and scars my letterure" (2073)), comes through Chaucer, who "fayn wolde han

---

[14] See above, 179–80.
[15] Jeanne E. Krochalis, "Hoccleve's Chaucer Portrait," *Chaucer Review* 21 (1986), 231–40; Jerome Mitchell, *Thomas Hoccleve: A Study in Early Fifteenth-Century English Poetic* (Urbana, Chicago, and London: University of Illinois Press, 1968), 110–15. Krochalis suggests part of Hoccleve's inspiration for including a portrait came from royal effigies (238–40).
[16] Spearing, *Medieval to Renaissance*, 34.

me taght" (2078). In both passages Chaucer is the center of traditional authority, like Cicero in rhetoric, like Aristotle (whom Hoccleve has just named as author of the *Secretum secretorum*) in philosophy, and like Virgil in poetry (2085–90). This displacement of Latin authority into the vernacular authority of Chaucer makes the authority of tradition more accessible to Hoccleve's audience. But it also solidifies that audience's investment in royal authority.

For to the extent that the textual is historicized, immediate political authority is strengthened. As Hoccleve elevates Chaucer to the status of an *auctor*, his insistence on the biographical makes the textual even more dependent on the actualities of historical existence. Chaucer's authority inheres most fully in his person; it does not survive complete in his texts alone. Though he is "universal fadir in science" (1964) and "firste fyndere of our faire langage" (4978) what Hoccleve learned from him he learned personally. The implication of the lament that Chaucer is no longer available for "consail and reed" is that once Chaucer is no longer alive and producing, the power of his texts to put the cultural world in order begins to fade. The final portrait, which abandons language altogether in favor of pictorial representation, takes this idea to its logical limit.

Vernacular authority is thus tied more directly to historical actuality than either the classical or the sacred. If authorizing the vernacular means a greater freedom from the past, it may also mean a greater subordination to the immediate *status quo*. These two tendencies are not necessarily opposed, for freedom from the past may be enabled by an increase in political empowerment. This was the case for Hoccleve's audience, and his canonization gave them a new, vernacular authority in the guise of the old. As the "Mirour of fructuous entendement," the "uniuersal fadir in science" (1963–64), Chaucer becomes the Aristotle to Henry's Alexander, the source of the communally held moral values to be embodied in the ideal prince.

The legitimacy of Henry is the cost of this new, vernacular access to discursive authority. Without an immediately available embodiment of moral order, Hoccleve cannot grant any moral privilege to the historically immediate. And if historical immediacy is without moral value, then so too is the vernacular. Hoccleve's celebration of the nascent English tradition embodied in Chaucer and the political authority embodied in Henry are the twin faces of the same moral

vision. As this vision empowers itself by exposing the assumptions of
the Latin traditions it inherits, it also solidifies its empowerment in
the figure of Henry. Henry must become the guarantor of moral
order because it is he who will become king.

Of course, the figure of Chaucer is no less exemplary and depends
no less on the discursive constructions of the exemplarist than the
figure of the prince does. Hoccleve adumbrates the tradition he
assigns to Chaucer as much through material drawn from Gower,
whom he also acknowledges, though much more briefly (1975–77).
He follows Gower in invoking the *Secretum secretorum* as the model for
his own poem, and, indeed, follows Gower in the very compilation of
a vernacular *Fürstenspiegel*. While he recounts many of the same
exempla that Gower uses in Book VII of the *Confessio*, his main source
is a text that Gower may not have known though Chaucer probably
did.[17] That text is the *Ludus schachorum*. The last Latin exemplum
collection substantially indebted for its tales to the *Policraticus*, its
political commitments are a good deal more ambiguous, although (or
perhaps because) its compiler, Jacobus de Cessolis was a Dominican.
Hoccleve's explicit acknowledgement of that fact (2110) is a nice
piece of self-conscious appropriation, setting off the purely lay status
of his own mendicancy, and affirming the moral authority he has
derived from clerical mendicancy. But Jacobus already displays
considerably more fascination for the inherently lay authority of
kingship than does John of Salisbury, and his exempla fit well with
the general commitment to royal absolutism Hoccleve takes from
Aegidius.

The *Ludus schachorum* begins with a fictionalized scene of public
instruction, which also purports to explain the origin of the game of
chess. It is invented by a philosopher at the court of the Babylonian
king Evilmerodag, a son of Nebuchadnazzar, who is cruel and
licentious, and executes any who dare to correct him. By interesting
the king in the game, the philosopher is able to show him his
obligations while explaining the rules.[18] Jacobus presents this ruse in
a complex manner, which insists on the king's power even as it
displays his correction.

---

[17] Jill Mann, *Chaucer and Medieval Estates Satire* (Cambridge: Cambridge University Press,
1973), 300.

[18] Ernst Kopke, ed., *Mittheilungen aus dem Handschriften der Ritter-Akademie zu Brandenburg A. H.,
II. Jacobus de Cessolis* (Brandenburg: Gustav Matthes, 1879), I, 1–3. Subsequent citations
will be given in the text.

Listening to his correction, for which he had slain many wise men, [the king] with a threatening command asked why the game had been invented. To which he replied "O my lord king, I desire that your life be glorious, which I cannot see, unless you love justice and are famed among the people for good habits. Therefore, I wish your regimen will be different, that you might first rule yourself, who has ruled others not with law but with violence. For it is unjust that you wish to control others when you cannot control yourself – remember, violent rule cannot long last.

audiens correctionem suam, propter quam multos sapientes occiderat, commintario praecepto philosophum interrogavit dicens, quare hunc ludum invenisset? Cui respondit: O domine mi rex, tuam vitam gloriosam desidero, quam videre non possum, nisi iustitia et bonis moribus insignitus a populo diligaris. Opto ergo te alium fore regimine, ut tibi prius domineris, qui non iure aliis sed violentia dominaris. Iniustum quippe est ut aliis imperare velis, cum tibi ipsi imperare non possis, et memento violenta imperia diu durare non posse. (I,3)

The ruse never loses its indirection. By the end of his explanation, the philosopher bluntly tells the king he is unjust, but even where he is most imperative he stresses the political efficacy of royal virtue rather than its obligation: "violent rule cannot long last." Moreover, his correction is framed entirely by his desire for the king's glory and he presents the change he recommends more as a self-generated ideological program than as a response to external constraint. The king's good manners and desire for justice will make him renowned (*insignitus*) among the people. The *Ludus schachorum* leaves this ambiguity between ideology and virtue unresolved, operating in the tension between the two. Its opening presents royal counsel as something which occurs concretely at court, under the pressure of a royal power that is always potentially beyond restraint, and is often so in actuality as well. The exchange I have just examined literally dramatizes counsel as a speech act – a transformation of royal power from threat to virtue that occurs in and through speech. As Jacobus retells the exempla he draws from the *Policraticus*, he often returns to their classical sources in search of details John represses, which dramatize precisely this loaded exchange between the power of kingship and the speech of counsel. Hoccleve exploits this aspect of the *Ludus schachorum* to the fullest.

Like Gower's, many of Hoccleve's exempla turn on a ruler's voluntary restraint of some power or prerogative otherwise freely available to him. While occasionally these are stories of self-sacrifice, such as that of Regulus, the Roman commander who convinced the senate to return him to execution in Carthage rather than complete an unfavorable exchange of prisoners (2248–96), more typically the restraint redounds to the ruler's advantage. For instance, there are two similar stories of Roman generals, Camillus (2584–2646) and Scipio Africanus (3676–3710). A schoolmaster in a city Camillus is besieging kidnaps the children of the wealthy citizens who employ him and offers them to Camillus to use as a bargaining chip. Camillus refuses, and when the citizens discover that he did, they decide to surrender in recognition of his great virtue. In the other story, Scipio is offered a virgin betrothed to a lord in Carthage, and his refusal brings about the same result, the surrender of the city. In both cases moral restraint effects a significant gain in political power, producing a sovereignty that had not existed before. Camillus and Scipio bend a hitherto refractory population to their will through the ideological power of example, through their personal enactment of a public moral narrative, acts of virtue that cannot be separated from the political positions they reinforce.

An even greater interdependence of the moral and the political occurs in Hoccleve's version of two of the most famous public exempla, Lycurgus and his Laws (2950–89) and the Phalarean Bull (3004–38). The first ends the section on Justice and the second begins the section on Pity. Hoccleve does all he can to intensify the representation of kingship as the source of moral value already implicit in both exempla. He juxtaposes them, and adds dialogue to moments, which even in Gower, had been primarily plot summary. He makes their protagonists anonymous, as if to focus attention on their political position. In both, private personal virtue is either moot, in the case of Lycurgus, or non-existent, in the case of Phalaris. Moral order is something they produce simply through their manipulation of political authority.

Expanding a suggestion that Jacobus makes briefly in summary, Hoccleve makes the simulation of the now anonymous "knyght" the result of a struggle with his people. After his "sharp lawes" are read to the "froward peple," they are "wondir wroth," and "wold han artyd [compelled] þis knyght hem repele, / Makyng ageyn him an haynous querele" (2950–61). Only then does the knight assign the authorship of the laws to Apollo: "I mad hem naght, it was god appollo; / And on my bak ... þe charge he leyde / To kepe hem; sires, what sey ye here-to? / As he me chargid hath riȝt so I do." (2963–66) But the struggle continues: "unto þat, anwered anon þe prees, / 'We wol hem naght admitten douteles'" (2967–68). At this point the knight introduces the second part of his ploy. Hoccleve gives it two full stanzas, almost entirely in direct quotation.

> "Wel," quod he, "þenne is gode, or ye hem breke,
> That unto god apollo I me dresse,
> To trete of þis matere, and with him speke, –
> With-owtyn him I may it naght redresse, –
> Biseche him wol I, of his gentilnesse,
> Repele hem, sen þat þei to streyte be,
> And do my dever riȝt wel, ȝe shul see.
>
> "But or I go, ye shul unto me swere
> þe lawes kepe til I agayn come,
> And Breke hem naght;" to which þei gan answere
> "Ȝee, ȝee, man, ȝee! We graunt it al and summe."
> þei made her oth, and he his wey hath nomme.   (2969–80)

As Gower had done before him, Hoccleve uses the knight's speech to insist on his manipulation of divine authority. The knight acts as if he were entirely a go-between. He meets his people's resistance with apparent compliance, acknowledging their ability to break the laws, and announcing his mission to Apollo as if he were to act entirely on their behalf. This "froward peple" confirm their fractiousness with the very energy of their response, "Ȝee, ȝee, man, ȝee!" In turn, this depiction of their anarchic energy justifies both the knight's deception, and the quick-witted and spontaneous manner in which he devises it. The lasting order he imposes on his people he enacts in and through speech. His speech is able to generate, out of its own spontaneous movement, authority beyond itself, and then to impose that authority on the resistance it faces. In this version of the story, Hoccleve foregrounds the ideological efficacy of royal authority by locating that authority squarely in the royal voice.

The same thing happens in the next exemplum. Drawing both from Gower and Jacobus, he explains the Bull's purpose in this way:

> ... þe kyng for to meve
> The lesse unto pitee, it made was so
> By sotil art þe dampned folk to greve
> þat whan to crye, hem compellyd hir woo,
> Hir woys was lyke a boles ever-mo,
> And nothyng lyke a mannys voise in soun ...   (3018–23)

The reason for the Bull's construction, to move the king the less to pity, he takes from Jacobus, but the exact sound the victims make he takes from Gower. Jacobus describes the sound as *feralis* (III, 11), while Gower calls it a "belwinge" (VII, 3322). Hoccleve's "Hir woys was lyke a boles ever mo," takes Gower's metonym even further, making explicit the co-optation of voice by machine, and the totality of the machine's ideological control. He then returns to Jacobus for the explicit account of the counselor's punishment, which Gower omits, conveying it by direct speech.

> ... han þe kyng, his cruel werk had seyne,
> þe craft of it commendith he ful wele;
> But þe entent he fully held a-gayne,
> And seyde, "þou þat art more cruel
> Than I, þe maydenhede of this Iuel
> Shalt preve anone; þis is my Iugement."
> And so as blyve he was þerin I-brent.　　　　　(3032–38)

Though the king's voice may be constructed for him, he always has the last word. This variation on the story's more usual point, that no one can surpass a tyrant in cruelty, brings out even more clearly the inherent orderliness the exemplum ascribes to kingship. The machine assumes that the tyrant will always strive to be as absolute as possible in his cruelty. Yet if he simply accepts it, he concedes the absoluteness of his prerogative to the counselor. If he rejects it entirely, he gives up the claim to cruelty which most effectively demonstrates that prerogative. So he turns the machine against its maker by having the last word, by acknowledging the Bull as a version of his voice, and then reclaiming that voice as his own. His prerogative remains an authorizing principle beyond any particular expression of his voice, but to which his voice alone can appeal.

Like Gower, Hoccleve uses these exempla to justify monarchy's ideological projections on the basis of the social order such projections ultimately produce. He replays this justification in even more complex fashion when, toward the end of the poem, he finally asks Henry for an annuity directly. He builds to the request slowly, as befits the moral grounds he has generated to support it. At the same time, he surrounds it with alternating moments of self-assertion and self-abnegation. The request occurs in the eleventh section of the poem, entitled *De Virtute Largitatis et De Vicio Prodigalitas*. This is the middle section of the three dealing with the management of wealth, which as a whole follows the section on personal virtues ending with magnanimity. Section 10 is entitled *Quod rex non debent felicitatem suam ponere in diviciis* ("That the king should not found his happiness on riches"), and section 12, *De Vicio Avaricie*. The section containing Hoccleve's request thus comes between two sections exhorting the king to generosity. He steps up his attacks on flattery throughout this part of the poem, reaffirming by contrast the authority of his own exchange with the prince. In an interesting reprise in the final part of the poem, he associates flattery and avarice, on the grounds that both produce false counsel (4915–21).

He adds a further contrast in section 11 itself, as he recommends largesse directly. He sets largesse off against the vice of prodigality, so that largesse becomes a kind of golden mean. His exhortations of the prince to this virtue support his request for an annuity; his attack on prodigality removes the taint of special pleading from his longer attacks on avarice. After an exemplum illustrating the evils of prodigality – John of Canacee, the longest in the collection (4180–354) – Hoccleve confesses to prodigality himself, and this confession forms the immediate preface to his entreaty. He needs the prince's help because he was prodigal in his youth. Offering the prince his own example is particularly presumptuous, especially since he is just about to request money. But the context he has established for this cross-identification enables him to make his presumption part of his larger vision of royal authority. Just as earlier, the prince would show himself a force beyond Fortune by rescuing Hoccleve, now he can become a force beyond prodigality. He will escape the vice (and danger) of giving too liberally precisely by giving to Hoccleve. He also gains the lesson which these clever maneuvers display about the plasticity of language at court. Requiring Prince Henry to put himself in Hoccleve's place immediately prior to receiving Hoccleve's request has the effect of demonstrating kingship's dependence on its own ideology and those, like Hoccleve, who maintain that ideology. The demonstration comes at the very moment where kingship is at its most powerful and unconstrained, that is during the supplication of a dependent. Hoccleve expects the prince to understand that this interdependence ultimately works in his favor. He also expects his larger audience to understand that the interdependence works in their favor as well. By identifying themselves with the king, the nobility and urban patriciate – the audience of the Chaucerian tradition – share the king's power, even when that power distinguishes him from them, because such power still distinguishes both him and them from all those below.

The exemplum of John of Canacee conveys this point in a particularly striking manner. One of the few exempla Hoccleve takes from Jacobus which does not have a monarchical protagonist, it requires from the prince another downward identification. John of Canacee is a rich bourgeois with two married daughters. Egged on by their continual flattery, he gives them gifts until all his wealth is gone, at which point they begin to treat him unkindly. Hitting upon a ruse to restore himself, he borrows 10,000 pounds from a friendly merchant, then contrives to count it where his daughters and their husbands can see him. When he promises to leave them all of it, they invite him to live with them. Just before his death he gets them to agree to make a number of bequests to religious orders in his name before opening the chest where he has led them to believe the money is kept. After they bury his corpse and pay the bequests they open the chest to find only

> ... passyngly greet sergeantes mace,
> In which ther gaily made was and I-wrought
> This same scripture: "I, John of Canace
> Make swhich testament here in þis place;
> Who berith charge of othir men, & is
> Of hem despised, slayn be he with this."   (4349–54)

In changing this object from the key of Jacobus's version to a sergeant's mace, Hoccleve provides a wonderful emblem of the power he offers both Henry and his audience. As a primitive weapon turned signifier of communal sovereignty, the mace embodies the power of ideology to produce material result. As the specific property of a sergeant, that is, a servant, or the representative of a bourgeois community (especially the sergeant of the House of Commons, if Hoccleve had that particular office in mind), this mace also embodies the particular capacity of such power to serve a pre-existing status quo. The inscription affirms this capacity in a subtler fashion. Directed at the problem of resistance to authority, it acknowledges authority's arbitrariness and contingency. Those who "berith charge of othir men" can be "despised" and by implication manipulated by them because such charge, or authority, is always ideologically constructed. But the point of the inscription is to reaffirm the material power of such authority, however ideologically contingent it may be. Those who bear charge of others can always draw on that power despite the contempt of those to whom they are superior. They should draw on it precisely to maintain their advantage, and root out the contempt, just as John himself does at the end of the tale. The inscription applies equally to John himself and to his daughters, yet in applying equally it always gives him the advantage.

The exemplum turns on his ability to use his daughters' own power of linguistic manipulation against them. They are taken in by the drama he stages with the money he borrowed from the merchant just as he was taken in by their flattery. This flattery, the appropriation of John's subject position, the construction of the voice he wanted to hear, erodes his wealth, and destroys the material power attached to that subject position. But because all subject positions are discursively constructed, John can manipulate those of his daughters. Even when his actual wealth is gone he retains a material advantage in the ideology that surrounds his position as patriarch. Once he realizes how ideological his position actually is – how vulnerable it is to manipulation – he can construct an ideological defense, one assured of success by virtue of the very materiality of the authority it defends.

The inscription also applies to the exchange Hoccleve proposes to Henry. Flattery and contempt are possibilities that threaten any exchange between ruler and dependent. Coming before Hoccleve's request, this exemplum acknowledges the danger and suggests its antidote: the use of material power for the continual reproduction of ideological advantage. Hoccleve insulates the prince from the example of John by interposing his identification, claiming immediately after this story that he himself was guilty of John's failing. But the protection is built into the story as well. The material advantage available to John is that much more available to Henry. If it requires a thoroughgoing acknowledgment of the contingency and ideological dependence of his own postion, it also promises continual reaffirmation of his power, so long as Henry recognizes that requirement.

The empowerment this scheme offers Hoccleve and the audience he represents is equally impressive. In return for their acquiescence to Henry's authority, they share in its production, a process that depends on the contingencies of the political and linguistic community they inhabit. Their submission to Henry's voice returns them a voice of their own specifically tied both to their own vernacular, and the form, narrative, taken to be most characteristic of it, and to the political status quo. This exchange is not so much a logical unity as it is two divergent tendencies held together by the shifting subject positions of Hoccleve's narratives. If there is a weakness to his various exemplary constructions of authority, it is that their interconnections remain largely implicit. It will be left to Lydgate to make those connections more explicit. He will do so in his own exemplum collection, the *Fall of Princes*. A version of Boccaccio's *De casibus*, it is governed by the trope of translation as the Regement is governed by the trope of voice.

TRANSLATION WITHOUT PRESUMPTION, OR, THE BIRTH OF
TRAGEDY OUT OF THE SPIRIT OF THE EXEMPLUM:
LYDGATE'S *FALL OF PRINCES*

Modern literary history usually takes Lydgate to mark the end, if not the exhaustion, of medieval poetry in England. Perverse as it may seem, in this chapter I will argue almost the contrary: that Lydgate should be seen as an important transitional, and in some ways, even innovative figure. Chaucer's initial installment at the head of the English canon owes a great deal to Lydgate's systematic efforts on his behalf. My reading of the *Fall of Princes* will argue that this fact should be regarded as part of a larger pattern, not just granted and dismissed. In canonizing Chaucer, Lydgate also helps institutionalize the peculiarly appropriative form of textual authority Chaucer embodies: vernacular and lay, yet claiming a spiritual prestige and ideological efficacy analogous to the Latin traditions of the Church. This quasi-sacral secular authority belongs to precisely that set of textual traditions modernity will come to call literary.

By today's perhaps inflated standards, Lydgate scholarship remains largely under-developed. It still carries the burden of the nineteenth-century verdict that he was a "voluminous, prosaic, driveling monk."[19] Even Derek Pearsall – whose 1970 study *John Lydgate* almost single-handedly made Lydgate's verse a respectable scholarly topic – feels obliged to apologize both for Lydgate's volume and his apparently prosaic lack of "poetic intensity."[20] But the past two decades in literary studies have made such issues seem less pressing. They have taught us that the definition of poetry as a particular kind of textual intensity, like the larger notion of literature

---

[19] Joseph Ritson, *Bibliographica Poetica* (London: 1802), 87; cited in Alain Renoir, *The Poetry of John Lydgate* (Cambridge, MA: Harvard University Press, 1967), 7.
[20] Derek Pearsall, *John Lydgate* (London: Routledge and Kegan Paul, 1970). See, for example, 1–4.

as an autonomous, self-evident activity, is itself culturally specific.[21] This change has also made other questions in relation to figures like Lydgate more interesting. If modernist ideals of poetic purity are historically contingent, where did they come from? Could they have unacknowledged debts to the very traditions they reject? I have been arguing throughout this study that modern literary ideals are closer to those of the later Middle Ages than they have usually cared to admit. I now want to argue that this proximity is most striking in Lydgate, the figure for whom it seems least likely.

Pearsall suggests Lydgate can be taken as "a comprehensive definition of the Middle Ages."[22] A. C. Spearing has recently argued somewhat more pointedly that Lydgate's relation to Chaucer should be understood under the trope of *tessera*, or completion.[23] Both of these suggestions accurately capture the spirit of Lydgate's encyclopedic ambition in the *Fall of Princes*. However, I think the specificity implicit in Spearing's claim should be foregrounded. Lydgate's ambitions are comprehensive and rebarbitive, but they are also exercised from a particular historical position in the interest of a particular audience, namely the lay audience of the Chaucerian tradition. This circumstance gives his work a transitional value well beyond what either he or Chaucer could have anticipated, or perhaps even desired. As we shall see, the very comprehensiveness of Lydgate's efforts authorized a depth of moral complexity in vernacular literature that in some ways remains in force even today. This claim may seem the height of paradox, given Lydgate's clerical position and his obvious commitment to the didactic. While I grant the paradox, I would argue that it originates not in my claim but in the cultural condition my claim describes. Literature in the English-speaking world has never relinquished the sacral aura which authorized its emergence at the end of the Middle Ages. Even in the twentieth century, when the literary characteristically presents itself as the secular epitome of a secular age, one of its greatest figures could describe the writer as "a priest of eternal imagination."[24] More

---

[21] The classic discussion of the contingent and historically variable significance of the term "literature" occurs in the introduction and first chapter of Terry Eagleton's *Introduction to Literary Theory* (Minneapolis: University of Minnesota Press, 1983), 1–53. For more recent discussions see Tony Bennet, *Outside Literature* (London and New York: Routledge, 1990), and Easthope, *Literary into Cultural Studies*.   [22] Pearsall, *John Lydgate*, 4.

[23] *Medieval to Renaissance*, 66–88. See above, 122.

[24] James Joyce, *A Portrait of the Artist as a Young Man*, (Harmondsworth: Penguin Books, 1976), 221.

recently, and much more poignantly, another major figure, caught unfortunately and unfairly in a religious crossfire of the first magnitude, could suggest the novel in response to the question, "Is nothing sacred?"[25]

The *Fall of Princes* was Lydgate's last major work, and his longest. He offers it as a translation of Laurence de Premierfait's *Des cas des nobles hommes et femmes*, a greatly amplified French version of Boccaccio's *De casibus*, compiled in its final form for the Duke of Berry sometime between 1405 and 1409. In fact the *Fall of Princes* is much more than a straightforward translation in the modern sense. Henry Bergen, the work's modern editor, describes it as a "paraphrase," but that term does not do it justice, either.[26] It is a version of the *De casibus* in the same way that the *Clerk's Tale* is a version of the Griselda story, or *Troilus and Criseyde* is a version of *Filostrato*. In addition to the myriad minor changes attendant upon translating a prose work into verse, Lydgate regularly adjusts Laurence, sometimes amplifying, more often reducing, and frequently supplementing what he finds in Laurence with material from a variety of other sources, including the *De casibus* and Boccaccio's other Latin works, Chaucer, Gower, and John of Salisbury. He also completely reworks the collection's didactic frame, drawing out and clarifying its connections to the *Fürstenspiegel*, then reformulating them to meet the circumstances of a recently established vernacular tradition, and an expanding lay reading public.

Like the *De casibus*, the *Fall of Princes* arranges its material in roughly chronological order from Adam and Eve to King John of France. It is divided into nine books, which grew progressively shorter as the work continued. Book I extends from Adam and Eve through the Theban and Trojan legends and the early part of the Old Testament (Nimrod and Samson) to Canace and Machaire. Book II begins with Saul, and Books II and III between them cover early Rome, and various Old Testament, Mesopotamian, and other Asian kings, ending with Artaxerxes and Darius. Book IV is concerned mainly with Alexander the Great and other Hellenic tyrants, and Book V with Alexander's aftermath and Rome and Carthage up to the defeat of Hannibal. Books VI and VII cover the early Empire

---

[25] Salman Rushdie, *Is Nothing Sacred?* (The Herbert Read Memorial Lecture, 6 February 1990) (No place of publication given: Granta (1990)).

[26] Henry Bergen, *Lydgate's Fall of Princes*, 4 vols. (London: Early English Text Society, 1924), v. I, xv.

and the coming of Christ, ending with the Fall of Jerusalem; Book VIII, Christian Rome and the adventures of Arthur; and Book IX, European history to the time of John.

The poem is dedicated to Humphrey, Duke of Gloucester, Henry V's younger brother, and Protector of England while Henry VI was a minor. Lydgate also tells us Humphrey commissioned it. He probably began work on it in 1431 and completed it by 1438 or 1439.[27] The dedication enables Lydgate to stage the poem as an act of public instruction in the *Fürstenspiegel*'s traditional style; it also enables him to fulfill the *Fürstenspiegel*'s traditional propagandistic role as well.[28] Most historians of this period agree that Humphrey was driven by royal ambitions throughout his life. During his nephew's minority he had mounted an aggressive but unsuccessful campaign to become *rector regis et regni*, with the privileges of an acting monarch.[29] In addition to the *Troy Book*, which Henry V had commissioned in 1412, Lydgate had already written a number of celebratory occasional poems for various members of the royal family, including the *Ballade to King Henry VI on His Coronation*, the *Roundell for the Coronation*, and the *Verses for the Triumphal Entry of King Henry VI into London*. Patronage from Humphrey went at least as far back to 1422 and *On Gloucester's Approaching Marriage*.[30] Since the commission from Henry V came just before his reign began, at the time he was also patronizing Hoccleve, it is tempting to see in Humphrey's patronage an imitation of his older brother, and a similar recognition of the political value of public affirmation in poetry. In all probability, Humphrey's patronage of Lydgate, like his many other efforts in this regard, was part of his continuing program to present himself as eminently monarchical, should the occasion only arise.

Nevertheless, the occasion did not, and this fact necessarily gives Humphrey's ostensibly monarchical role in the poem an ambiguity absent from Henry's role in the *Regement*. Whatever the frustrations

---

[27] Pearsall, *John Lydgate*, 223.
[28] I take Lydgate's claim that Humphrey commissioned the poem at face value, since there seems no obvious reason not to.
[29] See for instance, R. A. Griffiths, "The Sense of Dynasty in the Reign of Henry VI," in *Patronage, Pedigree, and Power in Later Medieval England*, ed. Charles Ross (Totowa, NJ: Rowman and Littlefield, 1979), 17–18; and "The Crown and the Royal Family in Later Medieval England," in *Kings and Nobles in the Later Middle Ages: A Tribute to Charles Ross*, ed. R. A. Griffiths and James Sherborn (New York: St. Martin's Press, 1986), 17–20; and E. F. Jacob, *The Fifteenth Century* (Oxford: Clarendon Press, 1961), 211–38.
[30] For a fuller account of Lydgate's commissions, see Pearsall, *Lydgate*, 160–91

this ambiguity might have caused Humphrey personally, it suited Lydgate's purposes perfectly. Humphrey's ambiguous status keeps him detached enough to occupy the position of a moral reader appalled at the blind excesses of power, and yet exalted enough to become the prince whose morality stands beyond correction, and who, in consequence, can set "a-side alle chaungis of Fortune."[31] The illicitness – indeed, the treason – of any actual aspirations in this direction only intensifies Humphrey's figural power in Lydgate's text. For the very illicitness of his pretensions to the throne exposes that dimension of monarchy which is irreducibly ideological and discursive – the dimension which the *Fürstenspiegel* articulates and supports. As Lydgate's exemplary reader, Humphrey makes more promiscuous than ever the identification between reader and monarch upon which the genre depends. And that very promiscuity will enable Lydgate to delineate the specifically lay authority of the Chaucerian tradition in a comprehensive and definitive form – more so than Hoccleve, and certainly more so than the master had ever done himself.

Lydgate systematically lays out an exemplary moral logic that operates fully within human history, a logic in which characteristic forms of lay action, the practices of monarchy, give rise to a characteristic form of lay textuality, vernacular poetry, which in turn authorizes future actions. This logic organizes every aspect of the poem, from his manipulation of its didactic frame to his deployment of individual narratives. A comprehensive reading of the *Fall of Princes* is beyond the scope of this study. However, it will be possible both to sketch Lydgate's conception of the relation between poetic and political authority, and to demonstrate how that conception affects one aspect of his exempla, namely, character. For the first, we will examine the work's frame tale, focusing mainly on the prologue to Book I. This prologue is substantial, nearly 500 lines long, and I concentrate on it in part for convenience. Lydgate uses it to lay out briefly the frame tale's major components. But this sustained attention to a small part of the poem will also afford me the opportunity to show that Lydgate is not quite as diffuse as he is accused of being.

I should begin by emphasizing that the frame tale is indeed a tale,

---

[31] John Lydgate, *Fall of Princes*, ed. Henry Bergen, 4 vols. (London: Early English Text Society, 1924) vol. 1, Book I, line 390, 11. All subsequent citations are from this edition. Book and line numbers will be given in the text.

a narrative, even if it is composed largely of moralizing explicits. For the frame tale is precisely a narrative of the process of moralization, just as the frame tale is in the *De casibus*. Lydgate makes the frame more elaborate but he does so precisely by historicizing it. That is, he characterizes his moralizing by subsuming it under the discrete textual practice which actually produces it: translation. He can moralize in this poem because he has translated, and he will define translation as a means of reproducing in a way that mirrors the exemplary – that is, as performative.

Translation involves both repetition and change: a change that aspires to the status of pure repetition, but a repetition that allows itself variation by virtue of that aspiration. Translation can allow itself change precisely because it does not seek it. Likewise, the exemplary author is one who gives moral virtue textual form; that is, who changes moral action into a moral text as a way of repeating it. The exemplary person is one who performs the actions mandated by a moral text; that is, who changes text into action as a way of repeating it. Lydgate will bring *translatio* and the exemplum together precisely by emphasizing the former's performative and moral dimensions – by locating it, like the exemplum, on the boundary between textuality and action.[32] At the same time, because *translatio* remains so textual in its orientation, using it as a way of defining lay authority enables Lydgate to make such authority a more purely textual matter. On the one hand, this change produces the encyclopedic didacticism so offensive to modern sensibility. On the other, it also produces an insistence on the autonomy of poetry modern scholars have almost entirely ignored.

Lydgate outlines his view of translation in the prologue to Book I, which may be divided into three parts. The first presents the poem as a translation of Laurence's translation of Boccaccio, then discusses the problem of translation more generally. The performative model Lydgate establishes in this part leads him to Chaucer, the master of the language into which he is doing his translating, and this specification leads him to Humphrey, his patron, dedicatee, and exemplar of political authority. He will characterize each of the distinct forms of authority Chaucer and Humphrey represent by reference to translation. Moreover, the broad interrelation between the textual and political his characterizations establish will enable

---

[32] Lydgate's emphasis on performance is entirely consistent with most medieval thinking about translation. See Copeland, *Rhetoric, Hermeneutics and Translation*, esp. 151–78.

him, as he moves in the rest of the frame tale, to imagine lay authority
on even broader terms, and to claim for poetry a moral autonomy
balanced by the moral competence of a national vernacular audience.
All of these elements are implicit from the very beginning. The
prologue's first stanza locates the poem on the terrain of Laurence's
text.

> He that whilom dede his diligence
> The book of Bochas in Frensh to translate
> Out of Latyn, he callid was Laurence;
> The tyme trewli remembrid and the date
> The yere whan kyng Iohn thoruh his mortal fate
> Was prisoner brouht to this regioun
> Whan he first gan on this translacioun ...   (I, 1–7)

Such archival neutrality, with its careful, albeit mistaken, chron-
ology, may seem no more than another instance of Lydgate's
notorious penchant for padding and tags. In fact, however, in this
case, the ostensibly pedantic insistence on the bibliographical
circumstances of Lydgate's source serves his larger purpose brilli-
antly. At the beginning of his text, he pictures the beginning of his
source-text. As that text is itself a translation, what he pictures is
Laurence thinking back to the completion of *his* original, Bochas's
book: "The tyme trewli remembrid and the date."[33] Laurence
marks that date with Boccaccio's final story, the capture of King John
of France by Edward the Black Prince in 1356. (The *De casibus* was
actually completed in 1363; Lydgate either did not know or chose to
disregard this fact.) This gambit not only reminds us that literary
artifacts, whatever their transhistorical ambitions, are always produced at specific historical moments, but also insists that such
material connections persist as they are transmitted into the future.
Boccaccio's text connects Laurence with the historical moment when
it was produced. Laurence's text in turn connects Lydgate to the
same moment.

There is still more. The materiality these connections ascribe to the
reinscription of tradition hold for Lydgate a specific affirmation of his
own moment and political community. Like both the *De casibus* and
the *Des cas*, this poem takes the French king's capture as its ending

---

[33] Bergen's marginal gloss of this stanza states that Lydgate thinks John's capture marks the
date of Laurence's text, but that reading is clearly untenable. Why would Laurence need to
remember his own present? And how could that present be contemporaneous with
Boccaccio?

point. That moment marked the high point of English achievement in the first stage of the Hundred Years War. The *Fall of Princes* was begun during the beginning of the third stage, Henry VI's campaign, which Lydgate explicitly mentions in this prologue when he introduces Duke Humphrey. By insisting on the Frenchness of Lydgate's antecedent, these lines display precisely the moral and textual continuity the *De casibus* tradition extracts from the discontinuities of history. Lydgate's respectful English translation of Laurence's French text demonstrates the commonality possible between two cultures even when they are in complete conflict.

Without ever ceasing to be respectful to Laurence's text, these lines define the commonality so that even it redounds to English advantage. As the mark of Anglo-French conflict, Edward's capture of John also marks a moment of English victory. In this way it anticipates the compliment the prologue is about to pay to Humphrey as English prince with a substantial contribution to make to the current war effort. It also anticipates the broader nationalist affirmations Lydgate will make later in the poem. In Book VIII, he will claim, inaccurately but revealingly, that Constantine was originally English (VIII, 1177). Constantine is the most heroic figure in the work, and only one of two who do not suffer Fortune's downturn. Shortly thereafter, Lydgate will devote over 500 celebratory lines to the career of Arthur, "Hedspryng of honour, of largesse cheef cisterne, / Merour of manhod, of noblesse the lanterne." (VIII, 2661–3206, 2855–56). He will also use the poem's ending, the capture of John, to rebuke Boccaccio for his intemperate remarks about English cowardice, pointing out, not unreasonably, that the capture of John is more convincing as evidence of English bravery (IX, 3162–96).

Beginning with Laurence also enables Lydgate to take advantage even here of his extended notion of translation. Though the material in the prologue is almost entirely his own, he presents his discussion of translation as if it were a simple recapitulation of Laurence's. The governing condition of this discussion is presumption. So long as translators approach their originals with humility and without presumption or envy they are justified in expanding and amending the originals (I, 8–42). These changes will both support the original and preserve it. (I, 78–98) One of the beauties of this notion is that it provides the justification itself for Lydgate's ascription of it to Laurence, when it is his own. He can do so because the ascription is

deferential rather than presumptuous. Of course, this deferential
gesture also enables him to take advantage of the very liberty this
ventriloquilized argument has granted him.

These subtleties in the argument's staging are more than matched
by the argument's substance. I quote at some length so that we may
examine this subtlety in detail. After pointing out that craftsmen can
"breke and renewe" the material they work on (I, 8–20), Laurence,
according to Lydgate, claims "clerkis" have a similar freedom:

> Thyng that was maad of auctours hem beforn,
> Thei may off newe fynde and fantasie,
> Out of old chaff trie out ful cleene corn,
> Make it more fresh and lusti to the eie,
> Ther subtil witt and ther labour applie,
> With ther colours agreable off hewe,
> Make olde thynges forto seeme newe.
>
> Afforn provydid that no presumpcioun
> In ther chaungyng have noon auctorite,
> And that meeknesse haue dominacioun,
> Fals Envie that she not present be;
> But that ther ground with parfit charite
> Conueied be to ther auantange,
> Trewli rootid a-myd of ther corage.   (I, 22–35)

While ostensibly stressing fidelity to the antecedent, these lines
actually give the translator an almost unlimited latitude for innovation.

The application of the traditional chaff and corn metaphor nearly
inverts its terms. The "corn," as the nub of doctrinal truth, should be
the antecedent term, since it pre-exists and determines the meaning
of whatever chaff is newly devised to represent it. Such inversions
were not uncommon in later medieval texts and do not finally
frustrate the logic of the metaphor, which, after all, is based on the
paradoxical and mysterious relation between the spiritual and the
literal. Like the Spirit, the corn is antecedent to its literal chaff, but
it is also eternally new and restorative, while the chaff can be
deadening. What makes Lydgate's inversion unusual is the way in
which it insists on associating the corn's newness with the superficial
and the inessential. The renovation of the "ful cleen corn" is a
product of "fantasie," which makes it "more fressh and lusti to the
eie": this appeal to the visual seems almost entirely carnal. And the
"subtil witt" and "labour" applied in the next line comes entirely

from the clerk doing the translating, not from the inherent truth which the corn is supposed to encapsulate. The final two lines of the stanza reinforce this point in at least three ways. The "colours agreable off hewe," in addition to recalling the carnality of the ocular metaphor in line 25, also define the corn's persuasive power as entirely rhetorical, while the final line firmly asserts that such power is strictly a matter of appearance: "Make old thynges for to *seeme newe.*"

With its injunction against presumption, the next stanza lays down the conditions limiting these prerogatives of innovation. But these conditions are exclusively moral, which leaves a translator's textual freedom intact. If the clause, "Afforn provydid that no presumpcioun / In ther changyng have noon auctorite," requires humility before the original text, it also takes the right to change the original for granted. So long as the changes do not grant presumption any authority, they are fully entitled to declare themselves faithful to the text they have changed. The oxymoronic formulation of the next clause, "that meeknesse have dominacioun," sums up the rhetorical power Lydgate claims for translators. They shall have dominance precisely through the attitude of meekness they bring to the text they translate. So long as they restrain presumption, they are free to expand or amend it in whatever way seems to them most in keeping with its spirit.

This notion of translation, both deferential and empowering – empowering precisely because it is deferential – will enable Lydgate to make considerable claims for himself, his text, his tradition, and his audience, without ever seeming to make any claim at all. It can do this because it imposes the same requirement of deference on those to whom Lydgate defers, beginning with Laurence. Laurence is doubly constrained. First, there is his respect for Bocaccio. "Thus Laurence fro hym envie excludid" (I, 36). Deciding to amend the text, nevertheless "first he forsook / Presumpcioun, and took to hym meeknesse" (I, 40–41). But second, there is also Laurence's constraint in relation to his audience.

> He in his tyme off cunnyng dede excelle
> In ther language, therfore he was requerid
> Off estatis, which gan hym eek compelle,
> A-mong hem holde off rethorik the welle,
> To undirfonge this labour they hym preie,
> And ther request he lowli dede obeie.   (I, 44–49)

Laurence's assumption of meekness is as much a social act as a
rhetorical one, and is equally empowering in both respects. Just as it
takes as its textual ground an authority amenable to amendment, it
takes as its social ground an audience eager for moral correction.
These two authorities Lydgate sets up for Laurence, Bochas's text,
and the "estatis," find their parallels in the textual and social
authorities he will establish for himself, Chaucer and Humphrey.
While his style cannot compare with that of Chaucer "Whom al this
land shold off riht preferre," (Pr., 251) his loyal submission to
Humphrey will make up the deficit. Humphrey commanded that
Lydgate

> This book translate, hym to do pleasaunce
> ...
> And with support off his magnificence,
> Undir the wyngis off his correcioun,
> Though that I have lak off eloquence,
> I shal procede in this translacioun,
> Fro me avoidyng al presumpcioun
> Lowli submytting everi hour & space
> Mi reud language to my lordis grace.   (I, 433, 435–41)

In the course of paying Humphrey the courtly compliments due a
patron, Lydgate simultaneously offers them as evidence of his humble
resistance to presumption generally, and thus clears poetic space for
himself, without in any way impugning his self-deprecating praise for
Chaucer. Nor are Chaucer or Boccaccio any less constrained than
Lydgate and Laurence.

Lydgate makes it quite clear that all his authorities owe their
authoritative status precisely to their own respect for previous
authority. He presents Bochas as a compiler, who "gadred out" of
"dyvers bookes ... / Off philisophres and many an old poete ... / The
fall of nobles in many dyvers lond" (I, 71–77), and he presents
Chaucer largely as a translator. He begins extremely deferentially,
declaring Chaucer the "cheeff poete off Breteyne ... / As he that was
of makyng sovereyne" (I, 247, 250). After lamenting his death for
one stanza, and placing him for three in a larger tradition of
authorities that includes Seneca, Cicero, Petrarch, and Boccaccio,
Lydgate devotes the remaining twelve stanzas (I, 273–357) of the
encomium to rehearsing Chaucer's canon. Of the sixteen works he
catalogs, eleven can be considered translations, either in the narrow,
modern sense, or in the more extended one Lydgate uses, and six he

explicitly identifies as such: *Troilus and Criseyde, Boece, House of Fame* (which he calls "Dante in English"), the *Romaunt*, the unattested *Mary Magdalen*, and the *Complaint of Mars* (which he calls the "Brooch of Vulcan"). The other five he lists that can be considered translations are the *Treatise of the Astrolabe*, the *Clerk's Tale, Melibee* (all three of which Chaucer treats as translations), the *Monk's Tale*, and the unattested *Ceix and Alcione*.[34] This catalog strongly implies that Chaucer's sovereignty as a maker inhered in his deference to the *auctors* which preceded him. To make is to translate, and the project Lydgate has in hand makes him Chaucer's peer.

Moreover, if Laurence's amendment of Boccaccio's work to more than double its original size is enough to merit recognition in its own right what must the 36,365 lines of the *Fall of Princes* do for Lydgate when set against the 775 lines of the *Monk's Tale*? Especially since Lydgate himself solidifies this comparison at the very end of the poem, in his last address to Humphrey. Proclaiming the imperfections of his own work, he once again invokes Chaucer, first in the company of Virgil, Homer, Dares, and Ovid, and then two stanzas later, in the company of Boccaccio and Petrarch:

> ... my mayster hadde nevir pere, –
> I mene Chauceer – in stooryes that he tolde;
> And he also wrot tragedyes olde.
>
> The Fal of Prynces gan pitously compleyne,
> As Petrark did, and also Iohn Bochas
> Laureat Fraunceys, poetys both tweyne
> Toold how pryncis for ther greet trespace
> Wer ovirthrowe, rehersyng al the caas,
> As Chaucer dide in the Monkys Tale.
> But I that stonde lowe doun in the vale,
>
> So greet a book in Ynglyssh to translate,
> Did it be constreynt and no presumpcioun,
> Born in a vyllage which callyd is Lydgate ... (IX, 3419–31])

He may stand in the vale, but Lydgate's great amplification of the project Chaucer set himself in the *Monk's Tale*, places him on the

---

[34] It does not seem likely that he means the *Book of the Duchess* by "Ceix and Alcione," since he lists that work as well, though it is possible the Ceix and Alcione portion of the work circulated separately. Besides the *Book of Duchess*, the other works he lists which are not translations are the *Parliament of Fowls*, the lost *Book of the Lion, Anelida and Arcite*, the *Legend of Good Women*, and the *Canterbury Tales* as a unit.

same plane as the poets he is eulogizing. His final adumbration of literary tradition concludes with the inscription of his own name. (And his identification of his village recalls the same gesture by Boccaccio in the *De casibus*.[35]) Though he accompanies this self-canonization with profuse declarations of his own shortcomings, even these demonstrate his worthiness, since he has made deference to predecessors and the forsaking of presumption the central criteria of poetic authority. As the final member of this canon, he is the most deferential, but he is also the one whose work is most comprehensive (he leaves Laurence completely out of this list), raising at least the possibility that he embodies the tradition's ultimate fulfillment.

Lydgate's implicit political claims are only slightly less exalted. The encomium to Chaucer ends with a broader invocation of the superiority of the past:

> ... these poetis I make off mencioun,
> Were bi old tyme had in gret deynte,
> With kingis, pryncis in every regioun,
> Gretli preferrid afftir ther degre...   (I, 358–61)

The point of this deference, however, is the celebration of Humphrey, whom the respect past monarchs paid to poets recalls. As Lydgate's dedication establishes his poem as a public act of instruction, it will also go even further than the *Regement of Princes* in its portrayal of the moralist's dependence on the prince. Commanding Lydgate to translate "The noble book off this John Bochas," (I, 423) Humphrey shows not only that he is in no real need of instruction, but can in fact take charge of producing the very text by which instruction should take place. Lydgate will cast him in this role in various ways throughout the poem. The most notable of these occurs in the prologue to Book II, where Humphrey directs that Lydgate add a moralizing envoy after each tragedy, and "to noble pryncis lowli it directe, / Bi othres fallyng thei myght themsilff correcte" (II, 153–54).

Humphrey is beyond "alle chaungis of Fortune" because he is already on the moralist's side, pre-empting his counsel. As an actual historical figure who has already internalized its precepts, he gives the *De casibus* tradition a positive purchase within history. If this portrayal grants Humphrey a pre-eminence among princes, it is nevertheless a pre-eminence Lydgate and his readers will share. For

[35] VI, i, 19; see above 130–31.

Humphrey's transcendence of moral correction is based precisely on his earnest desire for it. In leading up to the commission, Lydgate observes that as a "prynce ful myhti of puissance" (I, 373), Humphrey nevertheless "hath gret ioie with clerkis to comune" (I, 387). He especially enjoys reading books, which

> Makith a prynce to have experience,
> To knowe hymsilff, in many sundri wise,
> Wher he trespasith his errour to chastise. (I, 418–20)

As he makes himself more subordinate to his dedicatee than any previous writer in the *Fürstenspiegel* tradition, he paradoxically also makes his prince more subordinate to him. The power of this vision of lay authority lies precisely in its systematic requirement of constraint and submission. The requirement to submit is so general that it ends by affecting every position articulated.

These changes will also enable a more harmonious vision of the relations between Church and Crown, which after all was a longstanding feature of Lancastrian policy. In addition to defining Humphrey as a lover of learning and a seeker after moral improvement, Lydgate also defines him as a defender and champion "off hooli chirche," as evidenced by his active suppression of the Lollards (I, 400–13). Because Lydgate has already identified Humphrey as a source of moral order from within the laity, he need have no anxiety about the laity's relation to the authority of the Church. At the same time, and for the same reason, he accepts without question Humphrey's lay autonomy. He takes Humphrey's piety to be defined by his role as lay chastiser of heresy, not, as would have been the case for John of Salisbury, by his submission to clerical mandate.

Lydgate returns to this notion of harmony in his exemplum of Constantine, which occurs in neither Laurence nor Boccaccio. He clearly intends the addition as a dialogue with Gower, some of whose revisions to the *Vita S. Silvestri* he retains. He eliminates Gower's anticlericalism by dropping all reference to both the Donation and the angelic prophecy which followed it, but he retains Gower's notion of lay autonomy. He retains Gower's suppression of the retributive origins of Constantine's leprosy, and Gower's relocation of the opening scene to the palace. He also amplifies Gower's interest in the materiality of the piscina, devoting 21 lines (VIII, 1247–67) to Constantine's subsequent adornment of it with images of Christ and

John the Baptist in gold, pearls, and other gems. He then reinforces this metonymic demonstration of royal power supporting of clerical authority by returning to the *Vita S. Silvestri* for the details of Constantine's ecclesiological initiatives. He represses only the Donation, and while he retains its concomitant tearful prostration before Sylvester, he makes that purely symbolic. "This exaumple in open he hath shewed, / His staat imperial of meeknesse leid aside" (VIII, 1366–67). Lacking any material institutional counterpart, the example of meekness he provides by laying aside his imperial regalia effectively restricts itself to the purely spiritual. He exercises political leadership by offering his people an example of submission to the spiritual authority of an institution which affirms his political authority. Like Humphrey, he becomes a force beyond the mutability of Fortune, an association strengthened by Lydgate's assertions of his English origin, which Lydgate draws from the Arthurian tradition. With the exception of Theodosius, another imperial penitent, Constantine is the only protagonist in the entire collection who does not experience a fall.

The spiritual exemplarity Lydgate thus assigns to the figure of the monarch involves a more general broadening of the moral authority of the lay. Assigning to Bochas a claim Bochas never makes, he writes in the prologue to Book I,

> And as myn auctour list to comprehende, –
> This Iohn Bochas, bi gret auctorite, –
> It is almesse to correct and a-mende
> The vicious folk off every comounte
> And bi exaumplis which that notable be
> Off pryncis olde, that whilom dede fall,
> The lowere peeple from ther errour call.   (I, 204–10)

The prince's moral exemplarity has for immediate audience not just the court but the "lowere peeple" as a whole. This group is undifferentiated except for their distinction from the prince, whose exemplarity exerts a unifying moral pressure. In this passage Lydgate imagines the lay community in positive moral terms: as a unified entity whose moral regulation comes from within. Even if he defines royal exemplarity negatively, he does so in the conviction it is capable of amendment, and that conviction enables him to envision the lay community as a whole as amendable as well. He expects the laity as a whole to identify their moral status with that of the prince, in a way

that, explicitly at least, earlier compilers of *Fürstenspiegel* expected
mainly of the court. It is not that this broadening of identification
eliminates either the prince's privileges, or even the hierarchical
status of the court. On the contrary, if anything Lydgate intensifies
the power of hierarchy, precisely through this process of generalization.

In the next stanza, he continues:

> ... whan the suerd off vengeaunce eek doth bite
> Upon pryncis for ther transgressioun,
> The comon peeple in ther opynyoun,
> For verray dreede tremble don & quake,
> And bi such mene ther vices thei forsake.   (I, 213–17)

Trembling and quaking, the "comon peeple" are positively craven
in their instinctive subservience. The exempla of princes affects them
so strongly because they recognize implicitly their own vast inferiority. Nevertheless, that very sense of inferiority is also the
instrument through which they effect their identification with the
prince. It is how they put themselves in his place, and by so doing,
become morally self-corrective and self-regulative. The final line of
this stanza leaves no doubt on this point. The common people will
forsake their vices so long as royal exemplarity is brought to bear on
them in the proper manner.

This paradoxical broadening of audience gives an internal
coherence to the nationalist claims I have already mentioned. In
making this observation, I am fully aware that the term *nationalism*
has been used much too loosely in relation to later medieval culture.
I do not mean to imply the dominant sense of communal identity the
word later comes to signify. But it is worth noting Lydgate's claims of
English superiority occur in a poem that connects this broadened
sense of political community with claims of the moral authority
inherent in a specific form of linguistic community, that is, a tradition
of vernacular poetry. It is also worth noting that Lydgate marks the
emergence of both aspects of this incipient form of lay community by
engaging with two key moments from the *Policraticus*: John of
Salisbury's version of the corporate fiction, and his famous defense of
writing.

In his revision of the corporate fiction (II, 806–91), Lydgate keeps
two of the most distinctive features of John's version. The first is the
comprehensive elaboration of the correspondence between body

parts and estates. The second is the location of both prince and clergy in the head – the prince as "wit, memorie, and eyen off resoun" (II, 847), the clergy as the soul. In both cases, however, Lydgate reworks these details so as to emphasize the integrity and unity of the lay polity. His equation of reason with prince, soul with clergy, judges with eyes, nobility with arms and hands, and laborers with feet corresponds with some small variation to John's. But he also combines John's heart (the Senate) and stomach (financial officers) into a torso consisting of an "agregat off peeplis and degrees / Be parfit pes and unyte I-knet," including "meires, provostes & burgeis," and "Marchauntis also" (II, 863–67). His presentation of the conceit is shorter than John's, one hundred lines to two full books, and that enables him to make presentation of each of the members much more proportionate, about one stanza each, whereas John allotted as much as nineteen chapters to "the armed hand" (*milites* for John, "nobles" for Lydgate), and as little as one to the feet or laborers. Moreover John emphasizes the disproportion. The third estate is so large and various

that the commonwealth in the number of its feet exceeds not only the eight-footed crab but even the centipede, and because of their very multitude they cannot be enumerated. (243)

ut res publica non octipedes cancros sed et centipedes pedum numerositate transcendat, et quidem prae multitudine numerari non possunt... (VI, xx, 619)

By contrast Lydgate stresses proportionality. He ends his version with an evocation of unity and harmony, which, without ever denying the notion's essential hierarchy, stresses its mutuality:

> Thus first yiff pryncis governed been be riht,
> And knyhthod suffre the peeple to have no wrong,
> And trouthe in iuges shewe out his cleer liht,
> And feith in cites with love be drawe a-long,
> And hooli cherche in vertu be maad strong,
> And in his labour the plouh ne feyne nought, –
> Thanne be proporcioun this ymage is weel wrought.
>
> (II, 897–903)

This celebration of proportionate harmony is underwritten by the even more striking change Lydgate has made earlier on.

While he certainly retains the priority granted to clergy by their identification with the soul, this priority no longer has any real political importance, for he displaces John's hierocratism with notions of exemplarity he derives from Chaucer and Gower.

> This bodi must have a soule off liff
> To quyke the membris with gostli mociouns,
> Which shal be maad off folk contemplatiff,
> The cherche committed to ther pocessiouns
> Which bi ther hooli conversaciouns
> And good exaumples sholde as sterris shyne,
> Be grace and vertu the peeple tenlumyne.
>   ...
> For in ther techyng and predicaciouns
> Thei sholde trouthe to hih & low declare,
> And in ther office for no dreed ne spare
> Vices correcte, lich as thei ar holde,
> Sithe thei been heerdis off Cristes folde. (II, 876–82, 885–89)

Clerical authority here is not ecclesiological; it is barely doctrinal. Rather, like Chaucer's Parson, this clergy teaches by example. If, unlike Chaucer and Gower, Lydgate does not use this notion of exemplarity as the basis of an anti-clerical critique, he nevertheless accepts the narrow circumspection of ecclesiological privilege implicit in its premise. This clergy is Gower's "Mirour of ensamplerie," less an institution than an aggregate of moral "sterris," whose spiritual leadership depends on their own virtue more than the blanket sanction of their ecclesiological status.

As Lydgate defines this leadership more specifically in the next stanza, he restricts clerics to "techyng and predicaciouns" (as opposed to the curial duties envisaged by John of Salisbury). The rustic image of "heerdis off Cristes folde" and the assertion that "Thei sholde trouth to hih and low declare" both serve the same double function. They democratize the clergy's relation to the laity, but also restrict its role to spiritual instruction. If the clergy instructs high and low alike, it no longer has the special relationship to lay rulers on which the hierocratic counsel advocated by John of Salisbury depended. Its primary concern, rather, is moral correction, assisting the prince in maintaining the polity in proper moral order.

This understanding of clerical authority makes it equivalent to – one might even say interchangeable with – one aspect of his notion of lay authority, the textual, didactic aspect he associates with poetry. The equivalence enables him to fold his reworking of the corporate fiction nicely into his larger concerns. Not only does it affirm his

double status as cleric and lay poet, but it also reinforces the increased
moral authority he wants to bestow on poetry. Poetry as morally
constitutive is an idea to which he returns again and again, but most
notably in the second engagement with the *Policraticus*. Lydgate
places his defense of writing in the Prologue to Book IV, where he uses
it to introduce one of many moments where Boccaccio stops to take
stock of the progress of his labors. Like John of Salisbury, Lydgate
defines writing primarily by its power of duration. Writing is the
instrument which enables all forms of human order and authority to
last. Like John he also defines it as God's gift: "God sette writyng &
lettres in sentence, / Ageyn the dulnesse of our infirmyte"(IV,
29–30). But he stresses the secular and temporal benefits of this gift
much more than John. He repeatedly depicts writing as action in the
world, intensifying what was already a strong emphasis on the
performative. And he interpolates an account of poetry as a leading
example of writing's durative power.

   After a leisurely amplification of the pleasure of letters, *iocunditas
litterarum*, the idea John invokes in his first sentence, Lydgate comes
to the point in the fourth stanza.

> Lawe hadde perisshed, nadde be writyng;
> Our feith appalled, ner vertu of scripture;
> For al religioun and ordre of good lyvyng
> Takth ther exaumple be doctryn of lettrure.
> For writyng causeth, with helpe of portraiture,
> That thynges dirked, of old that wer begonne,
> To be remembred with this celestial sonne.   (IV, 22–28)

The *Policraticus* mentions the dependence of law and faith on writing,
but only as two in a series of such dependences. Here Lydgate focuses
on these two specifically, and he makes them analogous labels of the
two aspects of human existence, the secular and the sacral. Writing
makes possible "religion" and "ordre of good lyvyng" alike, and it
does so in a performative fashion. The "doctryn of lettrure" works
through example. As the phrase implies, "lettrure" is a teaching, an
activity. Its power to preserve should not be understood as that of a
neutral and empty vehicle, as if it were some airtight, transparent
container into which the truths of law and religion were installed.
Instead, it should be seen as the active conversion into more durable
form of other kinds of action, namely, the founding actions which
produce law and religion: that is, the "dirked" things which "of old
... wer begonne."

That human beings have this form of power they owe to God. Nevertheless, if writing is God's gift, only human labor can activate its power.

> Dilligence, cheef triumphatrice
> Of slogardie, necgligence & slouthe,
> Eek of memorye upholdere and norice
> And registreer to suppowaile trouthe,
> Hath of old labour (& ellis wer gret routhe)
> Brouhte thynges passid, notable in substaunce,
> Onli be writyng to newe remembrance.   (IV, 36–42)

Diligence achieves its mastery over humanity's degenerative tendencies, "slogardie, necgligence & slouthe" by and through writing. Lydgate highlights the interdependence of the relationship by declaring diligence achieves it mastery "onli be writyng." If writing waits for human labor to activate its power, it is nevertheless the only form such labor can take, if its aim is to preserve social and spiritual order. As the all-important gift of a scriptural God, writing both depends on, and demands human performance.

Lydgate moves quite easily from this global conception of writing to his more specific celebration of poetry. As a concretization of writing's power to endure, poetry becomes a distinct and autonomous form of textual authority.

> Writyng caused poetis to recure
> A name eternal, the laurer whan thei wan,
> In adamaunt grave perpetuelli tendure.
> Record I take of Virgile Mantuan,
> That wrot the armys & prowesse of the man
> Callid Eneas, whan he of hih corage
> Cam to Itaill from Dido of Cartage.   (IV, 64–70)

Writing gives poets an eternal name: it is not just the poetry that lasts, but the poet's name as well. In this, the poet is the beneficiary of God's gift, but God's gift makes him, as the source of textual authority, God's peer. The eternal name God gives makes him as ultimate and inevitable a principle of the regulation of the texts he produces as God is of scripture. As poetic *auctor par excellence*, and chronicler of what for medieval court culture was the most important act of historical foundation, Virgil provides Lydgate with the perfect illustration, as regards both the performative and the durative aspects of the notion of poetry he is propounding. But Virgil's pagan status is worthy of remark as well. If even pagan poets achieve eternal names – and all of the poets Lydgate goes on to discuss are pagan, with the exception of Petrarch – then poetic authority clearly is distinct from the divine authority with which its eternal status makes it coextensive.

The doctrine of poetic immortality has conventionally been taken to be a substitute for faith in divine authority. This passage shows how mistaken that idea is, as regards the later Middle Ages and Renaissance at least. Once can hardly say that Lydgate, in his glorification of poetry, is seeking a replacement for Holy Writ. On the contrary, he fully accepts, indeed celebrates scriptural authority. He merely wants to convey the prestige of that authority to poetry. It might be objected that Lydgate merely "remedievalizes" this notion, which, after all, he draws from Italian humanists like Petrarch and Boccaccio. But the objection will not stick. Aside from the highly dubious presumption that such writers were themselves seeking a substitute for God, this view ignores the fact that the doctrine of poetic immortality is essentially an appropriative notion. Its intelligibility depends on the religious notions of immortality it metaphorizes. If anyone is guilty of bad faith in this matter, it is not a putative "remedievalizer" like Lydgate, but the Romantic and post-Romantic literary thinkers who want to get rid of God and keep immortality. Lydgate's notion of poetry is appropriative on a grand scale, but its logic is coherent. Poetry translates moral action into textual authority. It provides, in the figure of the poet, a specifically historical source of authority, who is nevertheless eternally stable, and to whom those concerned with the exercise of lay power can always appeal. Poetry memorializes action; but it does so in order that past action can serve to regulate action in the future.

As the the facilitator of lay moral order, the poet has an obligation to exercise his craft as diligently and extensively as possible. This performative notion of poetry thus also underwrites Lydgate's encyclopedic ambitions. As he remarks in his prologue,

> These ookis grete be nat doun ihewe
> First at a stroke, but bi long processe,
> Nor longe stories a woord may not expresse.   (I, 96–98)

Moral order can be achieved within history, and poetry has a vital role to play in its achievement. The confidence Lydgate places in the moral value of human history gives his exempla and the long moralizing envoys an urgency they cannot have for those who do not share this confidence. Since moral order can be built within history out of history's own materials, Lydgate must attempt to include as much as possible. These stories must be retold, their moral dilemmas narrated fully, then drawn out and reformulated in the envoys. Nor is Lydgate's encyclopedic ambition incompetently undercut by his frequent disavowals of rhetorical colors, as has often been alleged.[36] The notion that amplification and a plain style are mutually exclusive derives from the mimetic ideals of high realism, in which the literary text is expected to achieve an approximation of the world its readers will recognize as real. Any portion of the text which does not somehow correspond to the object it depicts constitutes interference and waste. Lydgate's ambitions, however, are performative rather than mimetic. In fact, his rhetoric in this poem is less aureate than it is in some of his earlier work. But that is not because he is attempting to be more mimetic and failing. It is because he is engaged in what he understands as a moral struggle, one which requires the moral dilemmas of the past be recovered and memorialized. That is to say, he focuses his poetic attention on the point where textual authority meets historical action. His amplifications are designed to restage that confrontation as fully and as often as necessary.

Lydgate's moral poetic may seem to be at odds with his claim to be writing tragedies. For modern criticism has taken the hallmark of tragedy to be a certain kind of moral suspension and didactic neutrality. In the words of A. C. Bradley, it portrays "the self-division and intestinal warfare of the ethical substance, not so much the war of good with evil as the war of good with good."[37] The totalizing role Lydgate gives to the figure of Fortune has accordingly seemed too pat and inflexible to allow for intricate explorations of the "ethical substance" a humanist view like Bradley's requires. Nevertheless, humanist rejections of explicitly didactic versions of the tragic such as Lydgate's, claim too much flexibility for themselves and take too much away from those they reject. As Jonathan Dollimore has so convincingly demonstrated, the humanist view of tragedy has a moral vision of its own, one no less pat in many respects than the Christian didacticism it repudiates.[38] Indeed, in my view, it is more so. Lydgate's performative, exemplary conception of poetic authority

---

[36] For example, Pearsall, *Lydgate*, 7.
[37] A. C. Bradley, *Oxford Lectures on Poetry*, 2nd ed. (London: Macmillan, 1909), 71. Cited by Jonathan Dollimore in *Radical Tragedy: Religion, Ideology and Power in the Drama of Shakespeare and His Contemporaries* (Brighton: Harvester, 1984), 54.
[38] Dollimore, *Radical Tragedy*, 156–57.

does not require the same unified subject that humanism does. For this reason, I would also argue that Lydgate anticipates Renaissance tragedy not only as it is conceived in the narrow humanist sense, but also in the more decentered sense that Dollimore claims for it.

Lydgate's influence on Renaissance drama through the *Mirrour for Magistrates* (which presents itself as a continuation of the *Fall of Princes*) is a well-acknowledged, if not necessarily well-explored, fact. In the earlier part of this century, a number of scholarly accounts pressed the case for Lydgate's importance in the development of Renaissance tragedy, the most substantial of which was probably Willard Farnham's *Medieval Heritage of Elizabethan Tragedy*.[39] Based on relatively vague and reductive notions of transmission and influence, and driven by idealized notions of spiritual and textual authority, this case has been not so much refuted as forgotten. I want to revive it here, but on different, more specific grounds. I want to suggest that Lydgate's interest in the tragic was part of his larger interest in lay authority, both political and poetic. That interest defined authority as exemplary and therefore performative. If Lydgate's contribution to sixteenth- and seventeenth-century English culture can be attested most specifically by the *Mirrour for Magistrates*, that is because he played a larger role in the production of exemplary models of authority. Making poetry an autonomous, even eternal site for the exploration and production of moral order made way for increasingly elaborate explorations. Renaissance drama was to produce the figure who still stands today as the English canon's ultimate *auctor*; that he acquired that position is a result, in part, of the Chaucerian tradition's establishment of lay poetic authority, which it secured largely through the efforts of Lydgate.

In case it seems that this line of argument takes the notion of performance too literally, I would point out that I take it no more literally than did Lydgate himself. He was keenly interested in the relation between textual authority and dramatic performance, and he is the first major English author to leave a substantial body of dramatic work, primarily mummings, but including a pageant, and the poetry for Henry VI's *Triumphal Entry*. His mummings were performed both at court and before wealthy guildsmen and urban leaders. They celebrate the socially unifying force of royal and civic power and provide dramatic expressions of Lydgate's more general

[39] Willard Farnham, *Medieval Heritage of Elizabethan Tragedy*, 2nd ed. (Oxford: Basil Blackwell, 1959), esp. 160–72, 304–452.

participation in the poetic delineation of lay power. If Leonard Tennenhouse is right to argue that Shakespeare's drama "observed a transgressive logic" wherein "stagecraft collaborates with statecraft in producing spectacles of power," then Shakespeare was anticipated and in all probability enabled by Lydgate.[40]

Spectacles of royal power invite the viewer's identification with the monarch at their center. As I have already argued, such identification is essential to the *Fall of Princes*. By morally enjoining his readers to put themselves in the position of his exemplary monarchs, Lydgate implicitly offers them discursive participation in royal power. For he also enjoins them to participate in his moralizing. To the extent they moralize the princely falls they behold, they can control the process of identification, sharing the power, but protecting themselves from the punishment. It is in such carefully regulated identification that the humanist notions of tragedy begin. Moreover, in contrast to its operation within humanism, there is nothing hidden about this process in Lydgate. As I have been at pains to show, he is meticulously self-conscious in his broadening of the access to poetic authority. If it is true, as Dollimore argues, that Renaissance tragedy discloses "the mechanisms of state, of ideology and of power," the same thing is true of Lydgate and of the traditions which he exhaustively recapitulates.[41] It is true that the *Fall of Princes* is not the radically destabilizing artifact Dollimore takes Renaissance tragedy (almost universally!) to be. On the other hand, the fact that complex, self-conscious meditations on power and authority can already be found in Lydgate and his predecessors complicates Dollimore's frequent assumption that the very occurrence of such explorations in Renaissance tragedy is *prima facie* evidence of their destabilizing radicalism.

The connection between the *Fall of Princes* and Renaissance tragedy can be drawn even more tightly. One frequently finds in this work the complexity of character often assumed to be Renaissance tragedy's peculiar achievement. This claim may seem even more perverse than my previous ones, in view of both Lydgate's bad press, and the abiding modernist conviction that didacticism is a fatal enemy to character. Nevertheless, the complexity is there for anyone to see who only bothers to look, and the reason why it should be there is not far to seek. The characters in Renaissance tragedy are by no means average individuals. They are largely aristocratic and often

---

[40] Leonard Tennenhouse, *Power on Display: The Politics of Shakespeare's Genres* (New York and London: Methuen, 1986), 15.   [41] Dollimore, *Radical Tragedy*, 161.

royal. Their complexity, therefore, has less to do with some emergent commitment to mimetic realism, and more to do with the complexities of identification they offer a less socially privileged audience. The same thing is true of Lydgate.

He is frequently at pains to show that the pride which leads to a protagonist's downfall is nearly indistinguishable from the self-assertion that constitutes his heroism. Against clearly evil figures like Tarquin and Nero, and clearly virtuous ones like Zenobia or the Scipios, he sets extended explorations of more ambiguous figures like Cyrus, Alexander, Pompey, and Caesar. He presents their lives as constituted by the progressive accumulation of power, which inevitably violates some unarticulated boundary and results in their downfall. Because his attitude toward the early stage of this process is usually favorable, the overstepping comes to seem inevitable. His long celebration of Pompey's early career – which brings Rome out of the ruin of civil war with successive conquests of Lombardy, Sicily, Africa, Albania, Iberia, Syria, Phoenicia, Lebanon, Judea, and seven kingdoms between Caucausus and the Red Sea – concludes by comparisons to Alexander and Hercules:

> Peise his deedis, his conquestis marciall:
> Thries consul chose for his encres;
> Reed, ye shal fynde how he was egall
> To Alisaundre or to Hercules.
> Wher that evere he put hymsilff in pres,
> All cam to hand, concludyng, ye may see,
> To comoun proffit of Roome the cite. (VI, 2199–2205)

Pompey's heroism is entirely public. The exertions that make him equal to Alexander and Hercules are all connected to Rome's common profit. This equation governs both his trajectory as a character in the narrative and the identification he offers Lydgate's audience outside of it. Two stanzas later, the spirit of conquest, apparently of its own momentum, moves him to begin a series of actions opposed to the common interest. With "Cesar absent in Gaule," he decides, "He wolde have non that wer to hym semblable" (VI, 2214, 2219). He seizes sole legislative authority, depriving the absent Caesar of office, and precipitating the conflict which eventually would bring his downfall. The common interest which limits his self-assertion within the narrative takes control of that self-assertion outside of it. This exemplum offers Lydgate's readership a share both in the heroic power that enables Pompey's rise and in the even greater power of Fortune that forces his downfall. In making the latter a result of the former – that is, in making Pompey's downfall an inevitable expression of the overreaching that defines his heroism, Lydgate takes even the heroism away from him. For the inevitability which ties his rise to his downfall means that even when he acts in his own interest, he is actually acting in the interest of the moral law his career will illustrate. Since that moral law constitutes the discursive advantage Lydgate's audience holds over him, he ultimately acts in their interest, even when his heroism is at its most singular.

The example of Alexander defines the same dynamic in the emblem of the Gordian Knot. Once Alexander cut the knot, "Worldli presumpcioun gan make his herte bold" (IV, 1804). Yet the knot's preordained significance seems to make presumption the very quality the knot was designed to test. As Lydgate explains: "who that hadde science or kunnyng / That corious knotte to losne or untwyne, / Ouer Asie he sholde be crownid kyng" (IV, 1716–18). Having determined that

> The chaar [knot] with coordis was so enterlacid,
> That richeli stood in Iovys tabernacle,
> Which be his wit koude nat be unbracid,
> Nother be crafft nor no soleyn myracle...   (IV, 1723–26)

Alexander "Drouh out his suerd, wherof men hadde wonder, / Carf the knotte & cordis all assonder" (IV, 1728–29). Alexander's "science" consists in overthrowing science: the problem of the knot is not resolvable if one adheres strictly to the terms in which it is presented. Its solution can only come from one who does not feel constrained to play by the rules. That is precisely its point: to identify the conqueror who will be unconstrained by conventional standards, for no one else will be able to conquer Asia. Alexander's emblematic relation to the knot links his heroism and his downfall, and makes his heroism presumptuous in its very essence. The discursive control Lydgate's audience exercises over this presumption effectively gives it the power of violating the very moral law that constitutes its discursive advantage. With such violations the complexity of identification in his exempla reaches its full range. For these violations make the audience self-generating, giving it power over the moral law that constitutes it.

This doubleness can also be seen in those moments when Lydgate sustains a character's heroic integrity past the point of downfall. The most common instance is suicide, an ending to which Lydgate was inordinately attracted. He tends to treat suicide as an expression both of "disespair," and of defiance, a final, if empty, self-assertion against the inevitability of history. He condemns Hannibal's suicide, for example, as "bestiall," and "abhomynable to God & man" (V, 2148, 2156), but only after describing it as the expression of a "despiht" so great "That leuer he hadde, than bide in ther prisoun, / To moordre hymsilf be drynking off poisoun" (V, 2143–44). The very abomination of the act serves to indicate the extent of this "despiht," a despite fully consonant with heroism Hannibal demonstrates throughout the exemplum.

If we return to the story of Pompey, we can find an instance of tragic integrity sustained even after death. After his defeat at Thessaly, Pompey is betrayed in Egypt by Ptolemy and beheaded. When his head is presented to Caesar, the agent of justice whom Pompey had defrauded, Caesar

> Of his innat imperial excellence
> Brast out to weepe, & in his advertense
> Thouhte gret pite, a prince of so gret myht
> Sholde so be slayn, that was so good a knyht. (VI, 2489–92)

Confronted with graphic evidence of justice executed, Caesar's immediate reaction is not moral righteousness but pity. Caesar identifies with Pompey, giving his overreaching a moral weight equal to the law of Fortune which dictates his downfall. But this very identification subsumes Pompey's subjectivity as effectively as the beheading. Caesar has entirely aestheticized his rival, supplementing his actual victory over Pompey with a symbolic appropriation of Pompey's very resistance. Moreover, this appropriation displays the innateness of Caesar's "imperial excellence," an excellence Lydgate's audience only has to recognize to share.

The moral doubleness of this and similar moments in the *Fall of Princes* looks forward to such quintessentially tragic moments as the final soliloquies of Macbeth and Richard II, where the speaker maintains the integrity of his narrative viewpoint even as he recognizes the imminence of his destruction. There is the same insurmountable gap between subject position and narrative predicament, and the same expectation that the audience will find ideological unity in the recognition of the inevitability of the gap. I am not suggesting that Lydgate is as "good" as Shakespeare, whatever such a claim might mean. I am merely suggesting that

Shakespeare's excellence is not without its ideological specificity, and that on this point he shares that specificity with Lydgate. Considered as an ideological proposition, the moral ambiguity of the tragic hero cannot finally be separated from modern liberalism's abiding conviction that the needs of the individual are eternally at odds with the needs of the society. Lydgate's anticipation of this conviction calls into question the progressive halo with which modernity has usually crowned it. His more specific anticipation of Renaissance tragedy also calls into question the innovative status usually granted that genre even in the more qualified, less idealized terms of more recent accounts. If, for all of this, the image of Lydgate as a prosaic, driveling monk is still hard to shake, then perhaps that is because his anticipations of some of modernity's most cherished ideals threatens to make them seem prosaic as well.

The exemplum continues to be an important genre well into the Renaissance. The notion of exemplarity provides an important source of literary authority for much longer. Sidney in his *Apology*, and Spenser in the "Letter to Raleigh" both define poetic authority as exemplary. Fielding makes a similar suggestion for the novel in the preface to *Joseph Andrews*, albeit in more ironic terms. Exemplarity forms the conceptual base of such classic humanist defenses of the authority of literary discourse as W. K. Wimsatt's "Concrete Universal."[42] The "case study" or "case history" is the staple of half a dozen modern disciplines. If Peter Brooks is right to describe it as "a form of exemplary biography," then the connections between the case history and the *De casibus* tradition may be more than merely etymological. I end my account with Lydgate not because he represents some culmination, but precisely because he does not. He constitutes instead an important point of transition – important not least of all because it has been so neglected.

The same thing can be said of the medieval exemplum as a whole. As a classical form appropriated by the Western church, it lent authority to the emergent lay traditions of the later Middle Ages, particularly to the English tradition that begins with Chaucer. In so doing, it gave literary authority not only a sacral, but a sacerdotal cast that has persisted through modernity. The account of the exemplum I have offered owes part of its narrative coherence to claims about narrative and about the Middle Ages that some may

[42] W. K. Wimsatt, *The Verbal Icon: Studies in the Meaning of Poetry* (Lexington: University of Kentucky Press, 1954), 169–83.

find tendentious. In this I follow the spirit of my subject, which bases itself on narrative's polemical capacities. I have, nevertheless, been less interested in settling these large questions than with conveying their urgency as a stimulus to further discussion. The complex interrelations between narrative and authority, both past and present, have been neglected for too long. This study is offered in the hope that they will begin to attract the attention they deserve.

Bibliography

PRIMARY SOURCES

Aegidius Romanus (Egidio Colonna). *De regimine principum libri III*. Edited by F. Hieronymum Samaritanium. Rome: Bartholomaum Zannettum, 1607. Reprinted in Darmstadt by Scientia Verlag Aalen, 1967

An Alphabet of Tales. Edited by Mary Macleod Banks. 2 vols. London: Early English Text Society, 1904

Aquinas, Thomas. *De regimine principum, ad Regem Cypri*. Edited by Joseph Mathis. Torino and Rome: Marietti, 1948

On Kingship. Translated by Gerald B. Phelan; revised, with an introduction, by I. Th. Eschmann. Toronto: Pontifical Institute of Mediaeval Studies, 1949

Aristotle. *The Basic Works of Aristotle*. Edited by Richard McKeon. New York: Random House, 1947

Augustus Caesar. *Res gestae divi Augusti*. In *Documents Illustrating the Reigns of Augustus and Tiberius*. Collected by Victor Ehrenberg and A. H. M. Jones, 2nd edition. Oxford: Clarendon Press, 1955, reprinted 1976, 1–31

Boccaccio, Giovanni. *Decameron*. Edited by Vittore Branca. Milan: Arnoldo Mondadori, 1976

The Decameron. Translated by G. H. McWilliam. Harmondsworth: Penguin Books, 1972

De casibus virorum illustrium. Edited by Vittore Branca. Milan: Arnoldo Mondadori, 1983

Boethius. *The Consolation of Philosophy*. Translated by Richard Green. Indianapolis: The Bobbs-Merrill Co., 1962

Philosophiae consolatio. Edited by Ludwig Bieler. *Corpus Christianorum, Series Latina*, 94. Turnholt: Brepols, 1957

Cesarius of Heisterbach. *Caesarii Heisterbacensis monachi ordinis Cisterciensis dialogus miraculorum*. 2 vols. Edited by Joseph Strange. Cologne, Bonn and Brussels: H. Lempertz and Co., 1851

Die Fragment der Libri VIII miraculorum de Caesarius von Heisterbach. Edited by Aloys Meister. *Romische Quartalschrift für Christliche Alterthumskunde und für Kirchensgeschichte, Supplementheft* 13. Rome 1901

Cessolis, Jacobus de. *Mittheilungen aus dem Handschriften der Ritter-Akademie zu Brandenburg A. H., II. Jacobus de Cessolis.* Edited by Ernst Kopke. Brandenburg: Gustav Matthes, 1879

Chaucer, Geoffrey. *The Riverside Chaucer.* Edited by Larry D. Benson. 3rd edition. Boston: Houghton-Mifflin, 1987

Dante Alighieri. *Monarchy and Three Political Letters.* Translated by Donald Nicholl and Colin Hardie. London: Weidenfield and Nicolson, 1954

Étienne de Bourbon. *Anecdotes historiques, legendes et apologues tirés du recueil inédit d'Étienne de Bourbon.* Edited by A. Lecoy de la Marche. Paris: Librairie Renouard, 1877

Gauchi, Henri de. *Li Livres du gouvernement des rois.* Edited by Samuel Paul Molenaer. New York: Columbia University, 1899. Reprinted in New York by AMS Press, 1966

Gesta Romanorum. Edited by Hermann Oesterley. Berlin: Weidmannsche Buchhandlung, 1872

Gower, John. *The Complete Works of John Gower.* Vols. 2–3, *The English Works.* Edited by G. C. Macaulay. 4 vols. Oxford: The Clarendon Press, 1901

Gregory. *Gregoire le Grand: Dialogues.* Edited by Adalbert de Vogüé and translated into French by Paul Antin. Paris: Editions du Cerf, 1979

Hoccleve, Thomas. *Minor Works.* London: Early English Text Society, 1892
The Regement of Princes. Edited by Frederick J. Furnivall. London: Early English Text Society, 1897

John of Salisbury. *Ioannis Saresberiensis episcopi Carnotensis policratici sive "De nugis curialium et vestigiis philosphorum libri VIII".* Edited by Clement C. J. Webb. 2 vols. Oxford: Clarendon Press, 1909
Frivolities of Courtiers and Footprints of Philosophers. Translated by Joseph B. Pike. Minneapolis: University of Minnesota Press, 1938
The Statesman's Book. Translated, with an introduction, by John Dickinson. New York: Russell and Russell, 1963

Justinus, *Epitoma historiarum Phillipicarum.* Edited by Otto Seel. Stuttgart: Teubner, 1972

Liber exemplorum ad usum praedicantium. Edited by A. G. Little. Aberdeen: British Society of Franciscan Studies, 1908

Livy. *Books I and II.* Edited and translated by B. O. Foster. Cambridge: Loeb Classical Library, 1961

Lydgate, John. *Lydgate's Fall of Princes.* Edited by Henry Bergen. 4 Vols. London: Early English Text Society, 1924

Mannyng, Robert. *Handlyng Synne.* Edited by Idelle Sullens. Binghamton: Medieval and Renaissance Texts and Studies, 1983

Map, Walter. *De nugis curialium.* Edited and translated by M. R. James, revised by C. N. L. Brooke and R. A. B. Mynors. Oxford: Clarendon Press, 1983

Mombrizio, Bonino. *Sanctuarium, seu Vitae Sanctorum.* Milan: before 1480, reprinted in Paris: 1910

Odo of Cheriton. *Eudes de Cheriton et ses derivés.* Vol. 4 of *Les Fabulistes Latins*

(4 vols.). Edited by Leopold Hervieux. Paris: Librairie de Firmin-Didot et Co., 1896

Le Roman de Renart. Edited by Gaston Raynaud and Henri Lemaitre. Paris: 1914; reprinted, Geneva: Slatkine Reprints, 1975

Rotuli Parliamentorum. Edited by J. Strachey. London: 1767–83

Le Speculum laicorum. Edited by J.Th. Welter. Paris: Auguste Picard, 1914

La Tabula exemplorum secundum ordinem alphabeti. Edited by J. Th. Welter. Paris and Toulouse: E. H. Guitard, 1926

Vitry, Jacques de. *The Exempla or Illustrative Stories From the Sermones Vulgares of Jacques de Vitry*. London: Folklore Society, 1890

von der Vogelweide, Walther. *Werke*. Edited by Joerg Schaefer. Darmstadt: Wissenschaftliche Buchgesellschaft, 1972

SECONDARY SOURCES

Aarne, Antti. *The Motif Index of Folk Literature*. Revised and enlarged by Stith Thompson. Bloomington: University of Indiana Press, 1956

The Types of the Folk-Tale: A Classification and Bibliography. Translated and enlarged by Stith Thompson. Helsinki: FF Communications, 1928

Adorno, T. W., Else-Frenkel Brunswick, Daniel J. Levinson, R. Nevitt Sanford in collaboration with Betty Aron, Maria Hertz Levinson, and William Morrow. *The Authoritarian Personality*. New York: Harper and Row, 1950

Aers, David. "A Whisper in the Ear of Early Modernists, or, Reflections on Literary Critics Writing the 'History of the Subject,'" in *Culture and History 1350–1600*, ed. Aers, 177–200

Chaucer, Langland and the Creative Imagination. London: Routledge & Kegan Paul, 1980

Community, Gender and Individual Identity: English Writing 1360–1430. London and New York: Routledge, 1988

Aers, David, ed. *Culture and History 1350–1600: Essays on English Communities, Identities, and Writing*. Detroit: Wayne State University Press, 1992

Alfoldy, Geza. *The Social History of Rome*. Translated by David Branaud and Frank Pollock. Totowa, NJ: Barnes and Noble, 1985

Allen, Judson Boyce. *The Ethical Poetic of the Later Middle Ages: A Decorum of Convenient Distinction*. Toronto: University of Toronto Press, 1982

"The Ironic Fruyt: Chauntecleer as Figura." *Studies in Philology* 66 (1969), 25–35

"The Old Way and the Parson's Way: An Ironic Reading of the *Parson's Tale*." *Journal of Medieval and Renaissance Studies* 3 (1973), 255–71

Althusser, Louis. *Lenin and Philosophy*. Translated by Ben Brewster. New York: Monthly Review Press, 1971

Althusser, Louis, and Étienne Balibar. *Reading Capital*. Translated by Ben Brewster. London: Verso, 1979

Anderson, Perry. *Passages from Antiquity to Feudalism*. London: Verso, 1974

Arendt, Hannah. "What is Authority?" In *Between Past and Future: Eight Exercises in Political Thought*. Harmondsworth: Penguin Books, 1977

Arrathoon, Leigh, ed. *Chaucer and the Craft of Fiction*. Rochester, Mi.: Solaris Press, 1986.

Aston, Margaret. "'Caim's Castles': Poverty, Politics and Disendowment." In *The Church, Politics and Patronage in the Fifteenth Century*, ed. Dobson, 45–84.

Baker, Denise. "The Priesthood of Genius: A Study of the Medieval Tradition." *Speculum* 44 (1969), 568–84

Baldwin, John. *Masters, Princes, and Merchants: The Social Views of Peter the Chanter and His Circle*. 2 vols. Princeton: Princeton University Press, 1970

Baldwin, Ralph. *The Unity of the "Canterbury Tales"*. Copenhagen: Rosenkilde and Bassen, 1955

Benjamin, Walter. *Illuminations*. Edited by Hannah Arendt and translated by Harry Zohn. New York: Schocken, 1969

Bennet, Tony. *Outside Literature*. London and New York: Routledge, 1990

Benson, Larry D., and Theodore M. Andersson. *The Literary Context of Chaucer's Fabliaux*. Indianapolis: Bobbs-Merrill, 1971.

Benson, Robert L. "The Gelasian Doctrine: Uses and Transformations." In *La notion d'autorite au Moyen Age: Islam, Byzance, Occident; Colloques Internationaux de la Napoule, Session des 23–26 Octobre 1978*, ed. Makdisi, Sourdel, Sourdel-Thomine, 13–44.

Berges, Wilhelm. *Die Fürstenspiegel des hohen and späten Mittelalters*. Stuttgart: Hiersemann Verlag, 1938

Bergin, Thomas G. *Petrarch*. New York: Twayne, 1970

Bishop, Ian. "*The Nun's Priest's Tale* and the Liberal Arts." *Review of English Studies*, n.s. 30 (1979), 257–67

"The Narrative Art of the *Pardoner's Tale*." *Medium Aevum* 36 (1967), 15–24

Bloch, Marc. *Feudal Society*. Translated by L. A. Manyon. 2 vols. Chicago: University of Chicago Press, 1964

Bloch, R. Howard. *The Scandal of the Fabliaux*. Chicago and London: University of Chicago Press, 1986

Bloom, Harold. *The Anxiety of Influence*. New York: Oxford University Press, 1973

Boitani, Piero, ed. *Chaucer and the Italian Trecento*. Cambridge: Cambridge University Press, 1983

Boitani, Piero, and Jill Mann, eds. *Cambridge Chaucer Companion*. Cambridge: Cambridge University Press, 1988

Boyle, Leonard E. "The Fourth Lateran Council and Manuals of Popular Theology." In *The Popular Literature of Medieval England*, ed. Heffernan, 30–43

Brantlinger, Patrick. *Crusoe's Footprints: Cultural Studies in Britain and America*. New York and London: Routledge, 1990

Bremond, Claude, Jacques Le Goff, and Jean-Claude Schmitt. *L' " exemplum"*. Turnholt: Brepols, 1982

Brooke, Christopher N. L. *The Medieval Idea of Marriage*. Oxford: Oxford University Press, 1989

Brooks, Peter. *Reading for the Plot: Design and Intention in Narrative*. New York: Vintage Books, 1985

Brown, Carleton. "Mulier est Hominis Confusio." *Modern Language Notes* 35 (1920), 479–82

Brunt, P. A. *Social Conflicts in the Roman Republic*. London: Chatto & Windus, 1971

Bryan, W. F. and Germaine Dempster. *Sources and Analogues of Chaucer's Canterbury Tales*. London: Routledge and Kegan Paul, 1941; reissued 1958

Burlin, Robert B. *Chaucerian Fiction*. Princeton: Princeton University Press, 1977

Burns, J. H. *The Cambridge History of Medieval Political Thought c. 350–c. 1450*. Cambridge: Cambridge University Press, 1988

Burrow, John. "Autobiographical Poetry in the Middle Ages: The Case of Thomas Hoccleve." *Proceedings of the British Academy* 68 (1982), 389–412
    Ricardian Poetry. London: Routledge & Kegan Paul, 1971

Centre for Contemporary Cultural Studies, *On Ideology*. Birmingham: 1977; London: Hutchinson, 1978

Chenu, M. D. *Nature, Man, and Society in the Twelfth Century*. Edited and translated by Jerome Taylor and Lester K. Little. Chicago: University of Chicago Press, 1968

Classen, Albrecht. *Die Autobiographische Lyrik des Europäischen Spätmittelalters*. Amsterdam and Atlanta: Rodopi, 1991

Cohan, Steven, and Linda M. Shires. *Telling Stories*. New York and London: Routledge, 1988

Coleman, Janet. *Medieval Readers and Writers 1350–1400*. New York: Columbia University Press, 1981
    "English Culture in the Fourteenth Century." In *Chaucer and the Italian Trecento*: ed. Boitani, 33–63

Congar, Yves M.-J. "Aspects ecclésiologiques de la querelle entre mendiants et séculiers dans le second moitié du xiiie siècle et le début du xive." *Archives d'histoire doctrinale et littéraire du moyen âge*. 28 (1961): 35–151

Cook, G. H. *The English Mediaeval Parish Church*. London: Phoenix, 1954

Copeland, Rita. "Rhetoric and Vernacular Translation in the Middle Ages," *Studies in the Age of Chaucer* 9 (1987), 41–75
    Rhetoric, Hermeneutics and Translation in the Middle Ages. Cambridge: Cambridge University Press, 1991

Courcelle, Pierre. *La Consolation de Philosophie dans la tradition littéraire: Antécédents et postérité de Boèce*. Paris: Études Augustiennes, 1963

Culler, Jonathan. *The Pursuit of Signs: Semiotics, Literature, Deconstruction*. London and Henley: Routledge & Kegan Paul, 1981

Dahlberg, Charles. "Chaucer's Cock and Fox." *Journal of English and Germanic Philology* 53 (1954): 277–90

David, Alfred. *The Strumpet Muse: Art and Morals in Chaucer's Poetry.* Bloomington: Indiana University Press, 1976

de Ste. Croix, G. E. M. *The Class Struggle in the Ancient Greek World: from the Archaic Age to the Arab Conquests.* London: Duckworth, 1981

de Man, Paul. *Blindness and Insight.* Minneapolis: University of Minnesota Press, 1983

Decarreaux, Jean. *Monks and Civilization.* Translated by Charlotte Haldane. London: Allen and Unwin, 1967

Delany, Sheila. "'*Mulier est hominis confusio*': Chaucer's Anti-popular *Nun's Priest's Tale*." *Mosaic* 17 (1984), 1–8

Derrida, Jacques. *Of Grammatology.* Translated by Gayatri Chakravorty Spivak. Baltimore and London: The Johns Hopkins University Press, 1974

Di Lorenzo, Raymond D. "The Collection Form and the Art of Memory in the *Libellus super Ludo Schachorum* of Jacobus de Cessolis," *Mediaeval Studies* 35 (1973), 205–21

Dinshaw, Carolyn. *Chaucer's Sexual Poetics.* Madison: University of Wisconsin Press, 1989

"Rivalry, Rape and Manhood: Gower and Chaucer," in *Chaucer and Gower*, ed. Yeager, 130–52

Dobson, R. B., ed. *The Church, Politics and Patronage in the Fifteenth Century.* Gloucester: Alan Sutton Publishing, 1984

Dobson, R. B., ed. *The Peasants' Revolt of 1381.* London: Macmillan, 1970

Dollimore, Jonathan. *Radical Tragedy: Religion, Ideology and Power in the Drama of Shakespeare and His Contemporaries.* Brighton: Harvester, 1984

Donaldson, E. Talbot. *Speaking of Chaucer.* New York: Norton, 1970

Donovan, Mortimer. "The *moralite* of the Nun's Priest's Sermon." *Journal of English and Germanic Philology* 52 (1953), 493–508

Doyle, A. I. "A Survey of the Origins and Circulation of Theological Writings in English in the Fourteenth, Fifteenth, and Early Sixteenth Centuries, with Special Consideration of the Part of the Clergy Therein." Unpublished Ph.D. dissertation, Cambridge University, 2301–2302, 1951

Duby, Georges. *The Chivalrous Society.* Translated by Cynthia Postan. Berkeley and Los Angeles: University of California Press, 1980

The Knight, the Lady and the Priest: The Making of Modern Marriage in Medieval France. Translated by Barbara Bray. New York: Pantheon, 1983

Medieval Marriage. Translated by Elborg Forster. Baltimore and London: The Johns Hopkins University Press, 1978

The Three Estates: Feudal Society Imagined. Translated by Arthur Goldhammer. Chicago: Chicago University Press, 1980. Revised paperback editions, 1980, 1982, 1984

Easthope, Anthony. *Literary into Cultural Studies*. London and New York: Routledge, 1991

Edwards, A. S. G., and Derek Pearsall, "The Manuscripts of the Major English Poetic Texts." In *Book Production and Publishing in Britain 1375–1475*. Edited by Jeremy Griffiths and Derek Pearsall. Cambridge: Cambridge University Press, 1989

Engels, Friedrich. "On Authority." In *The Marx-Engels Reader*, ed. Tucker, 730–33

Erlich, Victor. *Russian Formalism: History and Doctrine*. New Haven: Yale University Press, 1981

Farnham, Willard. *Medieval Heritage of Elizabethan Tragedy*. 2nd edition. Oxford: Basil Blackwell, 1956

Ferster, Judith. *Chaucer and Interpretation*. Cambridge: Cambridge University Press, 1984

Finke, Laurie A. "'To Knytte Up al this Feste': The Parson's Rhetoric and the Ending of the *Canterbury Tales*." *Leeds Studies in English*, n.s. 15 (1984), 95–105

Finlayson, John. "The Satiric Mode of the *Parson's Tale*." *Chaucer Review* 6 (1971), 94–116

Fisher, John H. *John Gower: Moral Philosopher and Friend of Chaucer*. New York: New York University Press, 1964

Fleming, John V. "The Summoner's Prologue: An Iconographic Adjustment," *The Chaucer Review* 2 (1967), 95–107

Flinn, J. F. "Littérature bourgeoise et *Le Roman de Renart*." In *Aspects of the Medieval Animal Epic*, ed. E. Rombauts and A. Welkenhuysen, 11–23

Flores, Ralph. *The Rhetoric of Doubtful Authority: Deconstructive Reading of Self-Questioning Narratives, St. Augustine to Faulkner*. Ithaca and London: Cornell University Press, 1989

Foucault, Michel. "What is an Author?" In *Textual Strategies: Perspectives in Post-Structuralist Criticism*, ed. Harari, 141–60

Friedrich, Carl J. *Tradition and Authority*. New York, Washington, and London: Praeger, 1972

Gallacher, Patrick. *Love, the Word, and Mercury: A Reading of John Gower's "Confessio Amantis"*. Albuquerque: University of New Mexico Press, 1975

Genet, Jean-Phillipe. "Ecclesiastics and Political Theory in Late Medieval England: The End of a Monopoly." In *Church, Politics and Patronage*, ed. Dobson, 23–44

Four English Political Tracts of the Later Middle Ages. London: Royal Historical Society, 1973

Genette, Gerard. *Narrative Discourse: An Essay in Method*. Translated by Jane E. Lewin. Ithaca: Cornell University Press, 1980

Gilbert, Sandra M. and Susan Gubar. *The Madwoman in the Attic: the Woman Writer and the Nineteenth-Century Literary Imagination*. New Haven and London: Yale University Press, 1979

Gillespie, Vincent. "Vernacular Books of Religion." In *Book Production and Publishing in Britain 1375–1475*, ed. by Griffiths and Pearsall, 317–44

Godman, Peter. "Chaucer and Boccaccio's Latin Works." In *Chaucer and the Italian Trecento*, ed. Boitani, 269–95

Green, Richard Firth. *Poets and Princepleasers: Literature and the English Court in the Late Middle Ages*. Toronto, Buffalo, London: University of Toronto Press, 1980

Greetham, D. C. "Self-Referential Artifacts: Hoccleve's *Persona* as a Literary Device." *Modern Philology* 86 (1989), 242–51

Griffiths, Jeremy, and Derek Pearsall, eds. *Book Production and Publishing in Britain 1375–1475*. Cambridge: Cambridge University Press, 1989

Grudin, Michaela Paasche. "Chaucer's *Clerk's Tale* as Political Paradox," *Studies in the Age of Chaucer* 11 (1989), 68–91

Guillory, John. *Poetic Authority: Spenser, Milton, and Literary History*. New York, Columbia University Press, 1983

Haas, Renate. "Chaucer's *Monk's Tale*: An Ingenious Criticism of Early Humanist Conceptions of Tragedy." *Humanistica Lovaniensia* 36 (1987), 44–70

Hahn, Thomas, and Richard W. Kaeuper. "Text and Context: Chaucer's *Friar's Tale*." *Studies in the Age of Chaucer* 5 (1983), 67–109

Hall, Stuart. "The Hinterlands of Science: Ideology and The 'Sociology of Knowledge.'" In *On Ideology*, 9–33.

"The Toad in the Garden: Thatcherism among the Theorists." In *Marxism and the Interpretation of Culture*, ed. Nelson and Grossberg, 35–73

Hamilton, Marie P. "The Credentials of Chaucer's Pardoner." *Journal of English and Germanic Philology* 40 (1941), 48–72

Harari, Josue V., ed. *Textual Strategies: Perspectives in Post-Structuralist Criticism*. London: Methuen, 1980

Harding, Alan. *The Law Courts of Medieval England*. London: George Allen and Unwin; New York: Barnes and Noble, 1973

Harriss, G. L., ed. *Henry V: The Practices of Kingship*. Oxford: Oxford University Press, 1985

Heath, Peter. *Church and Realm 1272–1461*. London: Fontana, 1988

Heffernan, Thomas J., ed. *The Popular Literature of Medieval England*. Knoxville: University of Tennessee Press, 1985

Herbert, J. H. *Catalogue of Romances in the Department of Manuscripts in the British Museum*. London: printed by order of the Trustees, 1910, vol. 3.

Heyworth, P. L., ed. *Medieval Studies for J. A. W. Bennett*. Oxford: Clarendon Press, 1981.

Hilton, R. H. *The Decline of Serfdom in Medieval England*. London: Macmillan, 1983

Hiscoe, David. "The Ovidian Comic Strategy of Gower's *Confessio Amantis*." *Philological Quarterly* 64 (1985), 367–85

Howard, Donald R. *The Idea of the Canterbury Tales*. Berkeley: University of California Press, 1976

Hudson, Anne. *The Premature Reformation: Wycliffite Texts and Lollard History*. Oxford: Clarendon Press, 1988

Huppé, Bernard F. *A Reading of the Canterbury Tales*. Revised edition. Albany: State University of New York Press, 1967

Irigaray, Luce. *This Sex Which is Not One*. Translated by Catherine Porter, with Carolyn Burke. Ithaca: Cornell University Press, 1985

Itô, Masayoshi. *John Gower: Medieval Poet*. Tokyo: Shinozaki Shorin, 1976

Jolliffe, P. S. *A Checklist of Prose Writings of Spiritual Guidance*. Toronto: Pontifical Institute of Mediaeval Studies, 1974

Jones, R. H. *The Royal Policy of Richard II: Absolutism in the Later Middle Ages*. New York: Barnes and Noble, 1973

Jordan, Robert. *Chaucer and the Shape of Creation: The Aesthetic Possibilities of Inorganic Structure*. Cambridge, MA: Harvard University Press, 1967

Kantoriwicz, E. H. *The King's Two Bodies: A Study in Medieval Political Theology*. Princeton: Princeton University Press, 1957

Kaske, Carol V. "Getting Around the *Parson's Tale*: An Alternative to Allegory and Irony." In *Chaucer at Albany*, ed. Robbins, 147–77

Kaske, R. E. "The Knight's Interruption of the *Monk's Tale*." *ELH* 24 (1957), 249–68

Kawai, Michio, ed. *Language and Style in English Literature: Essays in Honour of Michio Masui*. Hiroshima: The English Research Association of Hiroshima, 1991

Kellogg, A. L., and L. A. Haselmayer. "Chaucer's Satire and the Pardoner," *Publication of the Modern Languages Association* 66 (1951), 251–77

Kemmler, Fritz. *"Exempla" in Context: A Historical and Critical Study of Robert Mannyng of Brunne's "Handlynge Synne"*. Tübingen: Gunter Narr Verlag, 1984

Kempton, Daniel. "Chaucer's *Tale of Melibee*: 'A Litel Thyng in Prose,'" *Genre* 21 (1988), 263–78

Kieckhefer, Richard. *Magic in the Middle Ages*. Cambridge: Cambridge University Press, 1989

Knapp, Peggy. *Chaucer and the Social Contest*. New York and London: Routledge, 1990

Knight, Stephen. *Geoffrey Chaucer*. Oxford: Basil Blackwell, 1986

Larrain, Jorge. *The Concept of Ideology*. London: Hutchinson, 1979
Marxism and Ideology. London: Macmillan, 1983

Lawton, David. *Chaucer's Narrators*. Cambridge: D. S. Brewer, 1985
"Dullness and the Fifteenth Century." *ELH* 54(1987), 761–99

Le Goff, Jacques. *The Medieval Imagination*. Translated by Arthur Goldhammer. Chicago and London: University of Chicago, 1988

Leicester, H. Marshall. *The Disenchanted Self: Representing the Subject in the "Canterbury Tales"*. Berkeley, Los Angeles and Oxford: University of California Press, 1990

Lepley, Douglas L. "The Monk's Boethian Tale." *Chaucer Review* 12 (1978), 162–70

360 *Bibliography*

Levitan, Alan. "The Parody of Pentecost in Chaucer's *Summoner's Tale.*" *University of Toronto Quarterly* 40 (1970–71), 236–46

Levy, Bernard. "Biblical Parody in the *Summoner's Tale.*" *Tenessee Studies in Literature* 11 (1966), 45–60

"The Meanings of the *Clerk's Tale.*" In *Chaucer and the Craft of Fiction*, ed. Arrathoon, 385–409

Levy, Bernard S., and George R. Adams, "Chauntecleer's Paradise Lost and Regained," *Mediaeval Studies* 29 (1967), 178–92

Lewis, C. S. *The Allegory of Love: A Study in Medieval Tradition.* Oxford: Oxford University Press, 1936

Liebeschutz, Hans. *Mediaeval Humanism in the Life and Writings of John of Salisbury.* London: The Warburg Institute, 1950

Linder, Amnon. "Ecclesia and Synagoga in the Medieval Myth of Constantine the Great." *Revue Belge de Philologie et d'Histoire* 54 (1976), 1019–60

"The Knowledge of John of Salisbury in the Later Middle Ages." *Studi Medievali* 18/2 (1977), 315–66

"The Myth of Constantine the Great in the West: Sources and Hagiographic Commemoration." *Studi Medievali*, 3rd ser., XVI (1975), 43–95

Macherey, Pierre. *A Theory of Literary Production.* Translated by Geoffrey Wall. London: Routledge and Kegan Paul, 1978

Macmullen, Ramsay. *Christianizing the Roman Empire (A. D. 100-400).* New Haven and London: Yale University Press, 1984

Makdisi, George, Dominique Sourdel, and Janine Sourdel-Thomine, eds. *La notion d'autorite au Moyen Age: Islam, Byzance, Occident; Colloques Internationaux de la Napoule, Session des 23–26 Octobre 1978.* Paris: Presses Universitaires de France, 1982

Mann, Jill. *Chaucer and Medieval Estates Satire.* Cambridge: Cambridge University Press, 1973

"The *Speculum Stultorum* and the *Nun's Priest's Tale.*" *Chaucer Review* 9 (1975), 262–82

Manning, Stephen. "The Nun's Priest's Morality and the Medieval Attitude toward Fables." *Journal of English and Germanic Philology* 59 (1960), 403–16

Manzalouai, M. A. "'Noght in the Registre of Venus': Gower's English Mirror for Princes." In *Medieval Studies for J. A. W. Bennett*, ed. Heyworth, 159–83

Marcuse, Herbert. *Studies in Critical Philosophy.* Translated by Joris de Bres. London: New Left Books, 1972

Markus, R. A. "Two Conceptions of Political Authority: Augustine, *De Civitate Dei*, XIX, 14–15, and Some Thirteenth Century Interpretations." *The Journal of Theological History*, n.s. 16 (1965), 68–100

Martin, Janet. "John of Salisbury as Classical Scholar." In *World of John of Salisbury*, ed. Wilks, 179–201.

Martines, Lauro. *Power and Imagination: City States in the Italian Renaissance.* New York: Alfred Knopf, 1979

Mazzotta, Giuseppe. *The World at Play in Boccaccio's " Decameron".* Princeton: Princeton University Press, 1986

McAlpine, Monica. "The Pardoner's Homosexuality and How it Matters," *Publication of the Modern Language Association* 95 (1980): 8–22

McFarlane, K. B. *Lancastrian Kings and Lollard Knights.* Oxford: Oxford University Press, 1972

The Nobility of Later Medieval England. Oxford: Clarendon Press, 1972

McKisack, May. *The Fourteenth Century.* Oxford: Clarendon Press, 1959

McLellan, David. *Ideology.* Minneapolis: University of Minnesota Press, 1986

McNeill, J. T., and H. M. Gamer. *Medieval Handbooks of Penance.* New York: Columbia University Press, 1938

Merrix, Robert P. "Sermon Structure in the *Pardoner's Tale.*" *Chaucer Review* 17 (1982), 35–49

Middleton, Anne. "The Clerk and His Tale: Some Literary Contexts." *Studies in the Age of Chaucer* 2 (1981), 121–50

"The Idea of Public Poetry in the Reign of Richard II." *Speculum* 53 (1979), 94–114

Miller, Jacqueline T. *Poetic License: Authority and Authorship in Medieval and Renaissance Contexts.* New York and Oxford: Oxford University Press, 1986

Millett, Bella. "Chaucer, Lollius, and the Medieval Theory of Authorship." In *Reconstructing Chaucer,* ed. Strohm and Heffernan, 93–115

Minnis, A. J. *Chaucer and Pagan Antiquity.* Cambridge: Cambridge University Press, 1982

Medieval Theory of Authorship: Scholastic Literary Attitudes in the Later Middle Ages. London: Scolar Press, 1984

Minnis, A. J., ed. *Gower's "Confessio Amantis": Responses and Reassessments.* Cambridge: D. S. Brewer, 1983

Mitchell, Juliet. *Psychoanalysis and Feminism.* New York: Vintage Books, 1975

Morse, Charlotte. "Exemplary Griselda," *Studies in the Age of Chaucer* 7 (1985), 51–86

Mosher, J. A. *The Exemplum in England.* New York: Columbia University Press, 1911

Murray, Alexander. *Reason and Society in the Middle Ages.* Oxford: Clarendon Press, 1978

Muscatine, Charles. *Chaucer and the French Tradition.* Berkeley: University of California Press, 1957

Nelson, Cary, and Lawrence Grossberg, eds. *Marxism and the Interpretation of Culture.* Urbana: University of Illinois Press, 1988

Nicholson, Peter. "The Analogues of Chaucer's *Friar's Tale.*" *English Language Notes* 17 (1979), 93–98

An Annotated Index to the Commentary on Gower's "Confessio Amantis".
Binghamton: Medieval and Renaissance Texts and Studies, 1989

"The Rypon Analogue of the *Friar's Tale.*" *The Chaucer Newsletter* 3:1
(1981), 1–2

Nordh, Arvast. "*Exemplum* in Martial." *Eranos* 52 (1954), 224–38

Ollson, Kurt. "Grammar, Manhood, and Tears: The Curiosity of
Chaucer's Monk." *Modern Philology* 76 (1978) 1–17

Oruch, Jack B. "Chaucer's Worldly Monk." *Criticism* 8 (1966), 280–88

Owst, G. R. *Literature and Pulpit in Medieval England.* 2nd edition. Oxford:
Blackwell, 1961

Preaching in Medieval England. 2nd edition. New York: Russell and Russell,
1965

Patterson, Lee. *Chaucer and the Subject of History.* Madison: University of
Wisconsin Press, 1991

Negotiating the Past: The Historical Understanding of Medieval Literature.
Madison: University of Wisconsin Press, 1987

"On the Margin: Postmodernism, Ironic History, and Medieval
Studies." *Speculum* 65 (1990), 87–108

"The 'Parson's Tale' and the Quitting of the 'Canterbury Tales.'"
Traditio 34 (1978), 331–80

"'What Man Artow?': Authorial Self-Definition in the *Tale of Sir Thopas*,
and the *Tale of Melibee.*" *Studies in the Age of Chaucer* 11 (1989), 117–75

Patterson, Lee, ed. *Literary Practice and Social Change in Britain 1380–1530.*
Berkeley, Los Angeles and Oxford: University of California Press, 1990

Payne, Robert O. *The Key of Remembrance: A Study of Chaucer's Poetics.* New
Haven and London: Yale University Press, 1963

Pearcy, Roy J. "Structural Models for the Fabliaux and the *Summoner's Tale*
Analogues," *Fabula* 15 (1974), 103–13

Pearsall, Derek. *The "Canterbury Tales".* London: George Allen and Unwin,
1985

"Gower's Narrative Art." *Publication of the Modern Languages Association* 81
(1966), 475–84

John Lydgate. London: Routledge and Kegan Paul, 1970

Pearsall, Derek, ed. *The Nun's Priest's Tale.* Vol. 2, pt 9 of *A Variorum Edition
of the Works of Geoffrey Chaucer.* Norman: University of Oklahoma Press,
1984

Peck, Russell A. *Kingship and Common Profit in Gower's "Confessio Amantis".*
Carbondale and Edwardsville: Southern Illinois Press, 1978

Pratt, Robert. "Chaucer and the Hand that Fed Him." *Speculum* 41 (1966),
619–42

"Three Old French Sources of the Nonnes Preestes Tale." *Speculum* 47
(1972), 422–44, 646–68

Price, Bennet J. "*Paradeigma* and *Exemplum* in Ancient Rhetorical Theory."
Unpublished Ph.D. dissertation, University of California, Berkeley,
1975

Powell, James M. *Albertanus of Brescia: The Pursuit of Happiness in the Early Thirteenth Century*. Philadelphia: University of Pennsylvania Press, 1992

Reiter, Rayna, ed. *Toward an Anthropology of Women*. New York and London: Monthly Review Press, 1975

Renoir, Alain. *The Poetry of John Lydgate*. Cambridge, MA: Harvard University Press, 1967

Rhodes, James F. "Motivation in Chaucer's *Pardoner's Tale*: Winner Take Nothing." *Chaucer Review* 16 (1982), 40–60

Richardson, Janette. *Blameth Nat Me: A Study of Imagery in Chaucer's Fabliaux*. The Hague: Mouton and Company, N. V., 1970

Robbins, Russell Hope, ed. *Chaucer at Albany*. New York: Burt Franklin, 1975

Robertson, D. W. "Chaucerian Tragedy." *ELH* 19 (1952), 1–37

"The Cultural Tradition of *Handlyng Synne*." *Speculum* 22 (1947), 162–85.

Preface to Chaucer. Princeton: Princeton University Press, 1962

Rombauts, E., and A. Welkenhuysen, eds. *Aspects of the Medieval Animal Epic: Proceedings of the International Conference, Louvain May 15–17, 1972* Louvain/Leuven: Leuven University Press; The Hague: Martinus Nijhoff, 1975.

Rosenwein, Barbara, and Lester K. Little. "Social Meaning in the Monastic and Mendicant Spiritualities." *Past and Present* 63 (1974), 4–32

Rubin, Gayle. "The Traffic in Women." In *Toward an Anthropology of Women*, ed. Reiter, 157–210

Said, Edward. *Beginnings: Intention and Method*. New York: Columbia University Press, 1985

Scanlon, Larry. "The Authority of Fable: Allegory and Irony in the *Nun's Priest's Tale*." *Exemplaria* I (1989): 43–51

"The King's Two Voices: Narrative and Power in Hoccleve's *Regement of Princes*." In *Literary Practice and Social Change*, ed. Patterson, 216–47

Sennett, Richard. *Authority*. New York: Alfred Knopf, 1980

Severs, J. Burke. *The Literary Relationships of Chaucer's "Clerkes Tale"*. New Haven: Yale University Press, 1942

Seymour, M. C. "Chaucer's Early Poem *De Casibus Virorum Illustrium*." *Chaucer Review* 24 (1989), 162–65

"Manuscripts of Hoccleve's *Regement of Princes*." *Edinburgh Bibliographical Transactions* IV, pt 7 (1974, sessions 1968–71), 253–97

Shallers, A. Paul. "The 'Nun's Priest's Tale': An Ironic Exemplum." *ELH* 42 (1975), 319–37

Shoaf, R. A. *Dante, Chaucer and the Currency of the Word*. Norman: Pilgrim Books, 1983

Silverman, Kaja. *The Subject of Semiotics*. Oxford and New York: Oxford University Press, 1983

Smalley, Beryl. *The Becket Conflict and the Schools*. Oxford: Basil Blackwell, 1973

English Friars and Antiquity in the Early Fourteenth Century. Oxford: Basil Blackwell, 1960

Southern, R. W. *The Making of the Middle Ages.* New Haven and London: Yale University Press, 1953

Medieval Humanism. Oxford: Basil Blackwell, 1970

Spearing, A. C. *Medieval to Renaissance in English Poetry.* Cambridge: Cambridge University Press, 1985

Stock, Brian. *The Implications of Literacy: Written Language and Models of Interpretation in the Eleventh and Twelfth Centuries.* Princeton: Princeton University Press, 1983

Listening for the Text: On the Uses of the Past. Baltimore and London: The Johns Hopkins University Press, 1990

Storm, Melvin. "The Pardoner's Invitation: Quaestor's Bag or Becket's Shrine?" *Publication of the Modern Languages Association* 97 (1982), 810–18

Straw, Carole. *Gregory the Great: Perfection in Imperfection.* Berkeley, Los Angeles, London: University of California Press, 1988

Strohm, Paul. "Chaucer's Audience." *Literature and History,* 5 (1977), 26–41

"Chaucer's Fifteenth-Century Audience and the Narrowing of the 'Chaucer Tradition.'" *Studies in the Age of Chaucer* 4 (1982), 3–32

"Form and Social Statement in *Confessio Amantis* and the *Canterbury Tales.*" *Studies in the Age of Chaucer* 1 (1979), 17–40

Social Chaucer. Cambridge, MA: Harvard University Press, 1989

Strohm, Paul, and Thomas J. Heffernan, ed. *Studies in the Age of Chaucer, Proceedings, No. 1, 1984: Reconstructing Chaucer.* Knoxville, TN: New Chaucer Society, 1984

Struve, Tilman. *Die Entwicklung der organologischen Staatsauffassung in Mittelalter.* Stuttgart: Anton Hiersemann, 1978

"The Importance of the Organism in the Political Theory of John of Salisbury." In *World of John of Salisbury,* ed. Wilks, 303–17

Szittya, Penn R. *The Antifraternal Tradition in Medieval Literature.* Princeton: Princeton University Press, 1986

"The Friar as False Apostle: Antifraternal Exegesis and the *Summoner's Tale.*" *Studies in Philology* 71 (1974), 19–46

Tennenhouse, Leonard. *Power on Display: The Politics of Shakespeare's Genres.* New York and London: Methuen, 1986

Tierney, Brian. *Religion, Law, and the Growth of Constitutional Thought 1150–1650.* Cambridge: Cambridge University Press, 1982

Todorov, Tzvetan. *The Poetics of Prose.* Translated by Richard Howard. Ithaca: Cornell University Press, 1977

Tubach, Frederick C. *Index Exemplorum: A Handbook of Medieval Religious Tales.* Helsinki: FF Communications, 1969

Tuck, Anthony. *Crown and Nobility 1272–1461.* Oxford: Basil Blackwell, 1986

Richard II and the English Nobility. London: Edward Arnold, 1973

Tucker, Robert C., ed. *The Marx-Engels Reader.* 2nd edition. New York and London: W. W. Norton, 1978

Tupper, Frederick. "Chaucer and the Seven Deadly Sins." *Publication of the Modern Language Association* 29 (1914), 93–128

Ullmann, Walter. "Boniface VIII and His Contemporary Scholarship." *The Journal of Theological Studies*, n.s. 27 (1976), 58–87

The Carolingian Renaissance and the Idea of Kingship. London: Methuen, 1969

The Growth of Papal Government in the Middle Ages. 3rd edition. London: Methuen, 1970

"The Influence of John of Salisbury on Medieval Italian Jurists." *English Historical Review* 59 (1944), 384–91

Principles of Government and Politics in the Middle Ages. London: Methuen & Co., 1961

Van Moos, Peter. *Geschichte als Topik: das rhetorische Exemplum von der Antike zur Neuzeit und die historiae im "Policraticus" Johanns von Salisbury*. Hildesheim, New York: G. Olds, 1988

"The Use of *Exempla* in the *Policraticus* of John of Salisbury." In *World of John of Salisbury*, ed. Wilks, 207–61

Vance, Eugene. "Chaucer's Pardoner: Relics, Discourse, and Frames of Propriety." *New Literary History* 20 (1989), 723–45

Wallace, David. "'Whan She Translated Was': A Chaucerian Critique of the Petrarchan Academy." In *Literary Practice and Social Change*, ed. Patterson, 156–215

Warren, W. L. *Henry II*. London: Eyre Methuen, 1973

Weber, Max. *The Theory of Social and Economic Organization*. Translated by A. N. Henderson and Talcott Parsons. New York: The Free Press; London: Collier-Macmillan, Ltd., 1964. Copyright, Oxford University Press, 1947

Welter, J.-Th. *L'exemplum dans la littérature religieuse et didactique du Moyen Age*. Geneva: Slatkine Reprints, 1973. Reprint of Paris-Toulouse edition of 1927

Wenzel, Siegfried. "Chaucer and the Language of Contemporary Preaching." *Studies in Philology* 73 (1976), 138–61

Wetherbee, Winthrop. "The Context of the *Monk's Tale*." In *Language and Style in English Literature*, ed. Kawai, 159–77

Wilkins, Ernest Hatch. *Studies in the Life and Works of Petrarch*. Cambridge, MA: Medieval Academy, 1955

Wilkinson, Bertie. *The Later Middle Ages in England*. London: Longmans, 1969

Wilks, M. J. *The Problem of Sovereignty in the Later Middle Ages*. Cambridge: Cambridge University Press, 1963

Wilks, M. J., ed. *The World of John of Salisbury*. Oxford: Basil Blackwell, 1984

Williams, Raymond. *Marxism and Literature*. Oxford: Oxford University Press, 1977

Yeager, R. F. "Aspects of Gluttony in Chaucer and Gower." *Philological Quarterly* 81 (1984), 48–53

John Gower's Poetic: The Search for a New Arion. Cambridge: D. S. Brewer, 1990

Yeager, R. F., ed. *Chaucer and Gower: Difference, Mutuality, Exchange.* Victoria, B. C.: English Literary Studies, 1991

ed. *Fifteenth-Century Studies.* Hamden: Archon Books, 1984

ed. *John Gower: Recent Readings.* Kalamazoo: Medieval Institute Publications, 1984

Zietlow, Paul N. "In Defense of the Summoner." *The Chaucer Review* 1 (1966), 4–19

Index

Aarne, Antti, 60n, 197
Abelard, 38, 91
Adam and Eve, 129, 223, 224, 324
Adams, George R., 230–31n
Adorno, T. W., 41–42n
Adrian IV, Pope, 99–100
Aegidius Romanus, 106, 128, 180, 314
   De regimine principum, 87, 106–18, 138,
     268, 283
Aers, David, 7n, 53, 192n, 195n
Aesop, 229
Albertanus of Brescia: *Liber consolationis et
   consilii*, 207, 213
alchemy, 277
Alcuin, 123
Alexander the Great, 277–83, 290–91, 292,
   313, 324
Alfody, Geza, 40n, 43n, 44n
allegory, 230–32, 243
Allen, Judson Boyce, 3n, 7n, 231n
Alphabet of Tales, 72, 74, 76, 77
Alphabetum narrationum, *see* Arnold of Liege
Althusser, Louis, 28, 35, 116
Ambrosiaster, 31
amplification, 324, 333, 340, 343
anachronism, 28–29, 47–48, 144, 228, 249
anarchy, 241–42
Anciaux, Paul, 73n
Andromache, 238
Annunciation, 279
anti-clericalism, 8–12, 230, 298–99
   Chaucer's, 145, 152, 158–60, 166–67,
     174–75, 192, 193, 205, 218, 220–21,
     262
   Gower's, 247, 250–52, 257–68, 275–76
   Lydgate's response to, 335–36, 339
   see also anti-fraternalism
anti-fraternalism, 148–49, 161, 164–66,
   171–74, 192
   principle of ecclesiastical economy in,
     165–66

Antiochus, 225
apostrophe, 200
Apollo, 287, 294
appropriation, 22–24, 75, 80, 83, 86, 87,
   90–93, 94–95, 137–38, 159, 193–94,
   207, 209, 228–29, 233, 321, 322, 342
Aquinas, Saint Thomas, 84–85, 87, 105–6,
   114
   De regno, 105, 114, 120, 121
Arendt, Hannah, 41–42, 52
Arion, 253–55
Aristotelianism, 84–87, 105–8, 113–17, 180,
   206, 210, 213
Aristotle, 32–33, 84–85, 87, 94–95, 105, 106,
   115–16, 279, 283, 292, 313
   Nichomachean Ethics, 115
   Politics, 107, 115–16, 283
   Rhetoric, 32
Arnold of Liège: *Alphabetum narrationum*,
   31–32, 70
   see also Alphabet of Tales
Arthurian tradition, 253, 336
Articles of Deposition, 139–41
Ashby, George, 138
Aston, Margaret, 9n
astrology, 277
auctor, 22, 24, 25, 38, 39–40, 45
   God as ultimate, 12
   as lay, vernacular category, 133, 142,
    179–80, 209, 299, 313, 344
auctor gentis, 40–41, 44
auctoritas, 5, 36, 38–46, 50–51, 70, 261,
   263
   hierocratic view of, 38, 257–58
   poet as source of, 144
   royalist view of, 39, 257–58
audience, 22, 63, 129, 141, 177, 190, 216,
   296, 319, 324, 331, 334–35, 347–48
   court as, 82, 143–44, 284
   "middle class" as, 143–44
   national, 328

Augustine, 9, 20, 85, 87, 268
  De doctrina Christiana, 277n
Augustinianism, 17, 84–87, 113–14, 180,
  184, 268
Augustus Caesar, 33, 42–43, 44
authority, 26, 28, 52, 177, 227, 234–35, 267,
  277, 305
  Christian, 6, 12, 24, 156, 176, 204, 212,
    215–16, 220
  classical, 212, 313
  clerical, 7, 14–15, 22, 45–46, 250–51, 336
  and death, 194, 204–5
  discursive or ideological construction of,
    274, 320–22
  Divine, 12, 273–77, 281, 282, 287–90, 317
  doctrinal, 13
  and the exemplum, 5
  king as source of, 81, 248
  lay (or vernacular), 22, 131, 141, 205,
    206, 210, 237, 247, 249, 279, 292,
    312–14, 322, 339, 344–45, 349–50
  of natural science, 205
  and poetry, 193, 195, 248
  political and textual, relation between,
    142, 302, 312–14, 318–19, 325, 332
  as power over the past, 37–38, 90–93
  royal, 191, 317
  textual, 210–11, 216, 220, 229
authorship, 52
autobiography, 299–300, 302–5, 310
avant-gardism, 228

Badby, John, 300n, 304
Baker, Denise, 255
Baldwin, John, 65n
Baldwin, Ralph, 6n
Ball, John, 17n
Balthasar, 226
Barthes, Roland, 52n
beast fable, 206, 229–30; politics of, 230,
  235–36
Becket, Thomas, 83, 88
Bede, 32
Beidler, Peter, 246n
begging poem, 300–1, 308
Benjamin, Walter, 194
Bennet, Tony, 323n
Benveniste, Emile, 35
Benson, Robert L., 45n, 50n
Bergen, Henry, 324, 328n
Berges, Wilhelm, 82n, 104n, 105n, 106n,
  138
Bergin, Thomas G., 122n
Bernard, St., 76
Berry, Duke of, 324

Betussi, Giuseppe, 119
Bible, 118, 209
  New Testament, 46, 49n
  Old Testament, 90, 93, 233, 291, 324
  II Corinthians, 117
  Daniel, 238
  Exodus, 238
  Hosea, 200
  John, 47
  Matthew, 8, 200
  Revelations, 49n
  Romans, 46, 117, 233
  II Timothy, 165
Bishop, Ian, 201, 238
blasphemy, 198–200
Bloch, Marc, 104
Bloch, R. Howard, 174n
Bloom, Harold, 122
body politic, *see* corporate fiction
Boethius, 89, 221–22
  Philosophiae consolatio, 123–26, 129, 216
Boccaccio, Giovanni, 25, 118, 177, 185,
  221–22, 223, 224, 324, 332, 342
  Decameron, 177–78
  Filostrato, 324
  see also De casibus virorum illustrium
Boniface VIII, 118, 264
  Unam Sanctam, 258
  see also Confessio Amantis
Boyle, Leonard E., 12n
Bradley, A. C., 343–44
Brantlinger, Patrick, 28n
Bremond, Claude, 4n, 31n, 63n, 66n
Bromyard, John, *Summa praedicantium*, 288n
Brooke, Christopher, 88n, 189n
Brooks, Peter, 31, 204–5, 349
Brown, Carleton, 239n
Brown, Elizabeth A. R., 101n
Brunt, P. A., 42, 43n, 99n
Brut, 253
Burlin, Robert B., 223, 231n
Burke, Linda Barney, 245n
Burrow, John, 3n, 29, 245, 299n, 300n
Butler, Judith, 188n

Caida de principes, 119
canonization (literary), 179–80, 299,
  312–14, 322, 332–34
Canterbury Tales, 3, 23, 24, 137, 206, 216,
  217, 299, 302, 333n
  clerical narrators in, 145
  Ellesmere manuscript of, 138n, 312
  Fragment I, 146
  Fragment II, 146
  Fragment III, 145, 146–47

Fragment IV, 145
Fragment VI, 145
Fragment VII, 145, 192, 206
individual tales: *Clerk's Tale*, 24, 137n,
   138, 145n, 146–47, 175–91, 208, 247,
   265, 291, 312, 324, 333; *Cook's Tale*,
   146; *Franklin's Tale*, 137; *Friar's Tale*,
   32, 137n, 145n, 147–63, 192; *General
   Prologue*, 8–12, 148, 205, 218, 220–21;
   Knight's Tale, 25, 146, 176; *Man of
   Law's Tale*, 137n, 146, 176, 246–47,
   296; *Melibee*, 24, 139, 205, 206–15,
   333; *Miller's Tale*, 25, 272; *Monk's
   Tale*, 24, 80, 119, 137n, 139, 205, 206,
   215–29, 333; *Nun's Priest's Tale*, 25, 80,
   137, 139, 192, 205, 206, 229–44;
   Pardoner's Prologue and Tale, 25, 137n,
   147–48, 192–205, 305; *Parson's Prologue*,
   5–6; *Parson's Tale*, 3–22, 24, 52, 54,
   184, 201, 248, 265, 297, 339; *Physician's
   Tale*, 137n, 176; *Prioress's Tale*, 24,
   137n, 176; *Retraction*, 3, 6, 23–24; *Sir
   Thopas*, 213; *Summoner's Tale*, 80, 137n,
   145n, 148–49, 160–75, 192, 205; *Wife
   of Bath's Prologue and Tale*, 25, 137n,
   177, 183
   see also Chaucer, Geoffrey
caritas, 255
Carolingian court, 86
Carruthers, Mary, 48–49
Carter, April, 41n
case study, 349
Cato, 238
Cavalcanti, Mainardo de, 120
Caxton, William, 119, 137n
Cesarius of Heisterbach, 248
   Dialogus miraculorum, 4n, 63, 65–66, 72,
   161
   Libri VIII miraculorum, 149–50, 152–53
Celestine (Pope), 258
Cessolis, Jacobus de: *Ludus schachorum*, 105,
   138, 288n, 314–15, 317, 318–19
character, 34–35, 326, 345–49
Charlemagne, 123
Chartres, School of, 248, 255
chastity, 292–96, 310
Chaucer, Geoffrey, 9–10, 13–15, 79–80,
   138, 208–9, 213–15, 221–22
   conservatism of, 11–12, 18–22, 184,
   211–12
   eulogies to, in *Regement of Princes*, 312–14
   eulogy to, in *Fall of Princes*, 332–34
   and fifteenth century, 22–26, 179, 219,
   298–99, 322, 327
   and Gower, 245–48, 262

and twentieth century, 24–26
Anelida and Arcite, 333n; *Boece*, 23, 222,
   333; *Book of the Duchess*, 23, 333n; *Book
   of the Lion*, 333; *Ceix and Alcione*
   (unattested), 333; *Complaint of Mars*,
   333; *House of Fame*, 23, 333; *Legend of
   Good Women*, 23, 333n; *Mary Magdalen*
   (unattested), 333; *Parliament of Fowls*,
   23, 333n; *Romaunt*, 333; *Treatise of the
   Astrolabe*, 333; *Troilus and Criseyde*, 23,
   324, 333
   see also Canterbury Tales
Chaucerian tradition, 3, 22–26, 81, 119,
   313–14, 326
   audience of, 141–45, 319, 321, 323
   and the Latin exemplum, 137–38, 248,
   349–50
   Gower's role in the establishment of,
   297–99, 314
cherl, 16–18
Chenu, M. D., 69n
Christ, 8–10, 199–201, 203, 265–66, 287–88,
   289–90, 324, 335
   the name of, 30–32
   as Word Made Flesh, 75, 78–79, 93–97
Christianity, 203, 218–19, 228–29
   as a form of atheism, 50
   appropriation of *auctoritas* by, 45–46
   conversion to, 31–32, 264–67
   doctrine of, 13–14, 31, 46, 71, 105, 109,
   268
   faith, 13
   grace, 19
   and idolatry, 275
   and magic, 277
   as New Law, 19, 46–47, 118
   and postmodernism, 51–52
   Redemption, 228
   subversive traditions of, 50
   textuality of, 46–52, 75, 77–79, 105
Church, the, 7, 9–10, 12, 13, 14, 31, 45, 58,
   74, 78, 100, 137, 220–21, 249, 296,
   298–99, 301, 322, 349–50
   and Crown, 85–86, 116, 249, 265–67, 335
   cultural politics of, 67–70
   ecclesiastical courts, 148, 152
   internationalization of, 69, 148
   and marriage, 188–89
   power to bind and loose, 149, 260
   proprietary, 147–49, 166, 174
   and textual production, 143
   as voice of communal instruction, 82–83
churls, 16–18, 170, 242
Cicero, 40n, 41–42, 89, 229, 313
   De oratore, 120

class, 15–22, 40–41, 65, 83, 86, 102, 107, 134, 163, 170, 176, 180, 265–66, 269, 282, 293, 296
in later medieval England, 142–45
see also churls; nobility
Classen, Abrecht, 299n
classical tradition, 90, 93–95
clergy, 7, 14, 32, 62–63, 70, 88–89, 101–2, 254–56, 257–58, 338
parochial and monastic, local orientation of, 148
secular, 165–66
close reading, 26
Cohan, Steven, 96n, 210n
Coleman, Janet, 9, 28, 139, 143–44
Colonna, Egidio, *see* Aegidius Romanus
communem opinionem, 112, 189
Communiloquium sive summa collationum, see John of Wales
communion, 69, 70, 75, 200
Confessio Amantis, 3, 25, 137, 139, 246–97, 299, 324
evil exempla in, 246–47, 296
Book I, 250, 255–57
Book II, 249, 250, 257
Book III, 267–68, 269–72
Book IV, 267–69, 272–74
Book V, 267–68, 274–77
Book VI, 267, 274–75, 277–82
Book VII, 138, 249, 267, 277, 278, 282–97, 314
Book VIII, 249, 296–97
Genius in, 79, 248–49, 250, 255–56, 275, 277, 278, 281–84, 292–94, 302
Prologue, 249–55, 258, 275
individual tales: Aeneas and Dido, 268, 272–73; Albinus and Rosemund, 247, 257; Alexander and the Knight, 290–91; Apollonius of Tyre, 296–97; Boniface, 250, 257–63, 267, 275, 289; Cambyses, Tale of, 286–87; Ceix and Alcione, 268; Constance, Tale of, 257n; David and Joab, 291; Demetrius and Perseaunt, 257; Demephon and Phyllis, 268; Donation of Constantine (Constantine and Sylvester), 250, 257–58, 260, 263–67, 335–36; False Bachelor, 257; Florent, Tale of, 257; Gideon, 291; Iphis and Araxarathen, 268, 274; Jason and Medea, 268; the Jew and the Pagan, 290; King, Wine, Woman, and Truth, 284–86; Lucrece, 293–95; Lycurgus and His Laws, 267, 287–90, 317; Mundus and Paulina, 257, 261; Nebuchadnezzar's Dream,

254; Nebuchadnezzar's Punishment, 257; Nectanabus, 267, 277–81, 289; Orestes, 271–72; Paris and Helen, 275, 276–77; The Phalarean Bull, 290–91, 317–18; Phoebus and Daphne, 267–68; Pompeius and the King of Armenia, 290; Pyramus and Thisbe, 267, 271; Pygmalion, 268, 273–74, 281; Saul and Agag, 291; Tarquin and Aruns, 294; Theseus and Ariadne, 268; Three Questions, Tale of, 257; Trojan Horse, 257; Trump of Death, 257; Ulysses and Penelope, 268, 272–73; Virginia, 293, 294–96; Vulcan and Venus, 268, 275, 276
see also Genius; Gower, John; Venus
confession, 12–13, 69, 70, 72–74, 77–78, 250, 276, 303–5, 319
Congar, Yves, M.-J., 147n
Constantine, 257, 263–64, 329
see also Constantine, Donation of
and under Confessio Amantis, *and* Fall of Princes
Constantine, Donation of, 32, 81, 93, 260, 263–67, 335–36
role of piscina in, 266–67, 335–36
royalist appropriation of, 257–58
Constitutio Constantini, 93, 263
contrition, 13
Cook, G. H., 11n
Copeland, Rita, 109n, 207n, 327n
corporate fiction, 92, 98–103, 108, 114, 140–41, 295
corpus Christi, 99
Cotton Cleopatra D. VIII (British Library), 149–50, 156
counseil (or counsel), 207, 210–12, 286, 304, 310, 318–19, 334–35
Courcelle, Pierre, 123n
court, as ideological site, 90, 97, 144, 170–71, 174–75, 205, 253, 284, 292, 301, 337
courteisye, 21
Crane, Thomas F., 32n
Croesus, 226, 238
Culler, Jonathan, 96, 200n
Cultural Studies, 28
Cupid, 270
cupiditas, 193

Dahlberg, Charles, 230–31n
damnation, 153–55
Daniel, 226, 254–55
Dante Alighieri, 122, 129, 333

De monarchia, 20, 118
Inferno, 264, 291
Dares, 333
De bono regimine principum, *see* Helinand de Froidment
De casibus tradition, 81, 87, 119, 219, 228, 256, 303, 334–35, 349
De casibus virorum illustrium, 119–34, 206, 215–16, 227, 250, 322, 324–25, 327–29, 331–34, 335, 340
as *Fürstenspiegel*, 119–22
see also Boccaccio, Giovanni
De falso credita et ementita Constantini Donatione, *see* Valla, Lorenzo, da
de Man, Paul, 227–28, 231
De nugis curialium, *see* Map, Walter
De regimine principum, *see* Aegidius Romanus, or Helinand de Froidment
De speculo Regis Edwardi III, *see* Islip, Simon
de Ste. Croix, G. E. M., 43–44
Dean, James, 245n
death, 194, 199–205
Decarreaux, Jean, 63n
deconstruction, 47–51
Delany, Sheila, 235
Derrida, Jacques, 47–51
Des cas des nobles hommes et femmes, *see* Laurent de Premierfait
Devil, the, 76–77, 154, 156–59, 223
Di Lorenzo, Raymond D., 105n
Dialogus cum Regis Edwardi III, *see* Peter of Blois
Dialogus miraculorum: *see* Cesarius of Heisterbach
dictum, 10, 34, 90, 95–96, 133, 224, 233
didacticism, 10, 18, 62–63, 206, 207, 233–34, 245–50, 255, 301, 323, 325, 339–40, 344, 345
différance, 51
Dinshaw, Carolyn, 6n, 176–77, 194–95, 196n, 205n, 247n
direct address, 309
discourse, 196–97, 198
Dollimore, Jonathan, 200, 343–44, 345
Donaldson, E. Talbot, 23n, 231n
Donovan, Mortimer, 230–31n
Doob, Penelope B. R., 299n
Doyle, A. I., 14n
dreams, 238–40
Dryden, John, 18
Duby, Georges, 101n, 189n, 221n

Eagleton, Terry, 322n
Easthope, Anthony, 28n, 323n

ecclesiology, 14, 24, 58, 70, 86, 117–18, 163–67, 172–75, 260, 263–64, 266, 339
Eco, Umberto, 47–48, 51
Edward, the Black Prince, 328–29
Edward, brother to Henry V, 300
Edward, son of Henry VI, 138
Egerton, Alix, 138
Eliot, T. S., 228
empathy, 17–22
Engels, Friedrich, 42n
Enlightenment, the, 51
Epicurus, 89
Epitoma historiarum Phillipicarum, *see* Justinus
Erlich, Victor, 96n
ernest, 137, 206
Eruditio regum et principum, *see* Guibert de Tournai
eschatology, 165
estates-satire, 10, 137
estates theory, 101, 250–52, 284, 338
Étienne de Bourbon, 72
Euclid, 174
Eusebius, 263
exegesis, 165, 167–68, 200, 233–34, 254
chaff and corn, 330–31
exegetical criticism, 3, 171–73, 200, 230–34
exempla, sermon (individual), "The Bad Priest," 75; "Bernard and the Parisian Clerks," 76; "Clerics Weighed Down with Mispronounced Words," 77; "Clerk's Confession," 77–78; "Confession in an Open Field," 72–74; "Confession to a Peasant," 72; "Devil Collects Idle Words," 77; "Devil Disguised as an Angel," 76; "Devils' Letter to Negligent Prelates," 76; "Devils and Psalm-Singing," 77; *De nomine Jhesu*, 30–32; "Host Hidden in a Box," 75; "How Christ appeared to his disciples," 58–63; "Jew and the Sign of the Cross," 71; "Pregnant Abbess," 72; "Return from the Dead after Confession to the Devil Disguised as Priest," 74; "Return from the Dead to Confess Unconfessed Sin," 74; "Return from the Dead for Mass," 74; "Thief who Said 'Ave Maria'," 72; "The Word Devils Fear," 78–79
exemplum, 25, 161–63, 198, 206, 216, 224, 349–50
analogues to the *Friar's Tale*, 149–53, 155
benevolent examples vs. evil ones, 81, 247–48

and Chaucerian narrative, 22, 81
Christ as, 9–10, 96–97
in classical rhetoric, 32–33, 34
in clerical commentary, 14–15, 31–32,
66–67, 194
collections of, 66, 82, 137n, 145, 206, 215,
248
definition of, new, 34
definitions of, previous, 4, 27–34
dominance in later Middle Ages, 3–4
and fable, 230, 232–33, 243
form vs. function, 27, 33–34
and modern scholarship, 26–29
monastic tradition of, 63–66, 248
in penitential tradition, 14
public exemplum, 57–58, 81–134,
137–38, 175, 215, 226, 248
sermon exemplum, 29, 57–80, 137–38,
150, 155, 230, 248
and translation, 327
for individual sermon exempla, see exempla,
sermon
exemplarity, 9–11, 108–11, 215, 251, 256,
267, 282, 289, 313–14, 326, 339, 344
and corporate fiction, 98, 141
see also exemplum, king, kingship

fable, 229, 232–35, 243
see also beast fable
fabliau, 57, 137, 161–62, 174–75, 206
fabula (story), 96
Facta et dicta memorabilia, see Valerius
Maximus
factum, 10, 34, 95–96, 133, 224, 233
Fall, the, 223, 227–28, 231
Fall of Princes, 3, 25, 119, 137, 139, 322–49
corporate fiction in, 337–40
defense of poetry in, 337, 340–42
eulogy to Chaucer in, 327
plan of, 324–25
prologue to Book I, 326–35, 336–37
individual exempla: Adam and Eve, 324;
Alexander, 324, 346, 347; Arthur, 324,
329; Caesar, 346; Constantine, 329,
335–36; Cyrus, 346; Hannibal, 324,
348; King John, 324, 325; Nero, 346;
Pompey, 346–47, 348; the Scipios, 346;
Tarquin, 346; Zenobia, 346
see also Lydgate, John
fame (*fama*), 131–33
Farnham, Willard, 344
Faus Semblant, 192
feminism, 28, 35, 40–41, 188, 292
Ferster, Judith, 176–77
Fielding, Henry: *Joseph Andrews*, 349

fin'amors, 255–56, 269–74, 292–93
Finke, Laurie A., 7n
Finlayson, John, 7n
Fish, Stanley, 231n
Fisher, John H., 246–47, 249, 289n
flattery, 235, 240–41, 242–43, 306–7,
319–21
Flinn, John, 230n, 235n
Flores, Ralph, 37n
Florus, 99n
folklore, 57–58, 60–63, 79, 197, 203
Formalism, 26, 27, 230–32
character in, 34–35
debates with exegetical (patristic)
criticism, 3, 230–32
Fortune, 121–27, 129–31, 216, 221–26, 229,
247, 301, 302–4, 306, 319, 326, 334,
336, 347, 348
Foucault, Michel, 37n, 52n
Francis, St., 65
Frank, R. W., 176
Frederick II, 257
Frère Lorens: *Somme-le-Roi*, 198
Freud, Sigmund, 188, 204–5
Friedrich, Carl J., 41n
Frontinus, 93
Fulk of Neuilly, 65
Furnivall, Frederick J., 300n
Furnivall, Lord, 300
Fürstenspiegel, 57, 81–84, 87–122, 206, 215,
240, 249, 257, 277, 278–79, 282–97,
300–2, 305–10, 314, 324, 337
dedications of, 106–7, 252–53, 308–9,
325–26, 334–35
in England, 138–39
inaccuracy as a term, 87
Parisian (or neo-Aristotelian) tradition of,
105–6, 122, 206, 210
Futurism, 228

Gallacher, Patrick, 246, 249n, 260,
287n
game, see narrative
Gamer, H. M., 12n
Gauchi, Henri de: *Li Livres du gouvernement
des rois*, 108
Gelasius, 38, 45, 50
gender, 15–16, 40–41, 107, 163, 176, 180,
269, 284, 293, 296
Genet, Jean-Phillipe, 105n, 109n, 138–39
Genette, Gerard, 35n, 302n
Genius, 248, 255
see also under Confessio Amantis
genre, 12
gentilesse, 268–69, 282

Gerald of Wales, 60
Gesta Romanorum, 287–88, 289
Gibbon, Edward, 43
Gilbert, Sandra M., 37n
Gillespie, Vincent, 14n
glossing, *see* exegesis
Gnostics, 50
Godfrey of Viterbo: *Pantheon*, 291
Godman, Peter, 215–16
Gordian Knot, 347
Gower, John, 25, 79, 145, 304
    as Amans, 250, 255, 276, 282, 284
    and Chaucer, 8–10, 245–48
    sophistication of, 263
    see also Confessio Amantis, Genius, Venus
Gramsci, Antonio, 35–36, 68–70
Green, Richard Firth, 123, 138n, 143–44
Greetham, D. C., 299n
Gregory I, 31, 63, 248
    Dialogues, 4n, 63–64, 65–66, 71
Griffiths, R. A., 325n
Grudin, Michaela Paasche, 178, 180
Gubar, Susan, 37n
Guibert de Tournai: *Eruditio regum et
    principum*, 104–5
Guillory, John, 37n

Haas, Renate, 216, 218–19, 222n
hagiography, 176
Hahn, Thomas, 148n
Hall, Louis Breuer, 119n
Hall, Stuart, 28n, 35–36
Hamilton, Marie P., 192n
Hamm, R. Wayne, 246n
Handlyng Synne: *see* Mannyng, Robert
Hannah, Ralph, III, 145n
Hansen, Elaine Tuttle, 176–77
Harding, Alan, 143n, 212n
Harriss, G. L., 301n
Hartung, Albert H., 208n
Haselmayer, L. A., 192n
Heath, Peter, 9n, 11n
Hector, 110
hegemony, 28, 35–36, 52, 68–70, 79, 83,
    85–86, 124, 134, 144
Heidegger, Martin, 228
Helinand de Froidment: *De regimine
    principum*, or *De bono regimine principum*,
    104
Henry I, 143
Henry II, 83, 88, 253
Henry IV (Bolingbroke), 139, 141, 250,
    253, 301
Henry V, 300–10, 312, 313–14, 319–22,
    325
Henry VI, 138, 325, 329

Henry of Lancaster, 301–2
Herbert, J. H., 162
Hercules, 225
heritability, 111–12, 182–83, 186–87, 189,
    286, 293
Herolt, Johannes: *Promptuarium exemplorum*,
    153n
hierarchy, 7, 19–22, 86, 89, 101–2, 186, 190,
    282, 284, 303, 337
hierocratism, 89, 91–97, 138, 339
Hilton, R. H., 142
Hiscoe, David, 245n
Hoccleve, Thomas, 25, 86, 298, 299–300,
    325
    La Male Regle, 303
    see also Regement of Princes
Homer, 299, 333
Howard, Donald R., 231n
Hudson, Anne, 8, 264n
humanism, 53–54, 84, 89, 97, 180, 185,
    218–19, 228–29
    modern, 343–44, 345
    politics of, 133–34
Humbertus Romanus, 31
Humphrey, Duke of Gloucester, 300,
    325–26, 329, 333, 334–35
Hundred Years War, 329
Huppé, Bernard F., 6n, 230n
hypocrisy, 148, 168

identity, 35, 63
ideology, 5, 28, 35–36, 52, 68, 84, 112–13,
    190–91, 195, 260, 269, 282, 302, 315,
    345
    see also kingship
immortality, poetic, 342
incest, 187–89, 246–47, 249, 269–71,
    296–97
In principio, 239
Investiture Crisis, 263
Institutio Trajani, 91–92, 101
Irigaray, Luce, 188n
irony, 160–61, 169–75, 200, 201, 227, 229,
    230–32, 235, 239–40, 243–44
Islip, Simon: *De speculo Regis Edwardi III*,
    138
Itô, Masayoshi, 246

Jacob, E. F., 325n
Jameson, Frederic, 58
Jesus, *see* Christ
Job, 178
Jochums, Mildred, 264n
jocunditas litterarum, 90–91, 132, 209, 340
John, St., 209
John the Baptist, 336

John, King, of France, 324–25, 328–29
John of Gaunt, 301
John of Salisbury, 86, 88, 116, 119, 148–49, 209, 314
  as originator of corporate fiction, 100
  Metalogicon, 38n
  see also *Policraticus*
John of Wales: *Communiloquium sive summa collationum*, 105, 161, 288n
Jolliffe, P. S., 12, 14n
Johnson, Dudley R., 226
Jones, R. H., 138n
jongleur, 174
Jordan, Robert, 6n
Joseph, 238
Joyce, James, 323
Judaic tradition, 50, 117–18, 233
Julius Caesar, 225
justice, 149–50, 156, 310
  adjudicatory ideal of, 212–13
  administration of in later medieval England, 142–43, 212–13
Justinus: *Epitoma historiarum Phillipicarum*, 287–89

Kantoriwicz, Ernst H., 98–99, 100, 118
Kaske, Carol V., 7n
Kaske, R. E., 216n, 220n
Kauper, Richard W., 148n
Kellogg, A. L., 192n
Kemmler, Fritz, 12n, 27, 65n
Kempton, Daniel, 207n
Kenelm, St., 238
Kerner, Max, 91–92n
Kieckhefer, Richard, 277n
king, 285
  relation to Church, 85–86, 89, 101–2
  dignity of, 310
  identification with, 326, 345
  and law, 93, 115–18, 139–41
  as source of lay authority, 81, 98, 103–4, 138, 143, 147, 176, 205, 206, 235, 311, 316–18
  and nobility, 282
  and poet, 249–50, 334–35
  voice of, 310–11, 317–18
  voluntas of, 139–41, 310
King, Stephen, 247
kingship, 25, 121–22, 182–83, 249–50, 256–57, 267
  and Chaucerian tradition, 145
  discursive construction of, 249–50, 252, 256
  exemplarity of, 82, 83, 87, 110–11, 128–29, 184, 283–84, 289, 292–93, 296, 310, 336–37, 345

ideology of, 141–45, 213, 234, 262, 319–22
  institutional features of, 20
  sacral, 86, 101, 108, 263, 292, 311
  self-regulating nature of, 190, 262–63, 265–67, 281–82, 286, 289, 315, 317–18, 337
  singularity of, 183–86, 190, 240–43, 291, 296, 318
Kittredge, G. L., 194–95
Kleineke, Wilhelm, 283n
Knapp, Peggy, 7n, 195n
Knight, Stephen, 7n, 158n, 211, 230n
Koester, Helmut, 46n
Krochalis, Jeanne, 312n
Kuczynski, Michael D., 246

Lacan, Jacques, 35
laicism, 11–12, 192, 250–51
laicization, 9, 14, 54, 87, 103–4, 166, 228–29, 239–40, 314, 339, 344, 349–50
  see also lay tradition
laity, 12, 13–15, 335, 336
Lancastrians, 145
  policy toward the Church, 298, 335
  dynastic rights of, 301
Langland, William, 152, 264
  Piers Plowman, 299
language, 155–58, 166–75, 195, 198–201, 233, 302, 321
  indirection, 175, 315
  sacred, 71, 77–80
  see also vernacular
Larrain, Jorge, 28n
Lateran Council, Fourth, 12, 69, 70
law, 89, 139–41, 212–13, 215, 310
  canon, 296
  divine, 287
  natural, 105–7, 116–18, 213
  royal, 284
  written, 115–18, 134, 143, 212
Lawton, David, 192n, 195, 301n
lay tradition, 129–34, 250–56, 328–29, 334–35, 337, 344–45, 349–50
Legenda Aurea, 264n
Le Goff, Jacques, 3n, 4n, 31n, 63n
Leicester, H. Marshall, 194–95
Lepley, Douglas L., 222n
Lévi Strauss, Claude, 188
Levitan, Alan, 171–73
Levy, Bernard, 171–73, 186, 230–31n
Lewis, C. S., 245, 249
liberalism, 85, 349
liberation theology, 50
Liber consolationis et consilii, see Albertanus of Brescia

Liber exemplorum ad usum praedicantium, 58–60, 72–74, 75
Libri VIII miraculorum, see Cesarius of Heisterbach
Liebeschutz, Hans, 88n
Lignano, Giovanni da, 179
limitour, 147–48
Lindner, Amnon, 138n, 263
lineage, 241
  see also heritability
Little, Lester K., 65n
Livre de Melibeé et de Dame Prudence, see Louens, Renaud de
Livre Griseldis, Le, 181
Livre de Melibeé et de Dame Prudence, Le, see Louens, Renaud de
Livy: *Ab urbe condita*, 33, 99–100, 294–95
Logos (God as Word), 49–50
Lollardy, 8–9, 155, 298, 304, 335
Lombard, Peter, 73n
Lords Appellant, 241
Louens, Renaud de: *Le Livre de Melibeé et de Dame Prudence*, 207, 213, 214
Louis IX, 104–5
Lucca, Tholomeus de, 105
Ludus schachorum, see Cessolis, Jacobus de
Luke, Saint, 209
Luther, Martin, 161n
Lydgate, John, 25, 145, 298
  aureate style of, 343
  encyclopedism of, 323, 327, 342–43
  and modern literary history, 322–23
  mummings of, 344–45
  works: *Ballade to King Henry VI on His Coronation*, 325; *On Gloucester's Approaching Marriage*, 325; *Roundell for the Coronation*, 325; *Troy Book*, 325; *Verses for the Triumphal Entry of King Henry VI into London*, 325, 344; *see also Fall of Princes*
Lyotard, Jean-François, 47

Macaulay, G. C., 263n, 264n, 275, 294
McFarlane, K. B., 142n, 301n
Macherey, Pierre, 116n
McLellan, David, 28n
McKisack, May, 140n
McNeill, J. T., 12n
McMillan, Douglas J., 299n
Macmullen, Ramsay, 50n
Macrobius: *Somnium Scipionis*, 110, 238
magic, 277–81
Mann, Jill, 231n, 314n
Manning, Stephen, 231n

Mannyng, Robert: *Handlynge Synne*, 12n, 14, 27, 79, 248
Manzalaoui, M. A., 138n, 279n
Map, Walter: *De nugis curialium*, 104
Marcuse, Herbert, 42n
Marie de France: *Fables*, 235
Mark, St., 209
Markus, R. A., 20n, 85n
marriage, 181–83, 188–90
  Church as regulator of, 188–89
Martin, Janet, 91–92, 99n
Martino, Francesco de, 45n
Marxism, 28, 35–36, 40–41, 42n, 52, 68–70
Mathews, William, 300n
Matthews, St., 209
mendicant orders (Dominican and Franciscan), 65, 162, 192, 314
  and class, 65, 170
  and a money economy, 164
  as perverters of speech, 166–67
  spirituality and ecclesiology of, 146–47, 159–65
Menenius Agrippa, 99
Merciless Parliament, 241
Mercury, 287
Merrix, Robert P., 197n
middle class, 142–45
Middleton, Anne, 143–44n, 176–77
Miehl, Dieter, 3
Miller, Jacqueline T., 37n, 38
Millet, Bella, 37n
Minnis, A. J., 37n, 222n, 283n
miracles, 62, 73–74, 75, 78–79, 81, 162
Mirror for Magistrates, A, 119, 344
Miskimmin, Alice, 299n
Mitchell, Jerome, 312n
Mitchell, Juliet, 188n
modernism, 47–48, 51–54, 228–29, 232, 245–47, 349
  high/low culture distinction in, 57–58
  its view of the Middle Ages, 52–54
  sacralization of literature in, 323–24
Mombrizio, Bonino: *Sanctuarium, seu Vitae Sanctorum*, 264–67
Mommsen, Theodor, 41
monarch, monarchy, *see* king, kingship
monasticism, 211; Benedictine, 63–64
money, 148, 172–73
Moore, R. I., 67–68
morality, 245–47; *see also* didacticism
Morse, Charlotte, 185n
Mosher, J. A., 4, 63n
Mum and the Sothsegger, 139
Murray, Alexander, 134n

Muscatine, Charles, 230, 243

narrative, 28, 77, 195, 200–5, 206–7,
   214–15, 224–25, 347
   agency in, 210
   and authority, 3, 95–97, 156, 191,
      226–27, 283, 300, 302–9, 350
   autonomy of, 193–94, 243–44, 302, 303
   complexity in, 3, 4, 144–45, 244, 348–49
   and doctrine, 15, 71, 109, 201
   as *game*, 137, 156, 161–62, 175, 206
   as language of the lay, 15, 22, 227, 321
   as source of order, 131
   and power, 100, 141
   and social location, 302, 308
   transformation in, 31, 61, 75, 307
narratology, 35, 96–97
nationalism, 329, 336–37
   see also audience
Nebuchadnezzar, 225, 226, 314
   see also under Confessio Amantis
Nero, 226
Nicholas III, 258
Nicholson, Peter, 149n, 153n, 155–56, 246n,
   263n, 289n
nobilitas, 112–13
nobility, 111–13, 116, 142–45, 170, 182–83,
   216, 236, 279, 282
Nordh, Arvast, 33n
nugae curialium, 88–89

oaths, 198–200, 305
   coronation, 310–11
Odo of Cheriton, 76, 230
Ollson, Kurt, 220
Oruch, Jack B., 216n
outridere, 218, 220–21
Ovid, 272, 285, 291, 333
   Fasti, 253
   Metamorphoses, 271
Owst, G. R., 149n, 150n, 162n

paradeigma, 32
parish, 10–11
Parliament, 20, 142–43
Pataria, 68
pathos, 179, 205
   see also pity; tale of pathos
paterfamilias, 40–41
patriarchy, 40–41, 187, 234, 280, 295–97,
   319–21
Patterson, Lee, 3n, 6, 12n, 14n, 18n, 53,
   146, 194–95, 199, 200n, 206n, 208n,
   232n

Paul, Saint, 46, 51, 93–96, 99, 117–18, 165,
   233, 264, 266
Payne, Robert O., 176
Pearcy, Roy J., 163n
Pearsall, Derek, 161, 163, 172–73, 230n,
   232, 245, 249n, 322–23, 325n, 343n
Peck, Russell, 246, 249n, 262, 289n
penetrans domos, 165, 166
penitential tradition, 12–15, 79, 198–99,
   248–49, 272
Pentecost, 171
performance (rhetorical or linguistic), 28,
   35–36, 141, 198–202, 257, 286, 311,
   327, 341–42, 344–45
Perrin, Norman, 46n
personification, 200–3
perversion, 195, 199–200
Peter, St., 266
Peter of Blois: *Dialogus cum Rege Heinrico*,
   138
Peter the Chanter, 65
Petrarch, 25, 122, 129, 131–34, 177, 185,
   219, 250, 333, 342
   Chaucer's eulogy to, 179–80, 312
   "Coronation Oration," 179
   De remediis utriusque fortune, 121
   De viris illustribus, 121
   Epistolae seniles, 177–78, 184
Petrarchan academy, 178, 185
Phaleas, 116
Pharisees, 8
Philip Augustus, 104
Philip the Fair, 106, 108, 118, 258
pity, 184, 265–66, 290–91, 310
   compared to Divine Grace, 290
Plantagenets, 253, 298
Plato, 116
Plutarch, 91–92
Plotinus, 110
poetry, autonomy of, 327, 328, 340–42, 344
   modernist ideal of, 322–23
Policraticus, 38n, 82, 86, 87, 88–105, 121,
   138, 233, 240, 250, 257, 315, 324
   exemplum of Codrus in, 93, 95, 97–98,
      290
   corporate fiction, version of, 101–3,
      337–39
   defense of letters, 90–91, 132, 250, 337,
      340
   influence of, 104–5, 138
   exemplum of Lycurgus in, 93, 95, 97–98,
      287–89, 290
   see also John of Salisbury
postmodernism, 29, 47–48, 51–52, 216, 300

post-structuralism, 26, 35
potestas, 5, 36, 38, 42, 51, 261–62, 263
Pound, Ezra, 228
power, 5, 17, 28, 40, 83–84, 89, 141, 179,
 188, 212, 214, 216, 229, 274, 280, 282,
 284–86, 292, 315, 319, 345
Powell, James M., 213
Pratt, Robert, 105n, 161n, 235n
prayer, 277
preaching, 163–64, 166; itinerant, 65
Premierfait, Laurence de: *Des cas des nobles
 hommes et femmes*, 119, 324, 327–34, 335
presentism, *see* anachronism
presumption, 329–35, 347
Price, Bennet J., 33n
primogeniture, 188–89, 236; *see also*
 heritability
prince, *see* king, kingship
Ptomely, 174

Quintillian, 33

realism, 343
Regement of Princes, 3, 25, 137, 139, 145,
 299–322, 325, 334
 illustrations in, 309–10, 312
 manuscripts of, 309–10, 312
 Prologue, 300, 302–8, 309, 312–13
 individual exempla: Camillus, 316; John
  of Canacee, 319–21; Lycurgus and His
  Laws, 316–17; The Phalarean Bull,
  316, 317–18; Regulus, 315–16; Scipio
  Africanus, 316
 see also Hoccleve, Thomas
relics, 196–97
Renaissance, 53–54, 84
 drama in, 343–46, 348–49
Renart le Contrefait, 240
Renoir, Alain, 322
rhetoric, 5, 7, 15, 84, 89–91, 98, 123–26,
 130–31, 175, 183, 246, 249, 283, 313,
 331, 343
Rhetorica ad Herennium, 34
Ricci, Pier Giorgio, 121n
Richard II, 138, 139–41, 208n, 240–43,
 253, 302–3, 306
Richard the Redeless, 139n
Richardson, Janette, 149n, 152n, 153n, 158
Rising of 1381, English, 241–42
Ritson, Joseph, 322
ritual, 12, 70–78, 277
Robert, King of Cyprus, 105, 120
Robertson, D. W., 3n, 53, 217n, 230–31n,
 238, 248n
Robinson, F. N., 217–18

Roman de Renart, 230, 235–36
Roman de Troie, 276
romance, 137, 176, 206, 268–74, 293
Romance of the Rose, 192, 248, 255
Romanticism, 51
Rome, ancient, political structure of, 39–44
Rosenwein, Barbara, 65n
royalism, 20, 24, 177
Rubin, Gayle, 188
Rushdie, Salman, 324–25
Rypon, Robert, 149–51

Said, Edward, 37n
Saint Amour, William, 165–66
Sanctuarium, seu Vitae Sanctorum, see
 Mombrizio, Bonino
sapientes, see vulgus
Scanlon, Larry, 141n, 231n
scatology, 161–62, 169–70, 172–75
Schmitt, Jean Claude, 4n, 31n, 63n
Secretum secretorum, 138, 278–79, 313, 314
Seneca, 226
Sennet, Richard, 42n
sententia (or *sentence*), 6, 81, 106, 121, 208–9,
 215, 222, 249
sermon (as discursive form), 197–98
Sermon on the Mount, 8
Severs, J. Burke, 177n, 178, 207n
Seymour, M. C., 217–18n, 309–10n
Shakespeare, William, 344, 345, 349
 Macbeth, 348
 Richard II, 348
Shallers, A. Paul, 231n, 240
Shires, Linda, 96n, 210n
Shoaf, R. A., 200
Sidney, Sir Philip: *Apology for Poesie*, 349
sin, 13, 16–19, 23, 198–99, 248
Sitz im Leben, 27
sjuzhet (narration), 96
Smalley, Beryl, 88n, 89n, 104n
Socrates, 116
Soner, Sir Henry, (Chancellor to Henry V),
 300
Southern, R. W., 63n, 89n, 104n, 143n
sovereignty, 18–20, 84–85, 101, 214, 320
Spearing, A. C., 23n, 122n, 153, 299n,
 301n, 312, 323
Speculum historiale, see Vincent de Beauvais
Speculum laicorum, 30, 67
Speculum stultorum, 230
speech act, 315; *see also* language,
 performance, rhetoric
Spenser, Edmund: "Letter to Raleigh,"
 349
Spiegel, Gabrielle M., 57n

Stasko, Nicolette, 274n
Steel, A. B., 140n
Stoicism, 125
Stock, Brian, 49n, 67–68, 197
strategemma, strategemmaticum, 93
Straw, Carole, 63–64n
Straw, Jack, 242
Street, Ethel, 289n
Stricker, Der, 149n
Strohm, Paul, 7n, 10n, 19, 24, 144n
Struve, Tilman, 98n, 100n
subjectivity, 12–13, 28, 35–36, 52, 195, 200, 202–3, 208, 215, 299–303, 321, 344, 348
subordination, 68, 71, 309
Suetonius, 33n
Sylvester, St., 93n, 257
    Vita Sancti Silvestri, 263–64, 266, 335–36
Szittya, Penn R., 147n, 148n, 165n, 166, 171–73

Tabula exemplorum secundum ordinem alphabeti, 78–79
tales of pathos, 176, 206
Tatlock, J. S. P., 217–18
Taylor, Archer, 149n
teleology, of medieval/humanist dichotomy, 84–87
    Whig, 140
Tennenhouse, Leonard, 345
tessera, 122, 323
textuality, 24, 190, 212, 232, 280
    and lay authority, 105–6, 122, 134, 138, 144–45, 210, 249
    and politics, 144–45
Thompson, Stith, 60n, 197
thral, 15–19
Tierney, Brian, 100
Til Eulenspiegel, 162–63
Todorov, Tzvetan, 61
tragedy, 216, 222, 224, 343–49
Trajan, 91
transcendental signified, 48–51
translation, 25, 183, 207–10, 213, 238–39, 327–34
Tubach, Frederick C., 70–71
Tuck, Anthony, 140, 241n
Twelve Tablets, 39, 40n
Tyler, Wat, 242
tyranny, 114–15, 140–41

Ullmann, Walter, 38, 84, 86n, 89n, 92n, 100n, 101n, 104n, 105n, 106n

Valerius Maximus: *Facta et dicta memorabilia*, 34, 287
Valla, Lorenzo da: *Da falso credita et ementita Constantini Donatione*, 257
Van Moos, Peter, 88n
Vegetius, 116
Venus, 250, 255, 273–77
vernacular, 27, 139, 321, 326
    authority of, 141–45, 313–14
Vescie à prestre, La, 162–63
vileynye, 21
Vincent de Beauvais: *Speculum historiale*, 104, 238–39
Virgil, 38, 45, 272, 313, 333, 341–42
Visconti, Bernabo, 217
vita apostolica, 69, 165
Vita Barlaam et Josaphat, 275
Vitry, Jacques de, 32n, 65, 70, 71, 74, 75–77
Vogelweide, Walther von der, 257–58, 263–64
voice, 7–8, 30, 140–41, 197, 207–9, 215, 224, 235, 237, 300, 302–4, 307, 311–12, 321
    of God, 260–61, 267, 279–82, 287–89
    see also king, voice of
vulgus, and *sapientes*, 133–34, 185

Wallace, David, 176–77, 178
Walsingham, Thomas, 242
Warren, W. L., 83n
Weber, Edwart, 289n
Weber, Max, 41n, 67–68
Welter, J.-Th., 31n, 67n, 71n
Wenzel, Siegfried, 6, 197–98n
Westmoreland, Countess of, 300
Wetherbee, Winthrop, 216, 219n, 257n
Wilkinson, Bertie, 140
Wilks, Michael, 84, 85
Williams, Raymond, 36n
Wimsatt, W. K., 349
Wycliff, John, 264; *see also* Lollardy
Wycliffitism, *see* Lollardy
Wynnere and Wastoure, 139

Yeager, R. F., 198, 245, 246n, 254n, 268n, 297
Ysengrimus, 230

Zaccaria, Vittorio, 119n
Ziegler, Jacob, 119
Zietlow, Paul, 160n